The Economics of Renewable Energy in the Gulf

T0270721

The Cooperation Council for the Arab States of the Gulf (GCC) has been at the epicenter of global energy markets because of its substantial endowment of hydrocarbons. Yet countries in the region have also stated their intent to be global leaders in renewable energy. This collection explores the drivers for the widespread adoption of renewable energy around the GCC, the need for renewable energy and the policy-economic factors that can create success.

All six countries within the GCC have plans to include renewable energy power generation in their energy mix for various reasons including: a growing demand for electricity because of increasing populations, an increasing government fiscal deficit due to inefficient subsidies, the need to diversify the economy and global pressure to meet climate change requirements. However, the decision of when and by how much to introduce renewable energy is fraught with complications. In this book, a stellar cast of regional policy and academic experts explore the reasons behind these renewable energy plans and the potential impediments to success, whether it be the declining cost of producing energy from hydrocarbons, an infrastructure which needs to be updated, social acceptance, lack of financing and even harsh weather. Weighing up all these factors, the book considers the route forward for renewable energy in the Gulf region.

The Economics of Renewable Energy in the Gulf offers an excellent examination of the adoption of renewable energy in the area. It will be of great interest to academic researchers and policy makers alike, particularly those working in the areas of energy economics, public policy and international relations.

Hisham M. Akhonbay is a research fellow in the Policy and Decision Science program at KAPSARC, Saudi Arabia. Working on GCC energy cooperation and research, he has been with KAPSARC since its inception. He was previously with the Center for Strategic and International Studies (CSIS) in Washington DC as a visiting fellow where he worked on the geopolitics of oil and authored a paper on Saudi Arabia's energy policy.

Routledge Explorations in Environmental Economics

Edited by Nick Hanley, University of Stirling, UK

47 **Economic Diversification Policies in Natural Resource Rich Economies**
Edited by Sami Mahroum and Yasser Al-Saleh

48 **The Impact of Climate Policy on Environmental and Economic Performance**
Evidence from Sweden
Rolf Färe, Shawna Grosskopf, Tommy Lundgren, Per-Olov Marklund and Wenchao Zhou

49 **Economics of International Environmental Agreements**
A Critical Approach
Edited by M. Özgür Kayalıca, Selim Çağatay and Hakan Mıhçı

50 **Environmental and Economic Impacts of Decarbonization**
Input–Output Studies on the Consequences of the 2015 Paris Agreements
Edited by Óscar Dejuán, Manfred Lenzen and María-Ángeles Cadarso

51 **Advances in Fisheries Bioeconomics**
Theory and Policy
Edited by Juan Carlos Seijo and Jon G. Sutinen

52 **Redesigning Petroleum Taxation**
Aligning Government and Investors in the UK
Emre Üşenmez

53 **National Pathways to Low Carbon Emission Economies**
Innovation Policies for Decarbonizing and Unlocking
Edited by Kurt Hübner

54 **The Economics of Renewable Energy in the Gulf**
Edited by Hisham M. Akhonbay

For more information about this series, please visit www.routledge.com/series/REEE

The Economics of Renewable Energy in the Gulf

Edited by Hisham M. Akhonbay

Routledge
Taylor & Francis Group

LONDON AND NEW YORK

First published 2019
by Routledge
2 Park Square, Milton Park, Abingdon, Oxon OX14 4RN

and by Routledge
52 Vanderbilt Avenue, New York, NY 10017

First issued in paperback 2020

Routledge is an imprint of the Taylor & Francis Group, an informa business

British Library Cataloguing-in-Publication Data
A catalogue record for this book is available from the British Library

Library of Congress Cataloging-in-Publication Data
Names: Akhonbay, Hisham M., 1978- editor.
Title: The economics of renewable energy in the Gulf / edited by
    Hisham M. Akhonbay.
Description: Milton Park, Abingdon, Oxon ; New York, NY:
    Routledge, 2019. | Series: Routledge explorations in
    environmental economics ; 54 | Includes bibliographical
    references and index.
Identifiers: LCCN 2018027454 (print) | LCCN 2018032399 (ebook) |
    ISBN 9780429434976 (Ebook) | ISBN 9781138351905 |
    ISBN 9781138351905 (hardback : alk. paper)
Subjects: LCSH: Energy development—Persian Gulf Region. |
    Renewable energy sources—Economic aspects—Persian Gulf
    Region. | Renewable energy sources—Government policy—
    Persian Gulf Region. | Energy policy—Persian Gulf Region.
Classification: LCC HD9502.P35 (ebook) | LCC HD9502.P35 E26
    2019 (print) | DDC 333.79/409536—dc23
LC record available at https://lccn.loc.gov/2018027454

ISBN 13: 978-0-367-58495-5 (pbk)
ISBN 13: 978-1-138-35190-5 (hbk)

Typeset in Bembo
by Swales & Willis Ltd, Exeter, Devon, UK

Contents

List of figures ix
List of tables xi
List of contributors xii
Foreword xviii
Acknowledgements xx

1 Introduction 1
HISHAM M. AKHONBAY AND MARILYN SMITH

Capturing the full potential of solar energy 3
Setting new policy frameworks for renewable energy 5
Energy system planning and integration to support renewables 6
Additional benefits of building a renewable energy sector 7

2 Overview of energy supply and demand in the GCC 10
DAVID WOGAN, IMTENAN AL-MUBARAK, ABDULLAH AL-BADI
AND SHREEKAR PRADHAN

Introduction 10
The Gulf Cooperation Council energy system 12
Energy demand and growth 12
Energy pricing 16
Carbon dioxide (CO_2) emissions 17
Energy transformation in the power and water sectors 17
Resources 24
Energy pricing as a barrier to coordination 30
Policies, targets and reforms 33
Conclusions 36

3 Economics of solar power in the GCC: assessing opportunities at residential and utility scales 41
AMRO M. ELSHURAFA AND WALID MATAR

Solar power in the GCC: weighing the costs and benefits 42
Examining motivations, barriers and potential breakthroughs 43

*Case study: the potential for solar electricity generation in
Saudi Arabia 46*
Which solar option delivers greater benefit in GCC contexts? 51
Conclusions 53

**4 Navigating the transition to renewable energy in
the GCC: lessons from the European Union**   **57**

MAHA ALSABBAGH AND ODEH AL-JAYYOUSI

Targets set, now time to move toward them 58
*State of GCC readiness for learning and ability to deploy
renewable energy 60*
*Case study: renewable energy deployment lessons from the
European Union experience 62*
Conclusions 72

5 Prioritizing renewable energy in a time of fiscal austerity   **77**

KAREN E. YOUNG

Introduction 78
*Fiscal constraint disrupts traditional roles of GCC
governments 79*
Rising energy demand supports the case for increased renewables 81
*Opportunities and risks for renewable energy investment in
GCC states 81*
*Legal frameworks, ownership structures and financial products:
what is working, what needs reform 86*
Case study of the United Arab Emirates 94
Conclusions 96

6 De-risking low carbon investments in the GCC   **100**

STEPHEN GITONGA AND WALID ALI

Global to regional overview of low carbon development 101
Renewable energy and climate action potential in the GCC 105
De-risking and scaling up low carbon investment in the GCC 106
The De-Risking Renewable Energy Investment methodology 108
*Applying the De-Risking Renewable Energy Investment methodology
to GCC countries 110*
*Future prospects for the Gulf to emerge as a hub for low carbon
investments 112*
Conclusions 116

7 **Policies to promote renewables in the Middle East and North Africa's resource rich economies** 120

RAHMATALLAH POUDINEH, ANUPAMA SEN AND BASSAM FATTOUH

Tapping into both hydrocarbon and renewable resources 121
The central role of incentives 123
Addressing barriers to renewable investment 130
Revising energy policy in the MENA 134
Conclusions 136

8 **Energy and climate policies to stimulate renewables deployment in GCC countries** 139

STEVE GRIFFITHS AND DANIAH ORKOUBI

Review of renewable energy deployment to date and its relevance
  to GCC countries 140
Targets set, now how to achieve them? 142
The energy and climate policy nexus, including energy pricing 142
Analysis: the context for renewable energy in the GCC 148
Policies to stimulate deployment of renewable energy in
  the GCC 155
Conclusions 160

9 **Potential impacts of solar energy integration on fuel mix strategies in Qatar** 167

MOIZ BOHRA, NASREDDINE EL-DEHAIBI, ANTONIO SANFILIPPO AND MARWAN KHRAISHEH

The potential for solar in power generation and electric transport 168
Analytical investigations of fuel mix strategies 171
A three step approach to calculate optimal fuel mix strategies 172
Results and discussion 178
Conclusions 183

10 **Renewable energy and its potential impact on GCC labor markets: opportunities and constraints** 188

SYLVAIN CÔTÉ

Can renewable energy deliver new hope for GCC youth? 189
Understanding the links between renewable energy and employment 193
The empirical evidence on employment and renewable energy 194

GCC labor markets: identifying the constraints 201
Potential policy actions 208
Conclusions 211

11 Forging a more centralized GCC renewable energy policy

216

OMAR AL-UBAYDLI, GHADA ABDULLA AND LAMA YASEEN

Introduction 217
Background: three GCC challenges 218
The GCC's current, decentralized approach to renewable energy 223
A more centralized GCC renewable energy policy 226
Conclusions 230

Index   235

Figures

2.1	GCC member states, disaggregated into regions	13
2.2	Total primary energy consumption from 1965–2015	15
2.3	Sectoral energy consumption, 2015	16
2.4	Breakdown of GHG emissions by energy subsectors in 2012	17
2.5	Power and water capacity by technology type	18
2.6	Installed desalination capacity by type	19
2.7	Estimated fuel mix for power and water sectors by GCC member states	20
2.8	Crude oil and gas production and exports	25
2.9	Map of GCC with trade linkages and quantities	28
2.10	Average direct solar irradiance for Saudi Arabia and Abu Dhabi during summer	29
2.11	Average wind speed for Saudi Arabia and Abu Dhabi during spring and fall	30
3.1	Analysis of the economics of residential solar in the GCC	48
3.2	2030 technology percentage shares in electricity generation by terawatt hours (TWh) under an immediate deregulation scenario	52
4.1	Overview of the methodology	63
4.2	Timeline showing main elements of EU renewables policies	65
5.1	Final energy consumption in the GCC, 2004–2014	82
5.2	Roll-out of privatization schemes in the GCC	90
6.1	Total annual new investments in clean energy worldwide, 2004–2015	102
6.2	Instruments for de-risking renewable energy investment	109
6.3	Pillars for making the GCC a hub for low carbon investments	113
7.1	A stylized model of renewable energy enhancement in the power sector	124
7.2	Renewable investment incentive spectrum	129
7.3	Levelized cost of electricity for renewables between 2010 and 2016	130
7.4	Risks faced by renewables investors in the MENA region	133

8.1	Growth of CO_2 emissions from fuel combustion in GCC countries	149
8.2	Sources of CO_2 emissions from fuel combustion in GCC countries	150
8.3	Distribution of total final energy consumption (TFEC) in MENA countries	151
9.1	Tradeoff curve for optimal fuel displacement strategy	180
10.1	Proportion of the population below 25 years of age in GCC countries, latest year available	190
10.2	Size of the total labor force in GCC countries, 2000–2014	190
10.3	Unemployment rates in GCC countries, youth vs total	191
10.4	Range of estimates on gross jobs per annual GWh generated	195
10.5	Projected direct jobs in renewable energy in GCC countries in 2030	196
10.6	Breakdown of direct jobs in renewable energy in 2030, by technology	197
10.7	Workforce required at different stages of a wind power project	198
10.8	Distribution of workforce requirements along a 50 MW solar PV value chain	199
10.9	Labor force composition in GCC countries, 2016	201
10.10	Employment rates of nationals and non-nationals in GCC countries	202
10.11	Working age population by level of education	202
10.12	Distribution of employed population (15 years of age and over) by nationality group according to industry activity	203
10.13	Labor distribution in Saudi Arabia, main sectoral industries, 2016	205
10.14	Distribution of university graduates across main fields of study	206
10.15	Share of vocational programs among upper secondary education programs, 2013	207
11.1	Gross domestic expenditure on R&D as a percentage of GDP, 2012	219
11.2	Researchers per million inhabitants, 2012	220

Tables

2.1	Estimated fuel consumption by power and water sectors	21
2.2	Electricity production in terawatt hours, consumption, and peak load	22
2.3	Annual desalinated water production and consumption	24
2.4	Regulated prices of selected fuels for the power and water sectors as of November 2016	31
2.5	Announced renewable energy and energy efficiency targets	33
4.1	Summary of the main policy elements, EU and GCC practices and lessons learned	71
5.1	Renewable energy projects, planned and underway in the GCC	83
5.2	GCC economic reform agenda 2015–2016	87
5.3	Prices for energy products: GCC and the United States	95
6.1	Energy share in GHG emissions in the GCC	106
6.2	GCC credit ratings	107
6.3	Current renewable energy capacity and proposed targets	111
7.1	MENA domestic targets for renewable energy	122
7.2	Renewable support mechanisms	127
8.1	Regulatory policy mechanisms for renewables deployment	144
8.2	GCC renewable energy plans and targets	152
8.3	GCC renewable energy policies	153
8.4	GCC intended nationally determined contributions	154
9.1	Qatar electricity generation forecasts for 2020 and 2030	169
9.2	Qatar's oil and gas subsidies for 2011–2013	175
9.3	CO_2 emissions from oil and gas	176
9.4	Description of variables and variable constraints	178
9.5	Base scenario with parameter values set for sensitivity analysis	179
9.6	Ranking of attributes	182
11.1	GCC country rankings, out of 144, for selected research indicators, 2015–2016	220

Contributors

Ghada Abdulla is an assistant researcher at the Bahrain Center for Strategic, International and Energy Studies. She holds an MSc in Economics from the London School of Economics and Political Science and a BSc in Economics and Finance from the University of York, UK. Her research focus is on the economics of the Gulf Corporation Council (GCC) countries, with a specific interest in the role of renewable energy for the economic diversification and sustainability of GCC economies.

Hisham M. Akhonbay is a research fellow at the King Abdullah Petroleum Studies and Research Center (KAPSARC) working in the area of GCC energy cooperation. He has been with KAPSARC since its inception and served in many roles, including collaboration and research. Previously, as a visiting fellow at the Center for Strategic and International Studies (CSIS) in Washington, DC, USA, Hisham focused on the geopolitics of oil and authored a paper on Energy Policy in Saudi Arabia. He holds an MBA from the American University and a BSc from George Washington University, both in the USA.

Abdullah Al-Badi is a professor in the Electrical & Computer Engineering Department, College of Engineering at the Sultan Qaboos University (SQU), Oman. He holds a BSc in Electrical Engineering from SQU (1991), and received his MSc (1993) and PhD (1998) in electrical machines and drives from UMIST, UK. Abdullah has published more than 100 papers in many well-known international journals and proceedings of refereed international conferences. He carried out several research projects on the effects of AC interference on pipelines, renewable energy, power system and electrical machines. He is a Senior Member of the Institute of Electrical Engineering and Electronics (IEEE) and an IEEE program evaluator for the Accreditation Board for Engineering and Technology (ABET).

Walid Ali (United Nations Development Programme [UNDP]) has over ten years of experience in country policy and program support on climate change and the environment and their links to issues of poverty reduction in least developed country (LDC) and crisis contexts. He has led the development and implementation of several of country-level flagship initiatives on climate change and the environment, funded by the Global Environment Facility (GEF) and the European Commission (EC). Walid's areas of expertise include UN Sustainable Development Goal (SDG) 13 on climate change, the COP21 Paris Agreement and new global climate finance mechanisms. He holds a PhD in Environment and Development and a Post-Doc in Environmental Economics.

Odeh Al-Jayyousi is Professor and Head of the Technology and Innovation Department at the Arabian Gulf University (AGU). Odeh holds a PhD in Urban Planning and Policy Analysis from the University of Illinois at Chicago, USA. He has more than 23 years' experience in conducting research and has engaged in collaborations with many international agencies such as the German Technical Cooperation Agency (GTZ), the United States Agency for International Development (USAID), World Bank (WB), the United Nations (UN) and the UN University (UNU), in areas such as water planning, the environment and policy analysis.

Imtenan Al-Mubarak is a research associate at KAPSARC, focusing on energy and economic policy, with an emphasis on Saudi Arabia, GCC countries and Northeast Asia. She holds a master's degree from DePaul University, Chicago, USA, and a Bachelor's degree from the University of Dammam, Saudi Arabia.

Maha Alsabbagh (Arabian Gulf University [AGU]) holds a PhD in Environment from the University of Leeds, UK. She has ten years' teaching experience and has conducted research for organizations such as the Centre for Environment and Development for the Arab Region and Europe (CEDARE), the United Nations Environment Programme (UNEP), the Arab Forum for Environment and Development (AFED) and the Regional Organization for the Protection of the Marine Environment (ROPME). In 2016, Maha was the recipient of a Rashid bin Humaid Award for Culture and Sciences (Environmental Science research) as well as a Venus International Women Award (VIWA) – Young Women Achiever, and she received a L'Oréal-UN Educational, Scientific and Cultural Organization (UNESCO) For Women in Science – Middle East Fellowship in 2015.

Omar Al-Ubaydli is the Program Director for International and Geo-Political Studies at the Bahrain Center for Strategic, International and Energy Studies, an affiliated associate professor of economics at George Mason University, Virginia, USA, and an affiliated senior research fellow at the Mercatus Center. Al-Ubaydli previously served as a member of the Commonwealth of Virginia's Joint Advisory Board of Economists and as a Visiting Professor of Economics at the University of Chicago, USA.

Moiz Bohra is a second year PhD student at Imperial College London. His research interests are in understanding the national energy system in Qatar and developing computer models to forecast infrastructure changes. He is a scholar under the Qatar Research Leadership Program, supported by the Qatar Foundation.

Sylvain Côté is currently Program Director and Senior Research Fellow in the Energy Demand, Efficiency and Productivity as well as in the Transport and Infrastructures Programs at KAPSARC, Saudi Arabia. Over the past 25 years, he has primarily conducted and directed macroeconomic and labour market research on a variety of issues, which were used to provide policy advice to governments. Sylvain previously worked at the Federal Government of Canada, the Organisation for Economic Co-operation and Development and the North American Commission for Labor Cooperation. He also taught labour economics at the University of Ottawa, Canada.

Nasreddine El-Dehaibi is currently pursuing a PhD in Mechanical Engineering from Stanford University, California, and obtained a master's in Energy Systems Engineering from the University of Michigan, both USA. He has internship experience in the oil and gas industry, and gradually moved into research focusing on renewables and sustainability. His research interests lie in understanding how product design can influence consumers to behave more sustainably.

Amro M. Elshurafa, a Research Fellow at KAPSARC, possesses 15 years' research experience in the fields of energy and technology, acquired on three continents. His research interests lie in renewable energy policy. Within that, Amro focuses on technology assessment, cost trends, supply chain development of the solar industry and how solar power interacts and affects conventional forms of generation. A registered professional engineer in Canada and a Senior Member of the IEEE, Amro is the author of 40+ peer-reviewed papers and reports, and the inventor of several patents. He holds a PhD in Electrical Engineering complemented by an MBA in Finance.

Bassam Fattouh is Director of the Oxford Institute for Energy Studies and Professor at the School of Oriental and African Studies, University of London, UK. He specializes in international oil pricing systems, OPEC pricing power, the security of Middle Eastern oil supplies, the dynamics of oil prices and oil price differentials. He has published extensively in academic and professional journals, and has served as a member of an independent expert group established to provide recommendations to the 12th International Energy Forum (IEF) Ministerial Meeting on strengthening the architecture of the producer-consumer dialogue. He acts as an adviser to governments and industry and is a regular speaker at international conferences.

Stephen Gitonga is a specialist at the United Nations Development Programme (UNDP), with more than 20 years' experience in sustainable energy, climate change and the environment. He has worked for the UNDP, for various international non-governmental organizations and for the Government of Kenya. Stephen is dedicated to spearheading action towards sustainable energy in the face of climate change and has gained extensive experience in programming, coordination and policy support for sustainable development at community, national, regional and global levels. His areas of expertise include design and management of programs, providing policy and programming advice and bringing extensive experience on local capacity development to energy and climate change issues.

Steve Griffiths is Interim Executive Vice President for Research at the Khalifa University of Science and Technology (KUST), Vice President for Research at the Masdar Institute of Science and Technology and Professor of Practice, all in Abu Dhabi. Dr. Griffiths has been elected and appointed to numerous energy policy and energy innovation positions, including the Zayed Future Energy Prize Selection Committee, the Global Energy Prize International Award Committee, *Energy Strategy Reviews* Editorial Board and Associate Editorship, and *Energy Transitions* Editorial Board and Associate Editorship. Dr. Griffiths holds a PhD in Chemical Engineering from the Massachusetts Institute of Technology (MIT) and an MBA from the MIT Sloan School of Management, both USA.

Marwan Khraisheh is a Senior Research Director and the Acting Executive Director of Qatar Foundation's Environment and Energy Research Institute (QEERI). Prior to joining the Qatar Foundation, he was the Founding Dean of the Masdar Institute of Science and Technology, Abu Dhabi, and a member of the Massachusetts Institute of Technology (MIT)-Masdar Joint Executive Committee. Dr. Khraisheh is a recipient of the US National Science Foundation CAREER Award. He is an elected Fellow of the American Society of Mechanical Engineers (ASME), an elected Fellow of the American Association for the Advancement of Science (AAAS) and an elected Member of the International Academy of Production Engineering (CIRP).

Walid Matar is a researcher at the King Abdullah Petroleum Studies and Research Center (KAPSARC) who specializes in developing energy systems models, particularly the KAPSARC Energy Model for Saudi Arabia and its satellite projects. He holds a master's degree in mechanical engineering from North Carolina State University, USA.

Daniah Orkoubi is a Senior Economist at the Ministry of Economy and Planning and the Centre for Strategic Development (CSD), Saudi Arabia. She holds a master's degree in Economics from University of South Florida in Tampa, USA. Daniah is a public policy and research expert with extensive international and government experience covering Arab countries in transition, including economic outlook and key challenges, labour market polices, the Saudi energy mix model and energy policies, and the Saudi national transformation program development.

Rahmatallah Poudineh is the Lead Senior Research Fellow of the electricity program at the Oxford Institute for Energy Studies (OIES), UK. He has several years' industrial experience and is the author of numerous scholarly articles, book chapters and reports, with a focus on industrial organization, policy and regulation of the energy sector. His works have appeared in several journals in the field, including *Energy Policy*, *Energy Strategy Reviews*, *Energy Economics* and *The Energy Journal*. Rahmatallah holds a PhD in Energy Economics from Durham University, UK.

Shreekar Pradhan is a senior research associate at KAPSARC, Saudi Arabia. His research interests include economic assessments of environmental and energy policies in partial equilibrium and general equilibrium modelling environment, with a focus on international trade and environment. He holds a PhD in Economics from the University of Tennessee at Knoxville, USA, and an MSc in Renewable Energy Engineering from the Tribhuvan University in Kathmandu, Nepal.

Antonio Sanfilippo is Research Director at the Qatar Environment & Energy Research Institute, where he leads the smart grid research program. From 2003 to 2014, he was Chief Scientist at the Pacific Northwest National Laboratory (United States Department of Energy), where he led projects for various government agencies including the Department of Homeland Security and the National Institutes of Health. Dr. Sanfilippo has also held positions as Research Director in the private sector and senior consultant at the European Commission. He holds an MPhil from Columbia University, USA, and a PhD from the University of Edinburgh, UK.

Anupama Sen is a Senior Research Fellow at the Oxford Institute for Energy Studies, UK, specializing in the applied economics of energy in developing countries. Her research has appeared in many peer-reviewed academic journals and professional publications such as *The Energy Journal* and *Gas Matters*, as well as in several book chapters and op-eds. She is a Fellow of the Cambridge Commonwealth Society and was a Visiting Fellow at Wolfson College, Cambridge, UK. She holds a BA from Mumbai University, India, an MSc from the London School of Economics and a PhD from Cambridge University, both UK.

Marilyn Smith is an editor and communications consultant specializing in the energy sector, providing services to organizations such as KAPSARC, the Edison Electric Institute, the International Energy Agency and the Asia-Pacific Energy Research Centre. She also serves as Executive Director of The Energy Action Project (EnAct / www.en-act.org), a multimedia project that brings together energy experts and journalists with the aim of raising awareness of energy poverty and boosting energy literacy.

David Wogan is a Research Associate at KAPSARC, Saudi Arabia, whose research focuses on modelling the economics of integrated energy systems, with a focus on electricity and water production in Saudi Arabia and the surrounding Gulf countries. Recent studies have focused on the impact of energy price reform on the technology and fuel mix of the Saudi electricity sector and the nexus of water, energy and agriculture. Ongoing projects include assessing efficient carbon mitigation pathways for meeting Saudi Arabia's commitments to the COP21 Paris Agreement and the value of electricity trade among countries in the Arabian Peninsula. Prior to joining KAPSARC, David led energy efficiency efforts at the municipally owned electric utility in Austin, Texas, and served at the White House Council on Environmental Quality on the Energy & Climate Change Directorate, both USA. David holds an MSc in Mechanical Engineering and a Master's of Public Affairs from the University of Texas at Austin, USA.

Lama Yaseen is a Senior Research Analyst at KAPSARC, Saudi Arabia. She holds a BSc in Computer Science from Effat University, Saudi Arabia, and specializes in data analysis and research tools development. She works mainly on the development and modelling of collective decision-making processes.

Karen E. Young is a Senior Resident Scholar at the Arab Gulf States Institute in Washington (AGSIW), USA. She was a Research Fellow at the Middle East Centre of the London School of Economics and Political Science in 2014–15, where she remains a non-resident Fellow. From 2009 to 2014, she was Assistant Professor of political science at the American University of Sharjah, UAE. Young is the author of *The Political Economy of Energy, Finance and Security in the United Arab Emirates: Between the Majilis and the Market*, published by Palgrave in 2014.

Foreword

With abundant sun, steady winds and vast tracts of land that are largely unused, transitioning to renewable energy sources might seem an obvious choice for countries in the Arabian Gulf. Indeed, all six countries belonging to the Cooperation Council for the Arab States of the Gulf – more commonly known as the Gulf Cooperation Council (GCC), comprising Bahrain, Kuwait, Oman, Qatar, Saudi Arabia and the United Arab Emirates – have announced ambitious plans to do so.

In reality, deploying renewables in this region is perhaps more complex than anywhere else in the world, as the rapid economic and social development realized in recent decades is directly linked to the region's vast hydrocarbon resources. Both oil and natural gas can be extracted and used domestically for very low costs and exported to global markets for profits that at times have led to substantial revenues, which governments redeploy through various social programs.

The potential for renewable energy in this region is vital to multiple areas of investigation being carried out by the King Abdullah Petroleum Studies and Research Center (KAPSARC), including the core theme of energy economics. To shed light on the topic, KAPSARC brought together a forum of experts from diverse research centers to develop the in-depth analysis presented here.

This publication demonstrates the value of regional cooperation. Through a series of workshops specific to renewable energy deployment in the GCC, participants identified areas of strength, outstanding technical challenges and policy actions needed to stimulate a thriving renewable energy sector, including energy sector reform and reducing the perception of risk in order to secure the substantial investment needed. This publication offers diverse perspectives, advances research and assesses the value of applying proven approaches to the GCC context. It is not intended to be comprehensive, but to deliver insights that are relevant to policymakers and other stakeholders.

Recognizing the diversity of stakeholders who need to engage in a GCC clean energy transition, this publication aims to strike an appropriate balance of academic rigor, thoughtful analysis and accessible presentation.

Adam Sieminski
President, King Abdullah Petroleum
Studies and Research Center
(KAPSARC)

David Hobbs
Head of Research, King Abdullah
Petroleum Studies and Research
Center (KAPSARC)

Acknowledgements

This publication was prepared by the King Abdullah Petroleum Studies and Research Center (KAPSARC) through close collaboration via a GCC Energy Experts Forum. The work was coordinated by KAPSARC and led by Hisham Akhonbay, Research Fellow, with the assistance of Lama Yaseen, Senior Research Analyst, and Imtenan Al-Mubarak, Research Associate. This team worked under the direction of Brian Efird, Director and Senior Research Fellow, and David Hobbs, Head of Research.

Contributing authors were strategically chosen to ensure that the rich expertise from within the GCC region would be coupled with insights from those who could bring impartial views and other perspectives. The authors include: Ghada Abdulla (Bahrain Center for Strategic, International and Energy Studies), Abdullah Al-Badi (Sultan Qaboos University), Walid Ali (United Nations Development Program), Odeh Al-Jayyousi (Arab Gulf University), Imtenan Al-Mubarak (KAPSARC), Maha Alsabbagh (Arabian Gulf University), Omar Al-Ubaydli (Bahrain Center for Strategic, International and Energy Studies; George Mason University; and Arab Gulf States Institute in Washington), Moiz Bohra (Imperial College London), Sylvain Côté (KAPSARC), Nasreddine El Dehaibi (Stanford University), Amro Elshurafa (KAPSARC), Bassam Fattouh (Oxford Institute for Economic Studies), Stephen Gitonga (UNDP), Steve Griffiths (Masdar Institute of Science and Technology), Marwan Khraisheh (Hamad Bin Khalifa University), Walid Matar (KAPSARC), Daniah Orkoubi (Ministry of Economy and Planning, Saudi Arabia), Rahmatallah Poudineh (OIES), Shreekar Pradhan (KAPSARC), Antonio Sanfilippo (Hamad Bin Khalifa University), Anupama Sen (OIES), Marilyn Smith (EnACT), David Wogan (KAPSARC), Lama Yaseen (KAPSARC) and Karen E. Young (Arab Gulf States Institute in Washington and London School of Economics). Concise biographies of authors are included in the list of contributors.

Sincere thanks to those individuals who agreed to review portions of the book during its development, including: Shahad Al-Arenan (KAPSARC), Turki Al-Shihri (National Renewable Energy Program (NREP) and associates at the Renewable Energy Project Development Office (REPDO), Abdullah Al-Tuwaijri (KAPSARC); Jorge Blazquez (KAPSARC), Marcelo Contestable (KAPSARC), Rolando Fuentes (KAPSARC), Samantha Gross (The Brooking

Institution), Lester Hunt (KAPSARC), Hussam Khonkar (King Abdulaziz City for Science and Technology), Daniel Mabrey (KAPSARC), Baltasar Manzano (KAPSARC), Abdulaziz Mohammed (Arab Gulf University), Roger Tissot (KAPSARC) and Hashim Zain (King Abdullah University of Science and Technology).

Similarly, the authors acknowledge the contributions of organizations and entities that provided access to data, agreed to be consulted, or reviewed content to ensure the unique characteristics of the GCC region were appropriately considered in this assessment of ways to stimulate a renewable energy transition in economies that have advanced economically and socially through exploitation of hydrocarbon resources. Specifically, we acknowledge the National Renewable Energy Program (NREP), the Kuwait Institute for Scientific Research (KISR) and the Arab Gulf University (AGU).

Marilyn Smith (consultant to KAPSARC) oversaw the editorial work required to ensure that the content of the book, at times rather technical and authored in diverse styles, would be rendered in a final document that is accurate to the authors' intent while also accessible to both expert and non-expert readers. Rajendran Ramasamy (KAPSARC) and consultants Ana Maria Coric, Kristine Douaud, Eloise Logan, Maria Sperling and Ghada Al-Shubaili assisted with efforts in the lead-up to final production.

1   Introduction

Hisham M. Akhonbay and Marilyn Smith

Ambitious plans to transition to a global low carbon energy system are emerging worldwide, particularly after the rapid ratification of the Paris Agreement, achieved in the context of the 21st Conference of the Parties (COP21) of the United Nations Framework Convention on Climate Change (UNFCCC). Many countries and other actors are forging ahead with their stated commitments, despite the withdrawal of the United States from the Paris Agreement. Also emerging are the associated challenges for low carbon energy, which are perhaps greatest in the region of the Arab Gulf where vast low-cost hydrocarbon resources have underpinned economic and social development in recent decades.

The potential for renewable energy is also vast in the six countries belonging to the Cooperation Council of the Arab States of the Gulf – more commonly known as the Gulf Cooperation Council (GCC), which is how it is identified here – Bahrain, Kuwait, Oman, Qatar, Saudi Arabia and the United Arab Emirates (UAE). The GCC area is well endowed with wind and solar resources. The annual solar potential is the equivalent of 2,000 kilowatt hours per square meter (kWh/sq m) in most areas. Developing just 1 per cent of the suitable area could result in 470 gigawatts (GW) of solar photovoltaic (PV) capacity and 60 GW of wind power (IRENA 2016). Additionally, the region has vast tracts of land that are largely unused, mitigating the challenge of competition for land for other activities. Recognizing that solar is likely to account for the major share of renewable energy development in the region, this publication focuses on the potential for solar energy in power generation.

With due consideration of global aspects, this publication probes the renewables transition within the national and regional dynamics of the GCC, examining the opportunities associated with such a transition and also seeking to identify and address related challenges. It is relatively easy to identify multiple motivations for renewable energy deployment in the GCC. Pursuing a comprehensive and coordinated strategy for renewable energy, and for solar power generation in particular, can reduce dependence on hydrocarbon feedstock, minimize fuel costs, and reduce carbon dioxide (CO_2) and other greenhouse gas (GHG) emissions, while also creating new industries and related employment opportunities. The outcome will assist the GCC transition to a more sustainable development path and optimize the value of the resource endowments of member countries.

Across the region, energy demand – particularly for electricity – is being boosted by increasing population and ongoing economic growth. As electricity generation is fueled almost exclusively by oil and gas, switching to renewable sources for domestic consumption is central to charting new pathways in recent visions or strategies published by GCC countries.

In the context of low oil prices on global markets substantially reducing GCC government revenues, the historical practice of providing power and water at below-market prices has become financially unsustainable. Deploying renewable energy for power generation domestically would make larger volumes of hydrocarbons available for export or for other higher value uses, effectively boosting government revenues while still promoting economic development. Stimulating a renewables sector could also satisfy a portion of national aims to diversify economies and stimulate employment of nationals. At the regional level, the existence of the interregional grid represents an untapped opportunity to optimize capacity, generation and transmission and distribution. Finally, all GCC countries are committed to the global objectives of the Paris Agreement, a core element of which is reducing GHG emissions. At present, GCC countries have very high per capita emissions compared with other developed countries; large-scale deployment of renewable energy and low carbon technologies can help to achieve stated goals.

The success of any major transformation or change initiative typically requires a long-term strategic vision, a well defined road map and a clear set of supporting policies. At present, each GCC country has stated goals for renewable energy deployment, either as a percentage of power generation or as a specific generating capacity. On the percentage of capacity side, by 2030 Kuwait aims for 15 per cent, Bahrain for 5 per cent, and Qatar for 20 per cent. The UAE has specified goals for each state, with Abu Dhabi aiming for 7 per cent capacity by 2020 and Dubai planning to install 5 GW of solar PV by 2040. Oman does not have any specific renewables target; rather, it pledged to reduce gas use in power generation by 5 per cent per kWh. Saudi Arabia specified capacity of 9.5 GW by 2023 and 54 GW by 2040.[1] This focus on renewables has resulted in $800 (USD) million of investments across the GCC in 2015; with 24 additional renewables projects planned, investment is expected to increase.

Intended as a reference for the many stakeholders that will be involved in deploying renewable energy in the GCC, this publication summarizes the current status of energy supply and demand in the region. It then examines renewable energy development to date, again with a focus on solar power generation. Acknowledging the underlying economic challenges of transitioning from low-cost hydrocarbons to renewable energy sources, the publication examines the macroeconomic benefits that governments could realize. In fact, it makes the case that the current context of fiscal restraint associated with low oil prices creates an unforeseen opportunity to initiate – albeit gradually – large-scale reform across the energy sector. Finally, several authors review the policy environment in the GCC and globally, with an eye toward understanding the instruments and mechanisms that have been shown to spur renewable energy deployment. This entails reviewing the pricing, legal, and regulatory structures with an emphasis on the social aspects, as well as the effectiveness of such measures when executed in a coordinated manner across the GCC states.

Capturing the full potential of solar energy

Demand for electricity in the GCC is projected to double by 2040. Increasing electricity generation to keep pace with rapid population growth and sustain economic growth while also curbing the region's high CO_2 and GHG emissions presents a massive challenge. In Chapter 2, David Wogan, Imtenan Al-Mubarak, Abdullah Al-Badi and Shreekar Pradhan set out the reality of demand growth in the GCC and demonstrate the need for GCC countries to take aggressive action away from oil- and gas-fired power generation. The chapter highlights the complexity of the GCC energy system, but also points to opportunities to make it more efficient through renewables integration and electricity trading. The remainder of the publication is dedicated to exploring different options to achieve the desired outcome by meeting part of the projected demand growth through renewable energy deployment.

The opportunity to capture multiple benefits by deploying renewable energy for power generation in the GCC is clear, yet the underlying economics remain a substantial challenge. In Chapter 3, Amro Elshurafa and Walid Matar analyze the costs and benefits from the perspectives of households – installing rooftop solar photovoltaics (PV) – and utilities, deploying large-scale PV or concentrating solar power (CSP). In both cases, the low rate of current tariffs serves as a strong disincentive for personal or private sector investment. Yet experts estimate that each gigawatt of renewable capacity installed in the GCC will reduce hydrocarbon demand by 3 million barrels (Mbbl) annually, delivering both economic and environmental gains. Shifting to a macroeconomic approach, the authors argue that under GCC economic structures, governments stand to gain the most from a low carbon transition and, hence, they should both lead efforts to deploy solar power and shoulder a large portion of the initial financial investment needed. They can also put in place reforms that will, over time, provide sufficient incentive for private investors also to engage. This premise underpins the analysis of the next set of chapters, and indeed the publication as a whole, which considers policies and mechanisms that can stimulate the transition.

If GCC governments are to take the lead in stimulating renewable energy deployment, it bears asking more precisely what role they could take, what tools they can apply and, indeed, is there any opportunity to gain from the experience of others who have gone before? In Chapter 4, Maha Alsabbagh and Odeh Al-Jayyousi examine the path followed by European Union (EU) countries, which saw wind and solar generation increase from just under 100 terawatt hours (TWh) in 2005 to over 400 TWh in 2015 (Eurostat 2015).

Acknowledging several fundamental differences between the EU and GCC contexts, the authors identify parallels that offer opportunities for GCC governments to move more quickly and also to avoid some missteps.

Their research highlights the lessons that characterize the transition in the EU. Most notably, policy formulation began as early as 1990, leading to the two foundational directives: the Renewable Electricity Directive of 2001 and the Renewable Energy Directive of 2009, which set out the specific goals of the Vision 20/20/20 initiative. The EU experience has been successful, in part, because the member states agreed to establish clear policies covering areas such as joint research, development and innovation, and to create common, yet flexible, regulatory measures. The policies coordinated efforts around energy efficiency, renewable energy and climate change mitigation/ abatement and adaptation.

The EU-GCC comparative analysis finds that GCC countries can benefit from establishing more robust and comprehensive national and regional policy frameworks and set specific measures to spur renewable energy deployment. The authors offer recommendations appropriate to the GCC context on how to fill the gaps.

The features that are unique to the GCC region, particularly in light of the current downturn in commodity prices, and the economic challenges associated with renewable energy deployment are investigated in Chapter 5 by Karen Young, who asserts that, in a dramatically changing context, governments need to reexamine their roles. Traditionally, GCC governments have been 'providers' of essential services including energy; their new role may be more akin to an entity that establishes an environment that allows the private sector to flourish and compete in a more liberalized energy market. As the cost of renewable energy deployment is beyond the capability of most GCC governments, attracting substantial investment from private companies, development banks and foreign direct investment agencies will be critical. Thus, to seize the opportunity of renewable energy, governments will need to implement economic and legal reforms that allow the private sector to participate more efficiently. Recent examples of successful public–private partnerships (PPPs) and independent power producers (IPPs) help build the case for the further opening up of the energy sector while innovations in financing, such as green bonds and *sukuks* (Islamic bonds), show strong potential for attracting capital.

Attracting financing to renewable energy projects remains a significant challenge in any context: the technologies, business models and prospects for adequate returns remain uncertain, so investment is perceived as having a higher risk than backing conventional energy capacity. As is evident in developing countries, this can drive up the cost of financing renewable energy by as much as 40 per cent against gas-fired plants, for example. Here again, governments can play a vital role. In Chapter 6, Stephen Gitonga and Walid Ali explain how a tool called De-risking Renewable Energy Investment, developed by the United Nations Development Program (UNDP), has helped governments in developing countries assess why renewable energy investment is perceived as high risk, and what regulatory and legal reforms might effectively 'de-risk' such investments. A case study from Tunisia demonstrates how the tool can be applied and suggests its potential for the GCC. The GCC will require as much as 72 GW to be installed between 2020 and 2040. While GCC countries have the substantial advantage of being in good financial standing, thus mitigating the risk of default, the private sector continues to perceive risk in non financial elements, including the lack of policies and regulations – for example, lack of transparency in procurement programs, difficulty in acquiring permits, nationally focused real estate laws and emerging labor issues. De-risking investment through policy reform, the authors suggest, could set the stage to make the GCC a low carbon investment hub.

Setting new policy frameworks for renewable energy

Tackling the policy environment is one the most important challenges when initiating large-scale renewable energy deployment. The next chapters investigate the possible policy instruments that could be implemented in order to make the intended plans operational.

Recognizing that renewables have effectively been 'locked out' of resource rich countries in the Middle East and North Africa (MENA), not only by low-cost hydrocarbon resources but by perceived risks and uncertainties, lack of necessary institutions and inadequate grid infrastructure, the Oxford Institute for Energy Studies authors (Rahmatallah Poudineh, Anupama Sen and Bassam Fattouh) set out in Chapter 7 how systematic policy reform can create an environment that stimulates deployment. Starting from the realities that large-scale deployment will require private investment, yet no investors will participate without sufficient economic incentive, this chapter addresses the need to enable a renewables market through pricing and subsidy reform across the electricity sector. Faced with the choice of completely eliminating existing price subsidies, which is politically challenging and would have severe economic impacts, or heavily incentivizing renewables to make them cost competitive, GCC countries bear a heavy financial burden either way. The more feasible approach, the authors suggest, is 'combinatorial', i.e., it involves partial reform of fossil fuel prices in the medium term, while providing partial government subsidies to renewable energy. The process of price reform would continue in the long term to bring prices across all energy generation technologies closer to economic cost. This will give strong signals to potential investors of the long-term aim to move toward a fully competitive energy market. In parallel, to attract investors, GCC countries will need to enhance grids, strengthen institutions and remove risks in the areas of politics, policy and regulation, technology, currency and liquidity, and creditworthy power off-takers.

Continuing on the theme of setting intermediate goals to achieve the final aim of meeting demand in a reliable, efficient, and sustainable manner, in Chapter 8 Steve Griffiths and Daniah Orkoubi probe the relationship between energy and climate change policy in creating effective market clearing mechanisms. They also examine the effects of explicit and implicit carbon pricing on renewable energy development. The chapter explores several policy instruments that could be applied in the GCC context: competitive supply long-term auctions, net metering, feed-in tariffs, carbon pricing and emissions trading schemes. (Net metering provides credit to customers with solar PV systems, via a special billing arrangement, for the full retail value of the electricity their system generates.)

Equally important is to properly design and execute the distribution mechanisms by which resulting funds could be allocated, such as green spending, green funds, and revenue recycling. Experience in the UAE shows that auctions have been effective in incentivizing the first wave of renewable energy projects in the region. Over the longer term, the most efficient and sustainable way to incentivize renewable energy in the GCC is by creating a market based system that allows supply and demand to interact, likely including measures such as explicit carbon pricing. Ultimately, the authors propose a phased approach to create – and over time strengthen – an integrated energy and climate policy framework. Early steps to promote distributed generation and solar water heating, in parallel with energy pricing reform, can help build a foundation for more aggressive action such as establishing a regional or sub regional emission trading scheme.

Energy system planning and integration to support renewables

Integrating renewable energy into conventional power systems requires substantial planning and strategic action to build up necessary infrastructure and eliminate existing institutional and market barriers. The following section explores innovative approaches to integration and assesses technical and policy considerations associated with realizing the potential of a more fully interconnected and optimally used grid in the GCC.

Targeting 20 per cent of electricity generation coming from renewables by 2030, Qatar is now considering how to optimize the savings and returns that both citizens and the government can derive from various fuel mix strategies. Moiz Bohra, Nasreddine El-Dehaibi, Antonio Sanfilippo and Marwan Khraisheh demonstrate in Chapter 9 how a cost utility function that accounts for six elements – oil and gas prices, oil and gas subsidies, the levelized cost of energy from gas and the introduction of a carbon tax – can inform policy decision-making. Acknowledging that the cost-savings from various fuel mix strategies depend strongly on the global hydrocarbon market, which is beyond the control of the Qatar government, the chapter comes to the conclusion that oil prices determine whether it is preferable to have renewables displace oil or gas. When oil is priced at $88 per barrel (/bbl) or higher, replacing oil with solar delivers higher savings; at a lower oil price, replacing gas is more advantageous. The point of the work is to demonstrate how governments can control endogenous factors to achieve best-case outcomes despite the exogenous factors affecting energy markets. As natural gas is the backbone of the Qatar economy, one of the most interesting scenarios to pursue is using gas-powered generation for electric vehicles (EVs) as a means to reduce oil consumption. The first step, then, may actually be to incentivize the adoption of EVs, even ahead of decarbonizing generation.

Additional benefits of building a renewable energy sector

While meeting growing demand is the primary motivation underpinning the build up of renewable energy capacity, other factors align well with GCC long-term goals such as creating jobs and stimulating new industries. In addition to exploring such benefits, the publication's final section examines the prospects for renewable energy to be a catalyst for further integration within the GCC and help move countries toward a more knowledge based economy.

With GCC countries looking to diversify their economies and boost employment of nationals, many agencies have investigated how a renewable energy transition could feed into these aims. A recent demographic shift means more than 50 per cent of the population in GCC countries is currently under the age of 25. While education and skill levels have improved among this young cohort – 20 to 25 years of age – unemployment rates within it are quite high, reaching 28 per cent in Saudi Arabia, 26 per cent in Bahrain, and 20 per cent in Oman. Many see renewable energy development as a potential boon to employment; indeed, renewable energy creates 0.65 jobs per gigawatt hour (/GWh) compared with just 0.15/GWh from conventional fossil fuel generation. Focusing on Saudi Arabia, analysis in Chapter 10 by Sylvain Côté goes behind the estimated number of jobs created to consider what types of workers will be needed and at what stages of development, installation, operation and eventual decommissioning. Joint effort between the government and the private sector will be needed to bridge the gap between what type of workers are needed in the renewables sector and the education paths and career aspirations of young Saudis. Attracting Saudis to the renewables sector will require concerted effort by departments of labor, education and vocational training to raise public awareness of opportunities and to ensure that nationals are equipped to step into the renewable energy workforce.

While shifting to renewable energy sources delivers many national benefits – and, indeed, requires national action – the opportunity to seize them might well be most efficiently achieved through regional cooperation. Countries in the GCC have made strides toward integrating the region economically and politically. Deployment of renewable energy can be another 'connection point' to further enhance cooperation. Transitioning to cleaner electricity systems will require substantial financial investment and significant skills buildup, including for research, development, innovation, and employment. At present, the region shows low levels of research and development (R&D) spending and output, as well as a lack of coordination of efforts. In Chapter 11, Omar Al-Ubaydli, Ghada Abdulla and Lama Yaseen make the case that coordinated policy action across all of these areas can help to spread the costs, avoid duplication of effort and deliver economies of scale and of scope while also supporting specialization to capture each country's comparative advantage. Reaching agreement on issues such as standards can help set the stage for participating as a bloc in larger consumer and producer markets. Finally, cooperation on renewables development can encourage further long-term collaboration to develop sustainable energy plans that appropriately consider the three key elements of energy policy: renewable energy, energy efficiency and climate change mitigation.

The GCC countries are resource rich economies that have used these endowments to drive economic and social progress over the past decades. Paradoxically, the hydrocarbon resources that spurred past development are now the major challenge that renewable energy must overcome to become competitive. If the region is to transition to a low carbon and environmentally friendly energy system that includes renewable energy, it will have to engage in far-reaching economic and regulatory reform that will send signals to the private sector to participate and encourage investments. This implies tackling several issues associated with pricing, regulatory and policy reforms. Technically, the region can accomplish the renewable targets recently set out in various vision and strategy documents. This publication provides insights to help policymakers develop a policy environment that will deliver their ambitious plans.

This edited volume, which collects the efforts of numerous government funded, GCC based energy researchers, can be considered a first step toward a more centralized renewables policy. The authors are confident that the impact of the volume will be greater than a collection of independently produced papers; by carefully coordinating efforts, the editorial team has sought to maximize complementarity among the different contributions and to minimize replication. We urge authorities to consider taking similar steps in the technological domain in an effort to realize isomorphic gains.

This collection of chapters brings together the efforts of several GCC based energy research centers. Its production has been accompanied and driven by workshops and interaction among these institutions that have created a shared understanding of the opportunities and challenges.

Note

1 The analysis contained within this book was completed in early 2017. The effort pre-dates the "Solar 2030" plan which was made official in March 2018 through a signed Memorandum of Understanding (MoU) between SoftBank and the Public Investment Fund of Saudi Arabia (Arab News 2018).

References

Arab News (2018) Saudi crown prince signs MoU with SoftBank to set up world's largest solar project. *Arab News.* www.arabnews.com/node/1274906/breaking-news (accessed May 16, 2018).

Eurostat (2015) Primary production of energy from renewable sources, EU-28, 1990–2015 F2. http://ec.europa.eu/eurostat/statistics-explained/index.php/File: Primary_production_of_energy_from_renewable_sources,_EU-28,_1990-2015_ F2.png (accessed May 16, 2018).

IRENA (2016) Website. http://irena.org/publications/2016/Jan/Renewable-Energy-Market-Analysis-The-GCC-Region (accessed May 16, 2018).

2 Overview of energy supply and demand in the GCC

David Wogan, Imtenan Al-Mubarak, Abdullah Al-Badi and Shreekar Pradhan

Abstract

The energy sector is a large contributor to the economic and social development in countries belonging to the Gulf Cooperation Council (GCC). It is also vital to meeting the water and food needs in a region that is predominantly hot and arid. Over the past several decades, access to abundant and low-cost energy has dramatically improved living standards and industrialization, ultimately leading to some of the highest growth in energy demand in the world. At present, virtually all electricity is generated using abundant, low-cost fossil fuels – primarily natural gas and oil. Should current trends continue, electricity demand will continue to rise, prompting a parallel increase in demand for these fuels. This chapter presents an overview of supply and demand in the GCC energy system, which is important for understanding how renewable energy can be integrated and optimized. It begins by describing the GCC energy system and the factors that contribute to energy demand. Its focus then turns to energy transformation in the electricity and water sectors. An assessment of fossil and renewable resources follows after which the next section addresses barriers to coordination in the form of government subsidized fuel prices and electricity tariffs. A sampling of existing energy policies, future targets, and power sector reforms is then covered and the chapter concludes with a discussion of opportunities and challenges of renewable energy in the context of the GCC.

Introduction

The energy sector is a large contributor to the economic and social development in countries belonging to the Gulf Cooperation Council (GCC). It is also vital to meeting the water and food needs in a region that is predominantly hot and arid. Over the past several decades, access to abundant and low-cost energy has dramatically improved living standards and industrialization, ultimately leading to some of the highest growth in energy demand in the world. At present, virtually all electricity is generated using abundant, low-cost fossil fuels – primarily natural gas and oil. Should current trends continue, electricity demand will continue to rise, prompting a parallel increase in demand for these fuels.

The utilities sectors, for the most part, are owned and operated by the governments, and a significant proportion of government expenditures is associated with delivering energy products at prices that are below market value – traditionally a mechanism of sharing the wealth of the region's resource endowment. As low prices on global oil markets have led to tighter national budgets in the region, GCC governments now face substantial challenges in keeping pace with increasing domestic energy and water demand.

With demand projected to continue rising as GCC populations increase and economic development continues, supplying energy in a more sustainable and economically efficient manner is a key priority for governments in the region.

Increasing the share of renewable resources in electricity production is part of an emerging fuel mix strategy to address the challenges in domestic energy sectors and to deliver co-benefits. Renewable generation could displace fossil generation, freeing those resources for higher value-added uses and for export – thus, ultimately, contributing to an uplift in government revenues. This would, in turn, contribute to meeting the Nationally Determined Contributions (NDCs) that GCC countries made under the COP21 Paris Agreement.

This chapter presents an overview of supply and demand in the GCC energy system, which is important to understanding how renewable energy can be integrated and optimized. It begins by describing the GCC energy system and the factors that contribute to energy demand. Its focus then turns to energy transformation in the electricity and water sectors. An assessment of fossil and renewable resources follows after which the subsequent section addresses barriers to coordination in the form of government subsidized fuel prices and electricity tariffs. A sampling of existing energy policies, future targets, and power sector reforms is then covered and the chapter concludes with a discussion of opportunities and challenges of renewable energy in the context of the GCC.

Policy relevant insights

- A strong link between electricity generation and water production is a unique feature of energy systems in the Gulf Cooperation Council (GCC) countries. While energy resources are abundant, water is scarce. To make informed policy decisions when developing plans to sustainably meet future demand for electricity and water, policymakers need to consider both resources together.
- GCC states are well endowed with fossil and renewable resources. To date, fossil energy has been exploited for export and domestic consumption, while use of renewable resources has contributed

(continued)

(continued)

negligibly to electricity supply. Renewable resources are well positioned to contribute to electricity supply, which aligns with new economic and environmental goals.

- Low energy prices continue to be a key barrier to greater penetration of renewable technologies in the GCC power and water sectors. Price reforms underway are expected to improve the cost-effectiveness of renewables.
- Electricity trade can be a key enabler to improve the economics of renewables in the GCC as it will create a larger market in which to integrate renewables. Utilizing the GCC Interconnector as a trading platform could enhance the economics of renewable technologies by better aligning supply with demand, both temporally and geographically.

The Gulf Cooperation Council energy system

Founded in 1981, the Gulf Cooperation Council (GCC) is a union of six states in the Arabian Peninsula: the Kingdom of Bahrain, the State of Kuwait, the Sultanate of Oman, the State of Qatar, the Kingdom of Saudi Arabia (KSA), and the United Arab Emirates (UAE) (GCC General Secretariat 2016). To capture the geographic variation of electricity and water production and consumption, this analysis disaggregates the six GCC states into 12 regions (Figure 2.1).

Bahrain, Kuwait and Qatar are represented as individual regions due to their small size. For simplicity, Oman is currently considered as a single region even though it has three electricity systems: the Main Interconnected System, which includes Muscat; the Dhofar Power System, which includes Salalah; and the Rural Areas System. Saudi Arabia is considered as four regions – east, west, south, and central – that correspond to the service areas defined by the Saudi Electricity Company (SEC). The UAE is represented as four regions: Abu Dhabi, Dubai, Sharjah, and the Federal Electricity and Water Authority (FEWA), which correspond to the regulatory authorities for the remaining four emirates.

Energy demand and growth

Within the GCC, there are substantial differences in the growth of total primary energy consumption from 1965 to 2015 for Kuwait, Qatar, Saudi Arabia, and the UAE (Figure 2.2) (BP 2017). All countries follow a similar trend, but magnitudes are different due to several factors including population, economic development, and urbanization.

GCC Energy System: Background

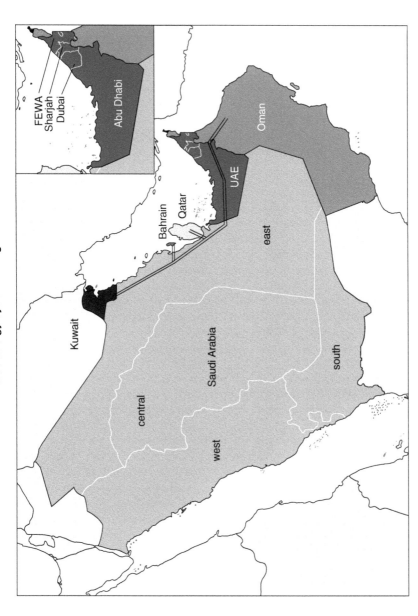

Figure 2.1 GCC member states, disaggregated into regions with GCC Interconnector shown in red (GCC Interconnection Authority, KAPSARC)

Population growth

In just 60 years, total population in the region has increased tenfold, from approximately 5 million in 1960 to 53 million in 2015. From 1990 onward, the GCC population more than doubled, from 21 million to 53 million (World Bank 2014). At present, Saudi Arabia is the most populous (31 million), followed by the UAE (9 million), Oman (4.5 million), Kuwait (4 million), Qatar (2 million), and Bahrain (1.4 million).

Two main factors have driven up population in the GCC region: high birth rates and high rates of labor migration. Across the GCC, foreign nationals represent 51 per cent of the total population, with particularly high expatriate population shares in the UAE (89 per cent), Qatar (86 per cent), and Kuwait (70 per cent). Saudi Arabia has the largest number of foreigners, but also the lowest expatriate ratio at 37 per cent.

Economic development

The discovery of oil spurred economic development in the GCC. In 1980, when the oil price peaked at around $102 per barrel (/bbl), GCC governments used the revenues resulting from exports to pursue aggressive economic and social development, including the development of large-scale infrastructure and the launch of heavy – i.e., energy intensive – industries such as petrochemicals and cement production. This expansion led to a staggering rate of energy consumption growth. As oil prices declined in 1986, the combination of lower demand and higher production created a supply glut that pushed the price down to less than $22/bbl (in today's prices). The consequence was a great loss in revenue for the GCC oil-producing economies.

The GCC economies have witnessed a similar boom and bust cycle in the past decade. Between 2002 and 2008, oil prices rose again to highs of $147/bbl and the combined GCC economy tripled in size to $1.1 trillion. The subsequent price drop, to around $30/bbl in 2014, shaved around $360 billion from the region's export revenue in 2015. Overall, high dependence on a volatile commodity has created an environment in which GCC economies are highly vulnerable to oil market cycles. In recent years, oil prices have been recovering from a low of $30/bbl to a monthly average of $40/bbl to $50/bbl, less than half of the 2014 peak ($112/bbl). The resulting lower public spending has slowed overall growth.

In response, GCC governments are increasing efforts to diversify their economies beyond hydrocarbons and have introduced several reform initiatives that focus on improving the medium-term fiscal outlook. Several megaprojects that should support growth in the near term have been announced, such as the Dubai World Expo 2020, the World Cup 2022 in Qatar, and the King Abdullah Economic City (KAEC).

Urbanization

Most of the GCC region is highly urbanized: on average, urban dwellers account for 80 per cent of the population, while both Kuwait and Qatar are almost 100 per cent urbanized. This has influenced GCC government spending to build road and public transportation networks, intercity highways, and industrial and economic cities.

In recent years, vehicle ownership rates in this region have increased rapidly. The number of commercial and personal vehicles in use has grown at an annualized rate of 7 per cent from 9.8 million in 2010 to an estimated 13.7 million in 2015. To curb energy consumption and reduce road traffic, GCC governments have invested in public transport infrastructure. The GCC wide railway network cost about $200bn and is scheduled to be completed in 2018. In addition, metro line construction projects were contracted in Riyadh, Abu Dhabi, Kuwait, Jeddah, Medina, and Mecca.

Urban planning is an important factor that influences both land use and transportation energy demand. In this region, substantial opportunity exists to make urban expansion more efficient and environmentally friendly.

The industrial sector accounts for the largest share of total final energy consumption in the GCC, representing half of all demand. The transport sector accounts for the second largest share (32 per cent), followed by the residential (10 per cent), commercial (5 per cent), and other sectors (2 per cent) (IRENA 2016).

In terms of energy consumption, the residential sector accounts for most of demand in almost all GCC countries (Figure 2.3) (Kingdom of Bahrain CIO 2012; ECRA 2014; Kuwait CSB 2015; OPWP 2015). The exceptions are Qatar, where industry is the largest consumer (67 per cent), and

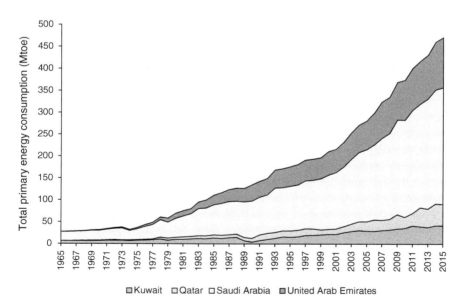

Figure 2.2 Total primary energy consumption from 1965–2015, million tonnes of oil equivalent (Mtoe) (BP *Statistical Review of World Energy* (2017), KAPSARC)

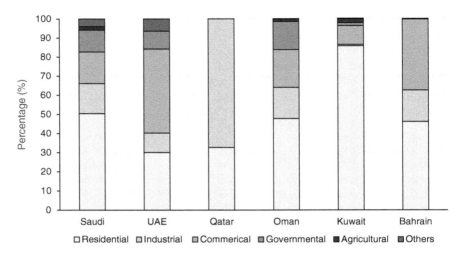

Figure 2.3 Sectoral energy consumption, 2015 (IRENA 2016)

the UAE, where the commercial sector is highest (43 per cent) (QEWC 2014; UAE Ministry of Energy 2015). Between 2003 and 2013, electricity consumption across the GCC region showed an average annual growth rate (AAGR) of 6 per cent to 7 per cent, largely driven by the residential sector which accounts for roughly 44 per cent of the region's total consumption (IRENA 2016).

Energy pricing

For the most part, governments control the energy assets underpinning GCC economic development. With the dual aims of ensuring energy access and supporting economic development, governments have followed a long-held policy of supplying domestic energy to citizens/residents and industries at very low prices.

At present, the GCC's electricity tariffs, which are regulated, are among the lowest in the world, with substantial subsidies offered to both utilities and end-consumers. In Saudi Arabia, for example, the state-owned SEC has long-term contracts with the government to purchase fuel for generation from state-owned Saudi Aramco at a fixed price. While slightly above marginal production costs, these tariffs are well below the market price. Electricity is then sold to consumers at subsidized prices. Subsidies and low prices currently cost GCC governments more than $160 billion annually in foregone revenues (World Bank 2014). This pricing scheme leads to high per capita consumption by fostering an environment characterized by low energy efficiency and lack of conservation. Energy subsidies in the power and water sectors are discussed in detail in the section on barriers to coordination.

Carbon dioxide (CO_2) emissions

The GCC produced 1.17 billion tonnes of CO_2 equivalent (tCO_2-e) in 2012, the bulk of which is associated with energy production and consumption. On average across the member states, energy related emissions are 95 per cent of total emissions, with agriculture, waste, and land use changes making up the remainder (WRI 2015). A breakdown of energy subsector emissions (Figure 2.4) shows that, collectively across the region, the power and water sectors emitted 438 million tonnes of CO_2 equivalent ($MtCO_2$-e).

The power and water sectors produce 43 per cent of emissions on average across the GCC, with the actual share being highest in Bahrain (76 per cent) and lowest in Oman (22 per cent). Substantial potential exists for the GCC to realize aggregate greenhouse gas (GHG) emissions reduction by improving the efficiency of the power and water fleet and introducing renewable capacity.

Energy transformation in the power and water sectors

Electricity and water production are inextricably linked in the GCC. Power plants typically produce a combination of power and desalinated water, with fossil fuels providing nearly all the input fuels. This linkage must be considered when analyzing ways to transform energy in the GCC.

Power and water capacities by technology

Two types of thermal power generation capacity are used in the GCC: power only units and cogeneration units, which produce power and use waste heat to

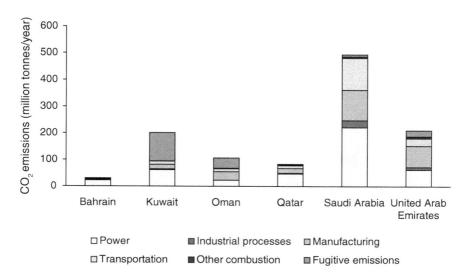

Figure 2.4 Breakdown of GHG emissions by energy subsectors in 2012 (World Resources Institute 2015)

desalinate seawater. Cogeneration uses steam, gas or combined-cycle turbines, together with various distillation techniques: multi-effect distillation (MED), multistage flash (MSF) units, or heat recovery steam generators (HRSG).

All GCC member states have a mix of power and water desalination capacity installed. With over 80.5 gigawatts (GW), Saudi Arabia has the largest installed power generation capacity, including desalination. Collectively, the UAE has the second largest installed capacity (nearly 29 GW), with more than half (15.5 GW) in the emirate of Abu Dhabi. The other countries have lower capacity, as follows: Kuwait (18.3 GW), Qatar (8.6 GW), Oman (7.8 GW), and Bahrain (3.0 GW). The technology mix for each country is shown in Figure 2.5.

At the end of 2015, total installed power capacity, including cogeneration, was 149 GW, of which 105 GW is thermal power only capacity. Single-cycle gas turbines – at 47 GW – have the largest share by technology type, while combined-cycle units represent 23 GW. Over 44 GW of cogeneration capacity is installed in the region, with Qatar and the UAE relying predominantly on this technology to meet power demand. Despite an abundance of solar radiation in the region, at the end of 2015 only 76 MW of photovoltaics (PV) were installed. (These are included but not visible in Figure 2.5). PV capacity represented 0.05 per cent of all installed capacity.

Some 82 per cent of cogeneration capacity is in the form of thermal cogeneration units, while more efficient reverse osmosis (RO) plants account for only 14 per cent. A key distinction between thermal cogeneration and RO plants is that the latter consume electricity to pump seawater through a membrane. Notably, Bahrain, Oman, and the three coastal regions of Saudi Arabia utilize RO technology. Kuwait and Qatar do not have any RO plants installed.

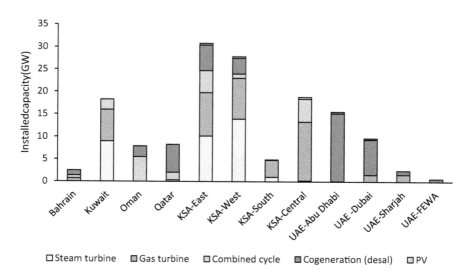

Figure 2.5 Power and water capacity by technology type

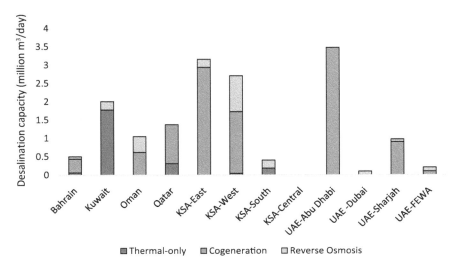

Figure 2.6 Installed desalination capacity by type (million cm/day) (Kingdom of
Bahrain EWA 2016, Kuwait MEW 2016b, OPWP 2015, QEWC 2014,
SEC 2015, ECRA 2014, ADWEC 2014, DEWA 2014, SEWA 2012,
UAE FEWA 2015, KAPSARC)

A small number of thermal water only plants, utilizing MED or MSF processes,
exist in Kuwait and in the southern region of Saudi Arabia. Figure 2.6 presents
desalination capacity, measured in cubic meters per day (cm/day), in terms of
thermal only, cogeneration and RO technologies.

States that have coupled power and water production almost exclusively
use thermal cogeneration. Many of these plants operate as baseload units that
produce a fixed amount of water and electricity to meet demand. Saudi Arabia
currently has variable cogeneration plants, in which the ratio of power and
water produced can be controlled. Bahrain, Saudi Arabia, and Oman have RO
and thermal desalination capacity; as these technologies do not produce electricity, more electricity generation capacity is available to meet power demand
independent of water production. This coupling of the power and water sectors must be considered when integrating renewables into the electricity mix.
If renewable capacity replaces thermal cogeneration plants, RO plants – which
consume electricity – would be needed to produce desalinated water.

Fuel mix for power and water

The power and water systems of the GCC states are supplied almost exclusively by fossil fuels, with natural gas supplying over 2.9 quadrillion British
thermal units (QBtu) annually, while crude oil, heavy fuel oil (HFO), and
diesel supply the remaining 1.9 QBtu. This breakdown is not surprising,

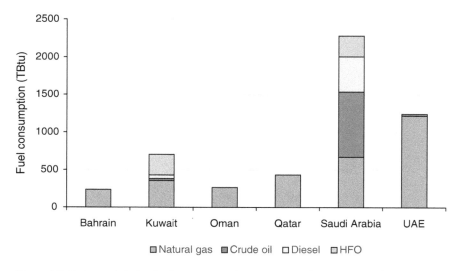

Figure 2.7 Estimated fuel mix for power and water sectors by GCC member states (Kingdom of Bahrain NOGA 2015, Kuwait MEW 2016b, OPWP 2015, QEWC 2014, ECRA 2014, UAE Ministry of Energy 2015, ADWEC 2014, DEWA 2014, SEWA 2012, UAE FEWA 2015, KAPSARC)

given the abundance of fossil fuel resources, described in more detail in the Resources section of this chapter. The share of fossil fuel types by member state is presented in Figure 2.7.

Water and power production in Saudi Arabia, the largest fuel consumer, consumes a significant amount of crude oil and oil products (diesel and heavy fuel oil) (SEC 2015). Kuwait consumes a mix of natural gas and heavy oil, with trace quantities of crude oil and diesel (Kuwait MEW 2016a). In Oman and Qatar, natural gas is the primary fuel (KAHRAMAA 2014; OPWP 2015). Bahrain consumes mostly natural gas and some diesel (Kingdom of Bahrain NOGA 2015). Estimated consumption by fuel source is presented in Table 2.1.

For the UAE, natural gas is the primary fuel for power and water production. In Abu Dhabi, the more than 689 trillion British thermal units (TBtu) of natural gas consumed account for over 99 per cent of all fuels consumed in 2015 (SCAD 2015). The fuel mix is essentially 100 per cent natural gas in Dubai, although an extremely small amount of diesel is used for testing and commissioning, according to the Dubai Electricity and Water Authority (DEWA) (DEWA 2014). The Sharjah region uses natural gas and a mix of heavy and light fuel oil (aggregated as HFO in Table 2.1) (SEWA 2012). FEWA consumes natural gas and a small volume of heavy fuel oil (UAE FEWA 2015; UAE Ministry of Energy 2015).

Table 2.1 Estimated fuel consumption by power and water sectors, trillion British thermal units (TBtu) (Kingdom of Bahrain NOGA 2015, Kuwait MEW 2016a, 2016b, OPWP 2015, QEWC 2014, ECRA 2014, UAE Ministry of Energy 2015, ADWEC 2014, DEWA 2014, SEWA 2012, UAE FEWS 2015, KAPSARC)

Country	Crude oil	Natural gas	Diesel	HFO	Total
Bahrain	–	235.3	–	–	235.3
Kuwait	26.3	354.6	46.9	274.3	702.1
Oman	–	264.2	–	–	264.2
Qatar	–	433.6	–	–	433.6
Saudi Arabia	865.1	670.3	469.8	275.0	2,280.1
UAE–Abu Dhabi	1.0	689.4	1.1	–	691.5
UAE–Dubai	> 0.0	467.0	0.7	–	467.8
UAE–Sharjah	–	59.2	–	16.9	76.1
UAE–FEWA	–	3.4	–	1.2	4.6
Total	**892.4**	**3,177.0**	**518.5**	**567.4**	**5,155.3**

Bahrain: Power is supplied by 1.7 GW of gas turbines and combined cycle units, along with 1.1 GW of cogeneration capacity for a total of 2.8 GW. These units, along with the Ras Abu Jarjur RO plant, have the capacity to supply 498,000 cm/day. Natural gas is the primary fuel source, nearly 90 per cent of which is consumed by the industrial sector (estimated from capacity of power plants) (Power Engineering International 2004; Kingdom of Bahrain CIO 2012; Kingdom of Bahrain EWA 2015; Kingdom of Bahrain NOGA 2015; HPC 2016; Power Technology 2016).

Kuwait: Power in Kuwait is produced through steam turbines, gas turbines and combined cycle gas turbines (CCGTs). Natural gas is the primary fuel consumed by the power sector. Thermal desalination plants consume natural gas exclusively. Kuwait has capacity to produce over 1.99 million cm/day of drinking water (Kuwait MEW, 2016b).

Oman: Nearly all power generating plants in Oman are CCGTs. Two-thirds of the capacity is made up of power only plants (5.8 GW) while one-third is thermal cogeneration (2.4 GW). The fuel mix is exclusively natural gas (OPWP 2015). Oman has the capacity to produce over 1.1 million cm/day of water, with three RO plants delivering 0.44 million cm/day.

Qatar: The Qatar Electricity and Water Company operates over 8.6 GW of power capacity, of which 72 per cent is thermal cogeneration, with the ability to produce up to 1.37 million cm/day of drinking water. All plants run on natural gas, with oil as a backup fuel. Approximately 433.6 TBtu of natural gas is consumed by power and water producers (KAHRAMAA 2014).

More than 1 GW of power capacity operates in the upstream, fertilizer, vinyl, and liquefied natural gas (LNG) industries (QEWC 2014).

Saudi Arabia: Saudi Arabia has over 82 GW of power only capacity installed, with gas turbines accounting for nearly half, and steam turbines and combined cycle units making up the remainder (ECRA 2014). There is a significant amount of thermal desalination capacity (9.4 GW) in the three regions adjacent to the Red Sea and the Arabian Gulf, with combined capacity to desalinate over 6.2 million cm/day. Most of the water capacity (78 per cent) is thermal based cogeneration; the remaining 22 per cent is RO (SWCC 2014).

UAE: Of nearly 29 GW of power generation capacity in the UAE, 24.9 GW is used to desalinate seawater. Most of the power and water capacity is in Abu Dhabi and Dubai, including 60 MW of solar photovoltaics (PV) (ADWEC 2014). Both Sharjah and FEWA have limited power generation capacity, and so purchase electricity from the Emirates National Grid. Combined cycle cogeneration technology accounts for nearly 73 per cent of capacity, followed by steam cogeneration (19 per cent) and RO (5 per cent).

Electricity production and consumption

For the most part, GCC member states consume electricity that is generated within national borders. The magnitude of production, consumption and peak loads are shown in Table 2.2.

Saudi Arabia produces over half of all electricity in the GCC. The Electricity and Cogeneration Regulatory Authority (ECRA) reported that 304.2 TWh

Table 2.2 Electricity production in terawatt hours (TWh), consumption (TWh), and peak load (GW) (Kingdom of Bahrain EWA 2016, Kuwait MEW 2016a, OPWP 2015, QEWC 2014, SEC 2015, ECRA 2014, ADWEC 2014, DEWA 2014, SEWA 2012, UAE FEWA 2015, KAPSARC)

Country	Production (TWh)	Consumption (TWh)	Peak load (GW)
Bahrain	14.1	12.6	2.9
Kuwait	68.3	60.5	12.8
Oman	31.3	31.3	6.1
Qatar	38.7	36.1	6.7
Saudi Arabia	304.2	274.5	56.6
UAE–Abu Dhabi	70.9	52.8	9.0
UAE–Dubai	39.6	38.4	7.2
UAE–Sharjah	5.7	10.2	2.2
UAE–FEWA	0.40	10.3	2.2
Total GCC	**573.2**	**526.7**	–

were produced in 2015, while 274.5 TWh were delivered to customers (ECRA 2014). In the UAE, Abu Dhabi produces over 70 TWh of electricity, roughly 18 TWh of which exceeds domestic demand and is sold to both Sharjah and FEWA. Sharjah imports nearly half of its power demand from the Emirates National Grid (SEWA 2012). Similarly, with less than 1 GW of capacity, FEWA consumes nearly 25 times more electricity than it produces (UAE FEWA 2015). Qatar produced over 38 TWh in 2014 (KAHRAMAA 2014). In Oman, total electricity production is reported as 31.3 TWh (OPWP 2015). (In the last two cases, consumption data are not available.)

Aggregate peak electricity demand in the GCC topped 104 GW in 2015, with Saudi Arabia (56.6 GW) representing over half of the demand and Bahrain having the lowest share at 2.92 (Kingdom of Bahrain CIO 2012; ECRA 2014). To date, the GCC Interconnector has been used primarily for reliability purposes, transferring power to meet peak load demands in Kuwait, for example. The GCC Interconnection Authority reported nearly 1 TWh in unscheduled exchanges occurred in 2014 (Al-Ibrahim 2015).

Water production and consumption

The importance of water and power production in the GCC is relevant to strategies to integrate more renewable energy. While cogeneration plants are an efficient use of waste heat, combining renewable electricity and RO plants could reduce natural gas consumption.

The region has one of the highest levels of water scarcity in the world. Surface water resources are very limited, existing only along the east and west coasts. In terms of renewable water supply, the region has the world's lowest availability, with only about 60 cm to 370 cm of annual freshwater available per capita. According to the *United Nations World Water Development Report 2016*, a country experiences 'water stress' when annual renewable water resources decrease below 1,700 cm per person per year. Rapid population growth and urbanization are putting pressure on the GCC's limited water resources, as is high per capita consumption, which ranges between 0.3 cm/day and 0.75 cm/day. In Saudi Arabia, about 84 per cent of the water used goes to agriculture, making it the main reason for the high per capita water use.

Recently, treated wastewater has been used to increase water availability. Some 84 per cent of all wastewater collected in this region goes through tertiary treatment.

Most GCC countries and regions are self-sufficient in terms of production and consumption of water resources, except for FEWA, which consumes nearly 24 million cm per year more than it produces. The majority (83 per cent) of Sharjah's water production is from desalination, of which only 10 per cent uses RO, with the remainder from thermal cogeneration (SEWA 2012). Table 2.3 summarizes water production and consumption for the GCC member states.

Interestingly, the emirate of Abu Dhabi consumes nearly as much water as the whole of Saudi Arabia (SWCC 2014; UAE Ministry of Energy 2015).

Table 2.3 Annual desalinated water production and consumption (million cm)
(Kingdom of Bahrain EWA 2016, Kuwait MEW 2016b, OPWP 2015,
QEWC 2014, SEC 2015, ECRA 2014, ADWEC 2014, DEWA 2014,
SEWA 2012, UAE FEWA 2015, KAPSARC)

Country	Production (million m³)	Consumption (million m³)
Bahrain	174.9	174.4
Kuwait	562.1	533.2
Oman	228.6	222.0
Qatar	495.0	495.0
Saudi Arabia	2,269.6	1,600.0
UAE–Abu Dhabi	1,170.5	1,154.0
UAE–Dubai	404.1	358.6
UAE–Sharjah	115.3	90.2
UAE–FEWA	66.5	90.5
Total GCC	**5,486.6**	**4,717.9**

Saudi Arabia consumption is estimated, taking note that 69 per cent of total
water production is by the Saline Water Conversion Corporation. Of 222
million cm consumed in 2015 in Oman, nearly half was met through RO technology (OPWP 2015; Oman PAEW 2015a). Qatar uses cogeneration plants
for nearly all of the 495 million cm of water produced (KAHRAMAA 2014).

Resources

The GCC is endowed with abundant fossil and renewable resources. To date,
states have mainly exploited their oil and gas resources; recently, all have published plans to increase the use of solar irradiation and wind resources. This
section begins with an overview of oil and gas production and trade, then
provides a brief assessment of solar and wind resources.

Oil and gas resources, including imports

Most oil and gas production in the GCC is concentrated in Saudi Arabia (primarily the eastern province), Qatar, Abu Dhabi, and Kuwait. Saudi Arabia is
the largest crude producer (3.7 billion bbls in 2015) and the second largest gas
producer (4.2 QBtu raw gas) after Qatar, which produced nearly 6.4 QBtu
(Saudi Aramco 2015; OPEC 2016). Kuwait produces over 1 billion bbls of
crude oil. In the UAE, Abu Dhabi is the primary source of domestic hydrocarbons. In recent years, Dubai's oil production has been declining, and the other
two regions of the UAE have negligible oil and gas production. Figure 2.8
illustrates the balance of domestic production, imports, and exports for crude
oil and natural gas.

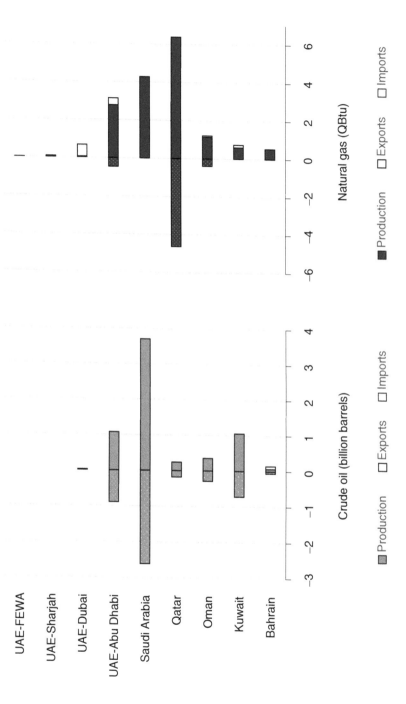

Figure 2.8 Crude oil and gas production and exports (OPEC 2016)

Production, imports, and exports for crude oil and natural gas for each country are as follows:

Bahrain: In 2015, Bahrain produced 73.6 million barrels (MMbbl) of crude oil. The country imported more oil (78.7 MMbbl) from Saudi Arabia than it produced, for a total supply of 152.3 MMbbl. Bahrain used crude oil in refining and exported 54.8 billion bbls in 2015. Gross natural gas production was reported as 0.76 QBtu in 2015, of which 28 per cent is reinjected for enhanced oil recovery and reservoir maintenance, leaving 0.55 QBtu of sales gas production (Kingdom of Bahrain NOGA 2015).

Kuwait: Kuwait produced 1.05 billion bbls of crude oil in 2015 (KOC 2015). The country produces a range of light to heavy crude grades, which are blended into a single grade. Kuwait exports crude oil with an American Petroleum Institute (API) gravity of 31, typical of medium Middle Eastern crude (SPE 2015). In 2015, Kuwait exported 720 MMbbl of crude oil, up from 690 MMbbl in 2013 (OPEC 2016).

Natural gas production in Kuwait is reported as 0.64 QBtu in 2015 (KOC 2015), of which around 1 per cent was flared or reinjected, leaving 0.60 QBtu of sales gas production (OPEC 2016). Kuwait does not export natural gas and has become increasingly reliant on LNG imports to meet domestic demand. Kuwait takes LNG delivery at Mina al-Ahmadi GasPort, which has a baseload capacity of 0.505 QBtu/day and peak capacity of 0.606 QBtu/day (Excelerate Energy 2016). In 2015, Kuwait imported 0.137 QBtu of LNG (OPEC 2016).

Oman: In 2015, Oman produced 358 MMbbl of crude oil and exported 287 MMbbl (NCSI Oman 2016; OPEC 2016). Natural gas production has grown to 1.13 QBtu, with 0.38 QBTU being exported (PDO 2015; OPEC 2016). One-third of the gas is supplied to power stations and desalination plants, over one-quarter to the Oman LNG liquefaction plant, 10 per cent to oil fields for enhanced oil recovery and the remainder to households and industries (SPE 2015). Oman is both an importer and exporter of natural gas. In 2015, according to the Oman LNG annual report, the country exported 0.38 QBtu of LNG while also importing 0.07 QBtu of natural gas from Qatar via the Dolphin pipeline (Oman LNG 2015; Dolphin Energy Ltd 2016). It has been reported that Oman is considering LNG imports to shore up domestic demand (Sergie and Dipaola 2015).

Qatar: Natural gas production and exports dominate Qatar's hydrocarbon output. Sales gas production was reported to be 6.4 QBtu in 2015. Natural gas is exported through liquefaction plants and the Dolphin pipeline, which connects to the UAE via the Tawelah Receiving Facility in Abu Dhabi. Natural gas exports totaled 4.6 QBtu in 2015, with 0.7 QBtu delivered by the pipeline (OPEC 2016). Of that amount, Abu Dhabi lifted

0.36 QBtu, Dubai lifted 0.26 QBtu, and Oman lifted the remaining 0.07 QBtu (Dolphin Energy Ltd 2016). Over 3.9 QBtu was sold as LNG on long-term and spot contracts. Qatar produced 230 MMbbl of crude oil in 2015, exporting 170 MMbbl (OPEC 2016).

Saudi Arabia: With production reaching 3.7 billion bbls in 2015, Saudi Arabia is the largest crude oil producer in the GCC. Crude oil exports amounted to 2.6 billion bbls in 2015. Saudi Arabia does not currently export or import natural gas: the entirety of the 2.9 QBtu produced is either reinjected into oil fields or consumed by industrial sectors such as power, water, and petrochemicals (Saudi Aramco 2015).

UAE: The second largest energy producer in the GCC (after Saudi Arabia), UAE energy production is led by the emirate of Abu Dhabi, which accounts for nearly all of the production and exports. In 2015, Abu Dhabi produced 1.07 billion bbls of crude oil of which it exported 890 MMbbl. The emirate produced 2.8 QBtu of natural gas in 2015, which was used to supply industrial sectors, produce liquefied fuels and products for export, and supply liquefaction trains (ADWEC 2014). Gas exports reached 0.47 QBtu in 2015, with 0.36 QBtu transiting through the Dolphin pipeline (Dolphin Energy Ltd 2016; OPEC 2016).

Dubai, by contrast, is not well endowed with hydrocarbon resources. Small volumes, 10 MMbbl of crude oil and 0.04 QBtu of natural gas, were produced in Dubai in 2013. The entirety of Dubai's crude production is exported as a medium gravity grade (SPE 2015). LNG is received at the Jebel Ali LNG Import Terminal (0.35 QBtu) (Excelerate Energy 2016).

The other two regions of the UAE, SEWA and FEWA, do not produce crude but do import natural gas.

GCC fossil resource trade

Natural gas and oil (at smaller volumes) are traded among GCC member states. The largest trade is between Qatar, UAE, and Oman. In 2004, Qatar began supplying gas to the northern UAE emirates via the Dolphin pipeline. The UAE then supplies gas to Oman via a connection between Fujairah and Oman. The Dolphin pipeline can now transport up to 56 million cubic meters/day (0.75 QBtu/year). Abu Dhabi lifts the most gas at 27.7 million cubic meters/day (0.36 QBtu/year), followed by Dubai with 20 million cubic meters/day (0.26 QBtu/year), and Oman with 5.6 million cubic meters/day (0.07 QBtu/year).

The only crude oil trade occurs between Saudi Arabia and Bahrain, with the latter importing 70 MMbbl in 2015, which exceeds the volume of its domestic production (Kingdom of Bahrain NOGA 2015). Figure 2.9 shows the trade linkages within the GCC.

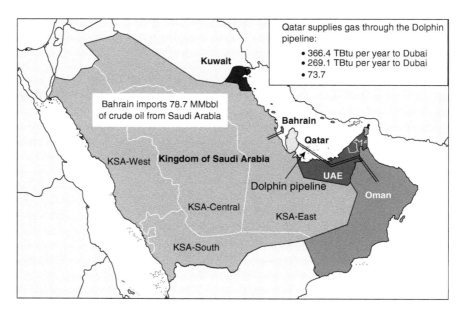

Qatar supplies gas through the Dolphin pipeline:
- 366.4 TBtu per year to Dubai
- 269.1 TBtu per year to Dubai
- 73.7

Bahrain imports 78.7 MMbbl of crude oil from Saudi Arabia

Kuwait

Bahrain

Qatar

KSA-West   **Kingdom of Saudi Arabia**

Dolphin pipeline

UAE

Oman

KSA-Central

KSA-East

KSA-South

Figure 2.9 Map of GCC with trade linkages and quantities (OPEC 2016, KAPSARC)

Renewable resources

The GCC is well endowed with renewable resources, making technologies such as solar photovoltaics (PV), concentrating solar power (CSP) and wind turbines attractive options for power generation. To date, the penetration of renewables has been marginal. (See 'Energy transformation in the power and water sectors' for discussion of power technologies.) Despite the small installed capacity of renewables, many member states have announced plans to expand renewable investments in the coming years (as discussed in 'Policies, targets, and reforms'). The following section presents selected data for solar and wind resources, to illustrate the potential for renewables.

Solar insolation and wind data for Saudi Arabia and the UAE have been collected to illustrate the temporal and geographic variation in these two resources. Data were collected from the National Renewable Energy Laboratory (NREL) database and are available for the four regions in Saudi Arabia and Abu Dhabi.

Solar power

To simplify analysis of the solar resource, hourly data were aggregated into eight discrete segments for three representative seasons. A more detailed discussion on the rationale behind this discretization is presented in Matar et al. (2017).

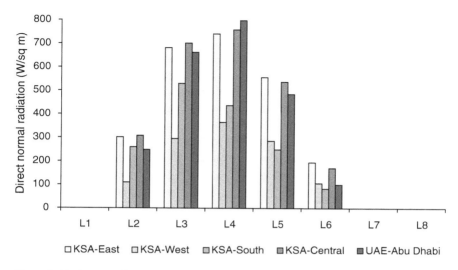

Figure 2.10 Average direct solar irradiance for Saudi Arabia and Abu Dhabi during summer (NREL, KAPSARC)

In Saudi Arabia, the south and central regions have the highest incidence of solar irradiance, although the level varies across seasons, from a low of 660 watts per sq m (W/sq m) in winter to 760 W/sq m in summer. Across all seasons, solar irradiance is consistently highest between 12:00 (noon) and 14:00 (Figure 2.10). Solar incidence for Abu Dhabi follows similar patterns but is slightly higher: about 700 W/sq. m in winter and 800 W/sq. m in summer, with the highest irradiance still occurring between 12:00 and 14:00. Average solar insolation for the four regions in Saudi Arabia and Abu Dhabi is shown in Figure 2.10.

Wind

Wind is available during all hourly segments across the GCC. In non coastal regions (e.g., KSA-Central), wind speeds peak in evening hours and decrease during daylight hours. Wind speed in coastal areas (e.g., KSA-East, Abu Dhabi) exhibits the opposite behavior, peaking during daylight hours.

Wind speed in Saudi Arabia varies significantly across regions and seasons. Across all regions and seasons, average wind speeds are higher between 14:00 and 17:00. The highest wind speed of nearly 8 meters per second (m/s) is found during this three hour period in the eastern region in spring and fall seasons (Figure 2.11). In summer, the highest wind speed in the eastern region is about 6.7 meters per second (m/s); in winter, it climbs to about 7.4 m/s. In Abu Dhabi, the highest wind speed also occurs between 14:00 and 17:00,

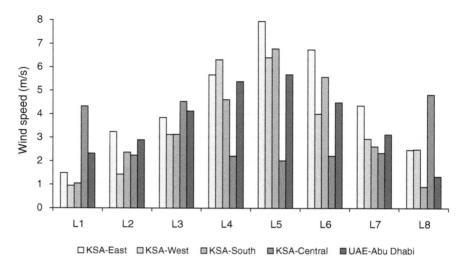

Figure 2.11 Average wind speed for Saudi Arabia and Abu Dhabi during spring and fall (Al Otaibi 2011, KAPSARC)

across all seasons. Wind speeds in Abu Dhabi are on an average lower than in Saudi Arabia; the highest wind speed is 5.8 m/s in summer, followed by 5.7 m/s in spring/fall, and 4.9 m/s in winter.

While not analyzed in depth in this chapter, Kuwait shows wind speeds suitable (i.e., greater than 5 m/s) for wind power development in some areas. Measurements for different locations in Kuwait show that the summer months have the strongest wind speeds (Al Otaibi 2011).

An integrated GCC energy system might be able to exploit the temporal and geographic variation in both solar and wind resources in the region. For example, utility scale PV farms in the western region of Saudi Arabia could feed in to the Interconnector and supply evening demand in Dubai or Muscat. Under such a scheme, the value of renewable capacity would increase: the potential demand it could satisfy is much larger than if limited to the host country.

Energy pricing as a barrier to coordination

Across the GCC, fuel prices to industry and tariffs to end-users are administered by governments: low-price energy products and services are considered a way of supporting domestic industries and maintaining the quality of life of its citizens. This chapter uses the term subsidies as defined by Lahn meaning "the gap between the regulated sales price of fuel and the cost of its supply" (Lahn 2016).

This section presents the fuel prices for the power and water sectors to illustrate the challenge of integrating individual energy systems. It does not explicitly examine energy products – electricity, petrol, diesel – or water tariffs.

At present, the regulated price of energy is a major barrier to renewable energy investments and to increased cooperation among the GCC member states. Low prices incentivize investment in less efficient technologies and discourage conservation, while also straining countries' finances (Fattouh and El-Katiri 2013; Fattouh and Sen 2016).

Industrial fuel prices

Fuel prices currently paid by industry are an important element of the economic barriers to increasing coordination among GCC energy systems. Because prices are not always transparent or published, it is difficult to assess the actual production costs for each member state. Knowing that subsidies do exist, it is logical for member states to be wary of exporting them. Depending on data availability, prices for the four input fuels for the power and water sectors are indicated in Table 2.4.

Bahrain: Reform is underway to gradually raise prices for natural gas and diesel. According to the 2015 Annual Report by the National Oil & Gas Authority, natural gas prices will rise from $2.50 per million British thermal units (MMBtu) in 2015 to $4/MMBtu in $0.25 increments each year. The price of natural gas as of April 1, 2016, is $2.75/MMBtu. The price of diesel as of January 1, 2016, is $0.40 per liter for domestic consumption. The value in Table 2.4 assumes that this price applies to industrial customers (Kingdom of Bahrain NOGA 2015).

Kuwait: Crude oil and natural gas are around two times more expensive in Kuwait than in Saudi Arabia, while HFO and diesel are three to four times more expensive (Kuwait MEW 2016).

Table 2.4 Regulated prices of selected fuels for the power and water sectors as of November 2016 (Kingdom of Bahrain NOGA 2015, Kuwait MEW 2016a, 2016b, OPWP 2015, QEWC 2014, *Saudi Gazette* 2015, Boersma and Griffiths 2016, Lahn 2016)

Country	Crude oil ($/bbl)	Natural gas ($/MMBtu)	Diesel ($/tonne)	HFO ($/tonne)
Bahrain	–	2.75	268.48	–
Kuwait	13.77	3.53	496.60	98.90
Oman	–	3.00	–	–
Qatar	–	1.00 to 2.00	–	–
Saudi Arabia	6.35	1.25	105.26	28.52
UAE	–	1.00 to 2.00	–	–

Oman: The power sector in Oman consumes natural gas, which recently doubled in price from $1.50/MMBtu in 2012 to $3/MMBtu in 2015 (OPWP 2015).

Qatar: Qatar's power producers consume natural gas. Independent power and water producers (IPWPs) pay between $1/MMBtu and $2/MMBtu depending on when they signed contracts with Qatar Petroleum.

Saudi Arabia: Saudi Arabia raised the price of industrial fuels in January 2016. The price of natural gas increased by 67 per cent, from $0.75/MMBtu to $1.25/MMBtu. The price of ethane, an important feedstock for the petrochemicals sector, increased from $1.25/MMBtu to $1.57/MMBtu, a 133 per cent increase. Diesel for industrial use experienced a fourfold increase to $105.26/t while the price of HFO doubled to $28.50/t. Arabian light crude oil increased by 50 per cent (Saudi Gazette 2015). Due to demand being greater than supply, natural gas volumes are allocated by the government; however, the level of allocations to individual industries is not reported. In the absence of a reported value, the utility sector's natural gas allocation is assumed to equal the consumption data provided by the SEC (see 'The Gulf Cooperation Council energy system').

UAE: It is difficult to ascertain prices paid by the utility sector in the UAE, as prices are not publicly available. As highlighted in 'Oil and gas resources, including imports', Abu Dhabi produces natural gas and receives deliveries from the Dolphin pipeline – reportedly at $1.30/MMBtu (Neuhof 2013). Dubai lifts gas from the Dolphin pipeline and receives LNG deliveries at the Jebel Ali terminal at spot prices. The price paid by utilities may be an average cost from all sources, or it may be that the price is maintained and the upstream sector takes a financial loss when selling fuel. Boersma and Griffiths report that the Abu Dhabi National Oil Company (ADNOC) calculates the production cost of associated gas at $1/MMBtu (Boersma and Griffiths 2016). Additionally, a recent study by Lahn estimated natural gas prices at between $1/MMBtu and $2/MMBtu (Lahn 2016).

Electricity and water tariffs

Electricity and water tariffs are undergoing reforms in the GCC to provide consumers with incentives to reduce consumption and to decrease government spending on subsidies. In September 2015, Qatar initiated a price hike for electricity and water. The UAE has also undertaken substantial tariff reforms. Several studies examine in detail recent subsidy reforms for electricity and water, as well as their impacts on demand (Boersma and Griffiths 2016; Fattouh and Sen 2016; Krane and Hung 2016; Lahn 2016; Wogan and Cote 2016).

Policies, targets and reforms

Taking account of their growing energy demand, GCC states have announced plans to both diversify electricity production by deploying renewable and nuclear capacity and to reduce demand through efficiency measures. This section outlines announced targets and reforms of the power and water sectors. Announced renewable energy and energy efficiency targets in the GCC are summarized in Table 2.5 (IRENA 2016; Oman PAEW 2015b; DSCE 2014).

Renewable energy mix

The GCC region is endowed with substantial renewable energy resources (as highlighted in Resources). Renewables based power generation has the potential to meet the GCC states' commitments to sustainable development while contributing to wider economic diversification goals. Collectively, the GCC countries have set a target to install 80 GW of renewable energy capacity by 2030, which is more than half of all existing conventional capacity.

Table 2.5 Announced renewable energy and energy efficiency targets (IRENA 2016, Oman PAEW 2015b, DSCE 2014)

Country	Renewable targets		Efficiency targets	
Bahrain	5% of installed capacity	2020		
Kuwait	CSP = 5.7 GW	2030	Improve generation	2020
	Solar PV = 4.6 GW	2030	efficiency by 5%	
	Wind = 0.7 GW	2030	Improve generation	2030
	15% of generation	2030	efficiency by 15%	
Oman	Currently preparing a long-term energy strategy			
Qatar	1.8 GW solar	2030	20% reduction in per capita electricity consumption	2017
	20% of generation	2030	30% reduction in per capita water consumption	2017
Saudi Arabia	9.5 GW = mix of wind, solar PV, CSP solar and waste-to-energy	2023	Reduce peak demand by 14%	2021
			Reduce electricity consumption by 8%	2021
UAE (no national target)	7% of installed capacity in Abu Dhabi	2020	Reduction in power consumption by 30%	2030
	25% of electricity supply in Dubai	2030		
	75% of electricity supply in Dubai	2050		

Saudi Arabia has a medium-term target of 9.5 GW of renewables by 2023. Qatar targets 20 per cent (1.8 GW) of capacity from renewables by 2030, by which time Kuwait is aiming for 5.3 GW (4.6 GW Solar PV and 0.7 GW Wind). The UAE has regional targets: in Dubai, 25 per cent of electricity will come from solar plants by 2030, while Abu Dhabi has a target for solar reaching 7 per cent of installed capacity by 2020. Bahrain aims to increase renewable energy to 5 per cent of total installed generation capacity by 2020.

Energy efficiency

Across the GCC region, administered prices for industries and consumers contribute to growing energy demand, in part because they disincentivize conscientious consumption. To temper demand growth, GCC member states, except Bahrain, have announced short- to long-term energy efficiency targets. By 2021, Saudi Arabia aims to reduce peak electricity demand by 14 per cent while also reducing overall electricity consumption by 8 per cent. The UAE has a long-term target of reducing energy consumption by 30 per cent by 2030. Qatar has an aggressive short-term target of 20 per cent reduction in per capita electricity consumption by 2017 (DEWA 2014). Kuwait has set targets to improve power generation efficiency by 5 per cent by 2020 and by 15 per cent by 2030.

Nuclear power

Following a feasibility study commissioned in 2006, two GCC countries have begun to seriously pursue nuclear power: the UAE and Saudi Arabia have gone as far as setting strategic nuclear power plans (WNA 2016). The UAE began building its first nuclear power plant in Abu Dhabi in 2012, with the first reactor due to come online in 2017; three additional reactors are expected to come online by 2020, for a total installed capacity of 5.6 GW (ENEC 2016). Saudi Arabia is considering constructing 16 nuclear power reactors amounting to 17 GW by 2040 to meet 15 per cent of the Kingdom's power demand (El-Katiri 2012). For comparison, the planned investments in renewables is almost four times more than planned nuclear capacity.

Power sector reforms

While GCC governments continue to play a significant role in the generation, transmission and distribution of electricity, all are in the process – albeit at different stages – of reforming their power sectors. Power sector reform can reduce overall demand – and thus the cost to governments of electricity supply – by incentivizing investment in more efficient technology and reducing end-consumer demand. All GCC countries have IPWPs and all are pursuing a structure in which a single buyer purchases electricity from generators. Some member states are much further on in the reform process. Oman, for example, has put in place laws to reform the power structure and established a plan for a spot power trading market. Saudi Arabia has approved plans for unbundling its state-owned electricity company, which, it is anticipated, will lower the cost of generation and reduce the financial burden on the Saudi government.

Bahrain: The power sector in Bahrain was vertically integrated until 2016, when the government privatized its generation stations. The Ministry of Electricity and Water Affairs oversees electricity generation, transmission, and distribution, through the Electricity and Water Authority. In March 2016, the ministry reduced subsidies to electricity and water consumption through an adjustment resolution on tariffs (Kingdom of Bahrain EWA 2016).

Kuwait: The Ministry of Electricity and Water is mostly responsible for electricity production, transmission, and distribution in Kuwait. In 2013, the Az-Zour North gas-fired power plant became Kuwait's first independent power plant, in which the Kuwaiti government holds a major share (60 per cent) (APICORP 2016).

Oman: Market reform in Oman was introduced through the Law for the Regulation and Privatization of Electricity and Related Water Sector in 2004 – known as the Sectoral Law – with the aim of unbundling the state-run power industry (OBG 2016). At present, IPWPs sell to the Oman Power and Water Procurement Company (OPWP). The Oman Electricity Transmission Company has sole responsibility for transmission while distribution is conducted via three companies: the Muscat Electricity Distribution Company (MEDC) and the Majan and Mazoon electricity companies. While OPWP purchases electricity from IPWPs by entering into power purchase agreements (PPAs), the transmission company is regulated by price controls, and no subsidies are involved. Direct subsidies are channeled through the distribution companies.

Qatar: The power sector in Qatar was reformed in 2000 by separating power generation and water production from their transmission and distribution. Currently, power generation and water production are carried out by the Qatar Electricity and Water Company (QEWC), a government corporation also known as KAHRAMAA, and by some IPWPs. The QEWC holds shares in these IPWPs, in most cases of more than 50 per cent (QEWC 2014). The QEWC is responsible for nearly all electricity generation and water supply, and its shares are publicly traded. Transmission and distribution of electricity and water are the sole responsibility of the QEWC. To meet the projected electricity and water demand, the QEWC is also actively involved in initiating and negotiating with IPWPs for the construction of additional production capacity (KAHRAMAA 2014; QEWC 2014).

Saudi Arabia: The Ministry of Energy oversees overall policies, plans and strategies for the electricity and water sectors in the Kingdom. An independent authority, the Electricity and Cogeneration Regulatory Authority (ECRA), oversees regulation of the electricity and water desalination industries. ECRA has approved plans for unbundling the power market structure, which is currently vertically integrated (ECRA 2014). As of 2017, the SEC is the utility company responsible for generation, transmission, and distribution of electricity; its stocks are publicly traded, although more than 81 per cent of SEC shares are owned by the Saudi government and Saudi Aramco. A new principal buyer, the Saudi Company for Purchasing Power, was established in 2017 (Roscoe 2017). Some large industrial consumers generate their own electricity and can sell surplus electricity to the SEC by connecting to the transmission grid. At the end of December 2015, the government announced a reform that increased electricity tariffs for the highest consumption tiers (Wogan and Cote 2016). Also, Saudi Aramco has announced an initial public offering of some of its equity, to be released in 2018.

UAE: The power sector in the UAE comprises regional autonomous entities that independently manage their power. Most of these regional entities have a vertically integrated power structure. Abu Dhabi is the exception in that generation, transmission and distribution function separately under an independent regulator (Abu Dhabi RSB 2013). Independent power producers (IPPs) generate nearly 96 per cent of Abu Dhabi's power, which the Abu Dhabi Water and Electricity Company purchases through bidding processes under power purchasing agreements (PPAs). Transmission of electricity and water is carried out by the Abu Dhabi Transmission and Dispatch Company.

Conclusions

The GCC states are well endowed with fossil and renewable resources. To date, fossil energy has been exploited for export and domestic consumption, while the use of renewable resources has been negligible in terms of total primary energy supply. As the region looks to diversify away from a fossil-centric energy mix, renewable resources are an attractive option that can deliver economic and environmental benefits.

Enhancing electricity trading can be an enabler to improve the economics of renewables in the GCC. Trading energy in the GCC is not new: natural gas has been traded along the Dolphin pipeline for over a decade while Bahrain imports crude oil from Saudi Arabia. Electricity, however, has not been traded as extensively. Despite the construction and operation of the GCC Interconnector, electricity is transferred primarily to maintain system reliability. Utilizing the Interconnector as a trading platform could improve the economics of renewable technologies by better aligning supply temporally and geographically with demand. For example, utility scale PV farms in the western region of Saudi Arabia could feed in to the Interconnector and supply evening demand in Dubai or Muscat.

However, low energy prices in the GCC have been, and continue to be, a major barrier to greater penetration of renewable technologies in the power and water sectors. Ongoing price reforms are expected to improve the cost-effectiveness of renewables. Recently announced targets in all six GCC states suggest that renewable resources will be a more prominent component of the region's future energy systems.

Acknowledgements

The authors would like to acknowledge Shreekar Pradhan and Shahad Al Bardi at KAPSARC for their assistance throughout the process of producing this chapter.

References

Abu Dhabi RSB (Abu Dhabi Regulation & Supervision Bureau) (2013) *Water and Electricity Sector Overview: 2010–2013*. Abu Dhabi RSB, Abu Dhabi. Accessed 10 Aug 2017. http://rsb.gov.ae/assets/documents/497/overview20102013.pdf.

ADWEC (Abu Dhabi Water and Electricity Company) (2014) *Statistical Leaflet*. AQWEC, Abu Dhabi. Accessed 10 Aug 2017. www.adwec.ae/Documents/Leaflet/Statistical%20Leaflet%202014.pdf.

Al-Ibrahim A (2015) GCC Interconnection: Opportunities and Challenges Working towards and Electricity Trade Price. In Wogan D, and Cote S (eds) *Opportunities and Challenges in Reforming Energy Prices in Gulf Cooperation Council Countries*. Riyadh. Accessed 24 July 2018. www.kapsarc.org/wp-content/uploads/2016/06/KS-1629-WB028A-Opportunities-and-Challenges-in-Reforming-Energy-Prices-in-GCC-Countries.pdf.

Al Otaibi S (2011) Energy Consumption in Kuwait: Prospects and Future Approaches. *Energy Policy* 39 (2): 637–43.

APICORP (Arab Petroleum Investments Corporation) (2016) *GCC Power Markets: Reliance on IPPs Set to Grow*. APICORP, Dammam, Saudi Arabia. Accessed 2 Nov 2016. http://apicorp-arabia.com/Research/EnergyResearch/2016/APICORP EnergyResearch_V01_N10_2016.pdf.

Boersma T, and Griffiths S (2016) *Reforming Energy Subsidies: Initial Lessons from the United Arab Emirates*. Brookings, Washington, DC. Accessed 10 Aug 2017. www.brookings.edu/wp-content/uploads/2016/01/esci_20160119_uae_energy_subsidies.pdf.

BP (2017) *Statistical Review of World Energy 2017*. BP, London. Accessed 10 Aug 2017. www.bp.com/content/dam/bp/en/corporate/pdf/energy-economics/statistical-review-2017/bp-statistical-review-of-world-energy-2017-full-report.pdf.

DEWA (Dubai Electricity and Water Authority) (2014) *DEWA Sustainability Report 2014*. Accessed 10 Aug 2017. www.dewa.gov.ae/en/customer/sustainability/conserve-now/sustainability-reports.

Dolphin Energy Ltd (2016) *Marketing and Distribution: Natural Gas*. Dolphin Energy, Abu Dhabi. Accessed 15 Oct 2016. http://home.dolphinenergy.com/en/17/marketing-and-distribution/natural-gas.

DSCE (Dubai Supreme Council of Energy) (2014) *The Dubai Integrated Energy Strategy 2030*. Accessed 18 Oct 2016. http://taqati.ae/dies-2030/.

ECRA (Electricity & Cogeneration Regulatory Authority) (2014) *Activities and Achievements of the Authority*. ECRA, Riyadh. Accessed 10 Aug 2017. www.ecra.gov.sa/en-us/MediaCenter/DocLib2/Lists/SubCategory_Library/7%20ECRA%20Annual%20Report%202014%20En.pdf.

El-Katiri L (2012) *The GCC and the Nuclear Question*. The Oxford Institute for Energy Studies, Oxford. Accessed 10 Aug 2017. www.oxfordenergy.org/wpcms/wp-content/uploads/2012/12/The-GCC-and-the-Nuclear-Question.pdf.

ENEC (Emirates Nuclear Energy Corporation) (2016) *Advanced Technology: Safety & Performance*. Accessed 6 Sep 2017. www.enec.gov.ae/barakah-npp/technology/.

Excelerate Energy (2016) *Mina Al-Ahmadi GasPort*. Accessed 16 Sep 2016. http://excelerateenergy.com/project/mina-al-ahmadi-gasport/.

Fattouh B, and El-Katiri L (2013) Energy Subsidies in the Middle East and North Africa. *Energy Strategy Reviews* 2 (1): 108–15.

Fattouh B, and Sen A (2016) *Striking the Right Balance? GCC Energy Pricing Reforms in a Low Price Environment*. The Oxford Institute for Energy Studies, Oxford. Accessed 10 Aug 2017. www.oxfordenergy.org/wpcms/wp-content/uploads/2016/04/Striking-the-Right-Balance-GCC-Energy-Pricing-Reforms-in-a-Low-Price-Environment.pdf.

GCC General Secretariat (2016) Home page. Accessed 5 Mar 2017. www.gcc-sg.org/en-us/Pages/default.aspx.

HPC (Hidd Power Company) (2016) *About Us. HPC, Bahrain*. Accessed 1 Nov 2016. http://hpc.com.bh/about-us.asp.

IRENA (The International Renewable Energy Agency) (2016) *Renewable Energy Market Analysis: The GCC Region*. IRENA, Abu Dhabi. Accessed 10 Aug 2017. www.irena.org/DocumentDownloads/Publications/IRENA_Market_GCC_2016.pdf.

KAHRAMAA (Qatar General Electricity & Water Corporation) (2014) *Statistics Report*. Accessed 08 Aug 2016. https://www.qewc.com/qewc/en/index.php/reports/category/16-2014.

Kingdom of Bahrain CIO (Kingdom of Bahrain Central Informatics Organisation) (2012) *Electricity Statistics*. Accessed 19 Jul 2016. www.cio.gov.bh/cio_eng/Stats_SubDetailed.aspx?subcatid=604.

Kingdom of Bahrain EWA (Kingdom of Bahrain Electricity and Water Authority) (2015) *Sitra Power and Water Station Visitor's Guide Booklet*. Accessed 8 Jun 2016. www.mew.gov.bh/media/pdf/2016/sitra%20-%20booklet.pdf.

Kingdom of Bahrain EWA (Kingdom of Bahrain Electricity and Water Authority) (2016) *Electricity and Water Tariff 2016*. EWA, Bahrain. Accessed 10 Aug 2017. www.ewa.bh/en/Customer/BillsTariffs/Documents/TariffEnglish.pdf.

Kingdom of Bahrain NOGA (Kingdom of Bahrain National Oil and Gas Authority) (2015) *Annual Report*. NOGA, Bahrain. Accessed 10 Aug 2017. www.noga.gov.bh/Publication/Annual_report_2015_EN.pdf.

KOC (Kuwait Oil Company) (2015) *Annual Report 2015–2016*. KOC, Kuwait. Accessed 10 Aug 2017. www.kockw.com/sites/EN/Annual%20Reports/2015-2016%20English.pdf.

Krane J, and Hung S Y (2016) *Energy Subsidy Reform in the Persian Gulf: The End of the Big Oil Giveaway*. Rice University's Baker Institute for Public Policy, Houston. Accessed 10 Aug 2017. www.bakerinstitute.org/media/files/research_document/0e7a6eb7/BI-Brief-042816-CES_GulfSubsidy.pdf.

Kuwait CSB (Kuwait Central Statistical Bureau) (2015) *Statistical Review*. Accessed 02 Sep 2016. www.csb.gov.kw/Socan_Statistic_EN.aspx?ID=19.

Kuwait MEW (Kuwait Ministry of Electricity and Water) (2016) *2016 Statistical Yearbook*. Kuwait MEW.

Kuwait MEW (Kuwait Ministry of Electricity and Water) (2016a) *2016 Statistical Yearbook – Electrical Energy*. Kuwait MEW.

Kuwait MEW (Kuwait Ministry of Electricity and Water) (2016b) *2016 Statistical Yearbook – Water*. Kuwait MEW.

Lahn G (2016) *Fuel, Food, and Utilities Price Reforms in the GCC: A Wake-up Call for Business*. Chatham House, London. Accessed 10 Aug 2017. www.chathamhouse. org/sites/files/chathamhouse/publications/research/Food%20Fuel%20and%20 Utilities%20Price%20Reforms%20in%20the%20GCC%20A%20Wake-up%20 Call%20for%20Business.pdf.

Matar W, Murphy F, Pierru A, et al. (2017) Efficient Industrial Energy Use: The First Step in Transitioning Saudi Arabia's Energy Mix. *Energy Policy* 105. Accessed 10 Aug 2017. http://ac.els-cdn.com/S0301421517301040/1-s2.0-S0301421517301040-main. pdf?_tid=1ed127ae-7dc4-11e7-b6bb-00000aab0f26&acdnat=1502366874_b60e035af-608cc7d750f5875657bd65a.

NCSI Oman (National Centre for Statistics and Information – Sultanate of Oman) (2016) *Development at a Glance*. Accessed 9 Sep 2016. www.ncsi.gov.om/Elibrary/ LibraryContentDoc/bar_Development%20At%20Glance%202015_8534bae5-4777-409c-a7dd-a330a0cdd9e6.pdf.

Neuhof F (2013) *Dolphin Energy Works with Qatar on Gas Expansion*. The National AE, Abu Dhabi. Accessed 10 Aug 2017. www.thenational.ae/business/dolphin-energy-works-with-qatar-on-gas-expansion-1.292415.

OBG (Oxford Business Group) (2016) *Oman's Electricity Regulator Extends Market Reforms*. Accessed 11 Oct 2016. www.oxfordbusinessgroup.com/analysis/spot-opportunity-electricity-regulator-looks-further-extend-market-reforms.

Oman LNG (Oman Liquified Natural Gas) (2015) *Annual Report*. Oman LNG, Oman. Accessed 10 Aug 2017. www.omanlng.com/en/Media/Documents/Annual Report/Oman%20LNG-AR%202015-English.pdf.

Oman PAEW (Oman Public Authority for Electricity and Water) (2015a) *Annual Report*. Oman PAEW, Oman. Accessed 10 Aug 2017. www.paew.gov.om/ getattachment/134fddb7-644e-4bd2-8e4e-61c2911782f0/Annual-Report-2015-English.

Oman PAEW (Oman Public Authority for Electricity and Water) (2015b) *Comprehensive National Energy Strategy*. Accessed 20 Nov 2016. www.paew.gov.om/ Our-role-in-Oman/Renewable-energy.

OPEC (Organization of the Petroleum Exporting Countries) (2016) *OPEC Annual Statistical Bulletin*. OPEC, Vienna. Accessed 10 Aug 2017. www.opec.org/opec_ web/static_files_project/media/downloads/publications/ASB2016.pdf.

OPWP (Oman Power and Water Procurement Company) (2015) *Annual Report*. OPWP, Oman. Accessed 10 Aug 2017. www.omanpwp.com/PDF/01-AR-2015-OPWP-Eng%20%287%29.pdf.

PDO (Petroleum Development Oman) (2015) *PDO Sustainability Report*. PDO, Oman. Accessed 10 Aug 2017. www.pdo.co.om/en/news/publications/Publications%20 Doc%20Library/_PublicationsFile_PDO%20Sustainability%20Report2014.pdf.

Power Engineering International (2004) *Al Ezzel: A First in Private Power for Bahrain*. Power Engineering International, London. Accessed 10 Aug 2017. www.power engineeringint.com/articles/mee/print/volume-1/issue-4/features/al-ezzel-a-first-in-private-power-for-bahrain.html.

Power Technology (2016) *Rifaa II Plant Upgrade, Bahrain.* Accessed 10 Aug 2016. www.power-technology.com/projects/rifaa/.

QEWC (Qatar Electricity and Water Company) (2014) *Annual Report.* QEWC, Qatar. Accessed 10 Aug 2017. www.qewc.com/qewc/en/index.php/reports/category/16-2014.

Roscoe A (2017) Saudi Arabia Establishes Principal Buyer for Electricity Sector. *Middle East Economic Digest* (MEED), Dubai. Accessed 10 Aug 2017. www.meed.com/sectors/power-and-water/power/saudi-arabia-establishes-principal-buyer-for-electricity-sector/5016400.article.

Saudi Aramco (2015) *Annual Report.* Saudi Aramco, Dhahran, Saudi Arabia. Accessed 10 Aug 2017. www.saudiaramco.com/content/dam/Publications/annual-review/2015/English/AR-2015-SaudiAramco-English-full.pdf.

Saudi Gazette (2015) GCC Energy Price Reform Still Long Road Ahead and Fraught with Risks. Accessed 10 Aug 2017. http://saudigazette.com.sa/article/146342/GCC-energy-price-reform-still-long-road-ahead-and-fraught-with-risks.

SCAD (Statistics Centre Abu Dhabi) (2015) *Energy and Water in Figures.* SCAD, Abu Dhabi. Accessed 10 Aug 2017. www.scad.ae/Release%20Documents/Energy%20and%20Water%20in%20Figures%202014%20-En%20-v5.pdf.

SEC (Saudi Electricity Company) (2015) *Annual Report.* SEC, Riyadh. Accessed 10 Aug 2017. www.se.com.sa/en-us/Pages/AnnualReports.aspx.

Sergie M, and Dipaola A (2015) Oman Said to Consider LNG Imports as Domestic Gas Use Surges. *Bloomberg.* Accessed 20 Sep 2016. www.bloomberg.com/news/articles/2015-08-30/oman-said-to-consider-importing-lng-as-domestic-gas-use-surges.

SEWA (Sharjah Electricity & Water Authority) (2012) *Statistics.* Accessed 22 Sep 2016. www.sewa.gov.ae/en/content.aspx?P=8Endvpatc3gylpBOCSt6ng% 3d%3 d&mid=RPiIoTtgdn4cwoW0%2bUAoBQ%3d%3d.

SPE (Strategies et Politiques Energétiques) (2015) *Arab Oil & Gas Directory.* Paris.

SWCC (Saline Water Conversion Corporation) (2014) *Annual Report.* Accessed 5 Sep 2017. www.swcc.gov.sa/english/MediaCenter/SWCCPublications/publication%20files/annual%20report%202014enc02348bb-a1d8-4029-bfe3-136fa70dab0b.pdf.

UAE FEWA (United Arab Emirates Federal Electricity & Water Authority) (2015) *Electricity Statistics.* Accessed 22 Sep 2016. www.fewa.gov.ae/en/OpenData/Documents/stat_elec_en2012.pdf.

UAE Ministry of Energy (2015) *Statistical Data for Electricity and Water 2013–2014.* Accessed 20 Sep 2016. www.moenr.gov.ae/assets/download/6f01f0a8/Statistical%20Data%20For%20Electricity%20and%20Water%20.pdf.aspx.

WNA (World Nuclear Association) (2016) *Emerging Nuclear Energy Countries.* WNA, London. Accessed 10 Aug 2017. www.world-nuclear.org/information-library/country-profiles/others/emerging-nuclear-energy-countries.aspx.

Wogan D, and Cote S (2016) *Opportunities and Challenges in Reforming Energy Prices in Gulf Cooperation Council Countries.* KAPSARC, Riyadh. Accessed 10 Aug 2017. www.kapsarc.org/wp-content/uploads/2016/06/KS-1629-WB028A-Opportunities-and-Challenges-in-Reforming-Energy-Prices-in-GCC-Countries.pdf.

World Bank (2014) *World Bank Middle East and North Africa Region MENA Economic Monitor: Corrosive Subsidies.* World Bank, Washington, DC. Accessed 10 Aug 2017. http://documents.worldbank.org/curated/en/922481468275944547/pdf/912100WP0Box380RSION0OCTOBER0402014.pdf.

WRI (World Resources Institute). 2015. CAIT Climate Data Explorer. Accessed 23 Jul 2018. www.wri.org/resources/data-visualizations/cait-climate-data-explorer.

3 Economics of solar power in the GCC

Assessing opportunities at residential and utility scales

Amro M. Elshurafa and Walid Matar

Abstract

This chapter assesses the economics of installing solar energy at both residential and utility scales in the countries of the Gulf Cooperation Council (GCC). When examining residential installations, the analysis focuses on the home-owner's finances; for utility scale deployment, investment needed for new generation and to ensure system reliability is assessed. Initial results show that in both situations, solar power is not economically viable at the present fuel and electricity prices.

Solar proponents in the GCC argue, however, that generating electricity from solar power can partially replace burning oil. Each barrel of avoided consumption for domestic electricity can potentially increase oil rents through additional exports, facilitate diversion of oil to higher value uses, or simply save and reserve resources for later use. As a rule of thumb, each gigawatt (GW) of solar installed in the GCC would avoid burning approximately 3 million barrels (Mbbl) of oil annually.

Thus, despite the rather poor forecasts produced when each sector is examined in isolation, this chapter demonstrates that viewing the situation from an economy wide perspective changes the equation. Applying a partial equilibrium model – which measures gains and losses incurred across diverse sectors – demonstrates that expanding solar deployment can deliver positive financial gains for the government's bottom line. In turn, this can benefit the broader economy.

Policy relevant insights

Analysis carried out in this chapter delivers insights regarding different types of policy instruments that can support the investment and deployment needed to capture the macroeconomic benefits of solar power in the GCC region.

(continued)

(continued)

- Fuel and electricity subsidies hinder the adoption of solar technologies; ongoing price reform in much of the GCC can accelerate their deployment.
- Given residential load profiles and the solar irradiation conditions prevailing in the GCC, to make solar photovoltaic (PV) economically attractive, electricity prices would need to rise to about $0.12 per kilowatt hour (/kWh) from current averages of $0.04/kWh.
- For utility scale solar, deploying both PV and concentrating solar power (CSP), rather than one or the other, would deliver the most attractive economic gains to the overall energy economy.

Solar power in the GCC: weighing the costs and benefits

Solar power installations, at both residential and utility scales, are gaining momentum worldwide. While large-scale solar farms capture the most public attention, the cumulative volume of small distributed generation – including residential systems – should not be overlooked: in 2015, solar photovoltaic (PV) systems with sizes up to 100 kilowatts (kW) represented 30 per cent of the 227 gigawatts (GW) installed globally (IHS 2015; REN21 2015).

Recent initiatives in countries belonging to the Gulf Cooperation Council (GCC) set clear, and in some cases quite ambitious, targets for solar energy. Yet to date this region remains glaringly absent in solar deployment statistics. At present, solar PV installations in GCC countries – including both residential and utility scale systems – account for less than 1 per cent of global installed capacity.

The harsh reality is that the natural resource endowment of GCC countries, comprising both abundant low-cost fossil fuels and high solar potential, creates an environment with particular economic challenges for a low carbon energy transition.

At present, fossil fuels meet virtually all the electricity demand in the GCC region. These oil-based economies generally levy no income taxes and provide electricity at low, administered prices. Historically, these low fuel costs have affected decisions by household and industry electricity customers, and by utilities themselves. Households have little incentive to be energy-conscious, while low energy prices give a competitive advantage to energy-intensive industries such as refining, petrochemicals, and cement manufacturing. Utilities have favored investment in open cycle gas turbines, which can be installed rapidly and at relatively low cost but are inefficient.

Several studies have been carried out on residential and utility scale solar in the GCC, some treating the region as a whole (Doukas et al. 2006; Alnaser and Alnaser 2011; Radhi 2011), while others focus on a single country (Alnaser 1995; Marafia 2001; Al-Badi et al. 2011; Hepbasli and Alsuhaibani 2011). All of these studies, though somewhat outdated, came to a similar conclusion: under the conditions during which they were carried out, solar PV was not economical in the region. There was general consensus that at least one of four conditions would have to change to produce a favorable equation: the oil price would need to be substantially higher than current local prices (around $100/barrel compared with $50/barrel to $60/barrel currently); the cost of solar systems would have to fall significantly; the price of electricity would have to rise; or governments would have to implement a cost associated with the climate externalities caused by electricity generation (i.e., a carbon price).

More recently, technological advances and market dynamics have brought down considerably the cost of solar modules. In 2005, the average selling price of modules was around $4.00 per watt (/W); by 2016, it had plummeted to $0.70/W. Over this period, technological advancements also enhanced the efficiencies of solar panels, so once installed, they deliver more electricity per unit of solar energy captured. Additionally, GCC countries have embarked on an energy price reform journey (IMF 2015), with some countries indeed raising their prices in early 2016. These developments warrant revisiting and updating the above-mentioned studies.

The analysis in this chapter focuses on the economic aspects of solar deployment in GCC countries, separately examining residential and large-scale installations, which have different stakeholders and different considerations. For residential, it assesses solar PV systems (in the range of 2kW to 8kW) from the perspective of the homeowner. Analysis of utility scale deployment covers the potential for both PV and concentrating solar power (CSP) technologies, considering the costs and benefits to both energy-intensive sectors (petrochemicals, cement, etc.) and utilities themselves.

Arriving at the conclusion that solar remains uneconomical for these groups, the chapter assesses the benefits to the wider economy, seeking to determine where policy interventions could change the equation sufficiently to make the economics attractive to support deployment across both PV and CSP at residential and utility scales. In essence, recognizing that the initial benefits, and many of the long-term ones, will accrue to the central government, the chapter identifies which costs it could bear as an alternative to the current practice of sharing oil wealth through low fossil fuel and electricity prices.

Examining motivations, barriers and potential breakthroughs

Although homeowners, investors in large-scale projects and governments may pursue solar installations for different reasons, the economic effectiveness of them undoubtedly exercises significant weight on such decisions. It would be difficult to promote installations if the homeowner, utility or the government does not economically benefit from them.

Many factors can motivate a homeowner to install a rooftop or backyard solar system, including environmental and financial concerns. Sometimes the person is driven more by social or cultural factors – even, for example, the desire to be perceived as technologically savvy, or as a 'first mover' (Schelly 2014). Overall, however, the financial aspect is usually the most influential (Kwan 2012; Rai and McAndrews 2012).

In the GCC context, this is a particularly important sector, as households account for around half of total electricity demand. In most contexts around the world where homeowners may be considering installing a rooftop solar system, the most compelling motivation is the opportunity to reduce – or eliminate, if storage is available – monthly power bills. In some cases, if the system can produce more electricity than the household consumes, the homeowner can even receive compensation for the amount 'exported' to the grid.

At present, residential customers in the GCC are charged low electricity tariffs of about \$0.04 per kilowatt hour (/kWh); thus, there is little, if any, economic stimulus for self-financed rooftop PV installation.

Utilities themselves can benefit from deployment of residential and utility scale solar as more distributed generation may reduce investment needs in transmission lines that carry power from generation plants to distribution lines and onward to customers. For utility scale applications of solar, the primary technology would be PV plants, although some CSP could be installed as well. In certain scenarios, e.g., when the peak load and maximum solar irradiation coincide, distributed and utility scale generation may contribute to shaving the peak and avoiding the startup of costly peak generators. The environmental aspect of solar energy, in terms of reducing fuel combustion emissions, is also a plus.

An inherent challenge, however, is that the intermittency of PV technologies – which currently lack any possibility for cost-effective electricity storage – creates the need to take additional steps to ensure system reliability. Additionally, bidirectional flow of electricity from distributed generation at the residential scale stresses transformers and results in more frequent maintenance (Borenstein 2012). Up to certain physical and economic limitations, this issue can be handled by the grid. But beyond the grid's capabilities, it typically means also investing in additional spinning reserves to provide backup from dispatchable generation to ensure sufficient ramping flexibility. The risk for utility companies is that the cost of establishing and managing a generation fleet that incorporates more solar and more backup generation may outweigh the value that can be derived from the saved oil.

To demonstrate how the outlook is altered by assessing the feasibility of solar from an approach that considers the whole energy economy, this chapter first examines the individual sectors, then applies aggregate approaches.

For the *residential sector*, it attempts to answer two main questions:

1   Given the combination of high solar irradiation, current solar system costs, load profiles, and low electricity prices, as well as other prevailing conditions in the GCC, can homeowners lower their energy bills by installing rooftop solar systems?
2   If the answer to Question 1 is 'no', what conditions are necessary to make solar economically justifiable?

For the *utility sector*, the chapter asks:

1   At current fuel prices in the GCC, how competitive is solar generation technology compared with conventional fossil fuel technologies?
2   If solar is not competitive, what price changes and/or forms of policy support would be needed to stimulate solar at the utility scale? What would the economic gains be then, if any?
3   What would the benefits of utilizing CSP be if utilities invested in this technology?

Despite the rather poor forecasts when the economics of solar for residential and utilities are examined in isolation, this chapter demonstrates that applying a perspective for the whole energy economy changes the equation. Broadly speaking, four motivators drive governments to pursue renewable energy: the opportunities to use existing resources more efficiently, to reduce carbon dioxide (CO_2) emissions, to achieve greater energy independence, and/or to boost the economy by creating a renewable energy industry. Solar deployment in the oil-rich countries of the GCC is largely considered to deliver economic gains. The reality of substantial declines in government revenues as global oil prices remain low, in parallel with significant energy demand growth, particularly for electricity, has prompted GCC governments to review their energy and economic policies. In a bid to use resources more efficiently, to reduce reliance on a single commodity, and curb energy consumption overall, several countries are currently embarking on a dual strategy of stimulating deployment of renewables, particularly solar, together with broad energy price reforms.

The chapter also acknowledges that, for a meaningful assessment, such numerical analysis must incorporate many factors, including solar capital costs, solar irradiation conditions, load curve, electricity prices, inflation, and others. Additionally, the analysis should consider a reasonable timeframe, as the benefits generally begin to materialize after a number of years. In fact, it shows that assessing utilities alone fails to appropriately consider how electricity is interwoven in the business functions of many economic sectors.

The chapter uses a bottom-up model to analyze various fuel pricing policy scenarios. In a business-as-usual scenario, it is clear that maintaining current pricing schemes would likely prompt deployment of combined cycle technologies to meet growing demand.

As previously noted, the economic aspect is of significant importance to homeowners. This explains why most government policy support mechanisms for solar deployment are financial. The three dominant incentive schemes all provide some financial 'reward'. Feed-in tariffs (FITs) offer a return on investment, with the utility paying the homeowner or industrial generator a predetermined amount for each unit of excess solar energy generated – i.e., units not consumed, that can be sent through the grid to another customer. Investment credits provide the homeowner, industrial entity, or utility with an up-front lump amount to aid in purchasing a solar system. The third approach of tax exemptions or credits is generally inapplicable in the GCC as there is little taxation (Parker 2008; Nelson et al. 2011; Mitscher and Rüther 2012; Moosavian et al. 2013).

One policy to facilitate both residential adoption and utility scale adoption is to raise electricity tariffs – including removing the subsidy – to a rate that makes solar attractive as an investment that delivers long-term savings. Given current capital requirements for solar systems, for example, this analysis suggests that the electricity price for industry would have to rise to approximately $0.08/kWh, compared with about $0.04/kWh currently, for solar to begin to be financially viable, assuming relatively high electricity consumption rates – which might fall as prices rise.

For utility scale deployment, however, strategic price reform that boosts the appeal of solar to other stakeholders could result in a positive bottom line for the government. The higher fuel prices and/or incentives reflected in the alternative policy scenarios provide the fuel-to-capital cost ratios necessary to lead to the emergence of PV and CSP by 2030. Depending on the valuation of the crude oil saved, this chapter shows overall economic benefits ranging from $50 billion to $275 billion between 2015 and 2030.

Using Saudi Arabia as a case study, this chapter assesses the economics of residential and utility scale solar in the region. The results demonstrate that economic benefits can be achieved if governments undertake to reform fuel prices and incentivize renewables.

Case study: the potential for solar electricity generation in Saudi Arabia

The following sections examine the potential for solar generation in Saudi Arabia, at both residential and utility scales, in order to provide insights relevant to broader deployment. The case study approach is plausible, as all GCC countries have very similar patterns on both aspects. To deliver a meaningful assessment, the analysis incorporates many other parameters, including loads, efficiencies and costs, for example. As is true of any modeling exercise seeking to produce insights and provide authoritative policy recommendations, these parameters need to be incorporated with a reasonable level of detail and accuracy.

Residential solar in Saudi Arabia

Residential solar deserves special attention in the GCC as households consume the lion's share of electricity generated. Qatar has the highest share

(57 per cent), followed by Saudi Arabia (49 per cent) and Oman (48 per cent) (AER 2014; ECRA 2015; KAHRAMAA 2015). Additionally, GCC countries have some of the highest per capita electricity consumption in the world, according to the World Energy Council (worldenergy.org) with Kuwait, Qatar, Saudi Arabia, and the United Arab Emirates (UAE) taking the top four spots, respectively. Without doubt, a contributing factor to this high consumption is that GCC countries fall at the opposite extremes in terms of electricity pricing, with household tariffs in Kuwait at a flat tariff of approximately $0.008/kWh, while Bahrain charges a maximum of $0.04/kWh and Qatar a maximum of $0.06/kWh. By comparison, the average price of electricity in the United States is $0.129/kWh.

To assess the economic potential for residential solar in GCC countries, this analysis uses the commercially available software HOMER. With respect to the load profile, the analysis employs a calibrated load profile using data provided from local electricity authorities in Saudi Arabia. Comparing these load profiles to others in the GCC, very similar patterns of general behavior are seen. The data show two peaks in the daily load profile: one near noon and one in the early evening. During the winter months only, the noon peak is lower than the evening peak; in summer, the peak trend is opposite (i.e., higher at noon). The study also distinguishes between weekdays and weekends.

Anticipating that the homeowner considering solar installation is interested in minimizing electricity costs, this study investigates only two options: 1) obtaining power from the grid only, or 2) installing a solar system and obtaining electricity from both the grid and the solar system.

For the financial aspect, the study uses the following assumptions: a solar system cost of $2.20/W, a discount rate of 5 per cent, and an inflation rate of 2 per cent as indicated by the Saudi Arabia Monetary Agency (sama.gov.sa). In technical terms, the efficiency of the solar cells is assumed to be 17 per cent, noting that cells lose 0.45 per cent of power output per each degree Centigrade of temperature increase. The analysis also assumes that the panels are fixed, i.e., they do not track the sun. The model tests different system capacities ranging from 2 kW to 8 kW in increments of 1 kW. A single scenario is run, assuming no policy support and no electricity exported to the grid, after which the model performs a sensitivity analysis.

Residential results

Based on the parameters and assumptions described, the modeling shows the least-cost option to acquire electricity supply based on the electricity price (horizontal axis) and energy consumption (vertical axis) (Figure 3.1). In Figure 3.1, the flags of the GCC countries are each placed to show the rate at the lowest tier that the consumer would pay in that country.

The light gray area of the figure depicts the conditions at which the consumer is better off buying electricity from the grid only. As the electricity price increases, however, it becomes economical to install a solar system, which is represented by the dark gray area. The level of consumption also plays a role.

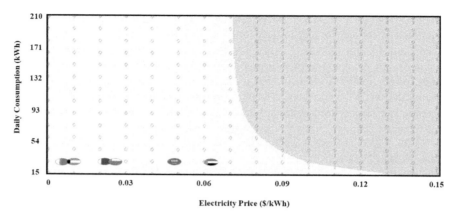

Figure 3.1 Analysis of the economics of residential solar in the GCC

Assumptions: CAPEX of solar system: $2.2/W; Operations & maintenance: $0.01/W/year; Discount rate: 5%; Inflation: 2%; Temperature effect on power output: −0.45%/°C; Nominal operation cell temperature: 50°C; Derating factor: 80%; Lifetime: 25 years; Solar conditions: Riyadh; Solar cell efficiency: 17%; Load curve: calibrated from real data distinguishing between summer and winter days, and between weekdays and weekends.

Notes: This visual aid summarizes conditions, under no policy support, at which a residential solar system would be financially advantageous for a homeowner in the GCC. The x-axis is the price of electricity in USD/kWh; the y-axis is daily load. In the light gray region, the home-owner is better off buying electricity from the grid only; in the dark gray region, the homeowner is better off installing a solar system. Numbers in the dark gray region represent the size of the solar system to be installed. The flags represent electricity prices at each consumption level in the respective country.

For example, if the electricity price rises to $0.10/kWh, and the consumption of the household reaches around 30 kWh/day, then installing a 2 kW system would be more economical compared with receiving power solely from the grid.

Clearly, based on the stated assumptions, it is not economic for homeowners anywhere in the GCC to install rooftop solar systems, except in Dubai, provided their consumption is high (~170 kWh/day or ~5,000 kWh/month). The values of 17 per cent for module efficiency and a discount rate of 5 per cent were intentionally chosen to favor solar energy systems: even with this favoritism, the economic case for residential solar is weak.

Solar starts to become viable only if electricity prices rise from the current rate of $0.04/kWh to around $0.12/kWh at low electricity consumption levels, or to around $0.08/kWh at high consumption levels (~1,800 kWh/month). It is worth noting, however, that if electricity prices rise, the consumer is expected to change behavior and use less electricity.

The reader can carry out a crude sensitivity analysis, qualitatively and visually, based on Figure 3.1. If the discount rate increases, for example, then the line separating the light gray and dark gray regions would move further to the right, showing solar to be even less attractive. By contrast, if the capital costs of the technology decrease, the line would move to the left: solar would become competitive at a lower electricity tariff.

Utility scale solar in Saudi Arabia

Most electricity in the GCC region is currently generated and distributed by state-owned operators, although there are some independent power producers (IPPs). These utilities plan to deliver electricity services for the least overall system cost. The economic conditions described above – growing demand and lower revenues from oil and gas resources – call into question the long-held practices of using fossil fuel for generation and supplying electricity at low prices.

In recent economic plans, GCC governments show strong interest in deploying renewable energy sources – particularly solar – at the utility scale. Diverse motivations are evident, including balancing fiscal budgets and heightened climate change concerns. Due to the large scale of deployment, the investment costs of solar technologies per unit of capacity are considerably lower for utilities compared with those in the residential sector.

Using the KAPSARC Energy Model (KEM) for Saudi Arabia (a partial equilibrium model for the Saudi energy economy; KAPSARC 2016b), the study models the reform of fuel prices paid by power utilities and incorporates the introduction of incentives to encourage investment in PV, CSP and nuclear power. This produces interesting insights as the model incorporates several sectors within the economy (electricity, water desalination, cement, petrochemicals, refining, etc.) and models the interactions between them. KEM follows the electricity sector's aim of minimizing the total power system cost.

The insights provided in this chapter also reflect investigation of the potential for utility scale renewable energy in the electricity sector in Saudi Arabia, primarily summarizing the work of Matar et al. (2015a, 2015b, 2015c). Although it focuses on Saudi Arabia, the results are applicable to most GCC countries, as they have similar opportunities to avail themselves of high solar radiation but also face common fuel pricing hurdles.

Fuel prices in the region, for example, have generally been set by the governments. Following a price increase in 2016, crude oil is currently sold to Saudi power utilities at $6.35/bbl and methane at $1.25 per million British thermal units (/MMBtu). The price of heavy fuel oil is even lower per unit of energy content. In the rest of the GCC, natural gas is often priced below international benchmarks (KAPSARC 2016a), with current prices ranging from $0.75/MMBtu in the UAE and Qatar to $1.50/MMBtu in Kuwait and $2.50/MMBtu in Bahrain. Oman is something of an exception in that gas is $3.00/MMBtu, higher even than the current U.S. market price at Henry Hub, Louisiana.

The current technology mix for electricity generation in Saudi Arabia reflects these low fuel prices: almost all power is generated by burning crude oil, refined oil products, and natural gas. A long history of low fuel prices – until

1998, gas was even lower, at \$0.50/MMBtu, rising to \$0.75/MMBtu in 2015 – favored installation of simple cycle gas turbines, because of their short lead time for construction and low investment cost. As growing electricity demand pushes up fossil fuel consumption, utilities are now upgrading simple cycle gas turbines to combined cycle gas turbine plants and installing new power capacity with higher thermal efficiency.

Utility scale results

Based on projected demand growth, KEM models all power generation capacity expansion between 2015 and 2032, taking into account construction lead times for all plant types. In the case of solar, anticipated future learning effects are reflected by decreasing costs of PV and CSP technologies. Five scenarios are tested in the model. The business-as-usual (BAU) scenario holds existing fuel prices constant in real terms until 2032. The four other scenarios reflect the introduction, beginning in 2015, of new policies as follows:

> **Immediate deregulation of fuel prices**: The prices of crude oil and oil products sold to utilities are set at projected international market values. Since natural gas is neither exported nor imported, the model uses a domestic market clearing price calculated by the authors.
>
> **Gradual deregulation of fuel prices**: The prices of fuels are gradually deregulated over an eight-year period.
>
> **Implicit fuel contracts**: Existing quantities of fuels consumed are allocated to the sectors at the administered prices while any incremental quantities demanded are valued at the deregulated prices. The quantities valued at the administered prices are phased out over an eight-year period.
>
> **Moderate price increase and investment credits**: Fuel prices are raised moderately and the government introduces investment credits for renewable and nuclear power technologies. This scenario aims to deliver to utilities similar fuel-to-capital cost ratios, and thus similar operational and investment decisions, to those they would encounter in a deregulation scenario.

These policy scenarios apply only to the primary supply and energy conversion sectors; electricity and transportation fuel prices for households and other end-users remain unchanged.

The model uses overall economic gain to gauge the efficacy of the alternative policy scenarios. This measure is defined as the sum of the annual differences between revenues in the overall economy and social cost relative to a case where fuel prices existing in 2015 remain unchanged. This sum is adjusted at a real social discount rate. In the GCC context, the economic gains are highly dependent on the value of the oil price. A sensitivity analysis of the results to the oil price, for example, found that immediate deregulation can – depending on how policymakers value the crude oil – generate $50 billion to $275 billion in economic gain from 2015 to 2030 (Matar et al. 2015a).

Examining the scenarios individually reveals more precise insights. Not surprisingly, continuation of existing policies, the BAU scenario, would deter any price-induced investment in renewable and nuclear power technologies. By contrast, the higher fuel prices and/or incentives in the alternative policy scenarios provide effective fuel-to-capital cost ratios and can be expected to stimulate the emergence of PV and CSP by 2030.

Immediate deregulation of fuel prices would render crude oil and refined products excessively expensive for electricity generation. When investment and operational decisions can be made based on deregulated prices, the higher economic value of oil as an export results in economic gains that prompt the sectors modeled to forgo its use. In effect, the potential to free up oil from the power sector stimulates deployment of PV and CSP.

The effect on natural gas is different: all of the alternative policy scenarios allow available gas to flow optimally, i.e., to where it adds the greatest value in the Kingdom's production sectors, based on the domestic market clearing price determined by the model. Yet the natural gas quantity allocated to each sector has implications for the prospects for renewable power technologies. (The study considers that natural gas is also required for producing fertilizer or for making cement products.) Depending on its projected availability to the entire economy, utilities would use all the natural gas possible, then satisfy remaining electricity demand with PV, CSP, and nuclear. For example, if natural gas supply to the Saudi economy is abundant – with this lack of scarcity leading to a lower price – power utilities could use it to fuel their plants. There would be no economic need for solar technologies. In essence, utilities would construct PV and CSP only if the natural gas supply were insufficient.

Perhaps of greatest relevance is the finding that most of the gains of immediate deregulation can also be attained, as in the last scenario, by slightly raising fuel prices to well below their deregulated values and offering financial support to the utilities for constructing PV, CSP and nuclear capacity (Matar et al. 2015c). Introducing investment credits reduces the cash outflows the utilities would have to shoulder in a deregulation scenario.

Graphing comparative cases in which oil saved is valued at market price or at half its projected value in 2030 shows very little difference between the two outcomes (Figure 3.2). Utilities invest in PV despite the additional system costs of maintaining spinning reserves to mitigate the effects of intermittency.

Which solar option delivers greater benefit in GCC contexts?

The analysis also assesses operational and policy nuances associated with installing PV and CSP as part of the local generation mix. In the utilities sector in general, CSP offers the major advantage in the long term in that it can

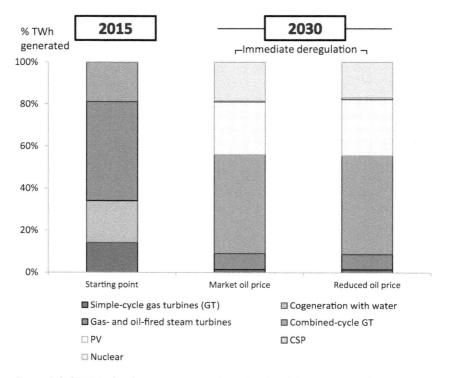

Figure 3.2 2030 technology percentage shares in electricity generation by terawatt hours (TWh) under an immediate deregulation scenario (adapted from Matar et al. 2015a)

support built-in thermal storage, something that PV cannot do. As electricity from the sun is generated, the operator can store it as heat and manage its later conversion to electricity, for example, when clouds intermittently block sunlight from reaching the panels, or after sunset. At present, PV without electricity storage is much less costly than CSP, but due to recent learning rates, the costs of various CSP technologies are declining at a faster rate than those for PV, which began the learning curve cost decline earlier.

Again using KEM, the study investigates the added value over the long term of incorporating CSP with thermal storage into the power generation mix. The thermal storage aspect means the utility would not need to maintain spinning reserves, as it would with PV. Over the longer term, the analysis indicates that even at higher costs, CSP will become economical in the late 2020s. Some estimates show that as much as 11.5 GW could come online in the Saudi system by 2030 (Matar et al. 2015c).

The results also show a complementary relationship between CSP and PV plants. Utilities can opt to operate PV plants during the day, with electricity feeding directly into the grid, while simultaneously running CSP plants at or even below capacity and storing solar energy as heat. The stored heat can be converted to electricity when PV is not sufficient – e.g., to satisfy early evening electricity peak demand – or cannot operate, primarily to meet night-time load. This way, solar energy can be exploited throughout most of the day and deliver electricity into the evening or night.

While all of the scenarios described above assume that CSP capacity does not contribute to the reserve margin requirement, this analysis also studied its prospects to fulfill this role, despite known physical limitations in ramping plants with thermal storage. The intention was to examine the potential added economic value to CSP if those restrictions were lifted. In this case, the scenario of immediately deregulating fuels was applied, considering that CSP with thermal storage can fully stand by to meet the reserve margin requirement. This added value resulted in its being economically feasible to install around 2 GW of additional capacity as compared with when ramping limitations are prohibitive.

The evidence of overall gains to the economy by implementing the analyzed policies does not suggest that utilities or energy-consuming firms sustain no additional costs. In all sectors, including the utilities, firms would have additional costs that reduce cash flows. Yet, in all the alternative scenarios, the incremental revenue of the aggregate system, mainly driven by the value of the avoided domestic oil consumption, exceeds the corresponding additional costs. The energy system as a whole will realize a substantial economic gain. Power and water utilities, however, will experience higher costs since fuel prices will increase while the price of their products will be unchanged. An investment credit policy aims to mitigate the utilities' costs by having the government bear a portion of the cost for the new renewable capacity. The resulting lower net revenues in the alternative policy scenarios may either be absorbed by the sectors themselves or be covered by financial transfers from the government.

If governments opt to pursue price reform and incentive schemes, they would seek the most cost-effective route. Even then, the decision may not be entirely straightforward, because associating a numerical value to CO_2 emissions and achieving other objectives, such as boosting employment for example, is not an exact science (Akella et al. 2009).

Conclusions

Intuitively, poor solar conditions and low electricity prices work against the case for solar installation whether PV or CSP, while high solar irradiation and high electricity prices create a convincing economic argument. When, as is the case in Saudi Arabia and across the GCC, one of these factors is favorable (high insolation) and the other is not (low prices), sound and detailed quantitative analysis must be carried out to arrive at a conclusive decision regarding the financial viability of installing solar systems.

Because of its low price, crude oil is used in great quantities to meet Saudi power demand: deploying solar technologies with the express aim of displacing its use would deliver additional gains to the government. Ultimately, the economic value of such gains will depend on the valuation of each barrel of avoided domestic consumption. The Kingdom would also realize gains from lower CO_2 emissions if natural gas and renewable technologies replace oil and refined products in electricity generation.

This analysis went beyond the factors of solar conditions and electricity prices to incorporate other equally important parameters, including consumption levels, capital costs, load profile and inflation. With a narrow focus on the economics of solar, the study did not investigate in any detail other challenges such as grid management and environmental implications.

From a residential perspective, the main finding is that solar is not yet financially justified for homeowners in the GCC, primarily because electricity tariffs are too low. While government reform of electricity subsidies – i.e., bringing tariffs up to market prices – could remedy this, the steep increase required, of up to $0.12/kWh from current rates of $0.04/kWh, is unlikely to be implemented immediately. Other options that GCC governments could use to promote residential installations include financial support to homeowners by either allowing them to sell back to the grid any excess electricity or providing generous investment credits to reduce upfront costs. These options, however, are economically inefficient because the governments would effectively be subsidizing both conventional and renewable electricity generation.

The quantitative exercise carried out here, as in any such exercise, is as accurate as the assumptions used. A word of caution is warranted for the analysis performed on the residential sector, which used a discount rate of 5 per cent. Many studies demonstrate that discount rates of at least 25 per cent are more indicative of real behavior for residential consumers (Harrison et al. 2002; Bruderer Enzler et al. 2014). At such high discount rates, it is unlikely any investment would ever be made. Consumers who are technologically savvy may invest in solar systems to achieve personal satisfaction. Financially mindful homeowners, however, may see little value in spending as much as $10,000 to install a solar system in order to save, for example, $100 every month, which translates to a relatively long payback period. As such, the discount rate depends to a great extent on the individual and can vary considerably. Although some may argue it is low, 5 per cent was intentionally chosen to show that even at such a discount rate, the economic case for residential solar in the GCC is considered weak. It bears repeating that this study does not consider environmental costs or benefits of the various feedstocks for electricity.

Optimism is greater for utility scale solar investments, even though low fuel prices currently offered by GCC governments to power utilities, including in the Saudi Arabia case, do not provide the necessary pricing signals to make PV – or in the next decade, CSP – worthwhile. However, raising fuel prices, as is currently being done in Saudi Arabia, will facilitate the emergence of solar technologies. Completely deregulating fuel prices would cause utility companies' near-term costs to increase drastically, likely having negative impacts on the sector. A controlled increase, in parallel with an investment credit policy through which the government bears a portion of the cost of new solar plants, is more feasible in the GCC context.

References

AER (Authority for Electricity Regulation, Oman) (2014) Annual report 2014. AER, Oman. www.aer-oman.org/pdfs/Annual%20Report%202014%20-%20Eng.pdf.. Accessed 17 Jul 2018.

Akella AK, Saini RP, and Sharma MP (2009) Social, economical and environmental impacts of renewable energy systems. *Renewable Energy* 34(2):390–396.

Al-Badi AH, Albadi MH, Al-Lawati AM et al. (2011) Economic perspective of PV electricity in Oman. *Energy* 36(1):226–232.

Alnaser WE (1995) Renewable energy resources in the state of Bahrain. *Applied Energy* 50(1):23–30.

Alnaser WE, and Alnaser NW (2011) The status of renewable energy in the GCC countries. *Renewable and Sustainable Energy Reviews* 15(6):3074–3098.

Borenstein S (2012) The private and public economics of renewable electricity generation. *Journal of Economic Perspectives* 26:67–92.

Bruderer Enzler H, Diekmann A, and Meyer R (2014) Subjective discount rates in the general population and their predictive power for energy saving behavior. *Energy Policy* 65:524–540.

Doukas H, Patlitzianas KD, Kagiannas AG et al. (2006) Renewable energy sources and rational use of energy development in the countries of GCC: Myth or reality? *Renewable Energy* 31(6):755–770.

ECRA (Electricity and Cogeneration Regulatory Authority) (2015) Activities and achievements of the authority in 2014. ECRA, Kingdom of Saudi Arabia, Riyadh. www.ecra.gov.sa/en-us/MediaCenter/DocLib2/Lists/SubCategory_Library/7%20 ECRA%20Annual%20Report%202014%20En.pdf. Accessed 17 Jul 2018.

Harrison GW, Lau MI, and Williams MB (2002) Estimating individual discount rates in Denmark: a field experiment. *American Economic Review* 92(5):1606–1617.

Hepbasli A, and Alsuhaibani Z (2011) A key review on present status and future directions of solar energy studies and applications in Saudi Arabia. *Renewable and Sustainable Energy Reviews* 15(9):5021–5050.

IHS (IHS Markit) (2015) Top solar power industry trends for 2015. IHS Market, London, UK. www.ihs.com/pdf/Top-Solar-Power-Industry-Trends-for-2015_21396311 0915583632.pdf. Accessed 18 Jul 2018.

IMF (International Monetary Fund) (2015). Energy price reforms in the GCC: what can be learned from international experiences? *Presented at annual meeting of ministers of finance and central bank governors, Doha, 10 Nov* 2015. www.imf.org/external/np/ pp/eng/2015/111015b.pdf. Accessed 18 Jul 2018.

KAHRAMAA (Qatar General Electricity and Water Corporation) (2015) Statistics report 2014. KAHRAMAA Publications, Qatar. www.km.com.qa/MediaCenter/ Publications/Kahramaa_Statistics%20Report%202014.pdf. Accessed 10 Feb 2016.

KAPSARC (King Abdullah Petroleum Studies and Research Center) (2016a) Opportunities and challenges in reforming energy prices in Gulf Cooperation Council countries. KAPSARC workshop brief KS-1629-WB028A. KAPSARC, Riyadh.

KAPSARC (2016b) The KAPSARC energy model for Saudi Arabia: Documentation of the model build called "KEM-SA_v9.16". KAPSARC, Riyadh. www.kapsarc. org/wp-content/uploads/2016/11/KEM-SA_documentation_v9.16.pdf. Accessed 18 Jul 2018.

Kwan CL (2012) Influence of local environmental, social, economic and political variables on the spatial distribution of residential solar PV arrays across the United States. *Energy Policy* 47:332–344.

Marafia A-H (2001) Feasibility study of photovoltaic technology in Qatar. *Renewable Energy* 24(3):565–567.

Matar W, Echeverri R, and Pierru A (2015a) The prospects for coal-fired power generation in Saudi Arabia. KAPSARC discussion paper KS-1528-DP022A. KAPSARC, Riyadh.

Matar W, Murphy F, Pierru A et al. (2015b) Lowering Saudi Arabia's fuel consumption and energy system costs without increasing end consumer prices. *Energy Economics* 49:558–569.

Matar W, Murphy F, Pierru A et al. (2015c) Efficient industrial energy use: the first step in transitioning Saudi Arabia's energy mix. KAPSARC discussion paper KS-1519-DP013A. KAPSARC, Riyadh.

Mitscher M, and Rüther R (2012) Economic performance and policies for grid-connected residential solar photovoltaic systems in Brazil. *Energy Policy* 49:688–694.

Moosavian SM, Rahim NA, Selvaraj J et al. (2013) Energy policy to promote photovoltaic generation. *Renewable and Sustainable Energy Reviews* 25:44–58.

Nelson T, Simshauser P, and Kelley S (2011) Australian residential solar feed-in tariffs: industry stimulus or regressive form of taxation? *Economic Analysis and Policy* 41(2):113–129.

Parker P (2008) Residential solar photovoltaic market stimulation: Japanese and Australian lessons for Canada. *Renewable and Sustainable Energy Reviews* 12(7):1944–1958.

Radhi H (2011) On the value of decentralised PV systems for the GCC residential sector. *Energy Policy* 39(4):2020–2027.

Rai V, and McAndrews K (2012) Decision-making and behavior change in residential adopters of solar PV. In: Fellows C (ed) *Proceedings of the world renewable energy forum*, Denver, CO, 13–17 May 2012.

REN21 (Renewable Energy Policy Network for the 21st Century) (2015) Global status report 2015. REN21, Paris. www.ren21.net/status-of-renewables/global-status-report/.

Schelly C (2014) Residential solar electricity adoption: what motivates, and what matters? A case study of early adopters. *Energy Research & Social Science* 2:183–191.

World Energy Council (www.worldenergy.org). Accessed 18 Jul 2018.

4 Navigating the transition to renewable energy in the GCC

Lessons from the European Union

Maha Alsabbagh and Odeh Al-Jayyousi

Abstract

As countries in the Gulf Cooperation Council (GCC) seek to boost use of renewable energy sources, it is valid to examine the experience of others that have already navigated the multiple challenges involved. This chapter offers insights from the European Union (EU) experience, which is particularly relevant as it involved collective action by multiple countries on a regional level.

The analysis identifies seven fundamental elements of EU policies for renewable energy from which the GCC can draw lessons, including: the use of mandatory targets; the legal and regulatory framework; support for research and development (R&D) and research and innovation (R&I); the design of both regulatory and voluntary measures; actions to boost public acceptance, including involvement in the policymaking process; and integrating renewables policy with the two other pillars of energy policy – energy efficiency and climate change. The EU experience highlights the importance of working collectively toward shared goals and developing regional approaches.

Policy relevant insights

- Collective action at the GCC level can stimulate deployment of renewable energy technologies at national levels.
- Collaborating to set a regional policy framework that covers renewable energy, energy efficiency and climate change, as well as R&D and R&I policies, could benefit all GCC countries.
- Mandatory renewables targets provide a stimulus for developing guidelines, preparing national action plans and ensuring periodic progress monitoring reports.
- Regulatory and voluntary measures need to be carefully designed, taking into account the socioeconomic and political context of each country.

(continued)

(continued)

- GCC countries need to design a renewable energy system that fits their context. While feed-in tariffs (FITs) have been more successful than quota based approaches in the European Union, achieving renewables targets in the GCC may require another approach.
- General guidelines on public participation are needed at the GCC level, especially where renewables projects are publicly funded.
- The GCC might consider the possibility of allowing the private sector, and even the general public, to contribute as producers of renewable energy.

Targets set, now time to move toward them

Despite being rich in fossil fuels, countries belonging to the Gulf Cooperation Council (GCC) have publicly announced ambitious plans to deploy renewable energy technologies. Although their targets are quite similar, progress to date varies from country to country in terms of developing policy frameworks, establishing infrastructure and building capacity. While some GCC countries have made efforts to create an enabling environment, scholars have identified significant gaps, primarily in the area of policy frameworks.

Given the interest in renewable energy in the GCC and the challenges associated with its deployment, it is logical to ask whether past efforts by others hold insights and/or lessons to help the GCC region move forward successfully and avoid missteps. The experience of the European Union (EU) is particularly relevant as it involves multiple countries at diverse stages yet working toward common goals. The European Union successfully increased renewable energy production from less than 75 million tonnes of oil equivalent (Mtoe) in 1990 to around 200 Mtoe in 2014 (Eurostat 2016), based on continuous efforts at both EU and member state levels. More specifically, final energy consumption from solar thermal in the EU 28 increased from 142 thousand tonnes of oil equivalent (ktoe) in 1990 to 2033 ktoe in 2015 (EuroStat 2016).

This chapter aims to answer the overarching question of what lessons GCC countries can draw from the EU experience to facilitate collective action for successful, regional deployment of renewable energy technologies. With a special focus on working collectively, it specifically addresses the following sub-questions:

- What main policy elements in the EU case study govern the deployment of renewable energy technologies?
- Compared with EU processes, what gaps are evident in the current GCC policy frameworks?

- What positive and negative lessons can GCC countries learn from the EU?
- How can GCC countries act collaboratively to foster deployment of renewable energy technologies?

In seeking to answer these questions, this chapter will help GCC countries navigate a path toward the successful achievement of their renewables goals.

Analysis of the EU process affirms that GCC countries can draw key lessons from its experience – including the importance of working collectively to set policies at the regional level and of providing guidance to ensure that member states can move in harmony toward agreed targets. It also identifies seven main elements of renewables policies that have contributed to progress to date in the European Union: mandatory renewables targets; the legal and regulatory framework; support for research and development (R&D) and research and innovation (R&I); both regulatory and voluntary measures; public acceptance; and the three pillars of the EU 2020 Energy Strategy (i.e., renewable energy, energy efficiency, and climate change).

- **Mandatory renewables targets**: Setting targets that must be met by the member states, rather than indicative targets, can accelerate the penetration of renewable energy technologies.
- **Legal and regulatory frameworks**: In addition to setting obligations in relation to the mandatory targets, these structures establish mechanisms to monitor progress and manage accountability.
- **R&D and R&I policies**: Such policies should seek to remove barriers to deployment of mature technologies and make them more cost-effective and to stimulate new research that considers all other technologies. They should also be part of an integrated approach covering training, education, and other relevant policies (Soriano and Mulatero 2011).
- **Regulatory and voluntary policy measures**: A carefully designed set of measures to promote deployment of renewable energy technologies must be tailored to the context. In the EU experience, a feed-in tariff (FIT) system quickly boosted renewables shares; other countries tried quota based systems, but with only limited success.
- **Public participation and acceptance**: Including the general public in the renewables policymaking process is vital to its acceptance of renewable energy.
- **Integrating renewable energy, energy efficiency, and climate change policies**: The EU 2020 Energy Strategy set clear targets and a clear timeframe for an integrated policy framework, based on these three pillars. Effective design plays an important role in how energy policies are perceived and carried forward.

Importantly, the chapter identifies some elements missing in the current GCC policy framework that have rarely been addressed in the literature, and investigates policy measures put in place by the European Union that could fill such gaps, in some cases with modifications. It starts from the premise that GCC countries can learn from the experience of others and sets out some best practices that will boost success while avoiding spending the substantial resources and time EU policymakers invested to test different practices.

The analysis also uncovers some inertia in terms of action towards targets in the GCC. In the current context of low oil prices and related economic constraints, new drivers for renewables deployment have emerged in the GCC region, including energy demand, environmental concerns and economic considerations (Doukas et al. 2006; Al-Mulali and Lee 2013; Munawwar and Ghedira 2014; Abdmouleh et al. 2015a; Lilliestam and Patt 2015). The rapidly increasing demand for energy, resulting from economic development and urbanization, prompts interest in energy sources other than fossil fuels. The commitment by most GCC countries, within the COP21 Paris Agreement, to reduce greenhouse gas (GHG) emissions by 2020 underpins the environmental driver. On the economic side, a key driver is the potential for renewables deployment to reduce domestic fossil fuel consumption and leave larger volumes available for sale in international markets. While currently low prices make this opportunity less compelling, renewables deployment can also help diversify the economy and create jobs, contributing as much as $200 billion per year to the GCC region by 2030 (KUNA 2016). These considerations, alone and together, are likely to accelerate the pace of action.

Perhaps of greatest relevance, the chapter focuses on the regional aspects of renewables deployment in the European Union and the GCC and provides recommendations at this level. This holistic approach is not evident in the extant literature. Noting the many differences between the EU and GCC regions, the chapter does not seek to compare the two regions, but rather to identify where experience gained in the European Union can help the GCC in its endeavors. As is the case with European countries having the European Commission as a central policy body, the existence of the GCC can facilitate collective work, with its Secretariat General taking a lead role in the successful deployment of renewable energy technologies.

GCC countries have a long history of collaboration with the EU, which may serve as a basis for assistance in establishing a sustainable energy market in the GCC (Patlitzianas et al. 2007). This chapter attempts to analyze how the GCC countries might learn from the EU's considerable experience in setting an enabling policy environment to support renewables deployment, which has been replicated in many countries worldwide (Lins 2013).

State of GCC readiness for learning and ability to deploy renewable energy

Globally, the share of renewable energy used in electricity generation has increased from 10.7 per cent in 1990 to 12.6 per cent in 2013 (IEA 2016), reflecting a doubling of the absolute volume of installed capacity (IEA 2016). Generally, three main factors drive this transition, including national and global goals to enhance energy security, reduce carbon dioxide (CO_2) emissions, and spur economic development (Muller et al. 2011).

Being rich in fossil fuels, which have long dominated worldwide energy supply for electricity generation (72 per cent) and overall final energy consumption (84 per cent), GCC countries had no concerns regarding energy security and were in no rush to adopt renewable energy technologies (Lilliestam and Patt 2015). Some showed early interest during the 1980s, for example, when Saudi Arabia conducted initial renewables research projects (Alnaser and Alnaser 2011; Hepbasli and Alsuhaibani 2011). Other studies assessed the potential of different renewable energy sources in the region (e.g., Alnaser and Alnaser 2011); reviewed policies and initiatives to support renewables deployment at the national level (e.g., Abdmouleh et al. 2015a); explored drivers for the adoption of renewable energy technologies (e.g., Doukas et al. 2006; Lilliestam and Patt 2015; Atalay et al. 2016); and estimated the costs and benefits of introducing renewable energy (e.g., Sgouridis et al. 2013).

Despite encouraging signs, renewables efforts in the GCC remain scattered. Also evident is a mismatch between the drivers of renewable energy adoption and the actions undertaken (Lilliestam and Patt 2015). In particular, obvious gaps exist in governance and policymaking (Patlitzianas et al. 2006; Munawwar and Ghedira 2014; Abdmouleh et al. 2015a; Lilliestam and Patt 2015; Mondal et al. 2016). Most experts agree that a clear roadmap is needed.

More recently, spurred by various factors such as low oil revenues and greater awareness of the need to reduce energy-related CO_2 emissions, GCC countries have initiated several renewables projects. A survey of experts finds a level of readiness not previously evident, although still in the low-to-medium range: the knowledge and expertise needed are readily available, a viable business case exists, and the general public will most likely be supportive (Lilliestam and Patt 2015).

GCC countries need to overcome several barriers to ensure successful implementation of renewable energy technologies, including governance, economic, social and technical factors (Patlizianas et al. 2006; Al-Badi et al. 2009; Al Hatmi et al. 2014; Munawwar and Ghedira 2014; Abdmouleh et al. 2015a; Al-Jayyousi 2015; Lilliestam and Patt 2015). The recent assessment of GCC readiness to adopt renewable energy technologies revealed low-to-medium national levels in terms of setting targets, establishing policy mechanisms, including for CO_2 emissions reduction, and public awareness (Mondal et al. 2016). Moreover, variations are evident in the progress of individual GCC countries toward renewables deployment: the United Arab Emirates (UAE) and Qatar are identified as leaders, while others have been described as 'laggards' (Atalay et al. 2016). The variations reflect progress on both political leadership and policy transfer mechanisms (Atalay et al. 2016).

Additionally, the fact that GCC energy markets are not yet liberalized has hindered renewables deployment to a degree. In recent years, some countries have initiated the liberalization process, including allowing private investors to participate (Lilliestam and Patt 2015). A similar situation still exists in the

European Union in that, despite an EU directive designed to prompt energy market liberalization, some "member states have been sluggish in implementing the EU directive" and "electricity markets are still dominated by few large electricity utilities" (Bohringer et al. 2016). This mix of liberalized and non-liberalized markets led to some concerns over access of new producers to the GCC market (Fouquet 2013). Nonetheless, Pollitt (2012) argues that it is not liberalization that will ensure the transition to a low carbon future, but rather the public's willingness to bear the cost of the transition. In the GCC context, liberalization alone is unlikely to ensure the transition to a low carbon future.

While a large body of literature suggests that regional and international cooperation is essential for deploying renewable energy technologies in the GCC context, to date such cooperation remains weak (Abdel Raouf and Loumi 2015). Some experts suggest that the GCC Secretariat could play a greater role in this (Abdel Raouf and Loumi 2015).

Several countries have already drawn on the EU experience to transfer knowledge gained, including Brazil (de Melo et al. 2016) and Sub Saharan Africa (Koskimäki 2012). This process, known as "policy transfer", is defined as a "process of using knowledge about policymaking from one setting and applying it to another" (Marsden and Stead 2011). The literature suggests that any policy is transferable from one country to another (Dolowitz and Marsh 2000) and includes all types of policies such as those relating to policy goals, content, instruments, programs, institutions, ideologies, ideas and attitudes and negative lessons (Dolowitz and Marsh 2000). The transfer can take various forms, ranging from total duplication (the entire policy is transferred) to general inspiration and learning from negative lessons (Keating and Cairney 2012). In addition, policy transfer can be either coercive – i.e., there is a compulsion to conform – or voluntary, where countries freely learn about each other's practices (Dolowitz and Marsh 2000; Keating and Cairney 2012). The process can be facilitated by policy networks (Stone 2001), which may be appropriate in the GCC region considering its networks with experts in RE, including within the European Union.

This chapter focuses on selected elements of renewables policy in the European Union, with the aim of examining experience relevant to the GCC region, including the value of collective action.

Case study: renewable energy deployment lessons from the European Union experience

Using a case study approach, this chapter probes the EU experience in deploying renewable energy technologies to assess whether any lessons learned may be transferable to the GCC region. The European Union was selected because it reflects joint effort by a union of countries to establish a suitable policy framework to support deployment of renewable energy technologies and to increase the share of renewable energy in the energy mix. Additionally, there is a well-established, cooperative energy relationship between the European

Union and the GCC region that goes back to 1988. More recently, in 2010 the EU-GCC Clean Energy Network program was launched, with EU funding; it is now in its second phase of implementation, aimed at facilitating knowledge transfer to the GCC region.

For the literature review specific to the case study, information on the EU and the GCC region was obtained from three main secondary sources in both Arabic and English. The first source was peer-reviewed published articles, mainly review papers, retrieved from the Web of Knowledge. The search did not define any timeframes. The second source was consultancy reports, restricted to well-known research institutes and organizations, such as the International Renewable Energy Agency (IRENA) and the Regional Center for Renewable Energy and Energy Efficiency (RCREEE), and others. The third source was official documents, including legislation related to renewable energy in both regions.

To achieve the aim of the chapter, the research was undertaken in four steps (Figure 4.1):

1 **Identify the main elements of renewables policies in the European Union** through a review of relevant literature that investigates both current and past policies to provide learning opportunities from the policy development process. After a screening process, the review focused on elements that had received the least coverage in the literature relating to renewable energy in the GCC region.

2 **Highlight the lessons learned from the EU experience** based on both negative and positive aspects of EU renewables policies.

3 **Present the current situation in the GCC region** based on a second literature review using different key words to focus narrowly on the region's performance with regard to the previously identified renewables policy aspects.

4 **Summarize how lessons learned in the European Union can be applied in the GCC region** and compare the state of renewables policies in the GCC region with those of the European Union.

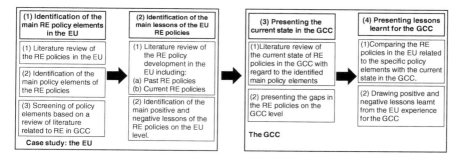

Figure 4.1 Overview of the methodology

The steps taken above identified seven main elements of renewables policies in the European Union: mandatory targets; the legal and regulatory framework; research and development (R&D) and research and innovation (R&I); both regulatory and voluntary measures; public acceptance; and the three pillars of energy policies – renewable energy, energy efficiency, and climate policies. The following section shows how the EU embeds these elements within its renewables policies and assesses whether these elements have been considered during the formulation of renewables policies in the GCC countries. A corresponding timeline shows the progressive introduction in the European Union of the main elements of renewables policies identified in the literature review (Figure 4.2).

Mandatory targets

The European Union showed early interest in the adoption of renewable energy technologies, launching the policy formulation process in the late 1990s by setting targets at the EU level (Fouquet 2013) (a detailed history of EU renewables policy development was published by Scarlat et al. 2015). Actual deployment started in 1997, following adoption of a white paper for a Community Strategy and Action Plan by the EU Council and Parliament (Scarlat et al. 2015), which set indicative targets to increase the share of renewable energy from 6 per cent to 12 per cent by 2010, with different targets for different renewable energy sources. The share of electricity generated from wind and photovoltaic (PV) sources has since significantly exceeded original targets (Scarlat et al. 2015).

Two directives were subsequently issued. The Renewable Electricity Directive (2001) set an indicative target of 21 per cent of energy from renewable energy sources by 2010. In fact, only 19.5 per cent was achieved, with hydro being the main source, followed by biomass and solar. The Directive on the Promotion of the Use of Biofuels and Other Renewable Fuels for Transport (2003) set a target to increase the share of biofuel to 5.75 per cent by 2010; ultimately, a share of 4.4 per cent was achieved (Scarlat et al. 2015).

In 2009, mandatory targets for EU member states were introduced, based on those specified in the Renewable Energy Directive. The overall target was a renewables share of 20 per cent of total energy consumption by 2020, with a specific target of 10 per cent for transport (Wyns et al. 2014; Scarlat et al. 2015). This overall renewables target is expected to be increased to 27 per cent by 2030 and 55 to 75 per cent by 2050 (Scarlat et al. 2015).

Importantly, the targets varied among countries according to current renewables deployment and each country's ability to increase its share in the overall energy mix (EC 2016).

Legal and regulatory frameworks

Each member state was obliged to develop a National Renewable Energy Action Plan and to set out a road map and measures to establish the required

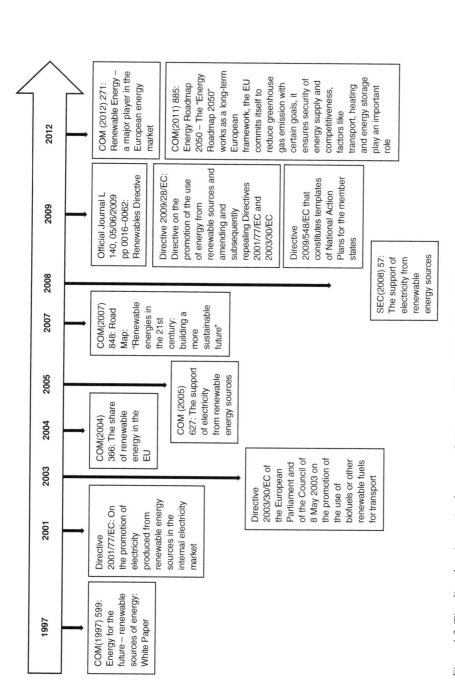

Figure 4.2 Timeline showing main elements of EU renewables policies (adapted from: Steinbeis Europa Zentrum and Karlsruhe Institute of Technology (n.d.); Langsdorf 2011; Sekercioglu and Yilmaz 2012; deLlano-Paz et al. 2015; Scarlat et al. 2015)

Notes: COM = Commission Communication; EC = European Commission; SEC = Staff Working Documents.

infrastructure to meet the targets. Additionally, member states have to report on progress every two years.

The Covenant of Mayors, launched in 2008, is an additional EU initiative that aims to involve cities in reaching the targets. It required cities to submit a sustainable energy action plan to the EU authority (Lombardi et al. 2016). Several tools were developed to support this initiative, including the European Local Energy Assistance (ELENA) program, which provides funding for technical support.

Some experts suggest that EU policies should now focus on demand management to achieve renewables targets (Fouquet 2013), using legislation and incentives to make households and buildings energy-neutral or even net energy producers. Several strategies, including smart metering and electronic control technologies, have sought to encourage behavioral change (Fouquet 2013).

At present, no such legislation exists at the GCC level, and formal renewables policy frameworks are lacking at the country level (Bhutto et al. 2014). Some GCC countries have announced new strategies, legislation or policies, including the Energy Policy for Abu Dhabi (2009), the Master Plan for Saudi Arabia (2012) and the national plan for renewable energy in Bahrain (2017) (Abdmouleh et al. 2015a; Jamil et al. 2016). Other GCC countries have renewables targets for 2020 and 2030 but have hardly any renewables strategies in place (Munawwar and Ghedira 2014; RCREEE 2015; IRENA 2016). To be successful, such targets "must be backed by dedicated policies and regulatory frameworks" (IRENA 2016).

As the EU case shows, establishing renewables policies and regulations, and stabilizing legal frameworks, are important aspects of successful implementation (Haas et al. 2011b; Fouquet 2013; Lins 2013; Wyns et al. 2014). These actions help to attract investment in renewable energy technologies and contribute to job creation (Lins 2013; Wyns et al. 2014).

Research, development and innovation

EU strategies for the energy sector have devoted special attention to R&D and R&I in renewable energies. In 2000, the European Commission launched the Lisbon Strategy, which focuses on technological capacity and innovation, with the aim of making Europe "the most competitive and dynamic knowledge based economy in the world, capable of sustainable economic growth with more and better jobs and greater social cohesion" (https:// portal.cor.europa.eu/europe2020/Profiles/Pages/TheLisbonStrategyinshort. aspx). The strategy initially focused on economic and social pillars; one year later, the environmental pillar was added. Since 2000, an increasing number of initiatives have been developed, such as the European Energy Research Alliance and the European Industrial Initiatives. Although advances in renewable energy technologies play a role in encouraging investment in renewable energy, stable policies are shown to play a greater role (Soriano and Mulatero 2011).

The two-phase EU Strategic Energy Technology Plan (EU SET-Plan) (2007) is the most relevant strategy for renewable energy at the EU level. The first phase focuses on how to remove barriers to the deployment of mature technologies and make them more cost-effective. It has a medium-term target to be achieved by 2020. The second phase sets a long-term target for 2050, based on research that considers all other technologies. A detailed review of R&D and R&I strategies and initiatives for renewable energy in the European Union emphasizes the need to strengthen the interlinkages between R&D and R&I strategies, and to enhance the effectiveness of those strategies by improving links between education and training (Soriano and Mulatero 2011).

Analysis of EU R&D and R&I strategies suggests that they should not be pursued in isolation, but rather be part of an integrated approach also covering training, education, and other relevant policies (Soriano and Mulatero 2011). Such strategies should focus on both supply and demand, and also address financial issues. Additionally, the organizational structure for R&D and R&I should include a centralized administration with effective information systems, along with a steering committee and key performance indicators (KPIs) to measure progress (Soriano and Mulatero 2011). Processes should be streamlined, as involving a large number of institutions and programs can add complexity.

Current recommendations for R&D strategies in the GCC reflect EU practices, including a focus on well established and mature technologies to reduce research spending (Patlitzianas et al. 2006). Additionally, previous experience in Saudi Arabia suggests a strategy placing the focus on the application of renewable energy in the region's context, rather than on research into basic renewable energy technologies (Hepbasli and Alsuhaibani 2011).

A review of the literature on GCC countries shows a lack of a regional R&D policy framework, as well as a lack of national R&D policies at both country and regional levels. In general, R&D expenditure for renewable energy in GCC countries is relatively low (Abdel Raouf and Loumi 2015), ranging from 0.04 per cent of GDP for Bahrain to 2.8 per cent of GDP for Qatar, whereas South Korea, for example, dedicates 3.6 per cent of its GDP to R&D (Higher Education Council 2014). However, R&D initiatives, projects, and centers exist in all GCC countries (Bachellerie 2012), and some cities have launched innovative renewables projects, such as Masdar City in Abu Dhabi (Reiche 2010; Jamil et al. 2016).

Regulatory measures

A review of measures implemented in the European Union to achieve renewables penetration targets reveals two main regulatory approaches: those driven by price and those driven by quantity (Haas et al. 2011a). An extensive body of literature provides in-depth analysis (e.g., Haas et al. 2011b; Lins 2013; Polzin et al. 2015). To provide insights into GCC countries, this chapter keeps a narrow focus on relevant positive and negative lessons from the EU experience, in which the FIT system and tradable green certificates have emerged as the main renewables regulatory policy measures. While FITs are a price-driven approach that delivers guaranteed revenues for investors and utilities, tradable certificates target a quantity of renewables penetration to be met by electricity generators or by consumers (Lipp 2007; Haas et al. 2011a).

To date, FIT systems are more widely used worldwide than tradable certificates (REN21 2015), perhaps reflecting that EU countries that adopted FITs were more successful in achieving renewables targets than those that adopted other measures (Haas et al. 2011a; Fouquet 2013; Lins 2013). France, for example, has shifted from competitive tendering to FITs. In contrast, the United Kingdom shifted from tendering to renewable obligations, but with little effect on achieving its target (Haas et al. 2011a; Wood and Dow 2011). In fact, only Sweden has successfully deployed renewable energy without FITs (Haas et al. 2011a).

Among many noted advantages associated with providing a guaranteed price, FITs allow non-traditional players, such as businesses or even households, to enter the electricity market (Lipp 2007). Considering that the legal and regulatory frameworks described above recommend greater involvement of more players in the process of renewables deployment, this is particularly relevant to the GCC region. In fact, Dubai recently announced that by 2030, all new buildings must include solar PV technology.

Tradable green certificates, by contrast, were found in the EU experience to be an unsuccessful strategy for renewables deployment (Fouquet 2013). As noted above, this system sets a target for renewables penetration to be met by the consumer or electricity generator. The public authority sets the minimum number of certificates to be obtained by the obligated party annually but leaves the market to set the price. This means that the obligated party can either generate the quantity of renewable energy needed to meet the certificates or purchase – i.e., trade – certificates from other parties that can generate more than their obligation (Fouquet 2013).

In the GCC, most experts prefer the FIT system (Lilliestam and Patt 2015), even though there are barriers to address when attempting to combine FITs with quota based measures (Jacobsen et al. 2014). One barrier, for example, is related to the support provided to the tenders. In the past, governments usually provided fixed support to the winning tender; newer tenders typically do not benefit from any fixed FIT (Jacobsen et al. 2014). Additionally, the design of any FIT system will influence its success (Fouquet 2013; Lins 2013; Polzin et al. 2015) and should be reviewed periodically. For instance, the tariff needs to be differentiated based on the technology used and, most importantly, the price applied should be fixed for a specified period of time, as such legal guarantees ensure investment security (Lins 2013). It is critical to build in a mechanism for the FIT price to evolve as the market does.

Except for the FIT system initiated to finance the Shams 1 project in Abu Dhabi, as yet none of the regulatory measures mentioned above are in place in any of the GCC countries (Lilliestam and Patt 2015; REN21 2015). Proposals to shift towards FITs and tradable green certificates are being developed in Saudi Arabia (Abdmouleh et al. 2015a), but some argue that FITs are unsuitable and recommend the use of tradable certificates (e.g., Abdmouleh et al. 2015b). The EU experience demonstrates that FITs can be successful (Al-Amir and Abu-Hijleh 2013; Ramli and Twaha 2015); in GCC countries, they could enable the private sector to contribute to electricity generation (Lilliestam and Patt 2015).

Participants in a survey on renewable energy in the GCC countries were significantly more supportive of FITs than other renewables policy measures (Lilliestam and Patt 2015), particularly the more experienced participants (Lilliestam and Patt 2015). Introducing an FIT system is believed to be a way to accelerate renewables deployment in Saudi Arabia (Ramli and Twaha 2015).

Voluntary measures

The EU experience clearly shows that no single policy will deliver successful renewables deployment; rather a strategic policy mix is required (Sovacool 2009).

Some voluntary policies aimed at promoting the use of renewable energy technologies can be highly complementary to the regulatory measures described above. Voluntary policies depend mainly on the willingness of consumers to pay for electricity generated from renewable energy sources and assume that consumers are willing to pay premium tariffs to protect the environment and reduce air pollution. Such policies can focus on the investment or the generation side of boosting renewable energy sources in the electricity sector. Examples of investment focused policies include donations and shareholder programs, whereas generation based policies include green electricity tariffs and labeling (Haas et al. 2011a). Such voluntary measures typically apply only to new projects; as learned from the EU experience, they should remain unchanged for a specific period (Haas et al. 2011a).

Again, no voluntary policy measures are observed in the GCC countries. This may reflect that such measures are considered to be an advanced level of renewables policy formulation and would be introduced later, or it could be the result of market constraints.

Public participation and acceptance

Public acceptance of renewable energy technologies and the policies to support them is extremely important. Case studies from the EU region demonstrate that public resistance can delay or even lead to cancellation of renewables projects (Hofman and Van der Gaast 2014).

To build such acceptance, the European Union ensures public participation in related activities through European Directive 2003/35/EC, which is based on the Aarhus Convention of 1998 (Hofman 2015). This includes ensuring access to information related to the environment and public participation in environment related policymaking. Several elements are set out to ensure successful public participation: awareness of climate change and renewable energy technologies; fairness of the policymaking process; costs and benefits of renewables projects; and local context (Hofman and van der Gaast 2014). This directive recognizes that, ultimately, the public will have to bear the cost of any government-funded project (Haas et al. 2011b). Not surprisingly, public acceptance is higher when costs are kept low (Haas et al. 2011b; Fouquet 2013).

Some EU countries, such as Denmark and Germany, have adopted community renewables projects in which the public participates directly in generation. Members of a community may, for example, form a legal structure to establish a renewables project in which electricity generated is then sold to the electricity authority or company, with profits distributed among the participants, in a bottom-up approach. In a more top-down approach, the public can purchase shares in existing renewables projects, thus becoming co-owners (Climate Policy Info Hub 2016).

Public participation in the policymaking process varies among GCC countries, but mainly takes the form of elected representatives acting on behalf of constituents in municipal councils or deputy councils. There is little opportunity for direct participation.

At present, there are no general guidelines at the GCC level covering public acceptance of and participation in renewables projects. The COP21 Paris Agreement, which all GCC countries signed and ratified, emphasizes public participation in policymaking and may be a driver for more active and representative participation in the future.

Three pillars of energy policies

Energy experts typically recognize the need to address three pillars when framing policies: economic efficiency, sustainability, and energy security (Lins 2013; Westphal 2014). This 'strategic triangle of energy policies' (Westphal 2014) is evident in the EU renewables policies, which link energy efficiency policies to the economic efficiency pillar and climate change policies to the sustainability pillar, while emphasizing renewables policies within the energy security pillar.

These three pillars are reflected in the EU 2020 Energy Strategy, established in 2010 by the EU Council, which sets EU level 2020 targets of having a renewables share of 20 per cent of the energy mix, improving energy efficiency by 20 per cent, and reducing GHG emissions by 20 per cent, compared with 1990 levels. They are also reflected in the more recent 2030 climate and energy framework adopted in 2014, which sets higher targets of 27 per cent for renewables' share of the energy mix, 27 per cent for improving energy efficiency and 40 per cent for the reduction of GHG emissions. This holistic approach ensures a balance among policies for renewables deployment, those designed to boost energy efficiency, and those targeting climate change.

General guidelines related to the environment exist at the GCC level, but these do not address climate change. Some climate change and energy efficiency

Table 4.1 Summary of the main policy elements, EU and GCC practices and lessons learned

Policy element	EU practice	GCC practice	Recommendations for action in the GCC
Mandatory targets	– Indicative targets to increase the share of renewable energy at the EU level were replaced by mandatory targets.	– No mandatory targets at the GCC level. – GCC countries have RE targets at the country level.	– Set mandatory targets to increase the share of renewable energy at the regional level.
Legal and regulatory framework	– A strategy and an action plan at the EU level with mandatory RE targets to be met by member states. – National RE action plans for EU member states.	– No RE policy framework at the GCC level. – Some GCC countries have developed RE targets and policies.	– Establish a policy framework at the regional level with indicative or mandatory RE targets. – Require that all countries develop action plans in support of regional policies. – Enlist countries that have already developed action plans to help those just beginning.
R&D and R&I	– Strategy at the EU level focusing on technological capacity and innovation. – Initiatives designed to achieve specific objectives established at the EU level.	– No R&D strategy at the GCC level. – R&D projects and initiatives exist in some GCC countries. – No R&I policies/strategies are in evidence in GCC countries.	– Establish an R&D policy framework at the GCC level. – Prepare initiatives targeting specific sectors.
Regulatory measures	– Application of FIT system to support RE technology deployment, which became widespread and delivered intended results. – Introduction of renewable obligations proved less effective and is now limited.	– No RE measures are in place at the country level, or at the GCC level.	– Focus on the design and implementation of an FIT system suitable to the GCC context.
Voluntary measures	– Introduction of a number of voluntary policies.	– No promotional or voluntary policies are in evidence.	– Establish a set of voluntary policies to promote renewable energy at the country level.
Public acceptance	– Public participation in energy policy-making at the EU level ensured through legislation.	– No mandatory legislation ensuring public participation at the GCC level is in evidence. – Various mechanisms exist for public participation at the national level, but GCC countries are at different stages.	– Introduce legislation at the GCC level to ensure public participation in the process of making energy policy.
Three pillars of energy policies	– RE policies are integrated with policies related to climate change and energy efficiency at the EU level. – These policies include mandatory targets to be met by member states. – Action plans to achieve the targets are developed at the member state level.	– No integrated policy is in evidence at the GCC level in relation to RE, climate change, or energy efficiency. – General Regulations of Environment in the GCC states, established in 1997, is in place. – Some relevant policies exist at the national level.	– Establish an integrated policy on RE, climate change, and energy efficiency at the GCC level.

policies are in place at the country level (IRENA 2016). To encourage collective action toward deployment of renewable energy technologies, there is a need to develop regional policies with regard to RE, energy efficiency and climate change.

To facilitate comparison of current practices in the EU and GCC regions, it is useful to summarize the main policy elements described above, including recommendations for action (Table 4.1).

Conclusions

Extensive literature review and qualitative research comparing the experience of the European Union in successfully deploying renewable energy technologies and early efforts in the GCC region reveal several lessons that may accelerate action and boost success in the GCC.

First, setting mandatory targets that each member state or country is required to meet is more effective than setting indicative targets. While collective effort can contribute greatly to reaching stated targets, allowing countries a high level of freedom in how they pursue these targets is preferable to highly prescriptive approaches. This implies the design of national action plans should be appropriate to each country's economic, social, and political context.

A second lesson reflects the value of developing R&D and R&I policies at the regional level (Hepbasli and Alsuhaibani 2011). Currently, all GCC countries have launched such projects, but no clear, relevant policies can be observed that ensure their long-term viability. Ultimately, the focus of such policies needs to match the capabilities, infrastructure and societal needs of each country. In the GCC context, starting with a focus on the application of renewable energy technologies is more likely to be fruitful than pursuing basic research would be.

The EU experience also highlights the importance of both regulatory and voluntary measures that support renewables policies. To date, in the GCC, regulatory measures are seen only at the state/provincial (non-national) level, while voluntary measures are largely absent. The EU experience brings forth the specific lesson that FIT systems proved more successful than quota based measures in deploying renewable energy technologies. In fact, some experts query why some EU countries are still considering the latter (Fouquet 2013). FIT systems seem to be preferred by those GCC countries that have started to put renewables policy measures in place. Existing literature attempts to identify the most appropriate design for the GCC countries (e.g., Ramli and Twaha 2015).

The fourth lesson relates to public participation and acceptance, which proved vital to the EU renewables policymaking process. As the public will be affected by any project implemented, its support is crucial for success. Different levels of public participation can be seen in GCC countries at present, suggesting that development of general guidelines at the GCC level would be useful.

Finally, the EU experience demonstrates that renewables policies should not be developed in isolation from other energy policies. An approach that integrates renewable energy with the two other pillars of climate change and energy efficiency is more likely to succeed. General guidelines related to the environment have been developed at the GCC level, which could stimulate regional guidelines to adopt a more holistic approach.

Across all these areas, GCC countries will need to act collectively to bring about the deployment of renewable energy technologies. Many regulations and technical specifications are already in place at the GCC level that will facilitate implementation of successful renewables policies at the national level. In parallel, introducing renewables policies at the regional level will help individual countries achieve their goals.

References

Abdel Raouf M, and Loumi M (eds) (2015) *The Green Economy in the Gulf.* Routledge, London.

Abdmouleh Z, Alammari RAM, and Gastli A (2015a) Recommendations on renewable energy policies for the GCC countries. *Renewable and Sustainable Energy Reviews* 50:1181–1191.

Abdmouleh Z, Alammari RAM, and Gastli A (2015b) Review of policies encouraging renewable energy integration & best practices. *Renewable and Sustainable Energy Reviews* 45:249–262.

Al-Amir J, and Abu-Hijleh B (2013) Strategies and policies from promoting the use of renewable energy resource in the UAE. *Renewable and Sustainable Energy Reviews* 26:660–667.

Al-Badi AH, Malik A, and Gastli A (2009) Assessment of renewable energy resources potential in Oman and identification of barrier to their significant utilization. *Renewable and Sustainable Energy Reviews* 13(9):2734–2739.

Al Hatmi Y, Tan CS, Al Badi A et al. (2014) Assessment of the consciousness levels on renewable energy resources in the Sultanate of Oman. *Renewable and Sustainable Energy Reviews* 40:1081–1089.

Al-Jayyousi O (2015) *Renewable Energy in the Arab World: Transfer of Knowledge and Prospects for Arab Cooperation.* Friedrich-Ebert-Stiftung Jordan & Iraq, Jordan. http://library.fes.de/pdf-files/bueros/amman/11667.pdf. Accessed 11 Aug 2016.

Al-Mulali U, and Lee JYM (2013) Estimating the impact of the financial development on energy consumption: evidence from the GCC (Gulf Cooperation Council) countries. *Energy* 60:215–221.

Alnaser WE, and Alnaser NW (2011) The status of renewable energy in the GCC countries. *Renewable and Sustainable Energy Reviews* 15(6):3074–3098.

Atalay Y, Biermann F, and Kalfagianni A (2016) Adoption of renewable energy technologies in oil-rich countries: explaining policy variation in the Gulf Cooperation Council states. *Renewable Energy* 85:206–214.

Bachellerie I (2012) *Renewable Energy in the GCC Countries: Resources, Potential, and Prospects.* Gulf Research Center, Jeddah, Saudi Arabia. http://library.fes.de/pdf-files/bueros/amman/09008.pdf. Accessed 11 Aug 2016.

Bhutto AW, Bazmi AA, Zahedi G, and Klemeš JJ (2014) A review of progress in renewable energy implementation in the Gulf Cooperation Council countries. *Journal of Cleaner Production* 71:168–180.

Bohringer C, Keller A, Bortolamedi M, and Seyffarth AR (2016) Good things do not always come in threes: On the excess cost of overlapping regulation in EU climate policy. *Energy Policy* 94:502–508.

Climate Policy Info Hub (2016) Community Energy Projects: Europe's Pioneering Task. http://climatepolicyinfohub.eu/community-energy-projects-europes-pioneering-task. Accessed 11 Aug 2016.

de Melo CA, de Martino Jannuzzi G, and Bajay SV (2016) Nonconventional renewable energy governance in Brazil: lessons to learn from the German experience. *Renewable and Sustainable Energy Reviews* 61:222–234.

deLlano-Paz F, Calvo-Silvosa A, Antelo S et al. (2015) The European low carbon mix for 2030: the role of renewable energy sources in an environmentally and socially efficient approach. *Renewable and Sustainable Energy Reviews* 48:49–61.

Dolowitz DP, and Marsh D (2000) Learning from abroad: the role of policy transfer in contemporary policy-making. *Governance* 13:5–23.

Doukas H, Patlitzianas KD, Kagiannas AG et al. (2006) Renewable energy sources and rationale use of energy development in the countries of GCC: myth or reality? *Renewable Energy* 31(6):755–770.

EC (European Commission) (2016). 2020 Climate and Energy Package. http://ec.europa.eu/clima/policies/strategies/2020/index_en.htm. Accessed 24 May 2017.

Eurostat (2016) Energy from renewable sources. http://ec.europa.eu/eurostat/statistics-explained/index.php/Energy_from_renewable_sources. Accessed 11 Aug 2016.

Fouquet D (2013) Policy instruments for renewable energy – from a European perspective. *Renewable Energy* 49:15–18.

Haas R, Panzer C, Resch G et al. (2011a) A historical review of promotion strategies for electricity from renewable energy sources in EU countries. *Renewable and Sustainable Energy Reviews* 15(2):1003–1034.

Haas R, Panzer C, Resch G et al. (2011b) Efficiency and effectiveness of promotion systems for electricity generation from renewable energy sources – lessons from EU countries. *Energy* 36(4):2186–2193.

Hepbasli A, and Alsuhaibani Z (2011) A key review on present status and future directions of solar energy studies and applications in Saudi Arabia. *Renewable and Sustainable Energy Reviews* 15(9):5021–5050.

Higher Education Council (2014) Bahrain National Research Strategy 2014–2024. http://moedu.gov.bh/hec/UploadFiles/Research%20Strategy%20%20Final-%20 16-10-2014.pdf. Accessed 3 May 2017.

Hofman E (2015) Public acceptance of renewable energy. www.polimp.eu/images/ publications/POLIMP_Briefing_note_01_20150311_Public_acceptance_of_ renewable_energy_1.pdf. Accessed 11 Aug 2016.

Hofman E, and van der Gaast W (2014) Acceleration of clean technology deployment within the EU: the role of social acceptance. http://polimp.eu/images/1st__ POLIMP_Policy_Brief_on_Public_Acceptance.pdf. Accessed 11 Aug 2016.

IEA (International Energy Agency) (2016) World: Balances for 2013. OECD/IEA, Paris. www.iea.org/statistics/statisticssearch/report/?country=WORLD&product= balances&year=2013. Accessed 11 Aug 2016.

IRENA (International Renewable Energy Agency) (2016) Renewable energy market analysis: the GCC region. IRENA, Abu Dhabi. www.irena.org/Document Downloads/Publications/IRENA_Market_GCC_2016.pdf. Accessed 11 Aug 2016.

Jacobsen H, Pade LL, Schröder ST et al. (2014) Cooperation mechanisms to achieve EU renewable targets. *Renewable Energy* 63:345–352.

Jamil M, Ahmad F, and Jeon YJ (2016) Renewable energy technologies adopted by the UAE: prospects and challenges – a comprehensive overview. *Renewable and Sustainable Energy Reviews* 55:1181–1194.

Keating M, and Cairney P (2012) Introduction: policy-making, learning and devolution. *Regional & Federal Studies* 22(3):239–250.

Koskimäki P-L (2012) Africa could take a leap to energy efficiency: what lessons could Sub-Saharan countries learn from European energy efficiency policy implementation? *Energy for Sustainable Development* 16(2):189–196.

KUNA (Kuwait News Agency) (2016) Diplomatic center expects Arab clean energy market to exceed $ 200 bln by '20. *KUNA*. www.kuna.net.kw/ArticleDetails. aspx?id=2506280&language=en. Accessed 11 Aug 2016.

Langsdorf S (2011) *EU Energy Policy: From the ECSC to the Energy Roadmap 2050.* Green European Foundation, Luxembourg. http://studylib.net/doc/18702348/ history-of-eu-energy-policy. Accessed 11 Aug 2016.

Lilliestam J, and Patt A (2015) Barriers, risks and policies for renewables in the Gulf States. *Energies* 8(8):8263–8285.

Lins C (2013) Learning from best practice – what European legislation and policy development can contribute to global growth of renewables. In: Hinrichs-Rahlwes R (ed.) *Sustainable Energy Policies for Europe*. CRC Press, London, pp 127–133.

Lipp J (2007) Lessons for effective renewable electricity policy from Denmark, Germany and the United Kingdom. *Energy Policy* 35(11):5481–5495.

Lombardi M, Pazienza P, and Rana R (2016) The EU environmental-energy policy for urban areas: The Covenant of Mayors, the ELENA program and the role of ESCos. *Energy Policy* 93:33–40.

Marsden G, and Stead D (2011) Policy transfer and learning in the field of transport: a review of concepts and evidence. *Transport Policy* 18(3):492–500.

Mondal MAH, Hawila D, Kennedy S et al. (2016) The GCC countries RE-readiness: strengths and gaps for development of renewable energy technologies. *Renewable and Sustainable Energy Reviews* 54:1114–1128.

Muller S, Brown A, and Olz S (2011) *Renewable Energy: Policy Considerations for Deploying Renewables*. OECD/IEA, Paris.www.iea.org/publications/freepublications/publication/Renew_Policies.pdf. Accessed 11 Aug 2016.

Munawwar S, and Ghedira H (2014) A review of renewable energy and solar industry growth in the GCC region. *Energy Procedia* 57:3191–3202.

Patlitzianas KD, Doukas H, and Askounis DT (2007) An assessment of the sustainable energy investments in the framework of the EU–GCC cooperation. *Renewable Energy* 32(10):1689–1704.

Patlitzianas KD, Doukas H, and Psarras J (2006) Enhancing renewable energy in the Arab States of the Gulf: constraints & efforts. *Energy Policy* 34(18):3719–3726.

Pollitt MG (2012) The role of policy in energy transitions: lessons from the energy liberalisation era. *Energy Policy* 50:128–137.

Polzin F, Migendt M, Täube FA et al. (2015) Public policy influence on renewable energy investments – a panel data study across OECD countries. *Energy Policy* 80:98–111.

Ramli MAM, and Twaha S (2015) Analysis of renewable energy feed-in tariffs in selected regions of the globe: lessons for Saudi Arabia. *Renewable and Sustainable Energy Reviews* 45:649–661.

RCREEE (Regional Center for Renewable Energy and Energy Efficiency) (2015) Arab Future Energy Index™ (AFEX) Renewable Energy 2015. www.rcreee.org/ projects/arab-future-energy-index%E2%84%A2-afex. Accessed 11 Aug 2016.

Reiche D (2010) Renewable energy policies in the Gulf countries: a case study of the carbon-neutral "Masdar City" in Abu Dhabi. *Energy Policy* 38(1):378–382.

REN21 (Renewable Energy Policy Network for the 21st Century) (2015) *Renewables 2015 Global Status Report 2015*. REN21, Paris. www.ren21.net/wp-content/uploads/2015/07/REN12-GSR2015_Onlinebook_low1.pdf. Accessed 11 Aug 2016.

Scarlat N, Dallemand J-F, Monforti-Ferrario F et al. (2015) Renewable energy policy framework and bioenergy contribution in the European Union – an overview from National Renewable Energy Action Plans and Progress Reports. *Renewable and Sustainable Energy Reviews* 51:969–985.

Sekercioglu S, and Yılmaz M (2012) Renewable energy perspectives in the frame of Turkey's and the EU's energy policies. *Energy Conversion and Management* 63:233–238.

Sgouridis S, Griffiths S, Kennedy S et al. (2013) A sustainable energy transition strategy for the United Arab Emirates: evaluation of options using an Integrated Energy Model. *Energy Strategy Reviews* 2(1):8–18.

Soriano F, and Mulatero F (2011) EU Research and Innovation (R and I) in renewable energies: the role of the Strategic Energy Technology Plan (SET-Plan). *Energy Policy* 39(6):3582–3590.

Sovacool BK (2009) The importance of comprehensiveness in renewable electricity and energy-efficiency policy. *Energy Policy* 37(4):1529–1541.

Steinbeis Europa Zentrum and Karlsruhe Institute of Technology (n.d.) Timeline of EU Energy and Climate Change Legislation. http://smartcities-infosystem.eu/sites/default/files/EU_policy_timeline.pdf. Accessed 11 Aug 2016.

Stone D (2001) Learning Lessons, Policy Transfer and the International Diffusion of Policy Ideas. CSGR Working Paper No. 69/01. Centre for the Study of Globalisation and Regionalisation (CSGR), University of Warwick, Coventry. www2.warwick.ac.uk/fac/soc/pais/research/researchcentres/csgr/papers/workingpapers/2001/wp6901.pdf. Accessed 11 Aug 2016.

Westphal K (2014) Institutional change in European natural gas markets and implications for energy security: lessons from the German case. *Energy Policy* 74:35–43.

Wood G, and Dow S (2011) What lessons have been learned in reforming the Renewables Obligation? An analysis of internal and external failures in UK renewable energy policy. *Energy Policy* 39(5):2228–2244.

Wyns T, Khatchadourian A, and Oberthür S (2014) *EU Governance of Renewable Energy post-2020 – Risks and Options*. Institute for European Studies, Brussel. www.ies.be/files/eu_renewable_energy_governance_post_2020.pdf. Accessed 11 Aug 2016.

5 Prioritizing renewable energy in a time of fiscal austerity

Karen E. Young

Abstract

Meeting stated targets to boost renewable energy in countries belonging to the Gulf Cooperation Council (GCC) presents multiple challenges, with attracting sufficient financing being a primary concern. With government budgets already constrained by low oil revenues, and electricity demand projected to grow rapidly, states will no longer be able to shoulder the full cost of building new capacity and continuing to supply electricity at substantially subsidized prices.

This chapter explores mechanisms by which GCC governments can secure private investment, including foreign direct investment (FDI), acknowledging specific challenges that arise from Islamic finance and identifying obstacles in policy that will need to be addressed. It also highlights steps some countries have taken, which demonstrate that investors are interested in the region.

Policy relevant insights

- GCC countries have new incentives to invest in renewable energy: as a way to preserve natural gas and oil resources for export revenue; as a means to create jobs in new technology; and as a tool to attract foreign investment.
- The fiscal reform efforts of GCC states will require some regulatory reform that may impact the ways in which foreign investors and state entities interact, particularly in large infrastructure projects in the energy sector.
- Renewable energies can attract different kinds of foreign investors, including those interested in products such as green bonds and *sukuks* (Islamic bonds).
- Recently established renewables organizations form a kind of foundational epistemic community for renewable energy, which can spur advance by individual countries and the GCC as a whole.

(continued)

(continued)

- Public-private partnerships (PPPs) show strong potential for reducing the financial burden of building and operating new capacity; effort will be needed to adjust existing legal frameworks that hamper their potential.
- Initial offerings of green bonds have proven successful as a financing mechanism that meets Islamic practices; GCC countries may consider building institutional capacity to expand their use.

Introduction

A substantial decline in oil revenues since late 2014 has pushed countries belonging to the GCC into a new era of fiscal austerity, compelling governments to consider how to finance many of their spending needs, including the financing of renewable energy production. Yet it has also created a changed policy environment for these oil-exporting countries, in which structural reforms are both necessary and politically feasible. There is general public acquiescence to the need for economic diversification away from oil revenues, as well as shifting to renewable energy sources for domestic consumption. For the most part, the recent introduction of subsidy reforms across the region – and subsequent increases in fuel, electricity and water prices – has been met with little confrontation.

The current restraints on fiscal policy due to the decline in oil revenues have created both a logic for reform and demand for savings in government expenditure, which renewables can provide. Renewables can create savings simply by allowing oil and gas resources to be dedicated to export, rather than domestic consumption. Yet these restraints also create some disincentives for government spending in infrastructure.

In an effort to analyze these simultaneous political and economic changes inside the Gulf region, this chapter has two aims. First, it describes the demand for and supply of renewable energy finance, in the context of global capital markets and as part of larger economic diversification goals set out by the six GCC states. As a second aim, the chapter seeks to contextualize the public policy goal of producing energy from renewable sources within the fiscal limits on government resources and the constraints of institutional frameworks.

The scale of financing needed to deploy renewable energy within the Gulf region will require investment by the states, as well as public-private partnerships (PPPs) including foreign direct investment (FDI). The opportunities for regulatory reform within the financial sector could provide incentives for innovative financing of renewable energy infrastructure.

The risks, however, are many; a steep increase in the global price of oil and gas could derail a diversification effort, while a sharp reduction in government outlays could create recession and worsen the investment climate for infrastructure development. The regulatory frameworks to encourage partnerships and foreign investment vary across the GCC, with many policies showing gaps in insolvency and dispute settlement processes. The short term could be an opportunity for renewable energy finance and innovation, as the global climate for infrastructure investment improves.

This chapter is organized as follows: it first explores the depth and diversity of the current fiscal crisis affecting the six GCC states. Second, it presents an analysis of the opportunities and risks associated with supporting the renewable energy sector in the region, with specific attention to the institutional frameworks in laws on finance and PPPs. Third, the chapter examines how a policy framework and industry support nexus can invigorate renewables policy and production, with a case study of the renewable energy landscape in the United Arab Emirates (UAE).

Fiscal constraint disrupts traditional roles of GCC governments

Historically, oil-exporting economies of the GCC have prioritized citizen welfare through an economic model that has seen the state as an engine of growth, a source of employment, and the provider of a range of social and economic benefits, including healthcare, housing, subsidized energy and free education. This is part of a social contract: in exchange for this generous welfare state, citizens accept limits on political voice and representation. This rentier model is abstract and there are certainly areas in which domestic politics are more complex and consultative, despite the resilience of authoritarian rule within the Gulf in the wake of 2011 uprisings (Young 2014). Besides political institutions, the societies are influenced by informal institutions, religious thought, and norms that maintain an affinity for the public provision of services.

In the harsh climate of the Gulf, citizens and residents rely on the state to provide the basics necessary for survival. The particularly precious commodities of water and energy are at the core of this social contract and have been consistently provided at highly subsidized prices. In fact, many Gulf citizens view the provision of water as tantamount to a state religious duty.

In the oil and gas boom decade of 2004–2013, wealth generated from oil and gas exports supported a model of state capitalism and enabled unprecedented growth in GCC state institutions (Ulrichsen 2016). The size of governments ballooned and massive projects were launched in infrastructure in roads, sea ports, power plants and airports. Additionally, new cities grew up rapidly, often populated by young citizens and expatriate workers.

More recently, a new era of low energy prices has emerged (El-Katiri 2016). The primary contributing factors are generally agreed to be more oil coming to the market while global demand growth weakened. Technological innovations made it possible to extract oil and gas from more difficult physical environments and also led to the shale oil revolution. Simultaneously, there was a slowdown in demand for oil and gas from the major consumers: economic growth slowed in Asia while the United States pursued a strategy of greater energy independence.

In 2014, the oil boom came to an abrupt end and all six GCC states found themselves in fiscal deficit – some for the first time in over a decade. Under this new fiscal reality, GCC countries have to cope with citizens who have become accustomed to government delivery of the necessary structural environment for economic growth, including readily available and low-priced sources of energy for electricity, water desalination and transport.

Production of electricity is a major cost to Gulf governments; as most generation is from oil or associated gas, it is also a major absorber of valuable export resources (IMF 2015). Additionally, as most of the states have very little access to a natural, clean water supply, one of the primary linkages in the energy system is cogeneration of power and water, using power for desalination of water.

Failure to provide these critical services would pose a direct threat to the state itself. Yet as national revenues plummeted, the cost, as a proportion of government spending, of providing these public goods has soared. In some cases, the current fiscal reality challenges the traditional social contracts of the state, including the ability to deliver economic opportunities and public goods (Gengler and Lambert 2016).

In the new Gulf fiscal reality post-2014 – and in the context of an economic reform agenda that has been unfolding since 2015 – a renewables strategy as an alternative to oil- and gas-fired electricity and desalination plants begins to make economic sense. Yet this agenda has to tackle long-standing beliefs that certain provisions, including water and electricity, are often viewed as rights, not commodities.

Recognizing that the reduction of subsidies for utilities poses a direct challenge to the existing social order, governments have been cautious in pursuing reform. Yet action undertaken by some has yet to create significant dissent.

After exploring the challenge of rising energy demand and the opportunity for renewables, this chapter outlines current efforts and the ongoing need to reform specific legal frameworks to better enable financing of large infrastructure investment, specifically renewable energy production, in each of the GCC states. This includes reducing subsidies for electricity and water, adopting proven mechanisms for privatization and finding ways to close funding gaps and secure financing. It also gives some background regarding private partners that could participate in developing large renewables projects, including the banking sector, international financial institutions, investors, and even contractors. In each section, some examples of recent reform are highlighted, but the range of examples is by no means exhaustive as efforts are underway across GCC states. A case study of the UAE provides a more complete picture of interrelated activity in a single state.

Rising energy demand supports the case for increased renewables

The drivers of rising energy demand in the GCC are quite straightforward: a population explosion, both citizens and foreign laborers, and rapid economic development over the last three decades have led to surging demand for electricity, for industrial and residential uses. As these societies grow, their needs for infrastructure and services are also expanding.

Governments have responded by devoting substantial resources to constructing cities, prioritizing housing and retail properties, but also creating the support infrastructure in roads, water, and electricity generation to connect them. While the previous oil boom of the 1970s prompted government expenditure to support subsidization of domestic energy consumption, largely in fuel, electricity and water, it did not create the same kind of domestically directed fiscal expenditure as seen during the recent boom.

For decades, electricity generation in the GCC has been dominated by gas- and oil-fired plants. As export revenues from hydrocarbons have sharply declined, it is becoming untenable to use cheap domestic energy production that carries a high opportunity cost in that it could otherwise be directed to export sales, domestic manufacturing of petrochemicals, or saved for later export. Furthermore, as transfer of energy among GCC states remains limited in both the transfer and exchange of electricity and the import and export of liquefied natural gas (LNG), states are forced to rely on – and potentially exhaust – domestic sources of energy (largely oil) rather than trading and mixing gas and solar energy for electricity generation, for example.

In the current context of low revenues from oil and gas, opportunity exists for renewable energy to play a substantial role in meeting this rising energy demand. But the opportunity is not without risks. To achieve stated renewable targets with minimal negative impacts, the GCC states will need to pursue assertive policy reform on multiple fronts simultaneously.

Opportunities and risks for renewable energy investment in GCC states

From the perspective of GCC governments, delivery of electricity is a priority for state development, for attracting foreign investment, and ultimately for state security. In the current fiscal context, GCC countries face a complex situation of opportunity and risk in terms of seeking to meet rising energy demand, achieve stated renewables targets, and financing such projects. Some opportunities and risks are regional; others reflect important differences within individual country cases.

Investment opportunities

Some GCC states have been considering renewables investments for many years, even during the exceptional boom years of high oil prices. Often, this

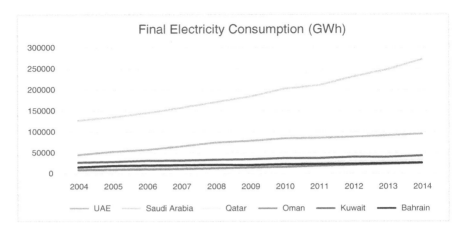

Figure 5.1 Final energy consumption in the GCC, 2004–2014 (www.iea.org/ statistics/statisticssearch/)

was led by projected demand growth (Figure 5.1). In 2010, for example, growth to 2015 was estimated at an increase of 80 per cent – a clear indication that demand would outstrip supply and that heavy reliance on gas-fired electric plants was no longer tenable. This prompted investigation of renewable energy markets in the GCC in 2010 (Alnaser and Alnaser 2011).

The development of renewable energy technologies, which is likely to lower their respective implementation costs, helps to solve several challenges facing the Gulf states. Tapping into an alternative source of energy for domestic use, for example, will allow governments to reserve oil and gas resources for more valuable export markets. Use of cleaner energy domestically will also reduce greenhouse gas (GHG) emissions that are harmful to the climate in the long term and thereby alleviate associated impacts. But perhaps most compelling is the opportunity to embrace localized technology to support research, innovation, and ultimately job growth.

Scholars examining the potential for adopting renewable energy technologies in the GCC present a multi-pronged argument that suggests various economic and social policy goals can be achieved with limited financial investment (Abdmouleh et al. 2015). The International Renewable Energy Agency (IRENA) claims that renewables industries in the Gulf states could create as many as 140,000 direct jobs every year (IRENA 2016). The IRENA report also stresses how Gulf policymakers have advocated for the creation of renewable energy agencies and research organizations to help stimulate demand and domestic support for the clean energy transition.

Recently established organizations form a kind of epistemic community for renewable energy, with front-runners including Masdar in the UAE, the Dubai Supreme Council of Energy, and in Saudi Arabia the King Abdullah

Table 5.1 Renewable energy projects, planned and underway in the GCC (IRENA, PWC)

Renewable energy projects in the GCC

Country	Technology	Number of projects	Project	Local developers/ops	Foreign developers/ops
United Arab Emirates	PV	9	Masdar City Solar PV Park	Masdar	Suntech Power Holdings, First Solar
			SunPower Masdar City	Masdar	SunPower
			Noor 1	Masdar	
			Shuaa Energy 1 (Phase 2)	DEWA	ACWA Power, TSK, NOMAC
			Moh'd Bin Rashid Al Maktoum Solar Power Plant (Phase 1)	DEWA	First Solar, Inc.
			Rooftop PV Program	DEWA	
			Moh'd Bin Rashid Al Maktoum Solar Power Plant (Phase 3)	DEWA	
			Solar Power Plant	Utico FZC	
			Bee'ah – Solar Energy Plant	Bee'ah	
	Waste to Energy	3	Waste to Energy Plant	CWM, TAQA	
			Al Warsan – Waste to Energy	Dubai Municipality	
			Waste to Energy Facility	Bee'ah	Chinook Sciences
	Wind	1	Sir Bani Yas Island	Masdar, TDIC	Vestas
	CSP	1	Shams 1	Masdar	Abengoa, Total
Kuwait	PV	2	Renewable Energy Complex	MEW, KISR	TSK
			Umm Gudair solar plant	KOC	Gestamp Solar
	Waste to Energy	1	Kabd Municipal Solid Waste project	KAPP, Kuwait Municipality	
	Wind	1	Renewable Energy Complex	MEW, KISR	TSK

(continued)

Table 5.1 (continued)

Renewable energy projects in the GCC

Country	Technology	Number of projects	Project	Local developers/ops	Foreign developers/ops
	Solar	2	Al-Abdaliya power plant	MEW	
			Renewable Energy Complex	MEW, KISR	TSK
Saudi Arabia	PV	6	North Park PV Project	Saudi Aramco, Sun & Life	Belectric
			Farsasan Island Solar Project	SEC	Showa Shell
			KAPSARC Solar Project (Phase 1)	Saudi Aramco	Canadian Solar
			KAPSARC Solar Project (Phase 2)	Saudi Aramco	Canadian Solar
			Tabuk Solar Plant	Saudi Aramco, Khled Juffali Co.	Soitec
			KAUST Solar Park	KAUST, National Solar Systems	Conergy
	CSP	1	Duba 1 ISCC Project	SEC	General Electric
	Solar	1	Waad Al Shammal	SEC	General Electric
Qatar	PV	1	KAHRAMAA – Solar Energy Power Plant	Kahramaa	
Bahrain	PV	2	PV Plant	BAPCO	
			Manama Solar Park	BAPCO, NOGA	Petra Solar
Oman	Solar	1	Miraah Solar Thermal Project	Petroleum Development Oman	GlassPoint Solar

Source: IRENA, PWC

Established projects

Projects being actively worked on

Stagnant projects/lack of information

City for Atomic and Renewable Energy (KACARE) and the King Abdullah Petroleum Studies and Research Center (KAPSARC). These efforts are amplified by private sector ventures such as the Arabian Company for Water and Power Development (ACWA) and the acquisition of Spanish solar company Fotowatio Renewable Ventures B.V. (FRV) by Saudi business Abdul Latif Jameel. The number of major renewable energy production facilities in use, in construction, or stalled within the GCC has grown rapidly (Table 5.1).

Investment risks

Despite aggressive goals and political will, GCC countries have encountered obstacles to embracing renewable energy in power generation. In light of new stresses on fiscal priorities, some evidence suggests GCC countries are backtracking on previous production targets. Despite new policy goals for sustainable domestic energy production, the economic reform process has put pressure on governments to prioritize social programs and public sector jobs over new renewable and clean energy targets and investments.

Price is also an obstacle, as building new power plants is expensive. In 2010, based on projects in the UAE, cost estimates for renewable electricity generation ranged from $0.27 per kilowatt hour (/kWh) for ground-mount photovoltaic (PV) solar to $0.35/kWh for roof-mount (Alnaser and Alnaser 2011). These costs were difficult to justify to investors when citizens paid roughly $0.01/kWh across the GCC, or even less in Qatar.

By January 2016, consultancies PwC and Eversheds advised clients that solar PV had become less costly than gas for new power projects in the Middle East. The Middle East Solar Industry Association estimated that LNG imports in the GCC would reach over 800 million cubic feet per day (MMcf/d) in 2016, at a cost of about $9 per million British thermal units (MMBtu), making the daily bill for GCC LNG imports of about $7 million, or about $2.7 billion a year, aside from the massive investments needed in infrastructure for combined cycle power plants (MESIA 2016). This puts the average cost of gas-fired electricity generation well above $0.05/kWh and much higher for peaking units that serve mainly summer loads (MESIA 2016).

In addition, these reports indicate that renewables have become politically more acceptable as part of an energy mix, rather than a replacement of other sources (Davies et al. 2016).

Ironically, a continued downward trend in the price of oil could discourage government spending in infrastructure overall, including solar power. At present, the political incentives for a renewable energy commitment are as compelling as the economic case. The more difficult targets will be standardizing distribution of electricity throughout the federation, which should be a shared goal of economic diversification and generating economic growth.

A kind of institutional inertia is another obstacle, in that renewable and clean energy production requires policy change and commitment. With some exceptions in the UAE, GCC governments have shown little public policy appetite for change. This is perhaps because vested interests in the oil and gas sectors tend to dominate energy ministries with set practices and preferences for power production, even when these preferences might be at odds with the overall goal of increasing oil and gas export revenue, which could be achieved by shifting to more renewables for domestic consumption.

In just five years, a clear shift in price and perception is evident, reflecting in part the decline in oil revenues, readiness among policymakers (Lilliestam and Patt 2015) and national utilities to embrace change, and a global change in finance mechanisms. Gulf states are clearly open to the idea of renewable and clean energy production, but they need two key elements to make it happen: domestic institutional commitment to policy change and financing, with an acceptable level of shared risk to the government and to local and/or foreign investors. Some hurdles in the regulation of risk-sharing between public and private enterprises are becoming evident as the tradition of state-owned utilities begins to shift towards partnership and private operation models.

Legal frameworks, ownership structures and financial products: what is working, what needs reform

The Gulf region, it would appear, is now ready for the idea of renewable energy and is prepared to secure the financing needed to make it feasible (Mondal et al. 2016). At present, however, the region has only a limited set of legal frameworks that allow potential partners to share risk in large infrastructure investments. Additionally, availability of and access to financial products, including Islamic bonds and other Sharia-compliant finance structures, varies across countries.

The necessity of legal and financial sector reform across the GCC states was evident before the current fiscal pressure heightened (Young 2015). Some states began implementing reform agendas years ago. For example, privatization of utilities – especially water – began in the late 1990s through local joint ventures between state-owned or state-related entities and private companies, often through build-operate-transfer (BOT) schemes.

The recent crisis has legitimated the reform logic, especially in diversification strategies that include renewables production targets, and intensified the speed of fiscal and labor market reforms. Given the pressing need for a more efficient and flexible kind of state-led growth, the reform process may now gain momentum. Recent action is evident on the two mechanisms Gulf states are considering to substantially lower the cost of providing energy and water: reduction of subsidies, and privatization (Table 5.2) (Lahn 2016). For some states, the challenge is more immediate than for others.

Ultimately, development of the legal and financial frameworks that enable shared investment will determine how large investments in energy and water provision will move forward. This section highlights various efforts in different countries to initiate reform.

Table 5.2 GCC economic reform agenda 2015–2016 (Arab Gulf States Institute in Washington, Gulf Economic Barometer)

Country	Water subsidy reduction	Electricity subsidy reduction	Fuel subsidy reduction	Utilities privatization/PPP
Bahrain			✓	
Kuwait	✓	✓	✓	
Oman		✓	✓	✓
Qatar	✓	✓	✓	
Kingdom of Saudi Arabia	✓		✓	✓
United Arab Emirates	✓	✓	✓	✓

Electricity and water subsidy reform

Relying on national hydrocarbon resources, which are in ready supply, GCC governments have been able to supply power and water to their customers at relatively low cost to national budgets. Additionally, keeping charges to customers low was seen as a way to share the wealth generated by resource revenues.

In Kuwait, water prices have been fixed for both nationals and non-nationals at the same rate for 40 years, thus becoming increasingly subsidized with the passing of time. In the 1970s, water was free to all households in Abu Dhabi; this changed somewhat in the early 1990s, also in a time of depressed oil prices, when non-nationals were made to pay for water. Current pricing is differentiated, with costs to Emirati nationals still highly subsidized and non-citizen residents paying much higher rates. Since mid-2016, the government of Bahrain has been negotiating with members of parliament to remove both water and electricity subsidies to non-nationals and private sector businesses.

Under the new fiscal constraints, pricing of water and electricity has become contentious. In the case of electricity, it is affected by factors such as the price of land, the lease of land, facility construction, and the ability to connect to a national grid system. Still, by the last quarter of 2016, all GCC states had embarked on a subsidy reform process, with differing levels of success in implementation.

Reform of ownership structures: privatization

Arab Gulf states are also amending laws on lending and forming new mechanisms to encourage private investment in utilities and infrastructure projects (see Figure 5.2).

One PPP model allows for joint or shared ownership of a plant between a government entity and a private investor or set of investors and/or developers or operators. Another option, the engineering, procurement and construction (EPC) model, sees joint participation only on the design and construction of the power plant itself; ownership remains solely in the hands of the state. The independent power producer (IPP) model separates construction and ownership of the plant from the electricity distributor but involves a contractual agreement on the purchase of the electricity to be generated.

Abu Dhabi launched the first PPP in the GCC water sector in 1999 with the creation of the Abu Dhabi Water and Electricity Authority (ADWEA). By 2010, some 95 per cent of desalinated water in Abu Dhabi was produced through PPPs (Lambert 2014).

In 2005, an Omani decree (Royal Decree 42/96) encouraged privatization by separating the Energy Ministry's responsibility for electricity generation from that of new entities that can participate in generation and distribution of power (IBP 2015). Under this type of privatization scheme, the state maintains its role in the procurement of power but privatizes generation and transmission to PPP entities.

Starting in 2014, new laws in Dubai and Kuwait granted ownership stakes in and revenues from assets to investors that fund origination costs for these kinds of infrastructure and utility projects (Ali and Masud 2014).

Various GCC countries have taken recent steps to amend or create new PPP regulations, develop outlines for BOT schemes, or stimulate full-on privatization proposals in which IPPs operate in place of – or in competition with – state-owned utilities.

In Saudi Arabia, where the state depends heavily on oil revenues for social spending and public sector salaries, the need for economic reform agenda is pressing. With substantially reduced revenue, the state has had to sell reserve assets and turn to debt issuance to cover expenses. The structure of the most recent fiscal budget aims to secure more revenues from fees and the sale of government assets, including the privatization and public offering of a share (mostly likely a 5 per cent stake) in Aramco, the state oil company.

Saudi Arabia has also announced the privatization of its airport in Jeddah, following the successful privatization (under a BOT scheme) of Medina airport in a 25-year concession led by Turkish holding group TAV Airports Holding Co in exchange for $1.2 billion (Trade Arabia 2016).

In water distribution, Saudi Arabia has a precedent for independent producers acting in partnership with the state utility (Shuaibah IWPP n.d.). In August 2014, the International Finance Corporation (IFC) invested $100 million in equity in Saudi Arabia's water and power project developer, the Arabian Company for Water and Power Development (ACWA) (Kiyasseh 2016). The investment also sought to spur regional development projects in the Middle East and North Africa by new private players.

Yet state interests in these limited companies, such as ACWA, demonstrate how the Saudi public sector has yet to fully release private operators and investors from its grasp. By late 2016, the Saudi Public Investment Fund had shown an interest in buying a stake in ACWA, which would limit the entity's ability to truly be a private developer in the Saudi domestic market (Al-Sayegh and Shamseddine 2016).

There is enormous wealth within Saudi state assets, but short-term liquidity could become a problem. To date, there is no PPP law in Saudi Arabia. Thus, it is not clear yet from the National Transformation Program or Vision 2030 how PPPs might move forward, or how privatizations will be managed as parts or assets of the Saudi Electricity Company (SEC), for example. The Kingdom has had some success with IPPs, but always with the SEC retaining a 50 per cent share.

Kuwait's advanced PPP law, established in 2014, led to development of the Kuwait Authority for Public Partnerships, which has a mandate to formalize government policy in this area. The law clearly sets out how external investors can participate in profit-sharing while also putting in place stringent rules on foreign ownership of shared ventures.

Article 13 of Law 116 of the 2014 PPP regulations requires, for example, that the equity of a public joint stock project be divided carefully among public authorities, winning investors and public subscription offers to Kuwaiti citizens. In a sell-off via PPP for any project of more than 60 million Kuwaiti dinars (KWD) (approximately \$150 million), the public authority is limited to no more than 24 per cent of an entity and the investor must take on at least 26 per cent of shares. The authority must offer 50 per cent of shares to Kuwaiti citizens in a public offering.

In this regulation, Kuwait has set two important precedents in its liberalization and efforts to attract foreign investment. First, it has prioritized and reserved opportunities for Kuwaiti citizens to benefit from the profit of sales of state assets. For example, if a utility is to be built under this scheme, the new company created would be more than 75 per cent investor owned, with the largest portion held by citizen investors. The government has been careful to sideline its own potential gains on such large investments – and to minimize its risks.

In comparison, frameworks for PPP investments are not nearly as developed in other parts of the GCC.

In Qatar, economic reform and privatization are included in an overall vision of good governance, according to the Emir's address to the 44th session of the Advisory Council in November 2015. As reported in the Qatar *Peninsula*, Emir Sheikh Tamim bin Hamad al Thani stressed the need to diversify the economy and to limit the state's competition with the private sector, including:

> [s]ubsidies for a number of these companies be ceased, and some to be privatized, and management of some be transferred to the private sector, and government corporations and companies not to compete with the private sector, and opportunities for this sector to implement government projects be enforced.
>
> (Peninsula 2015)

Qatar allows 100 per cent foreign ownership of corporate entities, but land rights are an issue. For utility providers, there is little competition, as the state-owned

Kingdom of Saudi Arabia

- No PPP legislation
- Under Saudi National Transformation Programme (NTP) includes the following initiatives:
  - *at least eight Independent Water Projects (IWPs);*
  - *two sewage treatment plants;*
  - *a 300 MW solar photovoltaic plant in Sakaka;*
  - *400 MW wind farm close to the Midyan Saudi Aramco gas plant;*
  - *privatization of 27 airports by the General Authority of Civil Aviation;*
  - *a waste management programme;*
  - *a healthcare programme, including privatization initially of up to nine hospitals; and*
  - *an education programme to encompass over 300 schools.*
- National Centre for Privatization (NCP) started operations in early 2017 to implement NTP plans and initiatives.

Kuwait

- Kuwait introduced PPP legislation: Law No. 7 of 2008.
- Introduced an updated Law No. 116 of 2014.
- First PPP project in Kuwait, Az Zour North Electricity & Water IWPP, awarded in 2013.

Oman

- No formal PPP model or legislation, however first draft of a legal framework expected to be delivered by mid-2017.
- In 2016, consortium of advisers was mandated to develop PPP legislation and create centralized oversight unit.

Bahrain

- No PPP legislation.
- First partnership in 2013 when Ministry of Housing signed PPP with Naseej real estate for housing development. Another real estate partnership in 2015, with Diyar Al Muharriq.

Qatar

- Qatar Chamber of Commerce began drafting legislation in November 2016.
- New PPP law put forward by Ministry of Economy and Commerce, expected to be implemented by mid-2017.

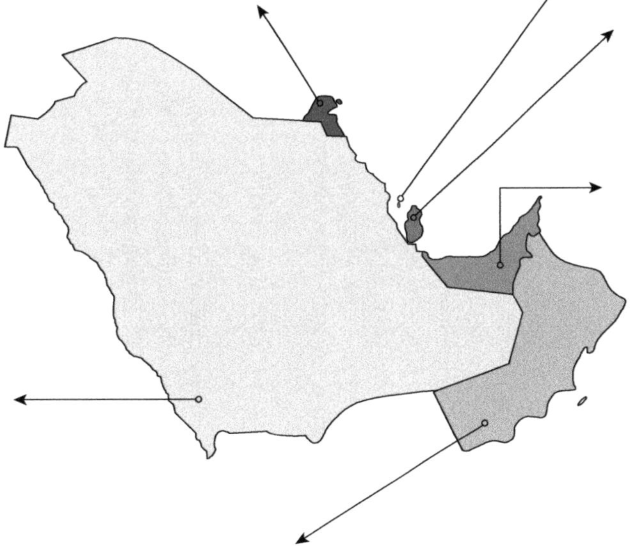

United Arab Emirates

- Dubai passed Law No. 22 in 2015.
- UAE Cabinet issued Resolution 1/1 in 2017, presented by Ministry of Finance, to outline PPP procedures, contracts, institutional structure, and life-cycle partnerships.

Figure 5.2 Roll-out of privatization schemes in the GCC

utility (Qatar General Electricity and Water Corporation, KAHRAMAA) dominates the market and controls grid access.

In the UAE, current law requires at least 51 per cent ownership by the state or a UAE national for any corporate entity, unless in a free zone, where private foreign businesses can operate without a local agent. The UAE has implemented many IPP models for electricity plants, as well as contracts for design and operation of large utilities, but does not allow outright ownership.

In the event that external financing is needed, each of these joint owner-ship structures raises questions of liability, creditworthiness and ownership of collateral.

Funding gaps and financing

Securing external financing has not been a major barrier to large renewables projects in the GCC. A list of recent renewables projects in the GCC that have used PPP finance models demonstrates strong industry and investor interest in the region.

Box 5.1   Renewable energy projects in the Gulf, based on PPP models

Facility	Description
Masdar City Solar PV Plant	Technology supplied by Suntech and First Solar
SunPower Masdar City	SunPower installed canopy structure on Masdar building
Shuaa Energy 1	ACWA, TSK, NOVAC
Mohammed Bin Rashid Al Maktoum Solar Power Plant	First Solar
Shagaya Renewable Energy Park	TSK provided with construction and installation
Umm Gudair Solar Plant	Gestamp Solar selected to build the facility
Saudi Aramco North PV Park	Solar Frontier
Farasan Island Solar Park	Showa Shell Sekiyu, Solar Frontier
Manama Solar Park	Petra Solar, Caspian Renewable Energy

One challenge to financing, however, is that states are confined by local Islamic law from extending interest payments to investors and, in return, cre-ating a source of collateral, in land or assets owned by the state, that can be dispersed in the event of bankruptcy or failure of a project.

In the GCC context, *sukuks* are one of the most important financing sources. These bonds meet the criteria of Islamic law in that they are not meant to accrue interest, but rather share the risk and ownership of tangible assets through a joint investment endeavor (Mahmoud 2016). 'Green sukuks' (or green bonds) are a novel financing option. These are targeted investments for an environmental purpose (Dubey et al. 2016), in which the 'green investment' is made in companies, projects and financial instruments that support projects in renewable energy, clean technology, or low carbon or climate-resilient actions. The projects are screened according to environmental, social, and governance criteria. These niche investment vehicles attract long-term investors and those with institutional commitments to environmentally friendly investments, as many large pension funds now prefer.

In Saudi Arabia, public sector entities, including the SEC, are using *sukuks* to fund new power plant construction. Smaller-scale ventures, especially in the solar PV market, have found it more difficult to secure financing or investments (IRENA 2016; NBAD et al. 2015). Some successful examples of government sourced funding exist, as in Dubai's plans to establish an AED 100 billion ($27 billion) Dubai Green Fund, providing soft loans for investors in the sector. The $3.2 billion Mohammed bin Rashid Al Maktoum Solar Park is self-funded by members of the Dubai Supreme Council of Energy. Masdar announced that, alongside the UK Green Investment Bank, it will invest up to AED 6 billion ($1.6 billion) in alternative energy projects (Meltzer et al. 2014).

In other GCC states, such as Oman and Bahrain, the funding gap could be more severe. According to the World Bank, in 2016 the ratio of debt to gross domestic product (GDP) in Bahrain was above 83 per cent, a dramatic increase from 44 per cent just in 2014. With such a high (by regional standards) debt-to-GDP ratio, Bahrain is now in breach of the GCC criteria for a currency union, though that system is far from implementation. At $107.20 per barrel in 2015, Bahrain's fiscal break-even price is much higher than most of its GCC neighbors (World Bank 2016).

Between late 2014 and the middle of 2016, Middle East and North Africa (MENA) oil exporters lost more than $800 billion in revenue compared with the boom years of 2003–2014, during which time governments had become comfortable with high levels of domestic spending (Batrawy 2016). The sharp downturn in fiscal positions has spurred changes in fiscal policy on energy, fuel, and water subsidies, and prompted the introduction of a plan for a value-added sales tax across the GCC.

Kuwait, like all GCC states, is struggling to meet fiscal outlays with a reduced oil revenue stream. It is, however, better positioned than many of its neighbors, as it has a lower break-even price for oil, partly because the country's geology makes its oil easily accessible. Perhaps more relevant to the current context, Kuwait has traditionally spent less on domestic infrastructure and large development projects, and over the last decade opted instead to direct much of its savings into its sovereign wealth funds. However, as investors lament and the World Bank *Ease of Doing Business* reports have tracked, Kuwait has been a difficult place to stimulate economic growth (Westall and Sleiman 2012). The resistance to spend on public works in a time of fiscal austerity might be viewed as prudent, but in fact Kuwait is now caught in a case of poor timing. Government spending commitments increased in 2015 to remedy the lag in infrastructure development – just as oil revenue dropped (Khaleej Times 2015). Kuwait has been on track since 2011 to increase its non-oil sources of revenue, though the recent decline in oil prices seems to have dampened the economy as a whole and diminished the diversification effort.

Considering they are all, to some degree, in the same boat, the six GCC states may be in a good position to share learning as they each navigate through this unfamiliar territory of structural reform. Potential partners from the international investment community are watching closely to gauge how these projects will be financed and how stable the partnerships can be. As seen in Saudi Arabia's partnership with the IFC, some are investing alongside renewable PPP ventures.

Some of the limitations of these products, and of financing in general for smaller-scale projects, reflects a relatively low level at present of institutional capacity within the local finance sector to evaluate risk and extend credit.

Renewable energy policy frameworks and industry support nexus

To achieve stated renewable targets, the current GCC policy environment must bring together a strengthening research and development (R&D) community and a nascent private sector of investors and developers. Important progress is already evident in key areas.

Local manufacturing, particularly in solar capacity, is growing and will likely expand further as the scale of projects increases and the possibility of feed-in from rooftop and smaller-scale solar electricity becomes technically feasible.

The policy frameworks to support growth in the renewables industry vary across the GCC and are still developing as new finance tools emerge and new legislation is passed to secure the transactions and investments. The primary motivation is to move away from solely state-owned investment in the power sector, starting with auction processes for procurement of both capacity and energy (Patlitzianas et al. 2006).

Response to reforms

Despite general recognition of the need for economic diversification and fiscal reform in the GCC, not all efforts have been well received. In fact, public criticism of reforms has prompted strong action, including one instance in which the Saudi government fired the minister for water after receiving complaints about tariff increases in April 2016 (Carey and Sabah 2016). The higher tariffs, however, remained in place.

Kuwait has shown a mix of measured steps forward and subsequent back-tracking, with the involvement of parliament and a court case that found the reduction of petrol (gasoline) subsidies to be illegal. On October 16, 2016, Kuwait's Emir Sheikh Sabah al-Ahmed al-Sabah dissolved Parliament, citing concerns about security and finances in an era of reduced oil revenue. The November 2016 elections, however, saw more members who were critical of the reform process voted into office (Diwan 2016).

To date, few GCC governments have been proactive in efforts to introduce conservation ethics and promote better public understanding of related issues such as the true cost of water and utilities, and the potential impact of renewables. Dubai is likely the most innovative in this sense, with a public campaign about conservation pre-dating the 2014 drop in oil prices, along with information about solar power plant construction and renewable targets (Aswad et al. 2013). Abu Dhabi has taken a longer and more protracted path towards a public articulation of its commitment to renewables and conservation, though efforts have vastly accelerated since 2011 (Krane 2012; Krane 2014). The UAE case is instructive in its early political and investment commitments to renewables, its efforts to institutionalize renewables policy as part of an effort to accommodate global norms through the headquarters of IRENA in Abu Dhabi, and its ability to seize on the economic rationale for energy price reform in a time of fiscal austerity.

Case study of the United Arab Emirates

To keep pace with demand growth, electricity generation in the UAE quintupled between 1991 and 2010, reflecting an average growth of 8.5 per cent per year.

The UAE's commitment to renewables production is driven primarily by economic and political motivations. In fact, the goal of economic growth and diversification is fiscally prudent and also politically salient to both domestic actors and to international allies and investors. Economic reform measures undertaken to date acknowledge that the traditional rentier Gulf economy does not work in the 21st century, because of drastic changes in demographics including rapid national and expatriate population growth, the reality of a finite supply of oil and the instability of global energy demand.

Various recent actions signal the UAE commitment to renewable energy. The decision to host the IRENA firmly established the UAE as a global leader in the clean energy transition, boosting the state's global brand and attracting industry. Similarly, Abu Dhabi's Masdar City – a planned city/research facility that relies on renewable energy – and Shams 1, the largest concentrating solar power (CSP) plant in the world, symbolize a political commitment to lead the emerging industry.

Other motivations for pursuing renewables in the UAE are perhaps more complex. More than 90 per cent of current electricity generation is from coal- or gas-fired plants. But unlike in neighboring Kuwait and Saudi Arabia, which are able to use domestic oil to produce as much as half of their electricity, the UAE imports nearly all of its natural gas supply from Qatar in long-term contracts. This requires a massive infrastructure investment. Energy independence for the UAE, at least from Qatari natural gas, may be both a political and economic objective. Saudi efforts to increase natural gas production follow a similar rationale (Mabro 2002).

Renewable energy, especially solar (whether PV or CSP), has become less expensive to produce. On the global market, solar technology now delivers power at prices comparable to conventional electricity plants (Table 5.3). While the economics of large-scale solar were not cost-saving at the time of constructing Shams 1 in Abu Dhabi, less than 10 years later the new 200 megawatt (MW) solar PV plant in Dubai, operated by ACWA, produces power at $0.059/kWh. Expanding solar power electricity generation now makes both political and economic sense, particularly since Gulf governments are reducing electricity subsidies to bring consumer prices, whether for renewable or conventionally produced electricity, more in line with international prices.

The rationale for solar power in the UAE is strengthened because of the structure of the federation and the individual emirate ownership of utilities. Abu Dhabi holds and produces as much as 94 per cent of the country's oil and 90 per cent of its natural gas, representing 8 per cent and 3.5 per cent of global reserves, respectively. Yet the UAE became a net importer of natural gas in 2008, because of the high demand for gas in oil production, electricity generation, and the difficult (high sulfur) composition of its domestic gas.

Dubai is somewhat unique among the emirates in that its economic model relies on trade and industry, rather than the export of oil. As such, electricity generation, and sale to consumers, is central to its ability to grow. This boosts

Table 5.3 Prices for energy products: GCC and the United States January–August 2015 (IMF 2015: www.imf.org/external/np/pp/eng/2015/111015b.pdf)

	Gasoline	Diesel	Natural gas	Electricity
	US dollars per liter		US dollars per MMBtu	US dollars per kWh
Bahrain	0.27	0.27	2.5	0.03
Kuwait	0.24	0.39	1.5	0.01
Oman	0.31	0.38	3	0.04
Qatar	0.27	0.27	0.75	0.05
Saudi Arabia	0.14	0.06	0.75	0.09
UAE	0.59	0.56	0.75	0.1
GCC average	0.3	0.32	1.54	0.05
GCC maximum	0.59	0.56	3	0.1
USA pre-tax	0.53	0.64	2.8	0.1

Sources: Prices in GCC countries come from GlobalPetrolPrices.com, government agencies, and country authorities. USA gasoline and diesel prices come from IEA. Natural gas price for the USA is spot prices at Henry Hub taken from World Bank Commodity Price Data. Electricity tariffs for the USA include taxes and come from US EIA. MMBtu stands for million British thermal units, kWh for kilowatt hour.

the incentive to develop renewable energy sources that require neither costly imported gas nor coal, with its dirty emissions.

The structure of the UAE federation, however, creates some impediments to efficient electricity distribution. The northern emirates, especially Sharjah, rely on an electricity grid that is managed from Abu Dhabi. In the summer months, Sharjah often experiences electricity shortages, although Abu Dhabi shows no correlated problem in generation. Solar energy production will require investment in connecting to the distribution grid and more efficient distribution among the emirates, but this problem needs to be resolved for the current supply as well, so it should not be considered an additional cost.

Renewable energy targets vary by emirate but are ambitious for the region. As of 2013, Dubai aimed for 5 per cent of renewable product by 2020 but has since committed to as much as 7 per cent, matching Abu Dhabi's 2020 target. Meeting these targets will require government commitment to investment in solar technology, new electricity plants, and infrastructure.

Conclusions

In the GCC transition to renewable energy, much is at stake. The sector has the potential to solve some very critical problems for Gulf states in cost-saving, preserving natural resources, and building new institutional pathways for policy problem-solving. But it will need to navigate a series of renegotiations between state, business and society.

As oil prices seem likely to stabilize at 'new normal' levels well below the highs of the last decade, and global growth is expected to be sluggish, GCC states will face more constraints in their fiscal policies and, in turn, their energy policies. Renewable energy now has the advantage of its cost-saving logic, especially when states are more willing to access external finance for its construction and distribution.

Additionally, opportunities for inter-governmental cooperation and feed-in to the regional GCC power grid could provide competition and cost-saving, while also fostering better cooperation among states. That said, greater cooperation could also increase tensions, especially when electricity generation and use are tied to long-term contracts and provision of natural gas. Any failed project, in construction completion or bankruptcy, will test legal systems and the new investment climate.

A future in which renewable energy is provided through PPPs and other schemes is new territory in Gulf state society relations. States will also face new tests of their abilities to manage new partnerships and structures of ownership of utilities and their distribution networks. The main test may be how citizens respond to price increases and new providers that are non-state entities. Citizens may demand better service delivery and blame governments, and new corporate entities, if they perceive any failures arising. The social contract may not be changing outright, but a negotiation is taking place that shifts the focus of Gulf society and leadership to prioritizing economic efficiency.

The current climate of fiscal austerity, in which all the GCC states face deficits due to declining oil and gas revenues, is stimulating a new consensus for economic reform. It could also prompt some important institutional changes in Gulf state political economy, including major changes in financial regulation and greater openness to foreign investment.

The effect is not a weakening of the state, but a more complex understanding of state business relations that acknowledges the usefulness of private sector funding and long-term investors, especially in bonds and *sukuks*. This shift in both governance and economic development policy for Arab Gulf states is a major change, which political analysts and investors will watch closely.

References

Abdmouleh Z, Alammari R, and Gastli A (2015) Recommendations on renewable energy policies for the GCC countries. *Renewable and Sustainable Energy Reviews* 50(2015):1181–1191.

Ali S, and Masud A (2014) The New Kuwait PPP Law. *Al Tamimi & Co.* www.tamimi.com/en/magazine/law-update/section-8/october-4/the-new-kuwait-ppp-law.html.

Alnaser WE, and Alnaser NW (2011) The status of renewable energy in the GCC countries. *Renewable and Sustainable Energy Reviews* 15:3074–3098.

Al-Sayegh H, and Shamseddine R (2016) Exclusive: Saudi sovereign fund PIF considers buying stake in power firm ACWA. *Reuters.* www.reuters.com/article/us-acwa-power-m-a-public-investment-fund-idUSKBN13911B.

Aswad NG, Al-Saleh Y, and Taleb H (2013) Clean energy awareness campaigns in the UAE: an awareness promoters perspective. *International Journal of Innovation and Knowledge Management in MENA* 2:131–156. www.researchgate.net/profile/Yasser_Alsaleh/publication/275299871_Clean_Energy_Awareness_Campaigns_in_the_UAE_An_Awareness_Promoters_Perspective/links/553744500cf268fd001892da.pdf.

Batrawy A (2016) IMF expects $500B loss for Mideast oil exporters. *USA Today.* www.usatoday.com/story/money/2016/04/25/imf-expects-500b-loss-mideast-oil-exporters/83487838/.

Carey G, and Sabah Z (2016) Saudi King fires water minister after complaints over tariffs. *Bloomberg News.* www.bloomberg.com/news/articles/2016-04-24/saudi-king-fires-water-minister-after-complaints-over-tariffs.

Davies M, Hodge B, Ahmad S et al. (2016) Developing renewable energy projects: a guide to achieving success in the Middle East. Eversheds and Pricewater Coopers, January. www.pwc.com/m1/en/publications/documents/eversheds-pwc-developing-renewable-energy-projects.pdf.

Diwan KS (2016) Kuwait's snap parliamentary elections bring return of the opposition. The Arab Gulf States Institute in Washington, Washington, DC. www.agsiw.org/kuwaits-snap-parliamentary-elections-bring-return-opposition/.

Dubey K, Fawkes S, Howarth N et al. (2016) Investing for Energy Productivity in the GCC: Financing the Transition. KAPSARC KS-1647-DP042A. KAPSARC, Riyadh. www.kapsarc.org/wp-content/uploads/2016/10/KS-1647-DP042A-Investing-for-Productivity-in-the-GCC-Financing-the-Transition.pdf.

El-Katiri L (2016) Vulnerability, resilience and reform: the GCC and the oil price crisis of 2014–2016. Columbia Center on Global Energy Policy, New York.

Gengler J, and Lambert L (2016) Renegotiating the ruling bargain: selling fiscal reform in the GCC. *The Middle East Journal* 70(2):321–329.

IBP (International Business Publication) (2015) *Oman: Energy Policy, Laws and Regulations Handbook, vol 1.* IBP Inc., Washington DC.

IMF (International Monetary Fund) (2015) Energy Price Reforms in the GCC – What Can be Learned From International Experience? www.imf.org/external/np/pp/eng/2015/111015b.pdf.

IRENA (International Renewable Energy Agency) (2016) Renewable Energy Market Analysis: The GCC Region. www.irena.org/DocumentDownloads/Publications/IRENA_Market_GCC_2016.pdf.

Khaleej Times (2015) Kuwait approves $10 billion infrastructure projects. *Khaleej Times.* www.khaleejtimes.com/region/kuwait/kuwait-approves-10-billion-infrastructure-projects.

Kiyasseh L (2016) Mobilizing private investment in Saudi infrastructure. The Arab Gulf States Institute in Washington, Washington, DC. www.agsiw.org/mobilizing-private-investment-saudi-infrastructure/.

Krane J (2012) The Political Economy of Abu Dhabi's Pursuits in Renewable Energy. JIME-IEE, Japan. https://jime.ieej.or.jp/en/publications/2012/0727.htm.

Krane J (2014) An expensive diversion: Abu Dhabi's renewable energy investments amid a context of challenging demand. James A. Baker III Institute for Public Policy of Rice University, Houston, Texas.

Lahn G (2016) Fuel, food and the utilities price reforms in the GCC: a wake-up call for business. Chatham House Research Paper. The Royal Institute of International Affairs, London. www.chathamhouse.org/publication/fuel-food-and-utilities-price-reforms-gcc-business.

Lambert LA (2014) Water, state power, and tribal politics in the GCC: the case of Kuwait and Abu Dhabi. Georgetown University, Doha, Qatar. https://repository.library.georgetown.edu/bitstream/handle/10822/711827/CIRSOccasionalPaper15LaurentALambert2014.pdf?sequence=4.

Lilliestam J, and Patt A (2015) Barriers, risks and policies for renewables in the Gulf states. *Energies* 8:8263–8285.

Mabro R (2002) Saudi Arabia's natural gas: a glimpse at complex issues. The Oxford Institute for Energy Studies, Oxford. www.oxfordenergy.org/publications/saudi-arabias-natural-gas-a-glimpse-at-complex-issues/.

Mahmoud M (2016) Islamic finance in a time of fiscal austerity. AGSIW Issue Paper #5. The Arab Gulf States Institute in Washington, Washington, DC. www.agsiw.org/wp-content/uploads/2016/06/Mai_Mahmoud_ONLINE-2.pdf.

Meltzer J, Hultman N, and Langley C (2014) Low carbon energy transitions in Qatar and the Gulf Cooperation Council region. *Brookings Papers on Economic Activity*, p. 48. www.brookings.edu/wp-content/uploads/2016/07/low-carbon-energy-transitions-qatar-meltzer-hultman-full.pdf.

MESIA (Middle East Solar Industry Association) (2016) Middle East Solar Outlook for 2016. MESIA. www.mesia.com/wp-content/uploads/2017/09/MESIA-Outlook-2016-web.pdf.

Mondal MAH, Hawila D, Kennedy S et al. (2016) The GCC countries RE-readiness: strengths and gaps for development of renewable energy technologies. *Renewable and Sustainable Energy Reviews* 54:1114–1128.

NBAD, University of Cambridge and PwC (2015) Financing the Future of Energy. *National Bank of Abu Dhabi, Abu Dhabi.* www.nbad.com/content/dam/NBAD/

documents/content-hub/sustainable-business/Financing-The-Future-Of-Energy-Report-2016.pdf.

Patlitzianas K, Doukas H, and Psarras J (2006) Enhancing renewable energy in the Arab States of the Gulf: constraints and efforts. *Energy Policy* 34:3719–3726.

Shuaibah IWPP (Independent Water & Power Project) (n.d.) SWEC Stakeholder Structure. www.shuaibahiwpp.com.

The Peninsula (2015) Emir inaugurates Advisory Council's 44th ordinary session. *The Peninsula*. www.thepeninsulaqatar.com/news/qatar/357519/emir-inaugurates-advisory-council-s-44th-ordinary-session.

Trade Arabia (2016) TAV to boost stake in Saudi airport operator. www.tradearabia.com/news/TTN_313180.html.

Ulrichsen K (2016) *The Gulf States in International Political Economy*. Palgrave Macmillan, New York, pp. 61–82.

Westall S and Sleiman M (2012) Mideast Money – Rich but backward: politics, oil poison Kuwait economy. *Reuters*. www.reuters.com/article/kuwait-economy-development-idUSL5E8M91RK20121114.

World Bank (2016) Bahrain's Economic Outlook – July 2016. World Bank, Washington, DC. www.worldbank.org/en/country/gcc/publication/economic-brief-bahrain-july-2016.

Young K (2014) *The Political Economy of Energy, Finance and Security in the United Arab Emirates: Between the Majilis and the Market*. Palgrave Macmillan, New York.

Young K (2015) Markets serving states: the institutional bases of financial governance in the Gulf Cooperation Council States. http://eprints.lse.ac.uk/63943/.

6 De-risking low carbon investments in the GCC

Stephen Gitonga and Walid Ali

Abstract

Setting the world on a truly climate friendly and sustainable development path will require huge investments in low carbon technologies, including in renewable energy. Approximately $13.5 trillion will be needed by 2030 to fully implement the Nationally Determined Contributions (NDCs), the main vehicle countries will use to collectively achieve the goals of the COP21 Paris Agreement.

Private and institutional investors control nearly $100 trillion of assets globally, but less than 1 per cent of this is currently invested directly in sustainable energy. As energy technologies and markets are evolving rapidly, investors are wary of risk and uncertainty. To mobilize capital toward the scaling up of low carbon solutions, governments will need to implement new and innovative policies that lower the perceived risks.

This chapter assesses the potential to apply the De-risking Renewable Energy Investment (DREI) methodology, pioneered by the United Nations Development Programme (UNDP),[1] to countries belonging to the Gulf Cooperation Council (GCC). Initially created for use in developing countries to identify and address barriers to investment through effective policy packages, the DREI methodology could help GCC countries more quickly mobilize available private sector investment for a low carbon pathway that includes action to expand renewable energy, improve energy efficiency and curb energy demand growth.

Policy relevant insights

While GCC governments can mobilize and attract large public investments, unlike other developing countries, this chapter highlights the importance of the private sector to scale up the transition to low carbon energy. The ambitious sustainable energy agenda of GCC governments will require strengthened partnerships. This chapter highlights how the

De-Risking Renewable Energy Investment (DREI) methodology in the unique context of the GCC can help accelerate the transition.

- A combination of existing and innovative public policy instruments by GCC governments can reduce perceived risks and mobilize capital toward deploying low carbon solutions.
- The DREI methodology can help each GCC country analyze existing de-risking instruments, identify what needs to be improved or added, explore the most effective options and implement the most effective package of public policy actions.
- Public institutional development in the GCC, including establishment of renewable energy centers of excellence, can also be informed by the DREI methodology.
- Scaling up private low carbon investments sets the foundation for long-term, national low carbon development paths that fulfill national priorities for energy security, economic diversification, and climate change mitigation.

Global to regional overview of low carbon development

Recent global political processes, such as the adoption in September 2015 of the Sustainable Development Goals (SDGs) by the United Nations General Assembly, and in December 2016 of the COP21 Paris Agreement by 194 countries, send strong signals of solid – and growing – political will to transition to a low carbon future. Already, multiple municipal, national, regional and international initiatives are underway. Yet achieving these goals on the global scale will require huge investments.

Nationally Determined Contributions (NDCs) are the main pillar in implementing the COP21 Paris Agreement. According to the International Energy Agency (IEA), full implementation of NDC pledges will require $13.5 trillion investment in energy efficiency and low carbon technologies, which is equivalent to 40 per cent of total energy sector investment to 2030 (IEA 2016). In sharp contrast, new investments in clean energy worldwide over the past 10 years have slowly climbed to a high of just $329 billion in 2015 (Figure 6.1).

The public sector cannot shoulder such huge investments alone; the goals can only be met if the private sector also becomes a substantial investor. An overarching challenge is that private investors base their decisions on analysis of possible risks and potential returns. As with any relatively new sector, both are rather uncertain at present in the key elements of a low carbon future -- i.e., renewable energy, energy efficiency and reduction of demand growth.

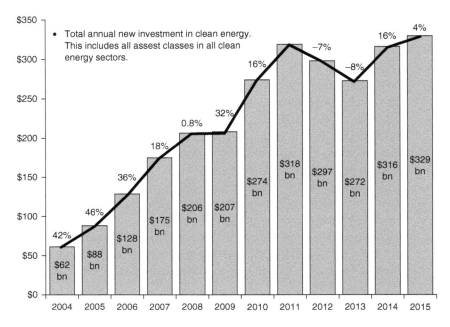

Figure 6.1 Total annual new investments in clean energy worldwide, 2004–2015
(Bloomberg New Energy Finance 2016)

Mobilizing capital at this order of magnitude will require new and innovative policies that lower the risk – i.e., 'de-risk'– that investors face in supporting the scale-up of low carbon solutions. Today, private and institutional investors control nearly $100 trillion of assets globally, but less than 1 per cent is invested directly in sustainable energy (Arezki et al. 2016). Renewable energy investment remains financially constrained, particularly in developing countries (IRENA 2012), owing to high investment costs and investment risks, which are typically compounded by policy, regulatory, financial, and informational barriers (World Bank 2016).

In developing countries, public interventions to remove barriers that hold back private sector renewables investment are fundamental. To address this problem, the UNDP has pioneered a new De-risking Renewable Energy Investment (DREI) methodology. The methodology aims to use policy instruments to reduce, transfer, or compensate for the high risks that private sector investors perceive in large-scale renewables investments. Experience shows that the basic pillars for encouraging private sector investments, particularly in developing countries, are a long-term policy regime coupled with 'packages' of public policy instruments that address the perceived investment risks.

The DREI methodology has been rolled out across a number of developing countries, including South Africa and Tunisia (Waissbein et al. 2013).

After applying it, countries report positive progress on private investment in renewable energy. Other countries in the region, including Egypt and Lebanon, have now expressed interest and initiated action to apply the methodology to help boost private renewables investment.

GCC countries are showing growing momentum toward deploying low carbon and renewable energy technologies, in part due to the aggressive global policy agenda now shaping public and political opinion on sustainable development. Considering that renewable energy sources currently supply only 1 per cent of electricity in the GCC (IRENA 2016), the ambitious aggregate renewables targets – approximately 72 gigawatts (GW) of power generation capacity to be installed over the time span from 2020 to 2040 – represents the need for massive investment (RCREEE 2016).

To achieve their respective national renewables targets, and indeed the NDCs that will contribute to sustained progress in implementing the COP21 Paris Agreement, GCC governments will need to incorporate into their overall development frameworks a range of policy instruments designed to de-risk clean energy investment. They will also need to take assertive action to catalyze private investments, including implementing development and investment policies that spur new opportunities and accelerate deployment of renewables investments.

This chapter first describes the DREI methodology, pioneered by the United Nations Development Programme (UNDP) to help developing countries address risks that block investment. Governments can use the methodology to analyze existing de-risking instruments, identify what needs to be improved or added and explore the most effective public policy actions to accelerate private sector involvement in a low carbon future.

Next, the chapter assesses the opportunity to apply the DREI methodology to support efforts to scale up low carbon investments in GCC countries. In stark contrast to other developing countries, those in the GCC region have high incomes, high rankings on the human development index, impressive credit ratings and high scores on the World Bank scale for ease of doing business. In this context, GCC governments should be able to mobilize and attract large private investments. Public and private investors, as well as development banks, are beginning to engage in sustainable energy investment in the GCC, yet it is clear that private sector players still perceive significant investment risks associated with low carbon technologies.

Applied to the GCC region, the DREI methodology identifies gaps in policy that undermine investor confidence. In helping governments pinpoint where they need to fill policy gaps, the methodology can help build the foundation for long-term low carbon development paths that fulfill national priorities, including diversification of economic growth, energy security, job creation and climate change mitigation. Finally, using the DREI methodology to assess the GCC region as a whole, the chapter investigates the future prospects for it to emerge as a hub for low carbon investments.

Additionally, governments could highlight the enormous and diverse opportunities to invest in low carbon technologies. The private sector can accelerate the shift towards low carbon investments across several areas, including scientific research and prototyping (research); fostering innovations and development (innovation); financing, investing and developing new commercial market niches (development); and technology transfer and accelerating technical capacity development (diffusion) (IEA 2010).

Countries in the GCC have undertaken numerous efforts to pursue low carbon development, including through pledging ambitious renewables investments (RCREEE 2016). These governments consider diversifying their domestic energy mix through renewable energy as a pressing policy priority, in concert with their national economic diversification plans (IRENA 2016). Renewable energy can help GCC economies meet rapidly growing energy demand associated with population and industrial growth, delivering sustainable energy services for socio-economic development. It can also contribute to energy security in the long term: as oil and gas are finite, diversifying energy resources reduces dependence on a single source. Renewable energy can also mitigate climate change by reducing energy-related emissions (Zwickel et al. 2015). Additionally, renewables can play a significant role in diversifying GCC economies and creating job opportunities, while boosting government revenues by preserving natural gas and oil for export. Ultimately, investment in renewable energy can deliver a wider range of benefits not only in terms of financial returns but also in relation to enhanced human development and improved health conditions, including through reduced air pollution in the short term and lower GHG emission impacts over the long term.

Box 6.1   Case study: De-risking Renewable Energy Investment in Tunisia

The Tunisian Solar Plan (TSP), Tunisia's official long-term plan for renewable energy, sets out ambitions to harness renewable energy sources to advance sustainable development. The plan includes specific 2030 targets for investment in wind energy, solar photovoltaic (PV) and concentrating solar power (CSP).

From 2013, through a project funded by the Global Environment Facility, UNDP helped the Government of Tunisia develop a Nationally Appropriate Mitigation Action plan for the TSP. The project is ongoing from 2015 and is planned for completion in 2019. The national implementing partner for the project is the Tunisian National Agency for Energy Conservation (*Agence Nationale pour la Maîtrise de l'Energie*).

As part of the project preparation activities, UNDP performed a DREI modeling analysis to identify a comprehensive set of public de-risking measures to achieve the 2030 TSP investment targets. The modeling identified nine different risk categories that contribute to higher financing costs in Tunisia. Power market risk, a main category, concerns risks relating to regulations and pricing mechanisms for renewable energy. Other categories that contribute to high financing costs included grid/transmission risk, counter-party risk, political risk and currency/macro-economic risk. The process resulted in quantitative data on the cost-effectiveness of various government measures, which in turn revealed the need to prioritize de-risking instruments to avoid resorting to premium prices to compensate for any residual risks. The priority measures identified included, for example, a well-designed regulatory framework, technical specifications for management of the electricity grid, and public loans for renewable energy developers.

In 2015, Tunisia's new renewable energy law entered into force. Having filled most of the identified gaps in public policy instruments, the law is expected to contribute to attracting investments in renewable energy, building on Tunisia's generally favorable business conditions. Currently, Tunisia is focusing on implementing the new law's provisions and creating a pipeline of private renewables projects. For instance, the smartly designed Tunisian net-metering scheme has already prompted deployment of small-scale PV in the residential sector with a total capacity of 23 megawatts (MW).

The Tunisia case shows that filling gaps in public policy is a continuous process. Not all gaps identified have yet been filled through public policy instruments; for example, the Tunisian power market still remains closed for large-scale private generation from renewable energy. Still, application of the DREI methodology in the NAMA plan played a key role in informing government interventions in renewables investments going forward. According to AFEX 2016, clear progress is evident. Since 2014, Tunisia has installed non hydro renewables capacity of about 265 MW, reaching a 6 per cent share of its energy mix.

(UNDP 2014; RCREEE 2016)

Renewable energy and climate action potential in the GCC

Establishing a favorable investment climate for renewable energy and low carbon technologies will be vital to GCC commitments to reduce GHG emissions within the COP21 Paris Agreement framework. Having small populations that are highly dependent on GHG intensive commodities for local economic development and for export, Qatar, UAE, Kuwait, and Bahrain are among the world's five highest per capita emitters (WRI 2005). Saudi Arabia ranks 15th in per capita GHG emissions (Baumert et al. 2005). Energy intensities in the GCC are also among the highest worldwide on the demand side, owing to the year-round need for air conditioning and low efficiency rates in energy consumption, particularly in the residential and commercial building sectors

Table 6.1 Energy share in GHG emissions in the GCC

GCC country	Share of energy-related activities in total GHG emissions (%)
Kingdom of Bahrain	77.0
Kuwait	95.3
United Arab Emirates (UAE)	88.0
Kingdom of Saudi Arabia (KSA)	66.0
Sultanate of Oman	60.0
Qatar	92.0

(Meltzer et al. 2014). Water desalination is another factor that drives up GCC energy consumption.

Energy-related activities, dominated by power generation, are the primary source of GHG emissions in the Arabian Gulf. (This chapter quotes official data as communicated by respective GCC countries in their latest National Communication processes) (Table 6.1). In Bahrain, energy-related sectors, including the combustion of fossil fuels and fugitive processes in oil and gas operations, accounted for approximately 77 per cent of total GHG emissions, with large shares attributed to industry (42 per cent) and power production (41 per cent) (Bahrain SNC 2012). In Kuwait, the energy sector accounts for 95.3 per cent of GHG emissions (Kuwait INC 2012).

Energy-related activities in the UAE accounted for approximately 88 per cent of GHG emissions in 2005 (UAE TNC 2012). Likewise, the energy sector in Saudi Arabia dominated GHG emissions, with high shares for electricity generation (33 per cent), road transport (22 per cent) and desalination (11 per cent) (KSA SNC 2011). In Oman, about 60 per cent of all GHG emissions are associated with the combustion of fossil fuels for electricity generation and desalination, and with fugitive emissions from the oil and gas sectors (Oman INDC 2013). Similarly, Qatar's energy sector accounted for about 92 per cent of total national GHG emissions (Qatar INC 2011).

De-risking and scaling up low carbon investment in the GCC

The transition to low carbon development involves shifting investments traditionally directed toward conventional energy to activities that will contribute to a sustainable and clean energy infrastructure, including renewable energy technologies and energy efficiency initiatives. Such a transition, however, is far from straightforward. At present, a range of policy, regulatory, institutional and financial barriers hinder mobilization of adequate capital investment, including from the private sector. These barriers result in high investment costs and risks, despite the rapid decline of renewable energy technology costs in the last decade. High financial costs including costs of equity and debt, operating costs, and investment costs such as depreciation make investment in renewable energy more expensive and less attractive to private entrepreneurs who often compare it with the lower costs – and consequently higher returns – on fossil fuel based energy investments (Waissbein et al. 2013).

The challenge is particularly great in developing countries because of the capital intensive nature of renewable investments and the underlying risks linked to renewable energy and climate policies. The financing costs for offshore wind in developing countries, for example, are 40 per cent higher than in developed countries, whereas the financing costs for gas are only 6 per cent higher in developing countries compared to developed ones (Waissbein et al. 2013).

GCC countries face a similar challenge, yet the situation is different in key ways. In recent years, GCC countries have demonstrated strong interest in deploying renewables, particularly to substitute for oil-generated electricity, which is heavily subsidized. They recognize this as a way of freeing up oil for export (Goldenberg 2016). A handful of large-scale renewables projects have been developed, underpinned by strong policy commitments, ambitious renewables targets, dedicated institutions and, indeed, substantial investments. In the UAE, for example, the auction of the 800 MW third phase of Mohammed bin Rashid Al Maktoum (MBR) Solar Park broke the world price record for a PPA when awarded to a Masdar-led consortium at a levelized cost of electricity (LCOE) of $0.0299 per kilowatt hour (/kWh) (World Energy Council 2016). This came after an earlier ground-breaking second phase of 200 MW, awarded to Saudi Arabia's ACWA Power led consortium at $0.0584/ kWh. In Saudi Arabia, the 50 MW solar PV plant considered by Taqnia for Saudi Electricity Company (SEC) received offers at $0.049/kWh (Borgmann 2016). More recently, Saudi Arabia invited expressions of interest to develop two solar PV power plants of 50 MW each, with the selection of the developer to be made through a competitive process.

For the most part, the substantial investments needed to launch these renewables projects, particularly in UAE, Qatar, and Saudi Arabia, have been from public sector resources. This reflects, at least in part, a fundamental difference between developing countries and the GCC area: GCC countries are generally ranked highly by the World Bank in ease of doing business and have good credit ratings, substantially changing the investment equation (Table 6.2).

Table 6.2 GCC credit ratings (Trading Economics 2017)

Country	S&P	Moody's	Fitch
UAE	AA	Aa2	AA
Kuwait	AA	Aa2	AA
Qatar	AA	Aa3	−AA
Saudi Arabia	A−	A1	AA+
Oman	BB+	Baa2	BBB
Bahrain	BB−	B1	BB+

The period 2015 to 2017 has seen GCC governments adjusting to loss of revenue from low oil prices by rebalancing budgets and renewing interest in involving the private sector in renewables investments. While financing has not been a constraint in the GCC in general, especially for government funded projects, the private sector has been much less engaged. Renewed interest in private sector investments opens new opportunities that require de-risking renewable energy investments in the region. Private investors perceive several factors as investment risks, such as: lack of clarity of procurement programs; shifting policies; difficulty in obtaining permits; constraining real estate laws, especially where foreign ownership is not allowed – specifically, lack of clarity on land ownership and leasing laws; and cumbersome labor issues. Some of these factors result in low carbon investment having high costs for the private sector (Dubey et al. 2016).

To capture the full potential for sustainable and low carbon energy deployment in the GCC, governments will need to undertake deliberate policy actions to remove barriers and address underlying perceived risks. Despite the impressive record of steps taken to attract low carbon investors, as yet none of the GCC countries has the full 'package' of public policy instruments needed to effectively attract private investors (Clean Energy Pipeline and Squire Sanders 2013).

The De-Risking Renewable Energy Investment methodology

To assist policymakers in developing countries who are seeking cost-effective ways to encourage private sector investment in large-scale renewables projects, UNDP has developed its de-risking methodology. The DREI tool was designed to systematically identify perceived barriers and associated risks so that policymakers can better enact public policy packages with targeted interventions. In the DREI approach, each policy intervention aims to reduce, transfer, or compensate for the risks identified. Its overall aim is to cost-effectively achieve a risk-return profile that catalyzes private sector investments at scale, eventually leading to reliable and affordable renewable energy solutions (Waissbein et al. 2013).

The methodology follows a four-stage process:

1   **Analyze the risk environment** to identify investment barriers and associated risks, especially within the regulatory policy framework.
2   **Assess public policy and select a mix of de-risking instruments** to address existing or perceived investor risks.
3   **Calculate the levelized cost of investments** to determine how reduced investment costs affect the life cycle cost of low carbon projects.
4   **Evaluate the process** to assess the selected public policy de-risking instruments using four performance metrics – investment leverage ratio, savings leverage ratio, end-user affordability, and carbon abatement – and sensitivity analyses.

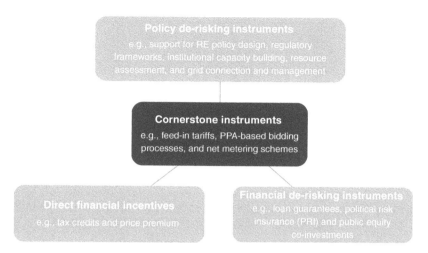

Figure 6.2 Instruments for de-risking renewable energy investment (Waissbein et al. 2013)

The outcome of this process is a package of public policy instruments meant to address the existing or perceived investor risks (Figure 6.2).

As per Figure 6.2, the methodology first considers cornerstone instruments: i.e., those that must be developed to catalyze renewables investments in a country; these are the minimum requirement that other public policies can be built upon. Based on experience in developing and developed countries, two main cornerstone instruments have been identified for their potential to transform markets and thereby attract greater private renewables investments. Both FITs and PPA-bidding processes facilitate investment in large-scale renewable energy projects, while net metering has been effective for the decentralized, stand-alone or rooftop renewables market. (Net metering provides credit to customers with solar PV systems, via a special billing arrangement, for the full retail value of the electricity their system generates.)

The methodology also identifies areas for intervention based on three categories of instruments: 1) policy de-risking instruments, 2) financial de-risking instruments, and 3) direct financial incentives.

1 **Policy de-risking instruments** *reduce* **investment risks**. Examples include institutional capacity building, resource assessments, long-term renewables targets, a streamlined permit process, improved operations and maintenance and skills development. A well-designed power market regulatory framework can also reduce risks.

2 **Financial de-risking instruments** *transfer* **investment risks to the public sector**. Such instruments include public loans, loan guarantees,

political risk insurance and public equity co-investments. In many cases, an instrument such as dedicated funds for renewables investments through a development bank is required to facilitate the use of financial de-risking instruments.

3   **Financial incentives** *compensate* **the private sector for taking the risk**. Direct subsidies for sustainable energy compensate investors for risks. Examples include FITs and private-public partnership (PPP) price premiums, tax credits, and carbon offsets. These incentives complement the policy and financial de-risking instruments.

The best outcomes occur when policymakers apply a package of instruments to address the risks to renewables investment in a systematic and integrated way.

The challenge is to identify – for any given context – the most effective package of public policy instruments that combines cornerstone instruments, policy and financial de-risking instruments and financial incentives. When measured against standalone instruments, such as paying direct financial incentives, allocating resources in an effective package of public policy de-risking instruments appears to be cost-effective.

Over time, de-risking can underpin the process of market transformation; indeed, policy instruments may need to be developed incrementally or in a phased approach before the market is fully transformed. Additionally, falling renewable energy technology costs provide a key opportunity for policymakers to explore innovative ways of addressing the high investment costs in developing countries.

Applying the De-Risking Renewable Energy Investment methodology to GCC countries

The DREI methodology has not yet been applied in the GCC context, but experience and results obtained in other regions suggest opportunity to apply it to catalyze private sector renewables investments. From a base of total installed renewable energy capacity of 190.4 MW in 2014, the six GCC countries have set ambitious targets for further deployment (Figure 6.3). Some countries have already enacted policies that support renewables deployment, including net metering in UAE, and independent power producers (IPPs) and power purchase agreements (PPAs) in Saudi Arabia. While all GCC countries face similar energy-related challenges, distinct national characteristics will influence their bids to transition to low carbon energy systems.

In each case, one key challenge is to develop a complete package of de-risking policy instruments that will attract private sector investment to accelerate and sustain the momentum of low carbon electricity production technologies and renewables deployment. The DREI methodology could help to refine the appropriate cornerstone instruments and sharpen the focus of policy or financial instruments or financial incentives. It could also be used as a tool to integrate renewables policies or strategies within the broader development

Table 6.3 Current renewable energy capacity (volume and share) and proposed targets (capacity/year) (IRENA 2016, 2017; RCREEE 2016)

Country	Total RE installed by 2014 (MW)	Total RE installed by 2016 (MW)	% of total installed capacity in GCC by 2014	% of total installed capacity in GCC by 2016	RE Target (MW / year)
Bahrain	6	6	2.75	2.00	250 / 2030
Kuwait	2	41	18.81	14.00	11,000 / 2030
Oman	1	1	0.46	0.35	
Qatar	43	44		15.70	1,800 / 2030
Saudi Arabia	36	48	19.72	17.20	54,000 / 2040
UAE	131	139	60.10	49.80	5,000 / 2030
Total	219	279	100.00	100.00	

policy process. As demonstrated in the following paragraphs, the methodology may well reveal that the ideal package of instruments will differ across the GCC countries.

Table 6.3 compares installed renewables capacity in the GCC over the period 2014 to 2016, based on IRENA published statistics for those two years. The trend has been positive, with upward movement of installed capacity across all GCC countries. The UAE holds the largest share of installed capacity followed by Saudi Arabia.

UAE: In 2016, the UAE had 49.8 per cent of installed renewable capacity within the GCC (IRENA 2017). The government has put in place several renewables de-risking instruments. IPP policy, for example, is a cornerstone instrument that was used successfully when the Dubai Electricity and Water Authority (DEWA) awarded the 800 MW third phase of the MBR Solar Park. Net metering policy enabled Dubai's Shams initiative to gain momentum in promoting small-scale distributed generation systems.

Saudi Arabia: The Kingdom has 17.2 per cent of the GCC's installed renewables capacity, based on 2016 data quoted in the IRENA report published in 2017. IPP policy is the cornerstone instrument and was first used to tender for two 50 MW projects in 2016. Other existing de-risking instruments include a dedicated institution for development of renewable energy, long-term policy and targets to attract renewables investments from the private sector. For instance, the King Abdullah City for Atomic and Renewable Energy (KACARE) leads the renewable energy sector. Due to its huge market size and high energy demand, coupled with strong resource potential and large land availability, Saudi Arabia has the largest potential in the GCC to attract private sector renewables investments.

Qatar: Based on the 2016 data in Table 6.3, Qatar ranks third at 15.7 per cent of installed renewable capacity in the GCC, with the public sector financing most investments (IRENA 2017). Among Arab countries, it ranks high in the global competitive index and in the ease of doing business index (RCREEE 2016). With a favorable business climate and available financial resources, Qatar has strong potential to attract private sector renewables investments.

Oman: IPP policy has been applied successfully in the power sector in Oman, but not much in the development of renewable energy. Plans are underway, however, to build one of the world's largest solar plants for enhanced oil recovery to extract heavy oil at the Amal oilfield (RCREEE 2016).

Bahrain: Renewables capacity in 2016 was 6MW, implying great potential for improvement if effective de-risking instruments could be put in place to attract private investments. Bahrain is in the process of developing its cornerstone instruments, including creating renewables targets, action plans and institutional frameworks. The country ranks 65 out of 189 countries in ease of doing business (RCREEE 2016).

Kuwait: Kuwait has an ambitious target to attract investment in renewable energy, aiming, for instance, to install over 2,000 MW of renewable energy capacity at the Shagaya park. It has put in place a public competitive bidding process as a cornerstone policy instrument; other de-risking instruments include long-term policy and commitment for renewables development. According to Table 6.3, Kuwait's installed renewables capacity has significantly jumped, from 2 MW in 2014 to 41 MW in 2016, the largest increase among GCC countries during that period. With de-risking, this trend can be strengthened.

GCC countries already have powerful de-risking instruments in place, but not enough to reduce the perceived risks and fully engage the private sector in renewables investments. Based on Figure 6.3, one can see that countries with more and clearer public policy, financial and regulatory instruments have higher levels of installed renewable energy capacity. The de-risking methodology could help them identify the optimal package of instruments needed to attract private sector renewables investment. Areas of focus could include development of institutional capacity and the necessary policy frameworks.

Future prospects for the Gulf to emerge as a hub for low carbon investments

The GCC's combination of a high level of solar radiation and huge potential market for renewable energy technologies creates the chance for this region to become a hub for low carbon investments. As noted above, each GCC

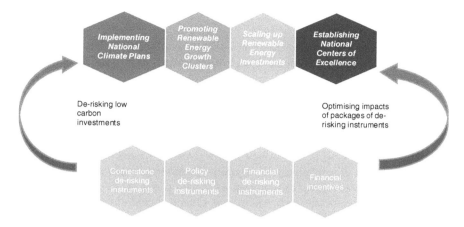

Figure 6.3 Pillars for making the GCC a hub for low carbon investments

country exhibits some distinct opportunities and challenges while also having common interests. In general, four pillars have been identified as vital to enable the GCC to emerge as a regional hub for low carbon investments, including: implementing national climate plans, scaling up renewables investments, promoting renewable energy technology clusters and establishing national centers of excellence (Figure 6.3). By helping GCC countries identify gaps in public policy instruments, the DREI methodology can accelerate this process of stimulating a hub. For instance, national centers of excellence can become spaces for innovation in developing cornerstone policy and financial de-risking instruments, and in identifying the optimal combination of financial incentives.

Implementing national climate plans

In the lead-up to the COP21 meeting in 2015, all GCC countries submitted intended nationally determined contributions (INDCs) to the UNFCCC, outlining their voluntary domestic climate actions. To reduce GHG emissions while also achieving national development goals, the INDCs included commitments to expand renewable energy, increase energy efficiency, and reduce energy consumption. These climate mitigation targets and commitments, which upon ratification of the COP21 Paris Agreement became Nationally Determined Contributions (NDCs), will shape the low carbon development path globally, including for GCC countries. Putting in place measures to scale up implementation of the NDCs demonstrates the political will to achieve low carbon development. The immediate challenges are to develop implementation strategies and to mobilize partners to raise the climate financing needed to achieve them. In the GCC context, the NDCs provide national climate policy frameworks with immense opportunities to accelerate the transition to low carbon development by further catalyzing private investments as a complement to public financing.

In that sense, many countries, particularly developing countries, will face enormous challenges to implement their NDC targets and to fulfill their commitments for transition towards low carbon economies. De-risking low emission investments will open up new opportunities to help scale up implementation of NDCs including through critical measures to mobilize new partners and raise additional financing to achieve the ambitious domestic climate policy goals across the GCC. Successful implementation of NDCs will require a package or packages of de-risking public policy instruments for increasing the efficiency and effectiveness of implemented programs. De-risking renewable energy and energy efficiency investments will help accelerate progress.

Two GCC countries, Saudi Arabia and Oman, included quantifiable mitigation targets in their NDCs. The NDC for Saudi Arabia commits to reducing GHG emissions by as much as 130 million tonnes of CO_2 equivalent ($MtCO_2e$) annually by 2030 compared with a business-as-usual trajectory, including by increasing the share of renewables in the energy mix. It should be noted that the commitment is contingent on a climate of economic growth, with a diversified portfolio of investments (KSA INDCs 2015). Oman's NDC committed to a 2 per cent reduction of GHG emissions relative to a business-as-usual scenario during the period 2020 to 2030, with mitigation potential of around 89 $MtCO_2$ equivalent. This reduction is expected to be achieved by increasing renewable shares in the energy mix, boosting the energy efficiency of industrial projects and establishing climate policies to support the transition to low carbon development paths (Oman INDCs 2015).

Other GCC countries instead outlined clear low-emission measures in their NDCs. The UAE set out several economic diversification opportunities with GHG mitigation potential, including targets for clean energy deployment, energy efficiency, decarbonizing transport, and expanding low carbon infrastructure. For example, the NDC sets a target of increasing the renewables share of the energy mix to 24 per cent by 2021, relative to 0.2 per cent in 2014 (UAE INDCs 2015). The NDC for Kuwait committed to pursuing actions to transition toward a low carbon economy and to avoid additional GHG emissions compared with business-as-usual, with quantifiable GHG emissions reduction to be communicated after the fact (Kuwait INDCs 2015). Bahrain's NDC focuses on reducing dependence on oil and gas in the financial, manufacturing and tourism sectors (Bahrain INDCs 2015), and outlines various strategies, plans, and actions for transitioning to a low-emission development path, such as energy efficiency, carbon capture and storage and renewable energy. Qatar had no clear mitigation targets in its NDC, but outlined contributions through environmental conservation, investments in energy efficiency and boosting shares of renewable energy and cleaner energy, including through use of natural gas (Qatar INDCs 2015).

Scale-up of renewable energy investment

Scaling up renewable energy could generate significant benefits for GCC countries, for example, replacing 400 million barrels (Mbbl) of oil for power production, reducing GHG emissions per capita by 8 per cent in 2030 and creating more than 200,000 direct jobs (IRENA 2016).

To secure the large private sector investments required, governments will need to set public policies that facilitate the engagement of private sector actors, such as commercial banks and venture capital firms.

Create renewable energy clusters

One way the GCC region can reduce renewables investment costs and risks for the private sector is by developing renewable energy clusters. Such clusters typically include universities and research institutions that support emerging private sector networks of developers, suppliers, financiers, and supply chain vendors that are bringing new ideas into the market. Ultimately, clusters could contribute to reducing low carbon investment costs and risks for private developers, and also reduce financial and insurance costs.

The Renewable Energy Program Development Office (REPDO) is the lead institution for developing the renewables sector in Saudi Arabia, working closely with other key institutional stakeholders such as the King Abdallah City for Atomic and Renewable Energy (KACARE), the Electricity and Cogeneration Regulatory Authority (ECRA), Saudi Aramco, and the Saudi Electricity Company (SEC). Universities in the GCC are also involved in various collaborative research activities to develop renewable energy technology suited to arid climates. These clusters could reduce dependence on renewable energy technology imports and create local, high-value jobs. Establishing a network of clusters in the GCC would facilitate sharing knowledge and research results and would help build an ecosystem that enables efficient functioning of an economically viable renewables market.

Establish national centers of excellence

Bringing public and private players together under the framework of national centers of excellence is an effective means of tackling priorities that are specific to a given country or shared across the GCC region, such as the energy-water nexus. These centers can play a key role in developing and implementing national policies and building up public-private partnerships (PPPs) to reduce the carbon footprints and energy intensity of sectors such as buildings, power and transport.

Several centers have already been established and can provide models for setting up others. In partnership with UNDP, Saudi Arabia launched the National Energy Efficiency Program, now the Saudi Energy Efficiency Center (SEEC), as the country's first center of excellence to scale up energy efficient technologies that can curb the pace of energy demand growth in key sectors while also reducing emissions. The UNDP has also been a key partner in the formation of the Bahrain Sustainable Energy Unit, the Dubai Carbon Center and the proposed Kuwait Energy Center, all of which are based on PPPs.

Using the DREI methodology as a tool in such centers to foster innovative public policy development and to attract low carbon investments could facilitate the establishment of renewable energy centers of excellence in the GCC. As GCC countries optimize their packages of public policy instruments, their efficiency in attracting low carbon investments is likely to increase. The DREI methodology can be applied to attract and leverage private sector investments and reinforce a stronger foundation for long-term low carbon development paths. Innovative partnerships with stakeholders to enhance policy and capacity development are a key ingredient to creating momentum.

Conclusions

De-risking private investment is vital to accelerating development, deployment and scale-up of low carbon technologies. In the somewhat unique context of the GCC, which comprises high income countries that enjoy high rankings on the human development index and on the World Bank ease of doing business scale, and have high creditworthiness with the three global credit rating agencies, it can be expected that private financing institutions and international and multilateral agencies will have a considerable willingness to lend. While this is a stark contrast to the situation in developing countries, where public financial constraints are a major barrier and investment risks are enormous, access to finance is not the only hurdle to investment in low carbon technologies.

Rather, in the GCC context, it is clear that to address the private sector's perceived risks, governments must make greater effort to identify and implement a package of public policy instruments that can reduce, transfer or compensate for investment risk. As demonstrated, the DREI methodology can be used to help each country analyze its existing de-risking instruments, identify what needs to be improved or added, explore the most effective options and implement the most effective package of public policy actions to accelerate private sector low carbon investments. In helping GCC countries establish effective regulatory frameworks, the methodology can help build the foundations for long-term low carbon development paths that fulfill national priorities for sustained and diversified economic growth, including local job creation, energy security and climate change mitigation.

Additional analysis will be needed to determine the magnitude of the financing costs of renewables investments by the private sector in the GCC context.

Note

1 Disclaimer: The views and opinions expressed here are solely those of the authors, and do not necessarily represent the opinions of the United Nations, UNDP, or their Member States.

References

Arezki R, Bolton P, Peters S et al. (2016) From Global Savings Glut to Financing Infrastructure: The Advent of Investment Platforms. IMF Working Paper WP 16/18. IMF, Washington, DC. www.imf.org/external/pubs/ft/wp/2016/wp1618.pdf.

Bahrain Intended Nationally Determined Contributions (Bahrain INDCs) (2015) www4.unfccc.int/Submissions/INDC/Published%20Documents/Bahrain/1/INDC_Kingdom_of_Bahrain.pdf.

Bahrain's Second National Communication to the UNFCCC (Bahrain SNC) (2012) http://unfccc.int/resource/docs/natc/bhrnc2.pdf.

Baumert KA, Herzog T, and Pershing J (2005) Navigating the Numbers: Greenhouse Gas Data and International Climate Policy. *World Resource* Institute Report, Washington, DC. http://pdf.wri.org/navigating_numbers.pdf.

Bloomberg New Energy Finance (2016) Clean Energy Pipeline. *Bloomberg NEF.* https://about.bnef.com/blog/clean-energy-defies-fossil-fuel-price-crash-to-attract-record-329bn-global-investment-in-2015/.

Borgmann M (2016) Dubai Shatters all Records for Cost of Solar with Earth's Largest Solar Power Plant. Apricum, Berlin. www.apricum-group.com/dubai-shatters-records-cost-solar-earths-largest-solar-power-plant/.

Clean Energy Pipeline and Squire Sanders (2013) *The Future of Renewable Energy in the MENA Region.* www.cleanenergypipeline.com/Resources/CE/ResearchReports/The%20Future%20for%20Renewable%20Energy%20in%20the%20MENA%20Region.pdf.

Dubey K, Fawkes S, Howarth N et al. (2016) Investing for Energy Productivity in the GCC: Financing the Transition. KAPSARC, Riyadh. www.kapsarc.org/wp-content/uploads/2015/10/KS-1647-DP042A-Investing-for-Productivity-in-the-GCC-Financing-the-Transition.pdf.

Goldenberg S (2016) Slump in Oil Prices Drives Green Energy Take-up in Top Exporting Nations. *The Guardian*, 20 January 2016. www.theguardian.com/environment/2016/jan/20/slump-in-oil-prices-drives-green-energy-take-up-in-top-exporting-nations.

IEA (2010) Transforming Innovation into Market Realistic Implementation Programmes. Workshop summary, 27–28 April 2010. Expert Group on R & D priority setting and evaluation. OECD/IEA, Paris. www.iea.org/media/workshops/2010/transforming innovation/Summary_Report.pdf.

IEA (2016) Energy, Climate Change and Environment, 2016 Insights. OECD/IEA, Paris. www.iea.org/publications/freepublications/publication/ECCE2016.pdf.

IRENA (International Renewable Energy Agency) (2012) Financial Mechanisms and Investment Frameworks for Renewables in Developing Countries. IRENA, Abu Dhabi. http://energy-base.org/wp-content/uploads/2013/11/IRENA-Financial-Mechanisms-and-Investment-Frameworks-for-Renewables-in-Developing-Countries.pdf.

IRENA (2016) Renewable Energy Market analysis in GCC countries. IRENA, Abu Dhabi. www.irena.org/DocumentDownloads/Publications/IRENA_Market_GCC_2016.pdf.

IRENA (2017) IRENA RE Capacity Statistics, IRENA, Abu Dhabi. www.irena.org/DocumentDownloads/Publications/IRENA_RE_Capacity_Statistics_2017.pdf.

Kingdom of Saudi Arabia. The Renewable Energy Project Development Office (REPDO) at www.powersaudiarabia.com.sa/web/index.html.

Kingdom of Saudi Arabia. Saudi Energy Efficient Center (SEEC) at www.seec.gov.sa/en.

Kingdom of Saudi Arabia Intended Nationally Determined Contributions under the UNFCCC (KSA INDCs) (2015) www4.unfccc.int/submissions/INDC/Published%20Documents/Saudi%20Arabia/1/KSA-INDCs%20English.pdf.

Kingdom of Saudi Arabia's Second National Communication to the UNFCCC (KSA SNC) (2011) http://unfccc.int/resource/docs/natc/saunc2.pdf.

Kuwait's Initial National Communication to the UNFCCC (Kuwait INC) (2012) http://unfccc.int/resource/docs/natc/kwtnc1.pdf.

Kuwait Intended Nationally Determined Contributions (Kuwait INDCs) (2015) www4.unfccc.int/Submissions/INDC/Published%20Documents/Kuwait/1/Kuwait_INDCs_English_Version.pdf.

Meltzer J, Hultman N, and Langley C (2014) *Low-Carbon Energy Transitions in Qatar and the Gulf Cooperation Council Region*. Global Economy and Development at Brookings, pp. 26–35. www.brookings.edu/wp-content/uploads/2016/07/03-low-carbon-energy-transitions-qatar-meltzer-hultman-chapter-3-1.pdf.

Qatar's Initial National Communication to the UNFCCC (Qatar INC) (2011) http://unfccc.int/resource/docs/natc/qatnc1.pdf.

Qatar's Intended Nationally Determined Contributions (Qatar INDCs) (2015) www4.unfccc.int/submissions/INDC/Published%20Documents/Qatar/1/Qatar%20INDCs%20Report%20-English.pdf.

RCREEE (Regional Centre for Renewable Energy and Energy Efficiency) (2016) Arab Future Energy Index (AFEX) Cairo, Egypt. www.rcreee.org/sites/default/files/final_afex_re_2016.pdf.

Sultanate of Oman's Initial National Communication to the UNFCCC (Oman INDC) (2013) http://unfccc.int/resource/docs/natc/omnnc1.pdf.

Sultanate of Oman's Intended Nationally Determined Contributions (Oman INDCs) (2015) www4.unfccc.int/submissions/INDC/Published%20Documents/Oman/1/OMAN%20INDCs.pdf.

Trading Economics (2017) at https://tradingeconomics.com/country-list/rating.

UNDP (United Nations Development Programme) (2014) Tunisia: De-risking Renewable Energy Investment. United Nations Development Programme, New York. www.undp.org/content/undp/en/home/librarypage/environment-energy/low_emission_climateresilientdevelopment/derisking-renewable-energy-investment/drei-tunisia.html.

United Arab Emirates Initial Nationally Determined Contributions (UAE INDCs) (2015) www4.unfccc.int/submissions/INDC/Published%20Documents/United%20Arab%20Emirates/1/UAE%20INDC%20-%2022%20October.pdf.

United Arab Emirates Third National Communication to the UNFCCC (UAE TNC) (2012) http://unfccc.int/resource/docs/natc/arenc3.pdf.

Waissbein O, Glemarec Y, Bayraktar H et al. (2013) De-risking Renewable Energy Investment. A Framework to Support Policymakers in Selecting Public Instruments to Promote Renewable Energy Investment in Developing Countries. United Nations Development Programme, New York. www.uncclearn.org/sites/default/files/inventory/undp702_0.pdf.

World Bank (2016) Climate Change Action Plan. April 7, 2016. http://pubdocs.worldbank.org/en/677331460056382875/WBG-Climate-Change-Action-Plan-public-version.pdf.

World Energy Council (2016) World Energy Focus. August 2016. www.slideshare. net/WEC_Italia/world-energy-focus-agosto-2016.

World Resources Institute (2015) *Navigating the Numbers: GHG Data and International Climate Policy*. Washington, DC: WRI.

Zwickel T, Eickemeier P, Hansen G et al. (2015) Intergovernmental Panel on Climate (IPCC) Special Report on Renewable Energy Sources and Climate Change Mitigation. Cambridge University Press, New York. www.ipcc.ch/report/srren/.

7 Policies to promote renewables in the Middle East and North Africa's resource rich economies

Rahmatallah Poudineh, Anupama Sen and Bassam Fattouh

Abstract

Hydrocarbon rich countries in the Middle East and North Africa (MENA) region have been slow to progress toward the penetration and scaling up of renewables. In addition to significant disincentives posed by general barriers to renewables deployment, countries in this region also face factors specific to their economic and political economy contexts. Renewables have been 'locked out' of many resource rich MENA energy systems as a result of plentiful low priced hydrocarbon fuels and the simultaneous presence of risk and uncertainties, weak institutions and inadequate grid infrastructure.

Given these distinctive characteristics, this chapter argues that the design of longer-term policies to promote renewables should carefully consider the balance of market and government roles in providing investment incentives for renewables, while simultaneously taking into account the barriers to renewables investment that are prevalent in these countries.

Policy relevant insights

To stimulate renewable energy deployment in MENA countries, governments will need to attract private investors, which implies ensuring sufficient economic incentive in the electricity sector – a substantial challenge considering the low end-user tariffs currently in place. Policy action across three key areas will be needed:

- Promoting renewable energy deployment through a combination of market and renewable subsidies, gradually moving towards fair competition for all generation options.
- Removing barriers to investment by ensuring grids across the region are adequate, connected, well managed, and resilient for renewable integration, strengthening institutions and addressing risks and uncertainties.

- Revising energy policy, including pricing and structural reform, with an integrated view of all energy sources.

Tapping into both hydrocarbon and renewable resources

In recent years, the resource rich economies of the Middle East and North Africa (MENA) have emerged as the focus of attention in global efforts towards the expansion of renewable energy. This has been accelerated specifically following the COP21 Paris Agreement, which came into force in November 2016, and according to which many countries, including the MENA resource rich countries, have committed to reducing their carbon footprints, compared with business–as–usual trajectories.

A point that may be worth considering before proceeding to the rest of this chapter is the rationale behind the idea that resource rich countries need to be concerned with renewable investment. Apart from climate change issues, economic diversification and job creation, at least two other important reasons underpin the argument for renewables in the MENA oil and gas economies. First, the emergence of shale oil in the United States (U.S.) has altered the global dynamics of the oil market, resulting in dampening prices and fierce competition for a potentially smaller market share. MENA countries aiming to monetize their hydrocarbon resources thus have the option of investing in renewables to meet domestic demand and thereby freeing up oil/gas for export. Second, at present, gas and petroleum products constitute almost 100 per cent of the fuel mix for power generation in these countries, with natural gas being the dominant fuel. In recent years, however, demand for gas has been outpacing the exploration and utilization of new reserves in many of these countries. Thus, if resource constraints make it impossible to meet growing demand through natural gas, it will be necessary to turn to oil or oil products, which have high opportunity costs in these countries. Investment in renewables can thus alleviate the pressure of domestic consumption of fossil fuels and boost export revenues.

The upside is that most MENA countries are 'double-blessed' when it comes to energy resources: along with massive fossil fuel reserves they have high potential for renewable energy, specifically solar power. Being concentrated in the 'global sunbelt', MENA countries have an estimated potential to generate 150,000 terawatt hours (TWh) annually with concentrating solar power (CSP) technology. Countries in the Gulf Cooperation Council (GCC) hold a large portion of this potential, with 56 per cent of their surface area estimated to be suitable for the deployment of wind energy and 59 per cent for solar (IRENA 2016a). This vastly exceeds the combined electricity consumption of GCC countries (470 TWh/year) and their combined primary energy demand of 4,400 TWh/year (Lilliestam and Patt 2015; IRENA 2016a).

Recognizing the need to invest in renewables as a strategy to achieve both fiscal and environmental sustainability, nearly all resource-rich MENA countries have announced long-term renewables targets (Table 7.1). Several projects are already operational, such as Abu Dhabi's 100 megawatt (MW) Shams CSP plant (generating since 2014) and the 13 MW phase 1 of Mohammed bin Rashid Al Maktoum (MBR), completed in 2013, while many others are in the pipeline. Other examples include: the United Arab Emirates' (UAE) Phase 2 (200 MW) and Phase 3 (800 MW) of Mohammed bin Rashid Al Maktoum and the Noor 1 solar photovoltaic (PV) plant (350 MW), Kuwait's Shagaya Solar Thermal project (50 MW) and Saudi Arabia's Al-Aflaj 50-MW solar PV plant.

Despite initial optimism, actual progress in the deployment, penetration and scaling up of renewable energy in the MENA region remains well behind the rest of the world. At present, non-hydro renewables make up nearly 7 per cent of installed electricity capacity in other high income countries, yet they are well below 1 per cent in the MENA region, barely on par even with low income countries (Poudineh et al. 2016). Indeed, renewables have arguably been 'locked out' of many resource rich MENA energy systems. The plentiful availability of low priced hydrocarbons has driven energy consumption to levels that are among the world's highest – three times the average of the world's high-income economies (World Bank 2016) – while a simultaneous rising dependence on hydrocarbon export revenues to fuel the domestic economy has further entrenched hydrocarbons within the energy system and economy, leaving little room for renewables to compete.

Considering the distinctive economic and political characteristics of the MENA's hydrocarbon economies – including the potential to reduce domestic consumption of resources that deliver higher value when traded on global markets – this chapter examines the design of longer-term policies to promote uptake of renewables. It investigates possible incentives for renewables

Table 7.1 MENA domestic targets for renewable energy (Poudineh et al. 2016)

	Target	Date
Kuwait	15% of electricity demand (generation)	2030
Saudi Arabia	9.5 gigawatts (GW) of renewable energy	2023
UAE	24% clean energy (including nuclear) in energy mix by 2021: Abu Dhabi = 7% of capacity by 2020; Dubai = 7% capacity by 2020 and 15% by 2030 (versus 'business-as-usual' scenario)	2021, 2030
Oman		–
Qatar	1.8 GW solar (16% of generation) by 2020; 10 GW solar PV by 2030	2020–2030
Bahrain	5% of installed capacity	2020
Iran	5 GW wind and solar capacity	2020
Algeria	20% of generation	2030

investment, while also taking account of investment barriers that have been encountered worldwide.

The key research question is: how can resource rich MENA economies develop policy frameworks to incentivize renewables within their unique economic and political contexts and also address the more general barriers to renewables deployment? The following section examines the importance of providing incentives within long-term policies to promote renewables in the MENA's hydrocarbon rich countries, after which we describe common barriers to renewables deployment. The need to revise energy policies in the region is the focus moving on from this, while the final section concludes with some overall policy insights. Ultimately, this chapter makes the case that MENA economies could benefit from the 'late-comer advantage' by drawing from international experience in the design of their renewables policies. This includes the importance of establishing renewables policies based on a balance of market incentives and explicit government support, through various policy instruments.

The central role of incentives

Historically, governments of the MENA region have been responsible for meeting all the investment requirements in the power sector. The current period of low oil prices has placed significant stress on these states' finances, prompting many of these governments to turn to the private sector. The benefits of involving the private sector, specifically as independent power producers (IPPs), include reducing pressure on public budgets by providing upfront capital, lowering electricity costs to consumers as competition can be exploited to incentivize efficiency and, finally, leveraging the skills, knowledge and competency of the private sector in project management and operation.

No private investment will take place, however, unless there is an economic incentive to do so and the renewables business is no exception. The revenue generated from renewable projects needs to be adequate and reliable so that investors can recoup their capital costs, plus a competitive return (Figure 7.1).

Some renewable technologies, such as onshore wind and solar photovoltaic (PV) modules, have experienced steep downward cost trajectories over recent years, making them competitive with conventional sources in some places. But, in many parts of the world, renewables are still relatively too expensive to compete with conventional generation. This implies that for the short to medium term, government intervention is necessary to stimulate the investment needed to move along the price curve.

Recent auctions demonstrate that solar PV is among the lowest cost technologies available for power generation in the MENA, reflecting the region's comparative advantage for solar irradiation and, in some cases, access to low cost finance. Clearly, solar power can be generated at a low cost.

Final cost to consumers, however, is a major challenge for both generators and investors. The widespread practice of extensive explicit and implicit fossil

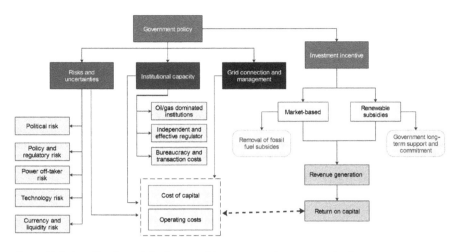

Figure 7.1 A stylized model of renewable energy enhancement in the power sector
(Poudineh et al. 2016)

fuel subsidies, often a part of the social contract between governments and
citizens, has resulted in electricity tariffs that are far below the cost of supply.
For instance, a recent auction in the United Arab Emirates (UAE) produced a
levelized cost of electricity (LCOE) at $0.0299 per kilowatt hour (/kWh), one
of the lowest LCOEs for solar energy both globally and in the MENA region
(Krupa and Poudineh 2017). Still, in many cases, the retail tariffs to final residential consumers are lower than generation costs – let alone the actual cost
of electricity supply, which includes the cost of generation plus transmission,
distribution and metering (Poudineh et al. 2016). In the GCC, retail residential
electricity tariffs range from as low as $0.07/kWh in Kuwait and $0.013/kWh
in Saudi Arabia to as high as $0.087/kWh in Abu Dhabi and $0.121/kWh in
Dubai. In fact, the UAE is the only country where solar energy is just about
competitive. It should also be noted that, in many cases, electricity tariffs are
differentiated, with expatriates paying higher rates than nationals.

This situation leaves policymakers in the region with two choices with
respect to providing incentives to stimulate private sector investment in
renewables. The first is to remove fossil fuel subsidies and, to the greatest
extent possible, internalize the cost of externalities in energy prices, thereby
correcting current market distortions. The second approach would be to tem-
porarily subsidize renewable resources to bring down their cost to a level at
which they can compete with fossil fuels – mainly gas but also oil – for power
generation. Further examination of these two approaches in the MENA context suggests that to realize the ambitious renewables targets set forth, neither
approach can be implemented in its pure form. Rather, countries will need to
apply a combinatorial approach in which current market distortions for fossil

fuels are gradually reduced while incentives for renewables are put in place. To move towards more liberalized electricity markets, MENA governments will need to both tailor their energy policies and fine tune them as their individual markets evolve.

Incentive through enabling markets

A major barrier for a pure market based renewables incentive is the competitive advantage given to fossil fuels through subsidies. Almost all MENA countries subsidize fossil fuels used for power generation, transport and industrial processes (Fattouh et al. 2016). Before the price adjustment in Saudi Arabia in late 2015, for instance, crude oil was sold to the power sector at $4.24 per barrel (/bbl) and methane and ethane at around $0.75 per million British thermal units (/MMBtu). Despite recent price increases, these remain among the lowest fossil fuel prices in the world for power generation. While these figures vary somewhat in countries across the region, they provide little or no incentive for investment in renewables as an alternative.

Getting actual subsidy measurements – and thus being able to assess their impact on investment – remains problematic as there is no commonly agreed definition of what constitutes a subsidy (El-Katiri and Fattouh 2015), even though various approaches do attempt to estimate the extent of fossil fuel subsidies. The so-called 'price-gap' approach, for instance, uses the difference between domestic and international fuel prices to estimate fossil fuel subsidies (Coady et al. 2015). Others point to the difference between the actual cost of electricity supply – i.e., LCOE from different fuels along with fixed network costs – and retail electricity tariffs as a measure of subsidies in the electricity sector (Poudineh et al. 2016; see also El-Katiri and Fattouh 2015 for a literature review on measurement of energy subsidies in the MENA region).

The figures that can be obtained from these approaches do suggest, however, that if domestic prices of fossil fuels were undistorted, it is very likely that the market would incentivize solar investment on its own or with minimal help from government subsidies. Therefore, the main challenge is how to reform energy prices to a level at which the market creates incentives for investment in alternative energy without government support. To appreciate this challenge, it is necessary to understand the logic of these subsidies.

The story of fossil fuel subsidies in MENA countries is more complex than the singular political element usually described in terms of the social contract by which governments agree to share wealth accrued from resource revenues in exchange for acquiring the privilege of extracting, managing, and distributing this natural capital. The 'social contract' argument correctly highlights the need for rent distribution, given the political structures in these countries. However, it reveals little or nothing about why a particular form of rent distribution, subsidizing fossil fuels in this case, would be chosen over other options. According to social welfare theory, for example, any rent in excess of basic administrative costs should be distributed as lump sums, or be used to finance essential services such as health care, compulsory education or their equivalent (Newbery 2016).

The choice to subsidize the commodity rather than follow social welfare theory for rent distribution is rooted in the distinct economic contexts of these resource rich countries. The first economic reason for not following social welfare theory in these countries is that they have limited capacity to invest resource rents locally in a profitable manner without causing inflation or other macroeconomic impacts. The second reason is that their populations often lack confidence that sovereign wealth funds provide benefits, mainly because the discount rate that the population applies tends to exceed the return to these funds (Newbery 2016).

Additionally, the abundance of low cost oil and gas has prompted these hydrocarbon rich economies to pursue industrial policies that focus on energy-intensive sectors such as petrochemicals, cement, steel and aluminum. The competitiveness and profitability of these industries is closely linked to changes in energy prices. Thus, once business models are created around the subsidies in place, it is very difficult to remove them without appropriate measures to mitigate their impacts on the public and the economy; those who benefit from subsidies are likely to resist any change to them.

Analysis using generic assumptions (EIA 2016) on the cost of generating 1 megawatt hour (MWh) of electricity from different technologies shows that on a levelized cost basis – without considering the cost of balancing and intermittency – solar becomes competitive as a source of generation only at an oil price of \$23/bbl or more, or of more than \$4/MMBtu for gas. This is based on a lowest cost LCOE for PV technology in the MENA of \$58/MWh (Poudineh et al. 2016). This point of competitive pricing may differ across individual MENA countries, but in all cases will increase when the cost of addressing the variability of renewable generation is taken into account. This suggests that given the current low level of fossil fuel prices in MENA domestic markets, enabling the market requires a considerable increase in the price of fossil fuels – something that is extremely challenging from a political perspective. With these considerations in mind, it is very unlikely that a renewables policy based on the complete removal of fossil fuel subsidies would be possible in the short to medium term.

This situation undermines investment in alternative energy. In short, enabling the market to provide incentives for renewables in MENA countries requires rationalizing the price of electricity and removing all forms of subsidies allocated to fossil fuels used for electricity generation.

Incentive through subsidizing renewables

If fossil fuels cannot be made more expensive relative to renewables by removing fossil fuel subsidies, the alternative approach is to subsidize renewables instead, effectively driving their cost down to a level that is competitive with fossil fuels. Design of such subsidies depends on various factors, but can be

Table 7.2 Renewable support mechanisms

Type of support mechanism		Example
Production oriented	Price based	Feed-in tariff, feed-in premium
	Quantity based	Auction (price is based on $/MWh)
Investment oriented	Price based	Grants
	Quantity based	Auction (price is based on $/MW)

broadly categorized as approaches targeting production and those targeting investment. These two forms can be further grouped as price based and quantity based models (Table 7.2).

In the production oriented approach, the subsidy is given for each unit of energy ($/kWh or $/MWh) that renewable resources generate. The investment oriented approach gives a subsidy to each unit of capacity ($/kW or $/MW) a generator installs. Under price based subsidies, the government sets the price and lets the market determine the quantity. Under quantity based subsidies, the government sets the target quantity and lets the market discover the price, for example through an auction.

With various models for renewables support schemes available, each government needs to choose one that satisfies a set of criteria within its own context. The six most critical criteria are as follows:

✓ Compatible with the structure of the electricity sector in the region
✓ Market oriented, when feasible
✓ Compatible with the scale of the project
✓ Covers most economic risks
✓ Compatible with the existing institutions
✓ Suitable for fiscally constrained countries

The question of whether to employ production or investment based support mechanisms depends on the characteristics of the country, including the design of the electricity market, the presence of necessary institutions and the degree of fiscal constraints. In liberalized electricity markets, production based schemes, such as feed-in tariffs (FITs), tend to distort price signals; however, as they spread the subsidy payment over the life of the asset, FITs can be quite effective in fiscally constrained countries. Investment based schemes tend to be suitable in liberalized power markets, but some forms, e.g., investment grants, place huge pressure on government budgets. Therefore, governments need to evaluate the scheme against the criteria mentioned above and choose those that are best suited for the electricity market and institutions in their countries.

To demonstrate how the above six criteria can be met in practice, it is useful to consider the two most popular support schemes: namely FITs, which are production and price based, and auctions which are investment (or production) and quantity based. FITs satisfy most of the criteria above, except that they are not suitable for large-scale projects. Because the price in this approach is set administratively, rather than being market based, if it is set too high it can become costly for large projects. Additionally, owing to a lack of transparency and incentives for cost reduction, it is susceptible to political intervention. Yet, FITs have been shown to be an effective way to incentivize investment in rooftop solar PV (household model), something that Germany's experience clearly endorses. (Also see Anaya and Pollitt (2015) for an analysis of Germany's experience with solar PV.)

An auction approach potentially meets all the above criteria: it can work within the current electricity market structures and is market-based; it is also scalable to different project sizes, covers most economic risks, and is compatible with the institutional structures and fiscal constraints in MENA countries. Therefore, depending on the process design and commodity procured – units of energy or units of capacity – auctioning is the most suitable approach to allocating scarce resources to promote renewables in resource rich MENA economies.

Given that electricity markets in MENA countries have not yet been liberalized – and thus do not need to be concerned with the market design for a heterogeneous set of technologies for renewables and conventional generation – a production based auction is in fact the most compatible approach within the economic and institutional context of these countries (Poudineh et al. 2016).

Despite the effectiveness of renewables support schemes to incentivize renewables in the MENA context, an overarching problem is that subsidizing renewables can become very costly, especially when the cost to government is added to existing fossil fuel subsidies. In an environment of low oil prices, dual subsidies may be impossible to sustain. In the MENA context, other factors must be considered. The decline in oil prices – and hence government revenues – since 2014 was preceded by an increase in government expenditures following the 'Arab Spring' as MENA governments announced social spending programs to pre-empt social unrest (Fattouh et al. 2016). Following the oil price decline, economic growth has also slowed and private sector activity has stalled. Overall, the ratio of debt to gross domestic product (GDP) has also increased considerably in recent years. Subsequently, some of these countries now find themselves on fiscally unsustainable paths. Fattouh et al. (2016) argues that fiscal pressures were building during the 2011–14 period of record high oil prices, as countries announced large increases in wages, employment benefits, social spending and infrastructure development programs following social unrest in some MENA countries. Under current conditions, a pure subsidy program for renewable investment would add a huge fiscal burden to already tight government budgets.

Incentive through the combinatorial approach

Given that complete removal of fossil fuel subsidies is not politically possible, at least in the short to medium term, and a full subsidy scheme to meet renewable targets would be prohibitively costly, what options remain for governments in MENA countries?

This section explores a practical, combinatorial approach in which incentives for renewable investment are partially provided through the market and partially through government subsidies (Figure 7.2). In this approach, governments would pursue an active plan to gradually adjust fossil fuel prices while also subsidizing renewables, with subsidies declining over time. Such an approach alleviates the pressure on government budgets, specifically during a low oil price environment, while anticipating that renewable electricity prices, especially for solar, will continue the descending cost trajectory seen over the last decade. If this trend continues, governments could adjust the speed of fossil fuel price reform to balance fiscal pressure against political acceptability.

The combinatorial approach is compatible with measures already taken in the region to reform energy prices and subsidize renewables. In the GCC, the UAE began to liberalize energy prices in 2008, although Emirati nationals remain largely shielded from increases in electricity prices. In 2016, Saudi Arabia initiated a gradual reform plan, which will see the price of most energy vectors – including natural gas, gasoline, diesel and electricity – adjusted upwards along with prices for water production, which is energy intensive. Kuwait, Oman and Bahrain also have plans to reform their energy prices in a gradual manner. Iran embarked on a drastic energy price reform in 2010, although it experienced significant challenges in subsequent years. The need for energy price reform is even recognized in politically unstable countries such as Iraq and Yemen, although no substantial measures have been carried out.

A trend that very much supports the combinatorial approach is that the LCOE of renewables has been on a descending cost trajectory over the last decade. Between 2010 and 2016, the costs of renewables have dropped significantly, specifically of those suitable for the MENA region, such as solar PV, solar thermal and onshore wind (Figure 7.3). A gradual increase of fossil fuel prices based on the removal of subsidies, alongside a gradual decline of renewables costs acts as a 'scissor' that progressively cuts the amount of subsidies needed for renewables. This provides a clear exit strategy for the government to wean itself off both fossil fuel and renewables subsidies in the future.

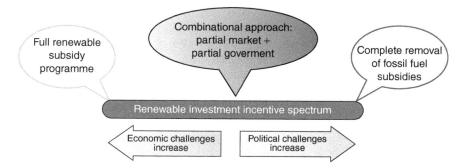

Figure 7.2 Renewable investment incentive spectrum

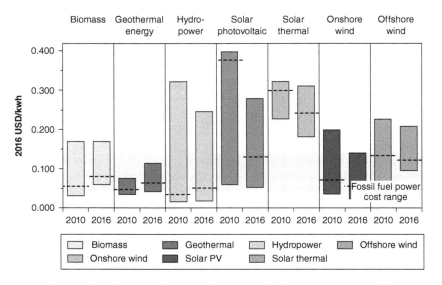

Figure 7.3 Levelized cost of electricity for renewables between 2010 and 2016
(IRENA 2016b)

Notes: All costs are in 2016 USD. Weighted average cost is 7.5 per cent for the Organisation for Economic Co-operation and Development (OECD) and China, and 10 per cent for the rest of the world. Image copyright IRENA.

Along with investment incentives, which can be provided through, for example, a combinatorial approach, government commitment is another key element for the creation of a vibrant renewable market in the MENA region. From the investors' point of view, evidence of ongoing government commitment to renewable policies is critical; anything less sends a wrong signal and induces significant uncertainty among potential investors. This could be alleviated if GCC governments were to demonstrate that recent renewables targets are not just announcements to 'showcase' compliance with international climate agreements, but rather form an integral part of overall strategies for energy, with the aim of decoupling development and economic growth from the ecological impacts of energy production and consumption. To further demonstrate real political will to promote renewables in the energy mix, governments can also design dedicated financial support mechanisms, such as priority lending, green banks, guidelines for issuing green bonds, convertible loans, etc.

Addressing barriers to renewable investment

In resource rich MENA countries, investment in renewable technologies is often hindered by three context specific barriers: grid inadequacy, institutional constraints and a well recognized set of risks and uncertainties. Examining these barriers in more detail creates opportunity to highlight their importance for penetration of renewables and identify mechanisms to remove them.

Grid connection, adequacy and management

Grid issues exist universally, but are more pronounced in developing and emerging economies. Grid connection is a recognized challenge in most MENA countries, where most grids have been set up to manage centralized thermal generation and may exhibit significant limitations as the share of decentralized generation, including renewables, increases. Unusually high levels of electricity loss are a sign of low adequacy and resiliency of MENA grids. Transmission and distribution (T&D) losses in countries such as Iran (15 per cent), Algeria (18 per cent), and Kuwait (12 per cent) are considerably higher than the world average of 8 per cent, let alone the rate of 6 per cent of advanced OECD countries (data from 2013, as reported in Poudineh et al. 2016).

A related issue is system operators that lack the training needed to competently manage power systems as the share of variable renewables increases – without resorting to curtailment. In China, for example, intermittent renewable capacity was added at a pace that exceeded the network operators' ability to dispatch it. Thus, as China's installed wind capacity reached around 138 gigawatts (GW) – more than the combined power capacity of Iran and Saudi Arabia – some 21 per cent of the potential was never called upon, as the grid could not manage its delivery. This is one of the highest rates of curtailment in the world (Renewable Energy World 2016).

Lack of interconnection with neighboring grids, or cases where such interconnections exist but are largely underutilized, also undermines the potential for renewables in the MENA region. At present, policymakers in the region tend to have a narrow view of interconnection as a tool for managing emergencies rather than a mechanism to optimize the power system and facilitate electricity trade. Experience in other regions shows that interconnection plays an important role in helping system operators manage variable generation without curtailment. For instance, Denmark's grid operator, Energinet, operates a power system with a considerable share of intermittent renewables in the form of wind power – 37.5 per cent of total electricity consumption in 2016 was generated by wind farms – by balancing the system through its linkages to neighboring Germany, Sweden and Norway.

Investors need to know up front whether the renewable projects they are considering will have secure grid connections, or whether the business model sufficiently covers any costs associated if network reinforcement is needed. Equally important is proof that the grid has sufficient capacity, and that the power system is flexible enough to integrate variable generation sources and is managed by competent operators. Additionally, depending on the type of support policy, renewables generators may need to have priority dispatch – for example, when the support scheme is not linked to the electricity market price, which is the case in the non-liberalized electricity systems of the MENA.

Experience shows that in the absence of power system flexibility and competent grid operators, renewables may face frequent curtailment, which reduces compensation and adversely affects their revenue streams, representing strong disincentives for potential investors. These issues are also important for lenders that base decisions for renewables projects on certainty about the revenue stream.

To date, only a few MENA countries have started to develop rules and regulations to facilitate connection and operation of renewable sources. Algeria and Iran, for example, have established rules for guaranteed grid connection, priority access and priority dispatch, and have developed detailed technical guidelines for connection of projects of various sizes at different voltage levels (Poudineh et al. 2016). Other countries still lag behind in this respect.

Institutional barriers

The success of any renewable policy adopted by a government, whether market based or not, depends, to a large degree, on the presence of administrative, economic and political institutions that can implement that policy. A core element is the need for an independent regulator that can design suitable regulatory frameworks for procurement and set out the necessary technical guidelines for integration of renewables within the existing power systems. At present in almost all MENA countries, the regulator is not independent of government and is thus susceptible to political influence.

Another potentially limiting factor is that renewables are handled within the same energy ministries that oversee the oil and gas industry. As fossil fuel exports constitute the main source of government revenue, and oil and gas trade dominates these economies, this 'all-under-one-roof' approach may be disadvantaging renewables. Over time, low cost and abundant fossil fuels have not only led to the buildup of energy-intensive industries, but also shaped the type of legal and economic institutions that have emerged. If renewables become a threat to the business model of traditional utilities, and to those who benefit from domestic subsidized fossil fuels, the progress of low carbon technologies will likely face resistance.

The bureaucratic processes associated with these institutions are often complex, particularly in relation to permitting processes, land leases, grid connections, environmental compliance, etc. Most MENA countries show little coordination among various governmental bodies linked to these issues and some have little experience in dealing with renewables technologies. This can lengthen the process of acquiring the documentation needed to apply for funding and begin construction, causing significant transaction costs. Financing is also a challenge as local financial institutions may either be unwilling to lend to renewables projects or have little experience in the renewables industry. Finally, the legal institutions are not strong enough and/or independent enough to earn the confidence of private investors, specifically in relation to dispute resolution between power offtakers and owners of renewables plants. One example of action that undermined confidence is Egypt's reversal, in May 2016, of permitting international arbitration for renewables projects.

Risks and uncertainties

The presence of risks and uncertainties in the operating environment for renewable technologies is a substantial concern for investors of renewable energy. Generally, five types of risks can be listed: political, policy and regulatory, technology, currency and liquidity, and power offtaker (Poudineh et al. 2016) (Figure 7.4). The degree to which investors are exposed to each type of risk can vary in different countries in the MENA region. For instance, some

Political risk

Political risks are related to the political events that have a negative impact on the value of investment including war, civil disturbance, sabotage, expropriation and non-honoring of contracts

Policy and regulatory risks

Policy and regulatory risks are those risks that are related to changes in investment incentives (for example, removal of renewable subsidies), network codes, grid connection costs model, and permitting processes

Technology risk

It is related to nascent renewable technologies and inexperienced and unskilled workers operating the facilities

Currency and liquidity risks

The currency risk pertains to the volatility of domestic currency. Risk of insufficient liquidity can happen if there is a mismatch between the time of revenue receipts and cost payments

Power off-taker risk

Risk of default and non-payment on the part of single buyer

Figure 7.4 Risks faced by renewables investors in the MENA region

countries have a better history of political stability, and thus lower political risk, whereas others – e.g., Iraq or Libya – have a high degree of political and security risks.

Risks and uncertainties increase the cost of capital, having negative impacts on the incentive for investment and making project financing more difficult to obtain. Governments can help reduce these risks by, for example, providing insurance and facilitating access to risk mitigation instruments such as credit guarantees, liquidity guarantees, currency risk hedging and local currency lending. In the absence of risk mitigation instruments and guarantees, the return on renewables investments may be insufficient to cover the risks, causing investors to forgo renewables investment opportunities altogether.

Providing insurance for currency and liquidity risks, as well as for power off-taker risks, is quite straightforward for MENA's resource rich countries. Most MENA governments have a policy of keeping exchange rates fixed in order to stabilize the economy and control domestic inflation. Additionally, the structure of the electricity supply industry is such that the power offtaker is often a state-owned company that can be bailed out by the government in the case of default. Reducing policy and regulatory risk is more challenging: frequent and unexpected change of renewables incentive models or regulatory models for renewables connection and management send a signal to potential investors that stability is lacking. To avoid surprising the market and thus build investor confidence, governments could consult with relevant stakeholders to design policy and to set out the plans and mechanisms to manage change.

Revising energy policy in the MENA

For many decades, energy policy in MENA countries has revolved around the abundant and low cost fossil fuels that have underpinned their economic growth and industrialization. The legacy of this period has been high domestic consumption and high-energy intensity. By the 2030s, the Middle East is expected to become the most energy intensive region in the world (BP Energy Outlook 2016). The MENA countries, together with those in the Asia-Pacific region, are expected to be the main drivers of energy demand growth over the next 20 years. This creates a situation in which many of the opportunities once offered by fossil fuels are now turning into liabilities, not least because increasing domestic demand accelerates the draw on the region's natural capital. Therefore, reassessing current energy policy has become a top priority for all MENA countries.

Revising energy policy has multiple dimensions, including energy price reform and structural reform of the energy sector, with an integrated view of all energy sources, rather than placing electricity, oil products and gas into separate silos. Traditional policies of separating energy carriers worked when end-markets could be easily separated but are now less appropriate. The potential for renewable energy as an alternative to using natural gas and oil, which could otherwise be exported, and for electricity to replace fossil fuels in most other end-markets – e.g., transport, heating, and cooling – requires that energy policies be developed in a more comprehensive and integrated manner.

To build stakeholder confidence, MENA governments could demonstrate their commitment by placing renewables alongside other energy sources in national energy policy strategies. This would also support the realization of more sustainable growth paths, improved productivity and industrial diversification. Going even further, MENA countries might consider energy and climate change policies together. This is especially relevant following the COP21 Paris Agreement, which highlights the need for decarbonization to become a focal point of national energy policies. There is also an economic rationale for combining energy and climate policy to support decarbonization: introducing specific renewables policies will affect the relative price of all other sources of energy and therefore impact the consumption level of fossil fuels. Energy efficiency policies can also alter the shape of the energy demand curve, which affects inter-fuel competition. Therefore, to minimize potential negative side effects that arise when energy and climate policy interact – and to optimize those effects that could be positive – these two policy areas need to be considered together.

With much of their electricity generation based on fossil fuels, MENA governments also need to implement appropriate policies to restructure their electricity supply industry. Until the late 1990s and early 2000s, most countries in the region had vertically integrated electricity sectors; several countries have since launched electricity reform legislation to transition away from this model. While the structure of electricity markets and degree of liberalization differs across the countries, most have retained variants of the vertically integrated, single buyer structure in which the state monopoly coexists with private generation companies (Poudineh et al. 2016). The reform laws of Iran (1999), Algeria (2002) and Saudi Arabia (2005) envision wholesale markets. The UAE (Abu Dhabi) reform law (1998) envisages disaggregated single buyers with bilateral trading and third party access. By contrast, the reform law of Kuwait (2008; 2010) is less ambitious and limited to IPPs in generation (Dyllick-Brenzinger and Finger 2013).

With energy market reform in its early stages in most MENA countries, the opportunity exists to design – from the outset – electricity markets and sectors around the incorporation of renewables. Given the distinct contexts of MENA economies, including the challenges of reconciling liberalization with decarbonization, in the transition phase the market structure for these hydrocarbon rich economies is likely to evolve into an unbundled, single buyer model rather than a fully liberalized model (Poudineh et al. 2016). In this structure, generation is structurally and financially unbundled from T&D, and the single buyer is the grid company, which does not own generation assets and is subject to regulation for non-discriminatory access and cost-efficiency improvements. This structure alleviates, to some degree, monopoly power and removes the perverse incentives of an integrated monopoly.

Conclusions

Hydrocarbon rich countries in the MENA region have shown slow progress towards the deployment and scaling up of renewables within their energy mixes, reflecting significant barriers posed by general obstacles and by factors specific to their economic and political contexts. This chapter argues that, to promote renewables, these countries will need to both remove barriers and create investment incentives. Moreover, policies to promote renewables in MENA countries should seek to strike a balance between government support and market incentives, aiming for an approach that is practically implementable.

In the near term and given the current economic and political reality of MENA countries, the complete removal of fossil fuel subsides would not be feasible, neither would implementation of a full government subsidy program for renewables. This supports the case for the combinatorial approach proposed in Poudineh et al. (2016) and described in this chapter, which suggests a partial adjustment of fossil fuel price, to align them with their opportunity cost, along with a partial government subsidy program as the most effective approach to create incentives for investment in renewables. This combination would balance the political acceptability of liberalizing energy prices against pressure on the government budget. In the long run, renewables costs may decline further and governments may be able to continue adjusting fossil fuel prices to bring them closer to their true economic costs. At some point governments may be able to completely phase out both fossil fuel and renewables subsidies.

The combinatorial approach resembles, in some ways, the current subsidy scheme for renewables in European countries, which is linked to electricity market prices. This means that renewables generators are compensated for the difference between the fixed guaranteed price and the price they receive from selling their energy in the wholesale market. This approach has two advantages. First, it fully integrates renewables into liberalized markets, as they need to actively participate in the electricity market. Second, governments can take advantage of electricity price movements: the need for subsidies declines as electricity prices increase. In the MENA region, where markets are not fully liberalized, the combinatorial approach offers compensation to renewables as the difference between a guaranteed price (which can be set through an auction) and the price at which the single buyer purchases electricity from subsidized fossil fuel plants. This price is set by governments in the region and is currently low because of fossil fuel subsidies. For MENA countries, the challenge is how to remove fossil fuel subsidies and increase the price of electricity, so that government subsidy for renewables declines.

At some point down the road MENA governments may decide to fully liberalize their electricity markets to improve efficiency, incentivize innovation and attract private sector capital and expertise at all segments of the supply chain, i.e., beyond just generation. The experience of developed economies in attempting to reconcile liberalization with decarbonization has not been particularly successful so far: often progress in one dimension has compromised the other. Therefore, MENA countries can exercise the 'late-comer advantage'; while now designing policy frameworks for renewable integration, they can tap into international experience and avoid missteps made by the early movers, primarily advanced OECD economies. This is particularly evident in the electricity sector, where OECD countries have found that liberalized markets originally designed for fossil fuels need to be adapted to accommodate intermittent renewables. It is now clear that both energy sources have inherently different characteristics that influence the system marginal cost and hence the market price in different ways (Keay et al. 2013). The adoption of an unbundled single buyer model in electricity provision at the very minimum, as discussed in this chapter, may be more suited to the distinct economic and political contexts of MENA countries. It may allow governments to self-select on the policy instrument spectrum and follow a dynamic combinatorial approach in policy design that balances market incentives and government support in the deployment and scaling up of renewables.

References

Anaya KL, and Pollitt M (2015) Integrating distributed generation: regulation and trends in three leading countries. EPRG Working Paper 1423, Cambridge Working Paper in Economics, University of Cambridge, Cambridge, UK.

BP Energy Outlook (2016) BP Energy Outlook country and regional insights – Middle East. www.bp.com/content/dam/bp/en/corporate/pdf/energy-economics/energy-outlook/bp-energy-outlook-2016.pdf. Accessed 23 Jul 2018.

Coady D, Parry I, Sears L et al. (2015) How large are global energy subsidies? IMF Working Paper WP/15/105, International Monetary Fund, Washington, DC.

Dyllick-Brenzinger RM, and Finger M (2013) Review of electricity sector reform in five large, oil and gas exporting MENA countries: current status and outlook. *Energy Strategy Reviews* 2:31–45.

EIA (US Energy Information Administration) (2016) How much coal, natural gas, or petroleum is used to generate a kilowatthour of electricity? www.eia.gov/tools/faqs/faq.cfm?id=667&t=6. Accessed 10 Aug 2017.

El-Katiri L, and Fattouh B (2015) A brief political economy of energy subsidies in the Middle East and North Africa. OIES Paper MEP 11, Oxford Institute for Energy Studies, Oxford, UK.

Fattouh B, Sen A, and Moerenhout T (2016) Striking the right balance? GCC energy price reforms in a low price environment. *Oxford Energy Comment*, Oxford Institute for Energy Studies, Oxford, UK.

IRENA (International Renewable Energy Agency) (2016a) *Renewable Energy Market Analysis – The GCC Region*. IRENA, Abu Dhabi. www.irena.org/Document Downloads/Publications/IRENA_Market_GCC_2016.pdf. Accessed Dec 2016.

IRENA (2016b) Levelised cost of electricity 2010–2016. IRENA Data Dashboard. http://resourceirena.irena.org/gateway/dashboard/?topic=3&subTopic=1057. Accessed 6 Apr 2017.

Keay M, Rhys J, and Robinson D (2013) Decarbonization of the electricity industry – is there still a place for markets? OIES Working Paper EL9, Oxford Institute for Energy Studies, Oxford, UK.

Krupa J, and Poudineh R (2017) Financing renewable electricity in the resource-rich countries of the Middle East and North Africa: a review. EL22, Oxford Institute for Energy Studies, Oxford, UK.

Lilliestam J, and Patt A (2015) Barriers, risks and policies for renewables in the Gulf States. *Energies* 8:8263–8285.

Newbery D (2016) Pricing electricity and supporting renewables in heavily energy subsidized economies. Cambridge Working Paper in Economics 1638, University of Cambridge, UK.

Poudineh R, Sen A, and Fattouh B (2016) Advancing renewable energy in resource-rich economies of the MENA. OIES Paper MEP 15, Oxford Institute for Energy Studies, Oxford, UK.

Renewable Energy World (2016) Wind power curtailment in China expected to increase in second half of 2016. www.renewableenergyworld.com/articles/2016/08/wind-power-curtailment-in-china-expected-to-increase-in-second-half-of-2016.html. Accessed 10 Aug 2017.

World Bank (2016) World Development Indicators. http://data.worldbank.org/data-catalog/world-development-indicators. Accessed Dec 2016.

8 Energy and climate policies to stimulate renewables deployment in GCC countries

Steve Griffiths and Daniah Orkoubi

Abstract

While all countries belonging to the Gulf Cooperation Council (GCC) have set targets for renewable energy deployment at national or local levels, progress to date has been minimal. Analysis of renewables deployment initiatives around the world shows that success is highest when stated targets are supported by well-defined policy frameworks that reflect the regional context.

This chapter investigates current trends in renewable energy and climate policy with the aim of helping to identify the most effective and feasible recommendations to catalyze renewables deployment in GCC countries. To develop an optimal policy framework, the chapter considers the GCC context across multiple dimensions, including the underlying motivations for adoption of renewable energy.

The findings show that the international policy trend of using renewables auctions to stimulate deployment is optimally suited to GCC countries. Furthermore, regional energy subsidy reforms currently underway may provide a foundation for future policy frameworks aimed at explicit carbon pricing to support regional renewables deployment. An emissions trading system (ETS) is proposed as the most viable mechanism for such carbon pricing. Thus, a phased approach is suggested to create – and over time strengthen – an integrated energy and climate policy framework.

Policy relevant insights

GCC countries are well positioned to implement policies that stimulate renewables adoption while also being aligned with international policy trends that are suitable for their social, economic and political contexts. The following points are relevant to stimulating advance through policy:

- Utility scale renewables auctioning for new power generation capacity is gaining traction as an optimal support measure in the region.

(continued)

(continued)

Auction design to ensure transparency and effectiveness is critical to ensuring the sustainability of the policy mechanism. To date, the first price, sealed bid auction format has proven appropriate for the region.

- In the near term, solar water heating (SWH) in the buildings sector also shows strong potential.
- Energy subsidy reforms already underway can support distributed renewable power. An approach, such as net metering, that does not require government financial support is more economically viable. Policy support is needed to establish necessary grid codes and infrastructure.
- Such energy subsidy reforms may pave the way for climate-oriented policies. Implicit carbon pricing through taxation of fuels already experiencing price increases is the most immediate possibility. An eventual ETS would require considerable new institutional capacity. GCC countries might be able to draw critical lessons by monitoring international ETS experiences in relevant geographies, such as China.

Review of renewable energy deployment to date and its relevance to GCC countries

The deployment of renewable energy technologies globally has increased considerably over the course of the past several years, in part due to favorable renewables support policies in numerous countries. By the start of 2016, such policies had been implemented in more than 146 countries, driven by concerns for energy security, energy system resiliency, economic development and climate change. The growing international concern for climate change and environmental sustainability has caused climate policy to become intertwined with energy policy in many countries, particularly following the international climate agreement signed by 195 countries at the 21st Conference of the Parties (COP21) to the United Nations Framework Convention on Climate Change (UNFCCC). As a result, integrated climate and energy policy tools, such as carbon pricing, will play a role in the further widespread deployment of renewable energy technology. Importantly, appropriate energy and climate policies are context specific and therefore must be considered within the unique circumstances of the regional, national, or subnational energy systems in which they are to be applied.

Although the six countries of the Gulf Cooperation Council (GCC) have abundant oil and natural gas reserves, energy system diversification through the adoption of renewable energy has become a key regional endeavor. An increasing imbalance between rising energy demand and low-cost sources of energy supply is a driving force behind this interest in renewables. Because of the substantial decrease in the cost of renewable energy technologies in recent years, particularly technologies to exploit abundant solar energy, renewables have become an attractive option for achieving energy security at low cost in many parts of the world. Although climate change mitigation does not appear to be central to the motivation for adopting renewables in the GCC, climate-oriented policies supportive of renewables deployment are relevant for consideration as part of an integrated package of policies to stimulate uptake of renewables.

Experience in other contexts demonstrates that stated renewables targets must be supported by defined policies and regulations that reflect the regional context and thus have the highest likelihood of achieving stated ambitions. This chapter reviews global trends in both renewable energy and climate policy, and then specifically focuses on the application of these trends to the GCC's evolving context. The chapter first assesses the intended role of renewable energy in defined regional energy strategies, then examines supportive renewables targets and policy measures already in place. Finally, the chapter identifies GCC sectors where renewables deployment is most relevant and proposes policies and regulations that afford the greatest opportunity for renewables in these sectors. The role of carbon pricing measures in supporting regional renewable energy adoption is also assessed with particular focus on energy subsidy reforms, carbon taxes and greenhouse gas (GHG) emissions trading. (For reference, the Kyoto Protocol regulates six GHGs: carbon dioxide (CO_2), methane (CH_4), nitrous oxide (N_2O), hydrofluorocarbons (HFCs), perfluorocarbons (PFCs), and sulfur hexafluoride (SF_6). The collective set of GHGs are often referred to as CO_2 equivalents (CO_2eq.).)

This chapter explores the applicable energy and climate policies for the GCC given the regional context and underlying motivations for renewables deployment. On the renewables policy side, internationally, a key trend is implementing renewables auctions to achieve lowest cost technology procurement. Climate policy, by contrast, focuses largely on carbon pricing with direct carbon taxes and emissions trading systems (ETS) being the dominant policy mechanisms. In the GCC, renewables auctions are fitting for the context while explicit carbon pricing is not, given the very high carbon emissions that currently exist in the region. Hence, the latter policy mechanism would need to be tailored as part of an overall policy package to be useful to regional adoption of renewable energy.

Based on the analysis provided in this work, a regional policy approach with near- and long-term components is suggested to catalyze deployment of renewables while creating strategic options for future policy frameworks with potentially broader impacts for both energy and climate. Specifically, near-term energy policy is proposed to focus on renewables auctions, complemented by continued energy subsidy reform efforts. Such auctions can stimulate rapid deployment of utility scale renewable energy, while energy subsidy reforms can enhance deployment of distributed renewables, providing a foundation for implicit and explicit carbon pricing. As social, economic, and political conditions in the region allow, implicit carbon pricing through energy taxation and ultimately explicit carbon pricing through an ETS may prove viable as a means to stimulate renewables adoption. This policy approach allows for renewable energy to achieve scale in the GCC based on purely economic drivers, with the opportunity for additional growth to be achieved by longer-term policy options.

Targets set, now how to achieve them?

As GCC countries have all stated their ambitions for greater adoption of renewable energy, their motivations for doing so are increasingly apparent. Renewable energy has become an economically competitive source of energy, particularly in the power sector, at a time when inexpensive sources of hydrocarbon based energy are in increasingly short supply and concerns for their impacts on the environment are stimulating the transition of many regional, national and local energy systems toward clean energy. Against this backdrop, this chapter specifically addresses the following research questions:

- What are the driving forces for the adoption of renewable energy globally and, more specifically, how do these driving forces relate to GCC countries?
- What are the major global trends in renewable energy and climate policy?
- How do the major global trends in renewable energy and climate policy relate to the GCC context?
- What is the optimal policy framework to catalyze renewables deployment in the GCC and how should this framework be tailored for the GCC context?
- What carbon pricing policies are most suitable for the GCC countries and how can these policies stimulate adoption of renewable energy?

To address these questions, this chapter begins with a review of recent energy and climate policies, followed by analysis of the policy frameworks most suitable for the GCC, given the regional context and related motivations for renewable energy. Discussion and conclusions offer a synthesis of the issues explored and yield policy relevant insights.

The energy and climate policy nexus, including energy pricing

Energy policy is fundamentally about political decisions for implementing programs to achieve energy related societal goals. An overarching societal goal is to manage the production and distribution of energy so that demand is met inclusively, reliably and cost-effectively, and with minimal environmental impact. Therefore, the relationship between energy policy and climate policy is particularly important. In fact, the need to ground climate policy discussions within an energy policy context has been discussed as a means of reinforcing the multiple benefits of developing low carbon economies, as opposed to the more narrow focus of reducing GHG emissions only for climate change mitigation (Bazilian et al. 2010).

At present, much of the literature on renewable energy and climate change makes little distinction between policies primarily focused on energy systems versus those targeting climate change mitigation (Luomi 2014; Michaels and Tal 2015). The key differentiating factor, then, between climate and energy policies is that climate-oriented policies tend to focus on the explicit pricing of GHG emissions, including ETS, carbon taxes, offset mechanisms and results based financing (RBF) schemes. (Note that an RBF approach provides a mitigation activity with financial support, once its emission reductions have been verified.) Energy-oriented policies, by contrast, do address GHG emissions, but implicitly through policy measures such as the elimination of fossil fuel subsidies, fossil energy taxes, financial support for clean energy, and obligations for clean energy. The European Union (EU) is perhaps the best example of a region with strong policies for both climate and renewable energy. Recent work concerning the EU has shown that the interaction of renewable energy and climate policies can be very positive when considered holistically, particularly when objectives beyond climate change mitigation are to be met (Lehmann and Gawel 2013; Gawel et al. 2014).

Regardless of the particular orientation of any given policy measure, an ideal policy package aims to ensure the availability of secure, affordable and reliable energy that supports robust economic development with minimal environmental impact (Hoppe et al. 2016). Hence, the optimal portfolio of policies for an economy should balance both energy and climate measures to varying degrees.

Renewable energy policies

Renewable energy is a key point of intersection between energy and climate policies. Targets for renewables deployment have become widespread: at the end of 2015, 173 countries had adopted at least one type of renewables target, more than four times the number in 2005. Perhaps more importantly, 146 countries had established renewables policies to support their targets (REN21 2016).

The cost-competitiveness of renewable energy, particularly for power generation, has complemented policy frameworks as an additional stimulus for renewables deployment. Biomass for power, hydropower, geothermal, solar photovoltaics (PV) and onshore wind are now all cost-competitive with fossil fuel based power generation in a number of geographies (IRENA 2015a; Lazard 2015) and further cost reductions are expected (IRENA 2015b; IRENA 2016c).

Although advances in all forms of renewable energy have been positive, renewables deployment in the power sector has been most significant. By the end of 2015, 114 countries had adopted renewables policies for the power sector as opposed to 66 countries with renewables policies in the transport sector and only 21 countries with renewables policies for heating and cooling (REN21 2016). An international policy focus on renewable power has driven much of the progress to date. It is now clear that these advances are influencing market conditions, and initial support mechanisms for renewable energy must be adapted to create a stable, attractive environment for renewable energy investments, while also ensuring a cost-effective and reliable energy system (IRENA 2014a; IEA-RETD 2016).

Support policies for renewable energy generally fall under the three broad themes of fiscal incentives, public financing, and regulation (IRENA 2012; Abdmouleh et al. 2015b). Fiscal incentives and public financing can support any aspects of the research, development, demonstration and deployment (RDD&D) life cycle in order to achieve technology push and market pull for renewable energy technologies. Regulations focus on market support for renewable energy and can relate to quantity, quality, price or access for renewable energy (Haas et al. 2011; IRENA 2012). More specifically, four main regulatory policy mechanisms are applied to stimulate renewable energy generation (Table 8.1).

Although these policies are differentiated by price determination and compensation schemes (Couture et al. 2015; Kylili and Fokaides 2015), there are many overlaps as well as variations in the actual implementation of each policy instrument (Couture et al. 2015). Specifically, both feed-in tariffs (FITs) and auctions in the form of tenders are designed to provide electricity offtake and

Table 8.1 Regulatory policy mechanisms for renewables deployment (Couture et al. 2015; Kylili and Fokaides 2015)

Policy mechanism	Type	Price determination	Compensation scheme
Feed-in-tariff (FIT) or feed-in-premium (FIP)	Price driven	Set administratively	Long-term, fixed price contracts
Tendering or auctions	Quantity driven	Competition among generators	Long-term, fixed price contracts
Tradable certificates	Quantity driven	Short-term fluctuations in credit and spot market prices	Variable pricing, depending on supply and demand conditions, and ability of generators to secure short-term contracts
Net metering	Access based	Pegged to the retail electricity rate	System output offsets retail electricity purchases and excess generation can be applied as a credit to future electricity purchases

price certainty for project developers. (While the terms auction and public tendering or competitive tendering are often used interchangeably, in this chapter, the scheme is referred to as an auction.) The primary difference between the mechanisms is that payment rates for FITs are predetermined by policymakers while auctions set the offtake price via competitive bidding. Because the cost of RE based electricity generation has, until recently, been considerably higher than that of fossil based power generation, the costs of renewable power FITs passed through to consumers became unsustainable in several European countries where FIT policies were implemented (Pyrgou et al. 2016). Auctions, by contrast, aim to minimize such consumer burdens through market based price discovery; this approach allows flexibility for prices to fall as costs of renewable energy technologies decline. Two challenges with auctions, however, are that they can come with significant administrative costs and so reduce the level of small-scale generation and private sector engagement that FITs have been effective at stimulating. Such considerations have led to much debate on optimal policy for various contexts (Becker and Fischer 2013).

The potential for market distortions and negative impacts on consumers from subsidies granted to renewable energy sources has prompted a trend in renewables policy design away from standard FITs and toward auctions (REN21 2016). The number of countries that adopted renewables auctions increased from 6 in 2005 to at least 60 by early 2015. Additionally, auctions were a major contributor to the average 9 per cent decline (in 2015) in worldwide prices for large-scale renewable electricity power purchase agreements (PPAs) (Anand 2016) and continue to contribute to rapidly falling PPA prices.

Another trend for renewable electricity is the design and implementation of hybrid policies specifically aimed at addressing the increasing cost-competitiveness of renewable energy technologies (Couture et al. 2015; Onifade 2016). Borrowing from a range of policy approaches, hybrid policies seek to achieve multiple goals, such as supporting a diversity of investors and project sizes, managing markets in which self-consumption of renewable energy has become less expensive than purchasing electricity from the grid and integrating renewable energy technologies into wholesale spot markets. Additionally, as the share of intermittent renewable energy increases, policies are evolving to account for the full system level costs incurred rather than just the levelized cost of electricity (LCOE), which is often calculated without considering wider system impacts. System level assessments are geographically specific and bring an important understanding of the true lifecycle costs of intermittent renewable energy, which in turn can help to inform effective policy (Hirth 2013; Khatib and Difiglio 2016).

The relative importance of these factors, and of other strategic and operational considerations, reflects the regional, national or subnational electricity market in which related policies are enacted. Hence, the most important action for policymakers is to understand deeply the context specific rationale for renewables deployment and ensure that polices are designed accordingly.

Climate change policies

Climate change has been known as a potential threat to the global economy since the mid 20th century, yet only in the early 1990s did it begin to receive significant attention. The 1992 Rio Earth Summit, where the UNFCCC was established, set the focus of all global climate negotiations. More than two decades later, in 2015, the UNFCCC mechanism brought together 195 countries to sign a new international climate agreement at the COP21 to limit global warming to well below 2°C above pre-industrial levels and pursue efforts to limit the increase to 1.5°C (Dagnet et al. 2016). Through intended nationally determined contributions (INDCs), the majority of countries globally have now committed to scaling up renewables and energy efficiency. An INDC outlines the post-2020 climate actions a country intends to take under the COP21 Paris Agreement; it becomes a Nationally Determined Contribution (NDC) when the country officially signs up to the Agreement.

Importantly, the COP21 Paris Agreement establishes a process through which countries put forward progressively more ambitious NDCs every five years post-2020 (Dagnet et al. 2016). As of June 2016, 169 INDCs had been submitted – the European Union submitted one INDC representing its 28 member countries – with 126 specifying a GHG target (WRI 2016). Notably, commitments to renewable energy have been prominent in the INDCs, with specific mention by 147 countries (REN21 2016). This strong emphasis on renewables deployment reflects the significant economic savings from reduced reliance on a fossil fuel based energy system, particularly when effort is taken to quantify the value of reduced indoor and outdoor air pollution and environmental degradation from the extraction and use of fossil resources, as well as the negative economic impacts of extreme weather events associated with climate change. The internalization of such real external costs is one of the top ten factors driving the acceleration of renewables deployment (IRENA 2016d).

While renewables deployment provides implicit benefits to climate change mitigation, the pricing of GHG emissions, particularly carbon dioxide (CO_2), is an explicit mitigation measure. CO_2 emissions from fossil fuel use and industrial processes represent two-thirds of global total GHG emissions, with the other sources of GHG emissions contributing the remaining third (Olivier et al. 2015). Because CO_2 is the primary GHG from fossil energy use, pricing of CO_2 or just 'carbon pricing', is the main topic of this chapter. More than 90 of the INDCs submitted by early 2016 included proposals for explicit carbon pricing, with this group of parties accounting for more than 61 per cent of total global GHG emissions (World Bank and Ecofys 2016). Emissions trading systems and direct carbon taxes are the main policy measures for explicit carbon pricing. By 2016, nearly 40 nations and more than 20 cities, states, and regions, together accounting for approximately 25 per cent of global GHG emissions, had implemented ETS and/or carbon tax schemes (World Bank and Ecofys 2016). Although the share of GHG emissions subject to carbon pricing schemes has tripled since 2012, the carbon prices observed vary significantly from less than $1 per ton of CO_2 equivalent (/tCO_2e) in Mexico to $130/$tCO_2e$ in Sweden (Kossoy et al. 2015). At present, 85 per cent of emissions are priced at less than $10/$CO_2e$, which is generally considered too low to stimulate concerted actions on climate change mitigation.

Regarding the use of funds generated by carbon pricing schemes, governments have opted for different modes of distribution, which may include (Carl and Fedor 2016):

- **Green spending** – investment in clean energy technologies, including RDD&D, as well as other initiatives aimed at GHG mitigation.
- **General funds** – bolstering of general government funds without allocation to a particular government program.
- **Revenue recycling** – programs for social support, which may include tax cuts, tax eliminations, or subsidies aimed at reducing the burden of carbon taxation to individuals and businesses.

To date, about 70 per cent of ETS mechanisms direct carbon revenues toward green spending while about 70 per cent of carbon tax mechanisms direct these revenues toward general funds and revenue recycling (Carl and Fedor 2016). Hence, even though all carbon pricing mechanisms are intended to stimulate adoption of renewables, ETS mechanisms may be considered more aligned with direct support for renewable energy technologies.

Energy pricing

Energy pricing is an important policy matter that intersects both renewable energy and climate policies. In many countries, fossil fuel subsidization is a key component of energy pricing policy, used to stimulate demand for energy from coal, natural gas and/or oil by putting the generation cost artificially below market levels. Arguments in favor of such subsidies suggest that they support energy access for the poor, offset commodity price fluctuations and spur economic development. In reality, however, they often provide much more financial benefit to the wealthy than to the poor while simultaneously absorbing financial resources that could be more productively deployed (Fattouh and El-Katiri 2013).

More and more countries are pursuing fossil fuel subsidy reform, increasing the costs to disincentivize their use and thereby stimulate demand for renewable energy and also reduce CO_2 emissions from fossil fuel based electricity generation (Charles et al. 2014). Recent modeling work from the International Institute for Sustainable Development (IISD) examined the opportunity for global energy subsidy reforms to support both GHG reductions and investment in clean energy technologies (Merrill et al. 2016). The findings suggest that, on a global level, removing fossil fuel subsidies could deliver a 10 per cent reduction in GHG emissions by 2025; if the resulting financial savings were reinvested in renewable energy, a 15 per cent reduction would be possible. The opportunity is particularly significant for countries in the Middle East and North Africa (MENA) region where, according to the International Monetary Fund (IMF), pre-tax energy subsidies in 2011 amounted to $237 billion, which represented approximately 48 per cent of global subsidies and 8.6 per cent of the region's gross domestic product (GDP) in the same year (Sdralevich et al. 2014). As reference, pre-tax subsidies are defined as the difference between the price consumers pay and the cost of supplying energy, while post-tax subsidies include the estimated cost of environmental damage and foregone consumption taxes that may rightfully be applied to energy products.

The need for energy subsidy reform in the MENA region has been widely documented and is critical for climate change mitigation, energy demand management and fiscal stability (Fattouh and El-Katiri 2013; Sdralevich et al. 2014; El-Katiri and Fattouh 2015; APICORP Energy Research 2016a). Within the MENA region, the ramifications of high energy subsidization include: the formation of energy-intensive industries that rely on low-cost energy for competitiveness; lack of incentive for energy efficiency in the industrial, power and water sectors; rapid growth in demand for primary fuels and electricity; growth in CO_2 emissions; and rapidly rising fiscal burdens (Fattouh and El-Katiri 2013; Sdralevich et al. 2014). Ultimately, it is the rising fiscal burden that has stimulated subsidy reform in MENA countries (Fattouh et al. 2016; Verme 2016).

Analysis: the context for renewable energy in the GCC

Increasing need for diversified sources of energy

GCC proven oil reserves are estimated at 493 billion barrels, representing 29 per cent of the global total and proven natural gas reserves are estimated at 42 trillion cubic meters (Tcm), representing 22 per cent of the global total (IRENA 2016e). Because of the GCC's abundant hydrocarbon reserves, the regional energy mix is dominated by oil and natural gas in the power, industrial, transportation and buildings sectors. Qatar, Oman, and the United Arab Emirates (UAE) use natural gas to meet more than 60 per cent of their primary energy needs and almost 100 per cent of their power needs (IRENA 2016e). Oil remains the principal means of meeting primary energy demand for power generation in Kuwait (60 per cent) and Saudi Arabia (40 per cent) (APICORP Energy Research 2016b). Domestic consumption of oil in the GCC has become problematic as it reduces the volumes available for export, creating a significant opportunity cost for oil-exporting countries while also having very negative climate impacts (Stevens and Lahn 2011).

Although GCC countries have substantial natural gas reserves, much of the gas from non-associated reserves is geologically challenging to extract, as it is either tightly bound or rich with hydrogen sulfide. This non-associated gas has estimated production costs of $3 per million British thermal units

(/MMBtu) to $9/MMBtu, as opposed to less than $1/MMBtu for gas from associated reserves that is consumed domestically (Krane 2015). Hence, all GCC countries, with the exception of Qatar, now face a shortage of cheap natural gas (Kombargi et al. 2010; UAE Crown Prince Court and Ministry of Foreign Affairs 2014; Krane and Wright 2014; Lahn 2016). The reasons for the shortage include:

- Rapid growth in demand for power;
- High usage of gas reserves for enhanced oil recovery;
- Heavy consumption of natural gas in the steel, aluminum and petrochemical industries;
- Technically challenging development of non-associated natural gas fields;
- Subsidized natural gas prices that make cost-effective development of non-associated natural gas fields difficult for international oil companies; Long-term natural gas export commitments in countries such as the UAE and Oman.

> (Kombargi et al. 2010; UAE Crown Prince Court and
> Ministry of Foreign Affairs 2014)

Given these circumstances, the UAE, Kuwait and Oman have turned to liquefied natural gas (LNG) imports while Saudi Arabia is considering this option (Lahn 2016; MEES 2016d). This is a clear sign that cost-effective, non-hydrocarbon energy sources are vitally needed in the region. From a climate perspective, heavy reliance on fossil fuels has made the GCC region one of the world's most carbon intensive on a per capita basis (Luomi 2014). CO_2 emissions from fuel combustion in the GCC nearly doubled between 2003 and 2013, with Saudi Arabia having the most substantial contribution (Figure 8.1). While electricity generation is a significant contributor to emissions in all GCC countries, manufacturing, construction, and the energy sector more broadly are also major sources (Figure 8.2).

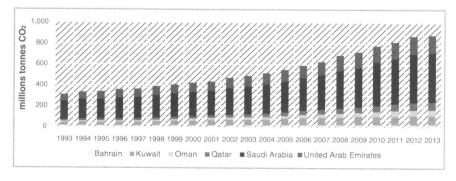

Figure 8.1 Growth of CO_2 emissions from fuel combustion in GCC countries (IEA 2015a)

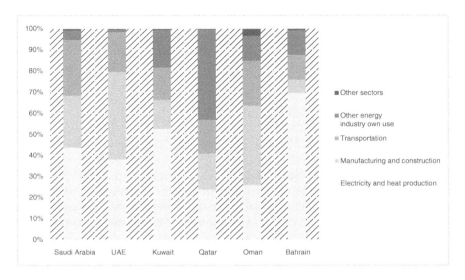

Figure 8.2 Sources of CO$_2$ emissions from fuel combustion in GCC countries (IEA 2015a)

Emissions from energy-intensive sectors – including crude oil production, petroleum refining, basic petrochemicals, ammonia, industrial gases, cement, plastics, metals, and construction – are a major challenge as these sectors spurred the region's economic growth (IMF 2016). The sectoral distribution of final energy demand shows very significant shares for industry as well as the use of energy resources as feedstock for products such as petrochemicals (Figure 8.3).

Motivations and ambitions for renewable energy in the GCC

As discussed in Chapter 2, multiple trends are driving the strong interest in renewable energy in the GCC. Several comprehensive reports published by international agencies highlight opportunities for renewable energy in the MENA region (REN21 et al. 2013; IRENA and League of Arab States 2014), and in the GCC more specifically (IRENA 2016e). Renewable energy in the GCC has been of academic interest to many authors considering policies that could stimulate its adoption (Alnaser and Alnaser 2011; Mezher et al. 2012; Al-Amir and Abu-Hijleh 2013; Bhutto et al. 2014; Abdmouleh et al. 2015a; Lilliestam and Patt 2015; Atalay et al. 2016). Others have developed economic top-down and technological bottom-up models to simulate policy impacts in the GCC (Sgouridis et al. 2013; Mondal et al. 2014; Matar et al. 2015; Griffiths and Mills 2016; Sgouridis et al. 2016). These studies show that while current renewables deployment in the GCC is minimal, the opportunity is large, particularly for solar energy. The social, economic, political, and energy demand contexts of the GCC are generally positive for attracting investments

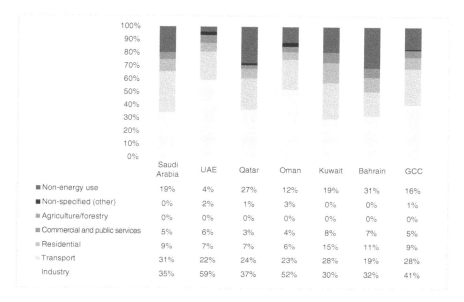

	Saudi Arabia	UAE	Qatar	Oman	Kuwait	Bahrain	GCC
■ Non-energy use	19%	4%	27%	12%	19%	31%	16%
■ Non-specified (other)	0%	2%	1%	3%	0%	0%	1%
■ Agriculture/forestry	0%	0%	0%	0%	0%	0%	0%
■ Commercial and public services	5%	6%	3%	4%	8%	7%	5%
■ Residential	9%	7%	7%	6%	15%	11%	9%
■ Transport	31%	22%	24%	23%	28%	19%	28%
Industry	35%	59%	37%	52%	30%	32%	41%

Figure 8.3 Distribution of total final energy consumption (TFEC) in MENA countries (IEA 2015b)

in renewables. Subsidized energy costs, however, are a major barrier to distributed renewable energy while utility scale deployments are hindered by legacy reliance on fossil based generation and lack of consideration for the opportunity costs associated with using fossil fuels to meet domestic energy demand.

Almost all GCC countries have set renewables targets, largely following the global trend of prioritizing the power sector (Table 8.2).

Regional targets for electricity generation from renewables range from no target in Oman to 25 per cent by 2030 in Dubai. As would be expected, based on regional renewable energy resources, capacity targets primarily relate only to solar and wind energy technologies (IRENA 2016a). Although renewable energy for the GCC power sector has promise, it is currently expected to play a very minimal role in industry and transportation. The International Renewable Energy Agency (IRENA) REMap 2030 assessment, which includes renewables opportunities in the UAE, Kuwait, and Saudi Arabia (IRENA 2016d), shows that transport is unlikely to have any significant contribution from renewable energy by 2030. This result is consistent across the GCC, given the national and subnational policy targets (Table 8.3) – which show only Qatar as having a national target for transport – the findings of IRENA's more detailed GCC assessment (IRENA 2016e) and the lack of consideration for renewables in Oman's transport sector (IRENA 2014b). Solar thermal energy for industrial process heat may be viable in the GCC, but its exploitation is not yet evident. In the near term, solar water heating (SWH) in the GCC buildings sector shows stronger potential.

Table 8.2 GCC renewable energy plans and targets (RCREEE 2015b; Fattouh and Sen 2016; REN21 2016)

| Country | RE strategy/ action plan/ program | Renewable energy targets | | | | Renewable power installed capacity and/or generation | Heating and cooling from renewable resources | Transportation energy from renewable resources |
		Primary energy from renewable resources	Final energy from renewable resources	Electricity generation from renewable resources	Technology specific share of electricity generation			
Bahrain				5% by 2030				
Kuwait				10% (no date)		Solar PV: 3.5 GW by 2030 CSP: 1.1 GW by 2030 Wind power: 3.1 GW by 2030		10% by 2020
Oman								
Qatar				2% by 2020 20% by 2030		Solar PV: 1.8 GW by 2014		
Saudi Arabia	Saudi Arabia Vision 2030*		4% by 2020			Unspecified renewable energy: 3.45 GW by 2020		
UAE	Dubai: Dubai Integrated Energy Strategy 2030		24% by 2021	No national target Abu Dhabi: 7% by 2020 Dubai: 7% by 2020 and 25% by 2030				

Table 8.3 GCC renewable energy policies (RCREEE 2015b; REN21 2016)

Country	Regulatory							Fiscal incentives and public financing				
	Feed-in tariff / premium payment	Electric utility quota/obligation/rps	Net metering/net billing	Transport obligation/mandate	Heat obligation/mandate	Tradable REC	Tendering	Capital subsidy, grant, or rebate	Investment or production tax credits	Reductions in sales, energy, VAT or other taxes	Energy production payment	Public investment, loans, or grants
Bahrain												o
Kuwait							o					
Oman												
Qatar												
Saudi Arabia												
UAE	●	▪*		●	▪*						●	●

Notes: o EXISTING NATIONAL (could also include subnational), ● EXISTING SUBNATIONAL (but no national), ▪ NEW (one or more policies of this type), R REVISED (one or more policies of this type), ▪* NEW SUBNATIONAL

While GCC countries have ambitious targets for adopting renewable energy in their power sectors, supporting policies and regulations are seriously lacking. With the exception of the UAE (particularly Dubai), supporting policy frameworks for renewables deployment are almost entirely absent (Table 8.3).

While several countries have recently released 'vision' documents that include renewables targets, few are backed up by published strategies and action plans. Thus, the motivations for renewable energy in the GCC are not transparent, but might include reducing energy related GHG emissions, enhancing energy security, boosting economic development, minimizing energy service costs – for both business and residential consumers – and improving energy service accessibility (Bazilian et al. 2010). Government objectives across GCC countries suggest that energy security and energy cost minimization are the primary drivers.

Some argue that a regional transition to clean energy can drive economic development through job creation (Sooriyaarachchi et al. 2015; IRENA 2016e), but the case is less than compelling as projections rely on renewables deployment targets that have yet to be backed by concrete strategies, road maps, policies and regulations. For instance, IRENA's clean energy job creation projections for the GCC were made before Saudi Arabia massively scaled back its renewables target from 54 gigawatts (GW) by 2032 to 9.5 GW by 2030

(MEES 2016c). Because 39 per cent of the IRENA employment projections are based on employment in Saudi Arabia, the figures seem highly optimistic, even though Saudi Arabia remains committed to job creation from renewable energy local content as part of Saudi Vision 2030 (MEES 2016b). GCC clean energy targets to date have generally lacked sufficient substance and stability to provide assurance that the clean energy sector will be central to regional economic diversification strategies. Also unclear is whether the installation, operation, and maintenance jobs (which are significant to renewables employment multipliers) are particularly desirable for GCC countries that need to create high-paying, knowledge-focused jobs for their citizens.

With regard to other possible motivations for renewable energy in the GCC, access to electricity is not a regional concern (AFED 2015) and climate change mitigation is not evident at the core of regional energy agendas. In fact, the INDCs of GCC countries show a lack of commitment to lowering GHG emissions (Dagnet et al. 2016). Only Oman has made a small and conditional GHG reduction commitment of 2 per cent relative to business-as-usual projections for 2030 (Table 8.4).

Table 8.4 GCC intended nationally determined contributions (INDCs)

Country	Unconditional target	Conditional target	Target year	Reference year	Conditions for implementation/ financial support required
Bahrain			N/A	N/A	Commitment depends highly on the level of international support in means of implementation
Kuwait			N/A	N/A	
Oman		2%	2030	Business as usual (BAU)	Implementation conditional on "the assistance that will be provided by the UNFCCC on finance, capacity building, and transfer of technology"
Qatar	Economic diversification of its economy away from hydrocarbons		2030	N/A	N/A

Saudi Arabia	Economic diversification that will deliver mitigation cobenefits of up to 130 MtCO$_2$e avoided annually by 2030	2030	N/A	N/A
United Arab Emirates	Pursuit of a portfolio of actions, including an increase of clean energy to 24% of the total energy mix		N/A	

Policies to stimulate deployment of renewable energy in the GCC

Analysis of the GCC energy landscape reveals that the regional driving force for renewables adoption is enhanced energy security at the lowest cost. It also seems clear that the regional focus is on options to reduce reliance on fossil based power generation to meet marginal demand more than for the multiple benefits of renewables deployment. Although climate change mitigation does not appear to be a key factor for renewables adoption, efforts to align carbon pricing policies with climate change mitigation policies can stimulate uptake of renewable energy uptake. The following sections assess energy and carbon pricing policies that could stimulate renewables deployment in the GCC. Among the policies outlined in this chapter, those considered most relevant to the GCC are highlighted.

Energy policies

Competitive renewable energy auctions

Experience in multiple countries shows renewables auctioning to be the most effective energy policy framework to stimulate deployment of low-cost, utility scale renewable power (IRENA 2013; IRENA and CEM 2015). In a renewables auction, the government issues a call for tenders to procure a certain capacity of renewables based electricity. Project developers participate in the auction by submitting a bid based on the per unit price of electricity at which they can deliver the project while acquiring an acceptable return on investment. The auctioning entity, usually the government, evaluates the bids on the basis of both price and other criteria, eventually signing a PPA with the successful bidder. Auctions differ from FIT schemes in that only selected project developers benefit from the support tariff and the tariff level is based on the prices indicated by the project developers in their bids during the auction process. Auctions can take several forms (IRENA 2013; Kylili and Fokaides 2015):

- **First price, sealed bid auction**: project developers submit sealed bids, and the awarded bidder pays the bid price. Usually, the auction aims to allocate a single project to a single developer.
- **Pay-as-bid, sealed bid auction**: project developers submit sealed bids, and the awarded bidders pay different prices for their awarded projects. Usually, the auction is seeking to acquire a total volume, which can be satisfied by multiple bidders.
- **Second price, sealed bid auction**: project developers submit sealed bids, and the awarded bidder pays the highest price of the losing bid.
- **Descending bid (or clock) auction**: starting from a high price, the auctioneer proposes multiple rounds of bidding with a slightly lower price in every new round; participants make their offers in terms of quantities they are willing to provide at the given price. The process continues until the quantity to be auctioned is reached at the lowest possible cost. Participants know each other's bids and can adjust accordingly as multiple bidding rounds proceed.
- **Hybrid auction**: a two-phase auction in which the first phase operates as a descending clock auction, followed by the second phase operating as a pay-as-bid, sealed bid auction.

The ability of auctions to deliver large-scale renewable electricity projects in a structured, cost-efficient and generally transparent manner is gaining increased interest globally. Recent auctions have achieved record low PPAs for utility scale solar PV in Peru ($0.048 per kilowatt hour [/kWh]), Mexico ($0.045/kWh), and Dubai ($0.0299/kWh) (IRENA 2016b). Beyond achieving low costs, auctions also offer design flexibility to suit a variety of contexts and enhanced certainty in both the price and quantity of renewable energy delivered. The resulting structured contracts also provide greater relative certainty as to how parties involved will share (or split) commitments and liabilities (IRENA and CEM 2015).

Auctions do have potential drawbacks, however, that include limited private sector and consumer engagement, relatively high administrative and transaction costs, and the possibility that a project will fail if awarded bidders prove unable to meet their delivery obligations (del Río and Linares 2014). A substantial amount of experience in auction design and implementation now makes it easier to avoid or minimize the inherent risks by following best practices (IRENA 2013; del Río and Linares 2014; IRENA and CEM 2015; Shrimali et al. 2016). Within the MENA context, Morocco and Dubai (UAE) recently completed first price, sealed bid auctions that can serve as case studies for regional implementation.

Morocco's auctions have a pre-qualification phase, in which the offering entity assesses the experience and financial and technical capacity of bidders, followed by an evaluation phase to select the winning bidder(s) according to their technical specifications, financial bid (financing and PPA), and contributions to local economic development (e.g., local content). Auctions to date have been technology specific, with wind projects receiving tariff commitments of 20 years and solar projects of 25 years. Compliance has been strict, with the PPAs clearly outlining penalties for delay and underperformance.

Assessment of Morocco's 160-megawatt (MW) Ouarzazate Noor 1 concentrating solar power (CSP) parabolic trough project shows that the auction was successful with 200 bidders engaging and a final awarded PPA of $0.189/kWh, which was 25 per cent lower than the price projected by the Moroccan Agency for Solar Energy (MASEN). At the time (2012), it was the lowest CSP tariff ever achieved (Carafa et al. 2016). The auction's success is attributed to policy development and financial de-risking. The former was achieved through the Moroccan government's clear policy commitment to develop solar energy, and its strong domestic institutional capacity to transform commitment into concrete projects. De-risking was achieved through the strong commitment of development finance institutions, government guarantee of necessary grid connections, and establishment of a solar resource profile for the Ouarzazate project site. Also important was the fact that MASEN would be part owner in the project company, ACWA Power Ouarzazate, as well as the electricity offtaker. Such assurances by the Moroccan government underpinned success in the next phases of the 500 MW Ouarzazate CSP project, including strong developer interest, and in PPAs declining further to $0.1567/kWh in the Noor 2 CSP project and $0.1541/kWh in the Noor 3 CSP project (MEED 2015).

Dubai has led in utility scale solar PV development. In March 2015, a PPA was signed for Dubai's first renewables independent power producer (IPP) as part of the second phase of the Mohammad bin Rashid Al Maktoum (MBR) Solar Park (Salman 2016a). The 25-year PPA for 200 MW of auctioned solar PV was signed at a record low price of $0.0584/kWh with electricity offtake scheduled to start in 2017. Similar to the success factors in Morocco, the Dubai Electricity and Water Authority (DEWA) is part owner (51 per cent) in the project consortium that won the bid and will be the electricity offtaker from a site that was established by the government. An auction in 2016 for the third phase of the MBR Park resulted in the lowest ever bid for solar PV of $0.0299/kWh (MEES 2016a). While this is a positive development with regard to solar pricing, which is a driving force for solar adoption in the GCC, the nearly 50 per cent reduction in tariff bids between 2015 and 2016 suggests that bidding has become extremely aggressive. Given that the lowest bidder and awarded consortium is led by Masdar, a UAE state-owned company, there is almost no chance of the project not being delivered. However, the extent of subsidization required to win the bid is unclear. Analysis of the PPA awarded by Dubai in 2015 suggests that the price of $0.0584/kWh was only achieved through extremely attractive financing terms offered by UAE banks, with debt financing at 86 per cent of the total project value at an interest rate near 4 per cent with a 27-year tenure. Also important were minimal costs for land and grid connection, as well as forward projections on improved technology performance from First Solar thin film panels to be deployed for the project in 2017. Given the many favorable factors required to achieve a price of less than $0.06/kWh, the sub $0.03/kWh prices currently being seen may be challenging to sustain.

Net metering for distributed renewables

High energy subsidies in place throughout the GCC undermine the cost-effectiveness of distributed renewables, particularly rooftop solar PV, in most locations. Therefore, policies directly aimed at deployment of distributed renewables, such as FITs and net metering, are not proposed as the optimal policies for stimulating regional uptake of renewable energy. As already stated, however, renewables auctions can be very limiting with regard to private sector engagement as small firms tend to be left out. For this reason, hybrid policies that include both FITs and auctions have been implemented in locations where both small and large renewables projects are desired (Couture et al. 2015).

The emirate of Dubai has implemented a net metering policy (Salman 2016b) and so stands out as one of the few MENA markets likely to see significant deployment of distributed solar power in the coming years. Anticipated electricity tariffs ranging from $0.08/kWh to $0.12/kWh for residential, commercial and industrial consumers will support uptake (Lahn 2016). The higher prices in Dubai, which are similar in all other UAE emirates except for Abu Dhabi, are for consumption levels more relevant to commercial and industrial consumers, making the economic potential for net metering most viable for these sectors (Griffiths and Mills 2016). Dubai's solar PV net metering policy, coupled with cost reflective electricity tariffs already in place, is anticipated to stimulate up to 1.5 GW of rooftop solar by 2030, thus playing a key role in the emirate's plan to have renewable energy generate 25 per cent of its electricity by 2030 and 75 per cent by 2050.

As GCC countries continue to implement energy subsidy reforms and the cost of distributed renewable energy continues to fall, other markets may find net metering an attractive option to reduce transaction costs and thus attract wider private sector engagement in distributed renewables.

Solar thermal in the buildings sector

The focus on cost for adoption of renewables in the GCC makes solar thermal for the buildings sector particularly relevant. Surprisingly, despite the excellent regional solar resources, no GCC country has yet to set a national target for solar water heating (SWH). Although SWH typically receives much less attention than solar power, it is a low-cost and effective means of improving energy performance in buildings (Urban et al. 2016). In Dubai, installation of solar water heaters to provide 75 per cent of domestic hot water requirements is mandatory in all new villas and labor accommodations

(RCREEE 2015a; Sgouridis et al. 2016). Given the cost-efficiency of SWH, similar SWH regulations should be implemented to counteract the reality that subsidized energy prices hinder deployment on a strictly economic basis.

Carbon pricing policies

The policies discussed to stimulate the adoption of renewable energy in the GCC are aimed at minimizing direct government financial outlays. Hence, these policy mechanisms are generally lacking any implicit or explicit price for carbon as they simply drive renewables adoption, based on cost-competitiveness relative to fossil energy sources. Carbon pricing policies, while being a fundamentally different mechanism from the policies described earlier, could be an effective means to stimulate adoption of renewable energy while simultaneously achieving broader regional imperatives for both energy and climate. Implementation of carbon pricing and related carbon intensity targets could deliver the following benefits (Lahn and Preston 2013):

- energy efficiency within the industrial, power and water sectors
- efficiency in energy consumption for buildings and vehicles
- stimulation of renewables deployment, and
- support for restructuring economies towards less energy-intensive sectors.

Two main policy options are most directly aligned with reducing carbon intensity. Under direct taxes on carbon emissions, emitters pay for the climate damage caused by their fuel use, with the tax serving as an incentive to switch to cleaner fuels. Emissions trading systems, often referred to as 'cap and trade' programs, set a target 'cap' on total emissions. The concept behind carbon trading, then, is that trading 'permits' are initially allocated or auctioned by the government, after which parties can buy, sell or trade the permits among themselves. For example, an entity that is unable to lower its own emissions can instead buy emission credits from another entity that can achieve higher reductions than strictly necessary under the larger plan to satisfy national or regional emission reduction targets. In effect, the carbon emissions become a commodity and have a market value among traders. At present, a direct carbon tax would be politically very challenging in the GCC, but other studies suggest that an ETS is potentially viable in the GCC context (Dargin 2010).

No MENA or GCC country has stated ambitions to establish a local or regional ETS (World Bank and Ecofys 2016), yet a recent study finds the region in an excellent position to develop a strong carbon market with binding caps that would cut emissions while also potentially generating revenue for renewables projects – and thus to take a lead in carbon trading globally. The region can look to examples in Europe, California (United States), Quebec (Canada) and Alberta (Canada) where ETS mechanisms have been implemented and are investing nearly 50 per cent (or more) of the funds generated in climate change mitigation technologies and approaches (Carl and Fedor 2016). The successes and failures of the EU ETS offer many lessons (de Perthuis and Trotignon 2014; Laing et al. 2014), but the ETS ambitions of China are perhaps most relevant to GCC countries.

China has launched ETS pilots in several provinces, with the ambition of developing a national ETS. Similarly, GCC countries could start with domestic pilots and expand to a regional system. A critical element in the opportunity to follow China's path, rather than try to adopt/adapt the EU experience, is that China, like the GCC countries, has a heavily regulated electricity sector and many state-owned enterprises (SOEs). This reality makes the design of an ETS particularly challenging in that regulatory and/or competition issues make it impossible for sectors with the highest emissions to directly pass carbon costs through to customers. Nonetheless, China has set specific short- and long-term carbon emission reduction targets and has launched ETS pilots in seven provinces, covering the electricity, industrial and buildings sectors (World Bank and Ecofys 2016). It can be anticipated that GCC countries would encounter the same major ETS design issues faced in the China pilots, including: strength of enforcement policies, design of the overall carbon cap, treatment of the electricity sector, strategy for allowance allocation, coverage of SOEs, management of allowance prices, and liquidity (Liu et al. 2015; Munnings et al. 2016).

Thus, an immediate policy suggestion for GCC countries is to monitor closely the implementation of China's ETS and identify successful practices that may be adopted. Among the practices to assess is how China has incorporated offsets for renewables projects into its trading schemes (Mo et al. 2016).

Realistically, national or regional ETS programs are a longer-term consideration for GCC countries. More actionable in the near term for the GCC are indirect carbon pricing measures, which include energy taxes and regulatory standards (OECD 2013). Although not energy taxation per se, energy subsidy reform is an important policy approach aligned with implicit carbon pricing (Kossoy et al. 2015). Following trends in the broader MENA region, subsidy reforms in the GCC since 2014 have been broad, covering natural gas, transport fuels, electricity and water (Fattouh et al. 2016; Lahn 2016). Further electricity pricing reforms will be important to stimulate regional adoption of distributed renewables. In parallel, increasing the cost of fossil fuels supplied to the power and water sectors will make renewables increasingly attractive.

Conclusions

Energy and climate policy are increasingly recognized as interrelated, particularly in the post-COP21 context in which reducing energy-related emissions is vital to climate change mitigation. Yet recently published visions and strategies to increase renewable energy in the GCC focus primarily on cost-effective power procurement, with the aim of ensuring energy security, as the driving force for renewables adoption. Climate change mitigation is not yet evident as central to the rationale for regional renewables adoption. If undertaken in a phased, step-wise manner, climate-oriented policies could begin to play a more important role. This chapter suggests catalyzing renewables deployment via a two-phase approach in which targeted energy policies are implemented immediately, followed by carbon pricing policies that build on energy subsidy reform efforts already underway.

With regard to near-term energy policies, GCC countries are well positioned to adopt the global trend of implementing renewables auctions to secure lowest cost energy supply in the power sector. As countries in the region, particularly Dubai and Morocco, gain experience with procuring large-scale power generation via auctions, the current approaches can be adapted to utility scale renewable energy procurement. Key elements of success to replicate include strong government support and, more specifically, provision of optimal project locations, certainty of grid access, and security of electricity offtake. These factors have attracted significant project developer interest while supporting access to low-cost project financing. If GCC countries can accelerate renewables deployment using the auction approach for utility scale projects, other forms of renewable energy, particularly distributed renewables, may be a future direction for the region. To quickly capture potential energy savings, SWH in buildings is a distributed renewables approach that should be supported immediately throughout the GCC, noting that appropriate regulations may need to be put in place given the low cost of current tariffs. Widespread adoption of distributed renewable power will require further energy subsidy reform so that electricity prices make support policies, such as net metering, economically viable.

Indeed, energy subsidy reforms are the first step toward leveraging a climate or carbon-oriented policy framework that can further stimulate renewables deployment in the region. For carbon pricing policies, a gradual and clearly defined pathway with both short- and long-term initiatives is essential.

In the short term, energy subsidy reform and pricing carbon emissions should be the primary focus. Energy subsidy reforms already being implemented throughout the GCC have the effect of indirectly increasing the cost of carbon emissions, and should be continued so that regional energy prices eventually become fully cost reflective. Placing a price on carbon emissions is a critical step that can directly and indirectly support renewables adoption. In the GCC, it may initially be done via taxes on fuels already subjected to subsidy reforms. Energy taxation is a clear form of implicit carbon pricing that would be foundational for explicit carbon pricing. Although it would be politically challenging for GCC countries to impose direct carbon emission taxes on sectors that are core to their economies, the dual benefits of generating government revenues and curtailing carbon emissions may, in time, make it more feasible.

Over the long term, GCC countries may be able to pursue implementation of ETS at the country and/or regional level for explicit carbon pricing to support renewables deployment, building on other forms of carbon pricing undertaken in the near term. Based on international practices, ETS funds could be linked to supporting clean energy technologies more directly than a straight carbon tax. The GCC could look to China, which has several pilot projects underway, for relevant ETS best practices, noting an important distinction. China has made strategic commitments to move toward a more service-oriented economy, i.e., away from energy-intensive industries, and has strategically planned carbon emission reductions to support this shift. GCC countries have yet to integrate climate and economic policies, perhaps because they are much further away from focusing on service-oriented industries for economic growth.

References

Abdmouleh Z, Alammari RAM, and Gastli A (2015a) Recommendations on renewable energy policies for the GCC countries. *Renewable and Sustainable Energy Reviews* 50:1181–1191.

Abdmouleh Z, Alammari RAM, and Gastli A (2015b) Review of policies encouraging renewable energy integration and best practices. *Renewable and Sustainable Energy Reviews* 45:249–262.

AFED (Arab Forum for Environment and Development) (2015) Arab environment: sustainable consumption. Annual report of Arab Forum for Environment and Development 2015. Technical Publications, Beirut.

Al-Amir J, and Abu-Hijleh B (2013) Strategies and policies from promoting the use of renewable energy resource in the UAE. *Renewable and Sustainable Energy Reviews* 26:660–667.

Alnaser WE, and Alnaser NW (2011) The status of renewable energy in the GCC countries. *Renewable and Sustainable Energy Reviews* 15(6):3074–3098.

Anand M (2016) Global solar demand monitor: Q2 2016, GTM Research. www.greentechmedia.com/research/report/global-solar-demand-monitor-q2-2016. Accessed Aug 2016.

APICORP Energy Research (2016a) Energy price reform in the GCC: Long road ahead. *APICORP Energy Research* 1(4), Arab Petroleum Investments Corporation.

APICORP Energy Research (2016b) MENA power investment: Finance and reform challenges. *APICORP Energy Research* 1(7), Arab Petroleum Investments Corporation.

Atalay Y, Biermann F, and Kalfagianni A (2016) Adoption of renewable energy technologies in oil-rich countries: explaining policy variation in the Gulf Cooperation Council states. *Renewable Energy* 85:206–214.

Bazilian M, Outhred H, Miller A et al. (2010) Opinion: An energy policy approach to climate change. *Energy for Sustainable Development* 14(4):253–255.

Becker B, and Fischer D (2013) Promoting renewable electricity generation in emerging economies. *Energy Policy* 56:446–455.

Bhutto AW, Bazmi AA, Zahedi G et al. (2014) A review of progress in renewable energy implementation in the Gulf Cooperation Council countries. *Journal of Cleaner Production* 71:168–180.

Carafa L, Frisari G, and Vidican G (2016) Electricity transition in the Middle East and North Africa: a de-risking governance approach. *Journal of Cleaner Production* 128:34–47.

Carl J, and Fedor D (2016) Tracking global carbon revenues: a survey of carbon taxes versus cap-and-trade in the real world. *Energy Policy* 96:50–77.

Charles C, Moerenhout T, and Bridle R (2014) The context of fossil-fuel subsidies in the GCC region and their impact on renewable energy development. International Institute for Sustainable Development, Winnipeg, Canada.

Couture TD, Jacobs D, Rickerson W et al. (2015) The next generation of renewable electricity policy. National Renewable Energy Laboratory (NREL), Golden, CO.

Dagnet Y, Waskow D, Elliott C et al. (2016) Staying on track from Paris: advancing the key elements of the Paris Agreement. World Resources Institute, Washington, DC.

Dargin J (2010) The development of a Gulf carbon platform: mapping out the Gulf Cooperation Council carbon exchange. Dubai School of Government, Harvard Kennedy School, Cambridge, MA.

de Perthuis C, and Trotignon R (2014) Governance of CO_2 markets: lessons from the EU ETS. *Energy Policy* 75:100–106.

del Río P, and Linares P (2014) Back to the future? Rethinking auctions for renewable electricity support. *Renewable and Sustainable Energy Reviews* 35:42–56.

El-Katiri L, and Fattouh B (2015) A brief political economy of energy subsidies in the Middle East and North Africa. Oxford Institute for Energy Studies, Oxford, UK.

Fattouh B, and El-Katiri L (2013) Energy subsidies in the Middle East and North Africa. *Energy Strategy Reviews* 2(1):108–115.

Fattouh B, and Sen A (2016) Saudi Arabia's Vision 2030, oil policy and the evolution of the energy sector. Oxford Institute for Energy Studies, Oxford.

Fattouh B, Sen A, and Moerenhout T (2016) Striking the right balance? GCC energy pricing reforms in a low price environment. Oxford Institute for Energy Studies, Oxford.

Gawel E, Strunz S, and Lehmann P (2014) A public choice view on the climate and energy policy mix in the EU: how do the emissions trading scheme and support for renewable energies interact? *Energy Policy* 64:175–182.

Griffiths S, and Mills R (2016) Potential of rooftop solar photovoltaics in the energy system evolution of the United Arab Emirates. *Energy Strategy Reviews* 9:1–7.

Haas R, Panzer C, Resch G et al. (2011) A historical review of promotion strategies for electricity from renewable energy sources in EU countries. *Renewable and Sustainable Energy Reviews* 15(2):1003–1034.

Hirth L (2013) The market value of variable renewables. The effect of solar wind power variability on their relative price. *Energy Economics* 38:218–236.

Hoppe T, Coenen F, and van den Berg M (2016) Illustrating the use of concepts from the discipline of policy studies in energy research: an explorative literature review. *Energy Research & Social Science* 21:12–32.

IEA (International Energy Agency) (2015a) CO_2 Emissions from Fuel Combustion, OECD/IEA, Paris.

IEA (2015b) Energy Balances of Non-OECD Countries 2015. OECD/IEA, Paris.

IEA-RETD (2016) RE TRANSITION: Transitioning to Policy Frameworks for Cost-Competitive Renewables. IEA Technology Collaboration Programme for Renewable Energy Technology Deployment (IEA-RETD), Utrecht, the Netherlands.

IMF (International Monetary Fund) (2016) Economic diversification in oil-exporting Arab countries. Paper presented at annual meeting of Arab ministers of finance, Manama, Bahrain, April 2016.

IRENA (International Renewable Energy Agency) (2012) Evaluating policies in support of the deployment of renewable power. IRENA, Abu Dhabi.

IRENA (2013) Renewable Energy Auctions in Developing Countries. IRENA, Abu Dhabi.

IRENA (2014a) Adapting Renewable Energy Policies to Dynamic Market Conditions. IRENA, Abu Dhabi.

IRENA (2014b) Sultanate of Oman: Renewables Readiness Assessment. IRENA, Abu Dhabi.

IRENA (2015a) Renewable Power Generation Costs in 2014. IRENA, Abu Dhabi.

IRENA (2015b) REthinking Energy: Renewable Energy and Climate Change. IRENA, Abu Dhabi.

IRENA (2016a) Investment opportunities in the GCC: Suitability maps for grid-connected and off-grid solar and wind projects. IRENA, Abu Dhabi.

IRENA (2016b) Letting in the Light: How solar Photovoltaics will Revolutionise the Electricity System. IRENA, Abu Dhabi.

IRENA (2016c) The Power to Change: Solar and Wind Cost Reduction Potential to 2025. IRENA, Abu Dhabi.

IRENA (2016d) REmap: Roadmap for a Renewable Energy Future, 2016 Edition. IRENA, Abu Dhabi.

IRENA (2016e) Renewable Energy Market Analysis: The GCC Region. IRENA, Abu Dhabi.

IRENA and CEM (Clean Energy Ministerial) (2015) Renewable Energy Auctions – A Guide to Design. IRENA, Abu Dhabi.

IRENA and League of Arab States (2014) Pan-Arab Renewable Energy Strategy 2030. IRENA, Abu Dhabi.

Khatib H, and Difiglio C (2016) Economics of nuclear and renewables. *Energy Policy* 96:740–750.

Kombargi R, Waterlander O, Sarraf G et al. (2010) Gas Shortage in the GCC: How to Bridge the Gap. Booz & Company, Abu Dhabi.

Kossoy A, Peszko G, Oppermann K et al. (2015) State and trends of carbon pricing 2015. World Bank, Washington, DC.

Krane J (2015) Stability versus sustainability: Energy policy in the Gulf monarchies. *Energy Journal* 36(4):1–21.

Krane J, and Wright S (2014) Qatar 'rises above' its region: geopolitics and the rejection of the GCC gas market. Research paper, Kuwait Programme on Development, Governance and Globalisation in the Gulf States. London School of Economics and Political Science, London.

Kylili A, and Fokaides PA (2015) Competitive auction mechanisms for the promotion renewable energy technologies: The case of the 50 MW photovoltaics projects in Cyprus. *Renewable and Sustainable Energy Reviews* 42:226–233.

Lahn G (2016) Fuel, Food and Utilities Price Reforms in the GCC A Wake-up Call for Business. Royal Institute of International Affairs, London.

Lahn G, and Preston F (2013) Targets to promote energy savings in the Gulf Cooperation Council states. *Energy Strategy Reviews* 2(1):19–30.

Laing T, Sato M, Grubb M et al. (2014) The effects and side-effects of the EU emissions trading scheme. *Wiley Interdisciplinary Reviews: Climate Change* 5(4):509–519.

Lazard (2015) Lazard levelized cost of energy analysis 9.0. Lazard, New York.

Lehmann P, and Gawel E (2013) Why should support schemes for renewable electricity complement the EU emissions trading scheme? *Energy Policy* 52:597–607.

Lilliestam J, and Patt A (2015) Barriers, risks and policies for renewables in the Gulf states. *Energies* 8(8):8263–8285.

Liu L, Chen C, Zhao Y et al. (2015) China's carbon-emissions trading: overview, challenges and future. *Renewable and Sustainable Energy Reviews* 49:254–266.

Luomi M (2014) Mainstreaming Climate Policy in the Gulf Cooperation Council States. Oxford Institute for Energy Studies, Oxford, UK.

Matar W, Murphy F, Pierru A et al. (2015) Lowering Saudi Arabia's fuel consumption and energy system costs without increasing end consumer prices. *Energy Economics* 49:558–569.

MEED (2015) MENA Power 2016: Investing in the Future. MEED, Dubai.

MEES (Middle East Economic Survey) (2016a) Dubai sets new PV cost benchmark in 800 MW phase three of solar park. *Middle East Economic Survey* 59(26):8.

MEES (2016b) Saudi Arabia's transformation plan already running out of time. *Middle East Economic Survey* 59(23):15–17.

MEES (2016c) Saudi kicks off new solar projects, gets realistic with long-term goals. *Middle East Economic Survey* 59(23):8.

MEES (2016d) Will the 'golden age of gas' ever arrive? *Middle East Economic Survey* 59(24):4–5.

Merrill L, Bassi AM, Bridle R et al. (2016) Tackling Fossil Fuel Subsidies and Climate Change: Levelling the Energy Playing Field. Nordic Council of Ministers, Copenhagen.

Mezher T, Dawelbait G, and Abbas Z (2012) Renewable energy policy options for Abu Dhabi: drivers and barriers. *Energy Policy* 42:315–328.

Michaels L, and Tal A (2015) Convergence and conflict with the 'National Interest': why Israel abandoned its climate policy. *Energy Policy* 87:480–485.

Mo J-L, Agnolucci P, Jiang M-R et al. (2016) The impact of Chinese carbon emission trading scheme (ETS) on low carbon energy (LCE) investment. *Energy Policy* 89:271–283.

Mondal MAH, Kennedy S, and Mezher T (2014) Long-term optimization of United Arab Emirates energy future: policy implications. *Applied Energy* 114:466–474.

Munnings C, Morgenstern RD, Wang Z et al. (2016) Assessing the design of three carbon trading pilot programs in China. *Energy Policy* 96:688–699.

OECD (Organisation for Economic Co-operation and Development) (2013) Climate and carbon: aligning prices and policies. OECD Publishing, Paris.

Olivier JGJ, Janssens-Maenhout G, Muntean M et al. (2015) Trends in Global CO_2 Emissions: 2015 Report. PBL Netherlands Environmental Assessment Agency, The Hague, the Netherlands.

Onifade TT (2016) Hybrid renewable energy support policy in the power sector: the contracts for difference and capacity market case study. *Energy Policy* 95:390–401.

Pyrgou A, Kylili A, and Fokaides PA (2016) The future of the Feed-in Tariff (FiT) scheme in Europe: the case of photovoltaics. *Energy Policy* 95:94–102.

RCREEE (Regional Center for Renewable Energy and Energy Efficiency) (2015a) Arab Future Energy Index 2015: Energy Efficiency. RCREEE, Cairo.

RCREEE (2015b) Arab Future Energy Index 2015: Renewable Energy. RCREEE, Cairo.

REN21 (Renewable Energy Policy Network for the 21st Century) (2016) Renewables 2016 Global Status Report. REN21 Secretariat, Paris.

REN21, IRENA (International Renewable Energy Agency), United Arab Emirates (2013) MENA Renewables Status Report. REN21 Secretariat, Paris.

Salman W (2016a) DEWA signs power purchase agreement and shareholder agreement for second-phase 200 MW PV plant at Mohammad bin Rashid Al Maktoum Solar Park. UAE State of Energy Report 2016. United Arab Emirates Ministry of Energy, Dubai.

Salman W (2016b) The Shams Dubai initiative. UAE State of Energy Report 2016. United Arab Emirates Ministry of Energy, Dubai.

Sdralevich C, Sab R, Zouhar Y et al. (2014) Subsidy Reform in the Middle East and North Africa: Recent Challenges and Progress Ahead. IMF, Washington, DC.

Sgouridis S, Abdullah A, Griffiths S et al. (2016) RE-mapping the UAE's energy transition: an economy-wide assessment of renewable energy options and their policy implications. *Renewable and Sustainable Energy Reviews* 55:1166–1180.

Sgouridis S, Griffiths S, Kennedy S et al. (2013) A sustainable energy transition strategy for the United Arab Emirates: evaluation of options using an Integrated Energy Model. *Energy Strategy Reviews* 2(1):8–18.

Shrimali G, Konda C, and Farooquee AA (2016) Designing renewable energy auctions for India: managing risks to maximize deployment and cost-effectiveness. *Renewable Energy* 97:656–670.

Sooriyaarachchi TM, Tsai IT, El Khatib S et al. (2015) Job creation potentials and skill requirements in PV, CSP, wind, water-to-energy and energy efficiency value chains. *Renewable and Sustainable Energy Reviews* 52:653–668.

Stevens P, and Lahn G (2011) Burning Oil to Keep Cool: The Hidden Energy Crisis in Saudi Arabia. Chatham House, London.

UAE Crown Prince Court and Ministry of Foreign Affairs (2014) Natural gas: an assessment of global trends and UAE development: a joint white paper (unpublished).

Urban F, Geall S, and Wang Y (2016) Solar PV and solar water heaters in China: different pathways to low carbon energy. *Renewable and Sustainable Energy Reviews* 64:531–542.

Verme P (2016) Subsidy reforms in the Middle East and North Africa region: a review. *Policy research* working paper 7754. World Bank Group, Washington, DC.

World Bank and Ecofys (2016) Carbon Pricing Watch 2016. World Bank, Washington, DC.

WRI (World Resources Institute) (2016) CAIT climate data explorer: Paris contributions map. https://cait.wri.org/indc/. Accessed 8 Aug 2016.

9 Potential impacts of solar energy integration on fuel mix strategies in Qatar

Moiz Bohra, Nasreddine El-Dehaibi, Antonio Sanfilippo and Marwan Khraisheh

Abstract

Qatar plans to generate 2 per cent of its electricity from solar energy by 2020 and 20 per cent by 2030. Considering the country's rapid projected electricity demand growth, this chapter analyzes the economics of deploying solar photovoltaic (PV) energy, specifically the cost savings that could be achieved by replacing oil and gas for electricity generation and for transport with solar energy.

The chapter develops a cost utility function, based on nonlinear programming (NLP), to optimize the savings/returns that both Qatari consumers and the Qatari government can derive from diverse fuel mix strategies. To establish the cost-effectiveness of any given fuel mix strategy, the chapter takes six factors into account: oil price; gas price; oil subsidy; gas subsidy; levelized capital and fixed operation and maintenance cost of energy from gas (gas LCO&M); and the introduction of a carbon tax.

Policy relevant insights

In the context of plummeting costs for solar photovoltaic (PV) energy, investments in solar energy to displace domestic use of oil and natural gas in Qatar is cost-effective in most hydrocarbon price scenarios. These findings suggest policy actions that could be taken to promote adoption of solar PV.

- Reduce or curtail subsidies for electricity generated from natural gas to level the field for solar energy.∗
- Maximize cost-savings achievable through solar PV adoption by aligning investments with the return opportunity, based on global oil prices:
  - when oil is lower than $90/barrel (bbl), deploy solar energy to displace more gas than oil; and

(continued)

(continued)

- ○ when oil is higher than $90/bbl, deploy solar energy to displace more oil than gas.

- Reinvest cost-savings achieved through solar PV adoption to help consumers switch to renewable energy technologies, such as building integrated PV and electric vehicles (EVs).
- Avoid building new gas-fired power stations to meet growing electricity demand, preferring the use of building integrated PV applications and solar power plants.

* This policy has been in place since September 2015, when the average residential tariff for electricity increased from $0.02 per kilowatt hour (/kWh) to $0.036/kWh.

The potential for solar in power generation and electric transport

Natural gas is the backbone of Qatar's economy. It generates more than half of the country's export revenue (Center for International Development at Harvard University n.d.), produces virtually all of the electricity in the country, and is a major feedstock for the downstream petrochemical industry. The prospect that renewable energy can economically displace domestic gas consumption and boost gas exports is therefore appealing. Similar arguments apply to the possibility of using renewable energy to reduce oil consumption.

This chapter analyzes cost–savings that Qatar could achieve by replacing oil and gas with solar photovoltaic (PV) energy. Such a replacement is mandated by Qatar's current national targets for solar energy adoption of 2 per cent of national electricity production by 2020 and 20 per cent by 2030 (REN21 2016, table R17). Using the electricity generation forecasting methodology and results described in Sanfilippo and Pederson (2016), the expected solar energy generation in 2020 and 2030 (measured in terawatt hours or TWh) can be estimated as shown in Table 9.1.[1]

Introducing solar energy could replace natural gas used for electricity production, either by cutting production at existing gas-fired power plants or displacing planned gas-fired power plants, and oil in transport through deployment of electric vehicles (EVs). The chapter aims to evaluate the cost utility of various fuel mix strategies in Qatar emerging from the use of solar PV for electricity generation to replace oil and gas.

To accomplish this goal, the analysis develops a cost utility function, based on nonlinear programming (NLP), to optimize the savings/returns that both Qatari consumers and the Qatari government can derive from diverse fuel mix

Table 9.1 Qatar electricity generation forecasts for 2020 and 2030 (see Sanfilippo and Pederson 2016 for 2020 forecast and methodology for 2030 forecasts)

2020			2030		
Total electricity generated	Qatar's national target for solar energy adoption (QNV 2008)	Electricity generated from solar	Total electricity generated	Qatar's national target for solar energy adoption (QNV 2008)	Electricity generated from solar
57.5 TWh	2%	1.15 TWh	61.9 TWh	20%	12.38 TWh

strategies. To establish the cost-effectiveness of any given fuel mix strategy, the chapter takes six factors into account: oil price; gas price; oil subsidy; gas subsidy; levelized capital and fixed operation and maintenance cost of energy from gas (gas LCO&M); and the introduction of a carbon tax. Sources of savings include the reduction of gas and oil subsidies, hypothetical carbon tax savings emerging from the reduction of domestic oil and gas consumption, and fixed cost reductions achieved by reducing electricity generation from natural gas.

The main research question addressed in this chapter is how can Qatar maximize savings by replacing domestic oil and gas consumption with utility scale solar energy? This question is answered by fulfilling three tasks:

1 Establish how much electricity production can be satisfied through solar energy in 2020 and 2030;
2 Determine the optimal distribution of solar PV energy in replacing oil and gas in terms of money saved per megawatt hour (MWh) of solar energy introduced in scenarios with diverse oil and gas prices, oil and gas subsidies, carbon tax amounts, and gas LCO&M costs; and
3 Individuate the relevant policy insights that emerge from the cost optimal distribution of solar PV energy, and the policy undertakings that such insights support.

Use of solar electricity generation could yield natural gas savings of 0.24 million tonnes of oil equivalent (Mtoe) in 2020 and 2.13 Mtoe by 2030 (Sanfilippo and Pederson 2016), with ensuing economic and environmental benefits. For example, the natural gas saved could be repurposed for additional natural gas trade to increase the country's revenues or be left untapped to extend the lifetime of the country's natural gas reserves. In terms of environmental benefits, such natural gas savings would reduce carbon dioxide (CO_2) emissions in Qatar by 0.51 million tonnes (Mt) by 2020 and 4.5 Mt by 2030 (Sanfilippo and Pederson 2016).

Alternatively, replacing oil with solar PV allows for growth in the EV market in Qatar. The oil savings would offer economic advantages by increasing oil sales with no additional extraction costs and yield even greater environmental benefits than gas savings since oil has a higher CO_2 emission coefficient than gas (117 pounds [lbs.] vs. 157.2 lbs. per million British thermal units [MMBtu]) (EIA 2016a). Additionally, such a prospect would help Qatar progress toward its plan to power 10 per cent of its transportation with renewable resources by 2020 (REN21 2016, Table R24).

The emerging results indicate that cost-savings per megawatt hour (/MWh) of solar energy introduced remain constant across the nationally mandated 2020 (lower) and 2030 (higher) PV adoption targets. Thanks to plummeting PV LCOE costs, investments in solar energy are cost-effective with most hydrocarbon price scenarios. When the price of oil is lower than $90 per oil barrel (bbl), fuel mix strategies in which solar energy replaces more gas than oil tend to offer higher savings/returns. When the price of oil is higher than $90/bbl, fuel mix strategies in which solar energy replaces more oil than gas tend offer higher savings/returns. The oil price has the greatest impact on savings/returns, closely followed by oil subsidy, while gas LCO&M, gas subsidy and the gas price have medium impact, and the carbon tax at $8 per tonne of carbon dioxide equivalent (tCO_2e) only has a marginal impact. The impacts of gas LCO&M and the carbon tax of up to $10/$tCO_2e$ on the cost-effectiveness of fuel mix strategies are far less linear as compared with other factors, and therefore less predictable as instruments of change.

The analysis does not consider government investments needed to support the introduction of electric vehicles (EVs) and additional costs for consumers. It is reasonable to assume that additional consumer costs would be offset by the lower energy cost per mile of EVs compared with internal combustion engine (ICE) vehicles and by reduced purchases of new ICE vehicles. In addition, EV charging stations require modest infrastructure investments as they can leverage the existing electrical grid and have low maintenance costs. For example, it costs about $1,000 to upgrade a home outlet or electric panel to build a home EV charging station (National Research Council 2015) and as little as $6,500 to build a direct current (DC) fast charging station (Ingram 2014). Annual maintenance costs vary between $25 and $50 per EV charging unit (May and Mattila 2009). By contrast, the cost of a gasoline station tends to be considerably higher, from several hundred thousand US dollars up to millions of dollars (Dean n.d.), with an average annual operational cost of $250,000 plus $160,000 to buy and stock products.[2] Therefore, building EV charging stations in place of new or refurbished gasoline stations may even reduce costs in the medium/long term.

As Qatar and other Gulf Cooperation Council (GCC) countries start implementing their national visions for solar energy adoption, determining which policies provide the best regulatory environment to achieve the specified targets is an important step. Such policies need to consider regulations and incentives that local policymakers can control, such as energy related subsidies and taxes, as well as global market conditions that set the price of fossil fuel and renewable energies. In light of increasing PV adoption, the chapter aims to provide an analytical platform to support decision-making about fuel mix policy in Qatar. This assessment provides policymakers with useful insights in determining which fuel mix strategies are more cost-effective when introducing policies that promote the use of solar energy.

Analytical investigations of fuel mix strategies

Studies of fuel mix strategies have focused on the development of mathematical models that analyze and optimize the environmental and economic benefits, energy security and power system efficiency of diverse fuel types. A review of these studies helps position the work described in this chapter with regard to the modeling approach chosen and its purpose.

One of the earliest fuel mix studies focused on environmental factors, suggesting that the primary stimulus of CO_2 emissions reduction is decreased manufacturing energy intensity due to higher efficiency in electricity generation and greater use of nuclear power in place of oil (Torvanger 1991). This study uses a Divisia index approach (Divisia 1926) to evaluate the reduction of CO_2 emissions in nine countries belonging to the Organisation for Economic Co-operation and Development (OECD) for the period 1973–1987, considering the use of four fuels (coal, oil, gas and nuclear) in six subsectors of manufacturing.

A study estimating pollutant emission scenarios in Malaysia for 2020 concluded that CO_2, sulfur dioxide (SO_2), and nitrogen oxide (NO_x) emissions would increase significantly based on the Fuel Diversification Strategy incorporated in the Malaysian Energy Policy in 1999 (Jafar et al. 2008). The Strategy targeted a gradual change in fuel use from 74.9 per cent gas, 9.7 per cent coal, 10.4 per cent hydro, and 5 per cent petroleum in 2000 to 40 per cent gas, 30 per cent hydro, 29 per cent coal, and 1 per cent petroleum by 2020. The assessment of CO_2, SO_2, and NOx emissions was carried out using Leontief's input-output framework, which is based on a three sector aggregation of the economy and estimates fuel emissions according to the guidelines issued by the Intergovernmental Panel on Climate Change (IPCC).

Widening the focus to include economic and power system efficiency factors, another study found that the dominance of combined cycle gas turbines (CCGTs) in the United Kingdom could be accounted for by correlating different fuels (coal, gas, and nuclear) with electricity costs and CO_2 emissions (Roques et al. 2008). This study uses the Mean-Variance Portfolio theory (Markowitz 1952) to identify optimal generation portfolios as characterized by fuel type, CO_2 emissions, and electricity price risk in liberalized electricity markets. While the study focuses on fossil and nuclear fuels, the approach could in principle be extended to include renewables.

Looking into power generation planning, a study developed for the Canary Islands highlighted inefficiencies of the electricity generating mix in terms of cost, risk and lack of diversification, suggesting the use of renewable energy sources and introduction of natural gas to generate electricity to increase efficiency and reduce CO_2 emissions (Marrero et al. 2010). This study also uses mean variance portfolio theory to assess the natural gas and renewables strategy proposed for the electricity industry in the 2006 energy plan of the Canaries, considering the average cost and the risk associated with the alternatives for electricity generation. Use of this approach for the problem addressed in this chapter would have to take into consideration that, as a major gas exporter, Qatar may have an advantage in using natural gas for electricity generation.

An evaluation of China's medium-term (2020) plans for power generation technologies and its power generation portfolio concludes that sustainable strategies can be achieved through energy conservation, energy efficiency and replacement of fossil fuels with renewable energy (Zhu and Fan 2010). This study measures the overall cost risk of the power generation portfolio as a function of the cost risk of each power generation technology. It also analyzes future scenarios that include fossil fuels, renewable energy and CO_2 emission constraints, and uses Pareto optimization to generate efficient fuel mix portfolios that enhance China's energy security.

Shifting the focus to efficiency of energy distribution, an evaluation of several energy scenarios that include solar, wind and biomass energy resources, singly or in combination, concludes that a significant reduction in energy losses can be achieved in all scenarios analyzed (Atwa et al. 2010). This study uses mixed integer NLP to optimize the allocation of different types of distributed renewable energy resources in the distribution system to minimize energy losses. The objective function that implements the optimization aims to minimize energy losses in the distribution system subject to network system constraints, including voltage limits, the feeders' capacity, the maximum penetration limit and the discrete size of the available distributed renewable energy resources.

A three step approach to calculate optimal fuel mix strategies

The objective of this study differs from past efforts, as it aims to establish the relative percentages of natural gas and oil that should be replaced by solar energy to maximize savings. The approach adopted is thus adjusted accordingly. In terms of mathematical modeling methods, this analysis follows Atwa et al. (2010) in using NLP as an optimization technique. More specifically, NLP is used to develop a function that measures the economic utility of diverse fuel mix scenarios emerging from the replacement of oil and natural gas with solar energy. The NLP objective function optimizes the shares of oil and gas replaced by solar energy to maximize returns in diverse scenarios, based on a number of exogenous variables, factors dependent on general market conditions such as oil and gas prices, gas LCO&M, and endogenous variables, which are those emerging from policy decisions such as oil/gas subsidies and a carbon tax. NLP is a process for solving an optimization problem constrained by a system of equalities and inequalities, where some constraints or the objective function itself are nonlinear (Bertsekas 1999). In this study, the objective function is nonlinear since most of the constraints, especially gas LCO&M and the carbon tax, exhibit nonlinear behavior.

Developing the utility function

To develop future scenarios, the study combines a range of exogenous and endogenous variables subject to a number of constraints determined by alternative variable values and the dependence among variables. The utility function optimizes the amount of oil and gas that should be replaced by solar for any scenario, based on three sources of savings: subsidy returns and electricity generation savings for the Qatari government; carbon tax savings for energy consumers in Qatar; and lower oil and gas consumption.

Subsidy returns

Subsidy returns are savings derived from displacing domestic oil and gas consumption with solar energy, thus increasing exports of oil and gas, as shown in equation (1), which defines the subsidy returns from oil and gas for any given fuel mix scenario. The 'oil replaced' and 'gas replaced' variables indicate how much oil and gas are replaced by solar energy. These replacements consider efficiencies for converting gas to electricity, and the energy use equivalence between gasoline powered and electric vehicles. Oil and gas prices are dictated by the international market price for each commodity, $/bbl for oil and $/MMBtu for gas. Subsidized prices are the purchasing price of oil and gas for local distributors, including Qatar Energy and Water Company (QEWC) and Qatar Fuel Company (Woqod). The subsidy return is calculated assuming that oil and gas replaced by solar energy are sold at international prices, of course assuming that global prices are not affected by the higher amount.

$$\text{subsidy returns} = \frac{\begin{array}{l} \text{oil replaced} * (\text{oil price} - \text{subsidized oil price}) + \\ \text{gas replaced} * (\text{gas price} - \text{subsidized gas price}) \end{array}}{\text{solar PV adopted}} \qquad (1)$$

Carbon tax savings

Carbon tax savings identify consumer savings emerging from the reduction of CO_2 emissions through the replacement of domestic oil and gas use with solar energy, as described in equation (2). CO_2 emissions from oil and gas are constants that define the amount of CO_2 emitted per unit of the commodity consumed (Table 9.3). The carbon tax is the hypothetical tax paid on CO_2 emissions ($/tCO_2$e). With continued pressure from international coalitions to adopt measures to mitigate the negative outcomes of climate change, it is important for Qatar to be prepared for a scenario in which an internationally binding carbon tax is enforced. Under such a scenario, carbon tax savings through solar energy adoption would generate consumer benefits, which increases the value of the utility function for a given fuel mix strategy. Carbon tax savings could also generate benefits for the Qatari government if countries around the world should start to tax CO_2 emissions from imported goods (Baker et al. 2017), by providing a credit to offset importing country taxes.

$$\text{carbon tax saving} = \frac{\left[\begin{array}{l}(\text{oil replaced} * CO_2 \text{ emissions from oil}) + \\ (\text{gas replaced} * CO_2 \text{ emissions from gas})\end{array}\right] * \text{carbon tax}}{\text{solar PV target}} \qquad (2)$$

Electricity generation savings

Savings from reduced gas fired electricity generation are achieved by partial replacement of electricity generation from natural gas with solar energy, as described in equation (3). Fuel costs are not added in equation (3) as these are already included in subsidy returns. The 'replaced gas powered electricity' variable is derived from the 'gas replaced' variable, considering efficiencies in the conversion of gas to electricity.

$$\text{electricity generation savings} = \frac{\text{replaced gas} - \text{powered electricity} * \text{gas LCO\&M}}{\text{solar PV target}} \qquad (3)$$

Total savings

The overall utility function in equation (4) evaluates the total return as USD saved per MWh of solar energy introduced, assuming Qatar will meet the 2020 and 2030 solar energy adoption targets. When the total returns are greater than the value of a given PV LCOE value, the adoption of solar energy creates a surplus and is therefore an economically viable option.

$$\text{total returns} = \text{subsidy returns} + \text{carbon tax saving} + \text{electricity generation savings} \qquad (4)$$

Defining variables and data

With reference to the cost-saving equations (1) through (3), six inputs are needed to determine the output of total returns from investing in solar. Some of these inputs are endogenous variables, the value setting of which is within Qatar's control, such as energy subsidies and carbon tax. Other inputs are exogenous variables, which are determined by global market conditions, such as oil and gas prices.

Endogenous variables: inputs under Qatar's control

OIL AND GAS SUBSIDIES

Government subsidies for domestic oil and gas are calculated using international market prices as reference points, using the International Energy Agency (IEA) Price-Gap approach shown in equation (5). In this formula, the reference price is the international market price, the end-user price is the domestic price after subsidies and the units consumed represent the amount of the commodity consumed domestically. Oil and gas subsidy data derived according to the IEA's Price Gap approach for 2011–2013 are shown in Table 9.2.

$$\text{subsidy} = (\text{reference price} - \text{end-user price}) * \text{units consumed} \qquad (5)$$

The subsidy price per unit of commodity was determined from the subsidies and domestic consumption figures shown in Table 9.2. This was then compared to the market price to determine the subsidy percentage. Total primary energy supply (TPES) was used to define domestic consumption for gas while total final consumption (TFC) was used for oil (IEA Data Services no date), because the TPES for oil includes exports of processed petrochemical goods that would not be included in the subsidies.

Given the historical level of subsidies shown in Table 9.2, this study estimates a range of potential subsidy levels the Qatari government could enact in the future. The boundary conditions for the oil and gas subsidy parameters used in the model are as shown in equations (6) and (7).

$$0 < \text{oil subsidy percentage} < 56 \text{ per cent} \qquad (6)$$

$$0 < \text{gas subsidy percentage} < 41 \text{ per cent} \qquad (7)$$

CARBON TAX

Given the historical and current subsidies on fossil energy in Qatar, the adoption of a carbon tax is unlikely. There is, however, a small possibility of an internationally binding carbon tax. In such an event, the amount of the carbon tax is expected to be modest, within the range of the European Emissions Trading System (European Energy Exchange Emission Allowances), which is used as a

Table 9.2 Qatar's oil and gas subsidies for 2011–2013

	Subsidies (GSI, IISD)	Domestic consumption (IEA Data Services)	Market price (IEA Data Services)	Subsidy percentage
Oil (ktoe)				
2011	$2.0 bn	5,440	$111/bbl	46.96
2012	$2.5 bn	6,785	$112/bbl	46.21
2013	$3.0 bn	6,729	$109/bbl	55.58
Gas (ktoe)				
2011	$1.86 bn	28,428	$4.00/MMBtu	41.25
2012	$1.60 bn	35,832	$2.75/MMBtu	40.95
2013	$1.5 bn	39,233	$3.73/MMBtu	25.85

Sources: Global Subsidies Initiative and International Institute for Sustainable Development (Charles et al. 2014); IEA database on oil and gas subsidies in Qatar (IEA Data Services no date).

Table 9.3 CO_2 emissions from oil and gas (EIA 2016b)

	Pounds of CO_2 emitted per MMBtu of energy produced
Oil	157
Gas	117

reference to define the potential range of carbon tax for this utility function, as shown in equation (8). The U.S. Energy Information Agency (EIA) values for CO_2 emissions from oil and gas are shown in Table 9.3.

$$0 < \text{carbon tax} < \$10 \text{ per tonne of } CO_2 \text{ equivalent (tCO}_2\text{e)} \qquad (8)$$

OIL/GAS SPLIT

The oil/gas split indicates how much oil and gas are replaced by solar energy. This variable is optimized using NLP programming to maximize savings and is fully within Qatar's control. Each setting of the relative quantities of oil and gas replaced by solar energy defines a different fuel-mix strategy. The oil/gas split can vary as indicated in equation (9), where 0 indicates that all of the solar energy generated replaces natural gas, and 1 indicates that all of it replaces oil.

$$0 < \text{oil-gas split} < 1 \qquad (9)$$

To determine how much oil or gas is replaced by solar energy, the study uses conversion efficiencies for natural gas to electricity and oil to electricity. The conversion efficiency from natural gas to electricity is 40 per cent, using the esti- mated average efficiency of natural gas-fired power plants in the United States (EIA 2016b). As the authors did not have access to data for Qatar's gas-fired power plants, data from U.S. plants were used. Factors such as high tempera- tures and humidity in Qatar may impact the efficiency of gas-fired power plants somewhat differently as compared with the U.S. This conversion efficiency was used to determine the total gas replaced by solar PV generation for any given oil/ gas split. The oil-to-electricity efficiency was determined by relating the equiva- lent miles per gallon of an EV (currently 50 kilowatt hours [kWh] per 100 miles) and a gasoline-powered car (on average about 150 kWh of gasoline energy equivalent per 100 miles). This calculation yielded a conversion efficiency from oil to electricity of 33 per cent (Murphy 2011), which was used to determine the total oil replaced by solar PV generation for any given oil/gas split.

Exogenous variables: inputs outside Qatar's control

OIL AND GAS PRICES

The oil price ranges in the study were determined with reference to a repre- sentative time series of Brent Crude Oil prices (Indexmundi Brent Crude Oil

Prices), with lower and upper bounds of $10 and $140 respectively, as shown in equation (10).

$$\$10/bbl > \text{oil prices} > \$140/bbl \tag{10}$$

As evidence shows that gas prices are partially correlated to oil prices, the study captured this dependency using Pearson's correlation coefficient to measure the linear dependence between oil and gas prices over the past 20 years (Alterman 2012). This dependency is defined in equation (11), where the oil-indexed gas price is determined by indexing 27.31 per cent of the gas price to 13 per cent of the oil price. The Henry Hub spot prices (Indexmundi Henry Hub Natural Gas Spot Prices) provided the time series for gas spot prices with a lower bound of $2 and an upper bound of $14, as shown in equation (12). The range of oil-indexed gas prices is shown in equation (13).

$$\text{oil-indexed gas price} = 27.31\% * 12\% \text{ of Oil Price} + 72.69\% *$$
$$\text{spot gas price} \tag{11}$$

$$\$2 / MMBtu > \text{spot gas prices} > \$14 / MMBtu \tag{12}$$

$$\$1.78\ MMBtu > \text{oil-indexed gas prices} > \$14.76 / MMBtu \tag{13}$$

GAS LCO&M

The levelized fixed and capital cost for natural gas-fired power plants (gas LCOE) can be defined using cost ranges for the various types of natural gas-fired power plants[3] expected to enter into service in 2022 (EIA 2017). Since the gas price is already included as a separate variable, the study removes fuel costs from total system LCOE, taking into account only the levelized capital and the fixed operation and maintenance (LCO&M) costs. Thus, instead of full system gas LCOE, the study uses the gas LCO&M cost, with lower and upper bound costs as shown in equation (14).

$$1.42\ ¢/kWh < \text{gas LCO\&M} < 4.36\ ¢/kWh \tag{14}$$

Generating scenarios with optimal fuel mixes

To advance the study to the next phase, plausible fuel mix scenarios were generated using a constrained scenario generation algorithm. This algorithm exhaustively creates configurations of all endogenous and exogenous input variables (Table 9.4), subject to three types of constraints: the upper and lower bounds of a variable (value range constraints); the number of values a variable can take within its range (value interval constraints); and dependencies among variables (dependencies constraints). Being one of the two optimization targets, the oil/gas split variable was not assigned value interval constraints. With this

Table 9.4 Description of variables and variable constraints

Variables	Value range constraints	Value interval constraints	Dependency constraints	Units
Endogenous variable				
Oil/gas split	$0 < x_1 < 1$	–	–	real
Oil subsidy	$0 < x_4 < 56$	5	Percentage of oil price	percentage
Gas subsidy	$0 < x_5 < 41$	5	Percentage of gas price	percentage
Carbon tax	$0 < x_6 < 10$	5	–	$/tCO_2$
Exogenous variables				
Gas LCO&M cost	$1.42 < x_7 < 4.36$	2	–	¢/kWh
Oil price	$10 < x_2 < 140$	14	–	$/bbl
Gas price	$1.78 < x_3 < 14.76$	13	Indexed to oil price	$/MMBtu

method, the modeling generated 45,500 scenarios, equaling the product of value interval constraints. In each scenario, the fuel mix ratio represented by the oil/gas split variable was optimized to maximize total savings. MATLAB was used as the computing software to perform both scenario generation and NLP optimization.

Results and discussion

The study results indicate that the ability of fuel mix strategies to yield higher cost savings depends strongly on the hydrocarbon market, which is beyond the control of the Qatar government. However, the choice of fuel mix strategy – i.e., as determined by the volumes of oil and gas to be replaced by solar energy – can be controlled by the government to maximize savings. For example, the study's utility function shows that when oil prices are about $88/bbl or greater, replacing oil with solar energy would yield higher savings, while when oil prices are lower than $88/bbl, higher savings would result from replacing gas. The impact of all other exogenous and endogenous factors on savings per MWh of solar energy introduced is established in a similar manner. The approach can thus help decision-makers determine which energy policies can be enacted on endogenous factors – e.g., relative quantities of oil and gas to replace with solar energy, level of oil/gas subsidies or carbon tax – given the current exogenous factors, e.g., oil/gas prices and gas LC+O&M cost, to maximize savings.

The remaining part of this section provides detailed analysis of the impact of each parameter on savings resulting from the introduction of solar energy to replace gas and oil, using two methods: sensitivity analysis and information gain. It also evaluates aggregates of the optimized scenario results, which point to common policy conclusions.

Parameter impact

Sensitivity analysis

In the next step, the study performs a 'one-factor-at-a-time' sensitivity analysis. It first sets a base scenario with fixed parameter values, as shown in Table 9.5, and then varies the value of each parameter at the opposite values of its range while other parameters remain fixed to verify the base returns for gas and oil replaced by solar energy.

OIL PRICE

To begin, the study observes base return changes when the oil price is altered while all other parameters remain unchanged (see Table 9.5). Per unit of energy contained, crude oil is typically more expensive than natural gas. For example, at $5/MMBtu, natural gas would cost $28/bbl of oil equivalent, which is in the low range of oil prices observed in the last 20 years. Thus, the commodity price of oil can be expected to play a major role in determining the returns obtained by displacing hydrocarbons with solar energy.

The boundary conditions for the oil price range from $10/bbl to $140/bbl (see Table 9.4). When the price of oil is $10/bbl, the optimal base return is $48/MWh of solar energy replacing gas. With the price of oil at $140/bbl, the optimal base return with all other parameters at their base values (see Table 9.5) is $81/MWh of solar energy replacing oil.

OIL SUBSIDY

The boundary conditions for the oil subsidy parameter range from 0 per cent to 56 per cent of market price (see Table 9.2). With oil subsidies at the

Table 9.5 Base scenario with parameter values set for sensitivity analysis

Parameter	Value	Unit
Oil price	50	$/bbl
Gas price	6	$/MMBtu
Oil subsidy	30	%
Gas subsidy	30	%
Carbon tax	5	$/tCO$_2$
Gas-powered electricity capital cost	0.03	$/kWh
Base returns (output)	47.6 (replacing gas with solar energy)	$/MWh
	31.3 (replacing oil with solar energy)	

bottom of the range (0 per cent) and all other parameters at their base values (see Table 9.5), the optimal base return is $48/MWh of solar energy replacing gas. With oil subsidies at the top of the range (56 per cent), the optimal base return is $55/MWh of solar energy replacing oil.

GAS PRICE

Boundary conditions for gas prices range from $1.78/MMBtu to $17.76/MMBtu. For a low gas price of $2/MMBtu (slightly below the Henry Hub price in July 2016), the replacement of gas with solar energy yields a base return of $37/MWh. If the gas price rises to $14/MMBtu, the base return increases to $68/MWh of solar energy replacing domestic gas.

OIL VERSUS GAS PRICES

Comparing oil and gas prices, it is possible to determine a tradeoff curve for optimal fuel displacement, as illustrated in Figure 9.1. This kind of analysis can be used to help identify the optimal fuel replacement choice in varied hydrocarbon price environments (which are beyond the control of the government), and indicate the expected returns on solar PV investments, at given subsidy

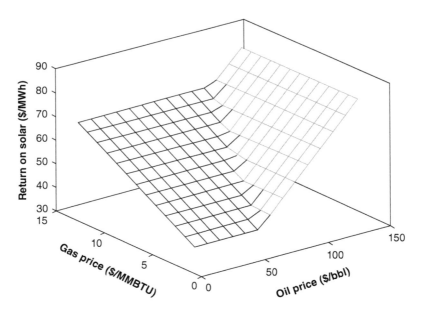

Figure 9.1 Tradeoff curve for optimal fuel displacement strategy

Note: Gas and oil prices vary, while other variables are fixed at the values in Table 9.5. The black region indicates higher savings when solar energy displaces gas, while the gray region indicates higher savings when solar energy displaces oil.

rates (which are set by the government) and fixed gas LCO&M (which is a known technology cost).

GAS SUBSIDY

Gas subsidies range between 0 per cent and 41 per cent of market price (see Table 9.4). In the base scenario (see Table 9.5), the base return for each MWh of solar energy replacing gas is $32 when there are no gas subsidies and $53 when the gas subsidy is at 41 per cent.

CARBON TAX

Given the historical and current subsidies on fossil fuel energy in Qatar, the adoption of a carbon tax is unlikely. There is, however, a small possibility of an internationally binding carbon tax. Thus, the study explores the effects of a low carbon tax of up to $10/tCO$_2$e in the base scenario (see Table 9.5). With no carbon tax, the resulting base return for each MWh of solar energy replacing gas is $45, while a carbon tax of $10/tCO$_2$e pushes it up to $50 per MWh. As there is not much difference in the returns obtained with no carbon tax or a tax of $10/tCO$_2$e, it follows that unless set at a much higher rate, a carbon tax is not an effective measure to incentivize renewables adoption in Qatar.

GAS LEVELIZED CAPITAL AND OPERATIONS AND MAINTENANCE COST

At $0.0142/kWh, the bottom range for gas LCO&M cost (see Table 9.4), the optimal base return is $32/MWh of solar energy replacing gas. At the gas LCO&M cost top range of $0.0436/kWh, the optimal base return is $61/MWh.

Using classification and information gain to assess variable impact As an additional way of establishing the relative impact of variables, the study first partitioned the 45,500 fuel mix scenarios into high, medium and low classes of achieved savings (total returns) using Bayesian classification. It then used information gain to establish the extent to which each variable contributes to identifying scenarios falling into each class. The information gain of a variable with respect to a class is the reduction in entropy (i.e., uncertainty) in the identification of the class when the value of the variable is known (Mitchell 1997). Therefore, the higher the information gain ratio (IGR) of an attribute, the higher its impact on the target class. For example, the entropy value of the 'oil price' with respect to the high saving classes of scenarios reveals whether the variable has a strong, medium or weak impact on high savings.

First, the study discretized the 45,500 fuel mix scenarios (see section on Generating scenarios with optimal fuel mixes) to obtain three values for the 'total returns' class ($ saved per MW of solar energy used): high (≥ $105.89), medium (≥ $60.05 and < $105.89), and low (< $60.05). The analysis then trained a classifier on 80 per cent of the discretized fuel mix scenarios data (72,800 instances) using the Bayesian network classifier in the Weka data mining environment (Bouckaert 2004; Witten and Frank 2005). This classifier uses information about oil and gas prices and subsidies, gas LCO&M, carbon tax, and oil/gas split to predict whether the value for the 'total returns' class of a given fuel mix scenario is high, medium or low. The study evaluated the classifier on an unseen portion of the data (20 per cent), using precision (lower false positives) and recall (lower false negatives) metrics to ensure that class assignment was done reliably. The evaluation yielded an average precision recall of 86 per cent, indicating that the model performs satisfactorily.

The study then applied the information gain algorithm in Weka (Witten and Frank 2005) to the discretized fuel mix scenario data to assess the relative impact of each attribute used in building the classifier (oil/gas price/subsidy, gas LCO&M cost, carbon tax, and oil/gas split) on the 'total returns' class. The IGR of an attribute with respect to a class is the reduction in entropy (i.e., uncertainty) of the value for the class when we know the value of the attribute (Mitchell 1997). The ranking of attributes provided by the IGR indicates that oil price has the strongest impact on the 'total returns' class, closely followed by oil subsidy and oil/gas split, while gas LCO&M cost, gas subsidy, and gas price have mild impacts, and carbon tax has marginal impact (Table 9.6).

Solution scenarios   By running the optimization model at several combinations across the input parameter space, it is possible to determine the behavior of the decision variable (fuel allocation) and the magnitude of returns under differing regimes. These can be aggregated into the three categories below. Each regime category provides diverse conditions for solar energy investments. Note that in the absence of probability data on the individual parameters, the study does not intend these scenarios to be considered as equally likely. They are merely first order tools for decision-making.

- **Low hydrocarbon prices and/or low subsidies**: Savings emerging from the replacement of fossil fuel with solar energy need to be above $30/

Table 9.6 Ranking of attributes

Attribute	Information gain ratio (IGR)	Relativized IGR (%)
Oil price	0.22248	28.7
Oil subsidy	0.18247	23.5
Oil/gas split	0.17207	22.2
LCO&M cost	0.07335	9.5
Gas subsidy	0.06303	8.1
Gas price	0.06057	7.8
Carbon tax	0.00220	0.3

MWh to cover of cost of the solar energy introduced. However, if a gas-fired plant is at the planning stage, a solar plant can economically replace it due to the large capital costs of gas-fired power plants. Electricity grid infrastructure needs to be upgraded to accommodate renewable generation.

○ *Recommendation*: Investing in solar is cost-effective only if it serves load beyond existing gas-fired capacity.

• **High gas prices and/or high gas subsidies**: The optimal returns occur when solar energy displaces natural gas ($37/MWh to $79/MWh based on gas prices, at 41 per cent domestic gas subsidy and $0.03/kWh fixed gas-fired electricity costs). Electricity grid infrastructure needs to be upgraded to accommodate renewable generation.

○ *Recommendation*: Investing in solar energy is cost-effective only if it serves load beyond existing gas-fired capacity.

• **High oil prices and/or high oil subsidies**: The optimal returns occur when solar energy displaces oil, thus increasing oil exports ($103/MWh when oil prices are at $100/bbl, and domestic oil subsidies are at 56 per cent). Electricity grid infrastructure needs to be upgraded to accommodate renewable generation. Additionally, electric transportation systems need to be developed and/or incentivized to reduce domestic oil demand.

○ *Recommendation*: Investing in solar energy can be cost-effective.

• **Low gas prices and high oil prices**: In this scenario, the use of gas-fired electricity to power EVs will reduce domestic oil demand, with a potentially rewarding windfall from oil saved. Thus, in high oil price scenarios, incentivizing the adoption of EVs even before decarbonizing the energy supply may yield economic, as well as environmental, benefits, although partial decarbonization of the energy supply is ultimately needed to meet the nationally mandated solar adoption targets.

Conclusions

Deployment of renewable energy technologies has been relatively slow in Qatar, due to the abundance of hydrocarbon resources and adequate power generation capacity. Opportunity exists, however, to use renewable energy – particularly solar – to meet growing domestic energy demand and thereby create a windfall in hydrocarbon resources. This work has analyzed the economics of investing in solar energy by determining the opportunity and technology costs of continuing the domestic use of hydrocarbons.

The results show that, based on current subsidy and tax structures, investing in solar power to replace oil and/or gas makes economic sense for a range of possible scenarios. This is especially due to the continuously falling costs of solar energy, which can generate returns in even a moderate hydrocarbon price environment. Assuming that the current low to moderate prices for both oil and gas will continue over the next several years, the optimal fuel allocation strategy is to replace gas-fired generation with solar energy.

The study also analyzed a scenario of low gas prices and high oil prices (near $100/bbl) and showed that the investment in gas-fired electricity to power EVs may be recovered by large returns from reducing domestic oil demand. Thus, in high oil price scenarios, incentivizing the adoption of EVs even before decarbonizing the electricity supply may yield economic, as well as environmental, benefits.

This chapter supports five main insights that could help inform policymaking in Qatar. First, in the context of plummeting PV LCOE costs, down to record lows of $0.0299/kWh (Clover 2016) and $0.0242/kWh (Graves 2016), investments in solar energy are cost-effective in most hydrocarbon price scenarios. With medium to low hydrocarbon prices, however, investments in solar energy are not cost-effective if the Qatari government maintains a strong subsidy structure for fossil fuels. For example, with gas prices at $6/MMBtu and 30 per cent gas subsidies (i.e., $1.8/MMBtu), the return on displaced natural gas would be positive only at LCO&M of $15/MWh of solar energy introduced, well below the current lowest reported PV costs ($24.20/MWh).

A third point is that when returns generated by displacing oil or gas are positive, they can be invested in solar energy to achieve planned targets of 2 per cent by 2020 and 20 per cent by 2030. Any additional returns could be used to support consumers switching to new renewable technologies such as building integrated PV and EVs.

While this chapter investigates scenarios, policymakers need to base decisions on reality. Consequently, the fourth finding is that investing in solar energy may not be cost-effective if a large natural gas generation capacity is currently unused, since the operational cost of natural gas plants remains lower than total costs for new solar plants. The economic appeal of solar energy projects is greater when they are competing with new natural gas power plants that require new capital investments. If sufficient natural gas plants are under construction to meet future electricity demands, the capital investment in these plants would be considered sunk costs, compared to having to invest in new solar energy plants. In this case, the only returns on investing in solar would be from increased hydrocarbon sales and possibly from displacing oil through electric vehicles.

Finally, while desirable from an environmental perspective, a carbon tax is not effective in incentivizing renewable energy in Qatar unless it is set at a range well beyond $10/tCO$_2$e. There are also political uncertainties surrounding the practicalities of an internationally binding carbon tax; however unlikely this may be, it may be considered more likely than a nationally imposed carbon tax.

Two limitations of this analysis warrant mention. First, it does not include the health impacts of clean technology. Thus, the air quality benefits of displacing gas-fired plants with solar energy, or replacing petrol-burning cars with EVs, have not been explored. Second, a detailed cost estimation of gas-powered plants, such as the ramping costs needed to meet peak loads, is not part of the analysis. However, given the ability of PV solar energy to meet afternoon peak loads, and evening peaks when paired with storage, any detailed analysis would improve the prospects of solar energy in Qatar.

Qatar might consider taking prompt action to commission new utility scale solar plants before its gas-fired energy infrastructure is locked in for the next two decades. As the integration of alternative energy does not require difficult alterations to the hydrocarbon subsidy structure, there are limited socio-political concerns regarding renewables integration over the medium term. Complementary changes on the demand side, such as switching to energy efficient devices and electric transportation, however, will require major societal outreach efforts, along with necessary changes to the pricing of energy. Qatar can benefit from growing regional expertise in alternative energy projects, while contributing to global efforts towards a sustainable energy future.

Notes

1 These forecasts are made under the assumption that the adoption of electric vehicles remains marginal.
2 See www.profitableventure.com/cost-start-a-gas-station/. Accessed 19 Jul 2018.
3 Conventional combined cycle, advanced combined cycle, and advanced combined cycle with carbon capture and storage.

References

Alterman S (2012) Natural gas price volatility in the UK and North America. The Oxford Institute for Energy Studies. www.oxfordenergy.org/wpcms/wp-content/uploads/2012/02/NG_60.pdf. Accessed 19 July 2018.

Atwa YM, El-Saadany EF, Salama MMA et al. (2010) Optimal renewable resources mix for distribution system energy loss minimization. *IEEE Transactions on Power Systems* 25(1):360–370.

Baker JA III, Feldstein M, Halstead T, Mankiw NG, Paulson HM Jr., Shultz GP, Stephenson T, Walton R (2017) The conservative case for carbon dividends. Climate Leadership Council. www.clcouncil.org/wp-content/uploads/2017/02/TheConservativeCaseforCarbonDividends.pdf. Accessed 10 Mar 2017.

Bertsekas DP (1999) *Nonlinear Programing (Second ed.).* Athena Scientific, Cambridge, MA.

Bouckaert RR (2004) Bayesian network classifiers in weka. Department of Computer Science, University of Waikato, Hamilton, New Zealand.

Center for International Development at Harvard University (no date) The Atlas of economic complexity. www.atlas.cid.harvard.edu. Accessed 30 Aug 2016.

Charles C, Moerenhout T, Bridle R (2014) The context of fossil-fuel subsidies in the GCC region and their impact on renewable energy development. Global Subsidies Initiative and International Institute for Sustainable Development, Winnipeg, MB. www.iisd.org/gsi/sites/default/files/ffs_gcc_context.pdf. Accessed 19 Jul 2018.

Climate Leadership Council: James A. Baker III, Martin Feldstein, Ted Halstead, N. Gregory Mankiw, Henry M. Paulson Jr., George P. Shultz, Thomas Stephenson,

Rob Walton (2017) The conservative case for carbon dividends. www.clcouncil. org. Accessed 19 Jul 2018.

Clover I (2016) Masdar selected by DEWA to lead consortium on 800 MW solar PV project in Dubai. PV Magazine, June 27, 2016. www.pv-magazine.com/2016/06/27/masdar-selected-by-dewa-to-lead-consortium-on-800-mw-solar-pv-project-in-dubai_100025158/. Accessed 19 Jul 2018.

Dean SL (no date) An introduction to buying a gas station. http://australia.businessesforsale.com/australian/search/gas-petrol-service-stations-for-sale/articles/an-introduction-to-buying-a-gas-station. Accessed 10 Mar 2017.

Divisia F (1926) L'indice monétaire et la théorie de la monnaie. *Revue d'Économie Politique* LX(1)49–81.

EIA (US Energy Information Administration) (2016a) Carbon dioxide emissions coefficients. www.eia.gov/environment/emissions/co2_vol_mass.cfm. Accessed 19 Jul 2018.

EIA (2016b) Frequently asked questions: how much carbon dioxide is produced when different fuels are burned? www.eia.gov/tools/faqs/faq.cfm?id=73&t=11. Accessed 31 Aug 2016.

EIA (2017) Levelized cost and levelized avoided cost of new generation resources in the Annual Energy Outlook 2017. www.eia.gov/forecasts/aeo/pdf/electricity_generation.pdf. Accessed 10 Mar 2017.

European Energy Exchange (EEX) Emission Allowances (no date). www.eex.com/en/market-data/environmental-markets/spot-market/european-emission-allowances#!/2016/08/31. Accessed 31 Aug 2016.

Graves L (2016) Marubeni-Jinko submit world-record low bid for 350MW Sweihan solar project in Abu Dhabi. *The National.* www.thenational.ae/business/energy/marubeni-jinko-submit-world-record-low-bid-for-350mw-sweihan-solar-project-in-abu-dhabi. Accessed 8 Oct 2016.

IEA (International Energy Agency) (no date) Fossil-fuel subsidies – methodology and assumptions: the price gap approach. International Energy Agency and World Energy Outlook. www.worldenergyoutlook.org/resources/energysubsidies/methodology/. Accessed 30 Aug 2016.

IEA (International Energy Agency) Data Services (no date). http://wds.iea.org. Accessed 31 Jul 2017.

Indexmundi Brent Crude Oil Prices. www.indexmundi.com/commodities/?commodity=crude-oil-brent. Accessed 31 Aug 2016.

Indexmundi Henry Hub Natural Gas Spot Prices. www.indexmundi.com/commodities/?commodity=natural-gas. Accessed 31 Aug 2016.

Ingram A (2014) BMW launches its own DC fast-charging station, priced at $6,500. *Green Car Report*, 28 Jul. www.greencarreports.com/news/1093548_bmw-launches-its-own-dc-fast-charging-station-priced-at-6500. Accessed 6 Jan 2017.

Jafar AH, Al-Amin AQ, Siwar C (2008) Environmental impact of alternative fuel mix in electricity generation in Malaysia. *Renewable Energy* 33(10):2229–2235.

Marrero GA, Ramos-Real FJ (2010) Electricity generation cost in isolated system: the complementarities of natural gas and renewables in the Canary Islands. *Renewable and Sustainable Energy Reviews* 14(9):2808–2818.

Markowitz HM (1952) Portfolio selection. *The Journal of Finance* 7(1):77–91.

May JW, Mattila M (2009) Plugging in: a stakeholder investment guide for public electric-vehicle charging infrastructure. Rocky Mountain Institute, Colorado.

www.10xe.orwww.10xe.org/Content/Files/Plugging%20In%20-%20A%20 Stakeholder%20Investment%20Guide.pdf. Accessed 19 Jul 2018.

Mitchell T (1997) *Machine Learning*. New York, McGraw Hill, p 55–58.

Murphy T (2011) MPG for electric cars? University of California San Diego. http:// physics.ucsd.edu/do-the-math/2011/08/mpg-for-electric-cars. Accessed 31 Aug 2016.

National Research Council (2015) Overcoming barriers to deployment of plug-in electric vehicles. National Academies Press, Washington, DC.

PV Magazine (2016) Third phase of Dubai's DEWA solar project attracts record low bid of US 2.99 c/kWh. *PV Magazine*, 2 May. www.pv-magazine.com/2016/05/02/ third-phase-of-dubais-dewa-solar-project-attracts-record-low-bid-of-us-2-99- centskwh_100024383/. Accessed 31 Aug 2016.

QNV (2008) Qatar National Vision 2030. www.mdps.gov.qa/en/qnv1. Accessed 31 Aug 2017.

REN21 (Renewable Energy Policy Network for the 21st Century) (2016) Renewables 2016 Global Status Report. REN21 Secretariat, Paris. www.ren21.net/status-of- renewables/global-status-report/. Accessed 19 Jul 2018.

Roques FA, Newbery, DM, Nuttall, WJ (2008) Fuel mix diversification incentives in liberalized electricity markets: A Mean-Variance Portfolio theory approach. *Energy Economics* 30(4):1831–1849.

Sanfilippo A, Pederson L (2016) Impacts of PV adoption in Qatar on natural gas exports to the Far East. In: Lester L, Efird B (eds) *Energy Relations and Policy Making in Asia: The benefits of mutual interdependence*. Palgrave Macmillan, Basingstoke, UK.

Torvanger A (1991) Manufacturing sector carbon dioxide emissions in nine OECD countries, 1973–87: a Divisia index decomposition to changes in fuel mix, emission coefficients, industry structure, energy intensities and international structure. *Energy Economics* 13(3):168–186.

Witten IH, Frank E (2005) *Data Mining: Practical Machine Learning Tools and Techniques*. Morgan Kaufmann Publishers, Burlington, MA.

Zhu L, Fan Y (2010) Optimization of China's generating portfolio and policy implica- tions based on portfolio theory. *Energy* 35(3):1391–1402.

10 Renewable energy and its potential impact on GCC labor markets

Opportunities and constraints

Sylvain Côté

Abstract

Beyond the opportunity to deploy renewable energy as a means to meet future energy demand and climate change obligations, governments in countries belonging to the Gulf Cooperation Council (GCC) increasingly see the clean energy transition as a way to diversify their economies and increase employment. While multiple studies provide positive estimates regarding job creation in the renewable energy sector, few have accounted for labor market particularities or the social context of the GCC region. Given the evolution and nature of the GCC labor markets, the implications of these constraints are important as they could represent a missed opportunity for new employment in an emerging sector for a young and rising population.

After briefly assessing projected employment opportunities associated with renewables deployment, this chapter explores some of the supply-side constraints in GCC labor markets and highlights areas in which targeted policy action by governments could help alleviate the anticipated skills gap. In particular, policy action is needed to address asymmetrical labor market information, sectoral and occupational biases, and corresponding needs in education and training.

Policy relevant insights

Deployment of renewable energy in the GCC is expected to create up to 140,000 jobs (IRENA 2016b) of diverse skill levels annually. Yet specific barriers, such as labor market information asymmetry, occupational and sectoral biases and a shortage of adequate skills, may play a role in preventing GCC nationals from taking advantage of these job opportunities. To alleviate these constraints, GCC governments could build on recent efforts to:

- Further expand technical and vocational training.
- Continue working closely with schools, colleges and universities to ensure that potential job seekers have the necessary information about the career opportunities renewable energy might bring.
- Integrate skills development for the renewable energy sector into wider training and skills development policy, rather than isolating it.
- Further promote a comprehensive approach to policy, involving several stakeholders, to better assess training needs associated with the renewable energy sector.

Can renewable energy deliver new hope for GCC youth?

Driven by both oil and gas revenues and growth oriented policies, the Gulf Cooperation Council (GCC) region has experienced tremendous socio-economic development in recent decades. While the six member countries – Bahrain, Kuwait, Oman, Qatar, Saudi Arabia and the United Arab Emirates (UAE) – have greatly benefited from their endowment of oil and gas, the recent collapse in oil prices, combined with a demographic shift, has amplified fiscal challenges and increased existing pressures on labor markets. In addition to diversifying the energy mix while meeting future energy demand and climate change obligations, the deployment of renewables is increasingly identified by policymakers as offering prospects for increased employment in a broad range of sectors and occupations.

With about half of national populations in the GCC being under 25 years of age (Figure 10.1), finding ways to activate the young cohort into the labor market provides the opportunity for a 'demographic dividend'. This situation occurs when the labor force grows relative to the population dependent on it, resulting in a boost to productivity. It is also expected that per capita income will grow more rapidly during this period. Although the demographic change will be felt across all GCC countries to varying degrees, it is in Saudi Arabia where the ramifications will be the most important: some estimates show that up to 4.5 million young Saudis will be of working age by 2030 (McKinsey Global Institute 2015: 5).

So far, it has been difficult for GCC governments to turn this potential into a dividend. Even though Gulf economies have demonstrated a strong capacity to create jobs over the past decade – a development that is notably reflected in the growth of their respective labor forces (Figure 10.2) – unemployment among nationals has remained high for the past several years. This condition of joblessness has predominantly been concentrated among new entrants to

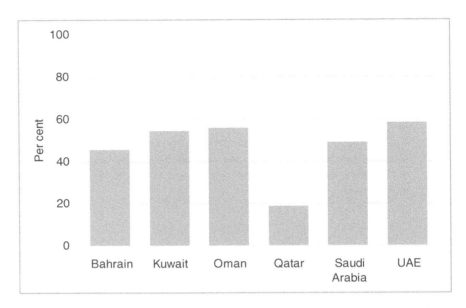

Figure 10.1 Proportion of the population below 25 years of age in GCC countries, latest year available (GCC national statistical offices; UAE refers to Abu Dhabi)

Source: Information & E-Government Authority, Bahrain (2017); Public Authority for Civil Information, Kuwait (2017); General Directorate of Civil Status, Oman (2014); Annual Bulletin of Labor Force Sample survey 2015 and Women and Men in the State of Qatar 2016, Qatar (2015); GaStat, Demographic Survey, Saudi Arabia (2017; Statistics Centre of Abu Dhabi, UAE (2015)

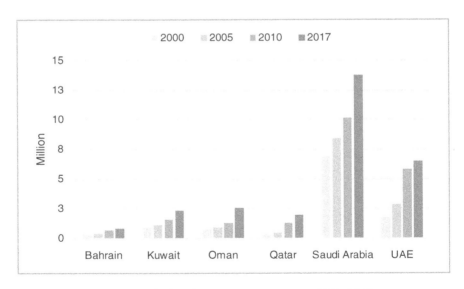

Figure 10.2 Size of the total labor force in GCC countries, 2000–2014

Source: World Bank, World Development Indicators.

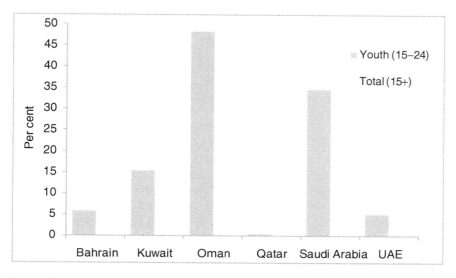

Figure 10.3 Unemployment rates in GCC countries, youth vs total
Source: World Bank, World Development Indicators.

the labor market, i.e., young people. Unemployment rates for this cohort are particularly high in Oman (48 per cent), Saudi Arabia (35 per cent) and Kuwait (16 per cent) (Figure 10.3). These high rates imply that an unexploited growth potential exists among the national populations in these countries.

At present, foreign workers fill about two-thirds of typical entry level jobs. Although all GCC governments have introduced various plans to indigenize their labor force in recent years (Box 10.1), high youth unemployment suggests that more can be done to capitalize on the potential of their youth populations. Indeed, with the workforce forecasted to grow rapidly, a sizable number of GCC nationals could further inflate the already high level of joblessness and slow the development of existing and new economic sectors.

This chapter explores the potential for the transition to renewable energy to create employment opportunities for nationals as well as value added work to support them. While past policies of rent distribution have led, among others, to inefficient use and misallocation of resources and a highly segmented labor market, taking advantage of opportunities in the renewable energy sector will require a more efficient allocation of human resources. To maximize the potential employment prospects offered by renewable energy, action will be needed to address constraints through human capital development and the adoption of active labor market programs and policies – particularly regarding the domestic labor force.

Box 10.1   Labor nationalization initiatives, and vision frameworks

To address, at least partially, demographic pressures and the relatively low level of economic diversification, in recent years all GCC countries launched different nationalization policy initiatives to stimulate private sector activity and job creation.

Saudi Arabia's ambitious Vision 2030 strategic plans include more than tripling non-oil revenues by 2030, and creating more than 450,000 jobs in the private sector by 2020. In addition, the Nitaqat program establishes quotas for Saudi labor across sectors.

National strategies from other GCC countries similarly aim to diversify economies away from dependence on the oil and gas sector and to further encourage nationals to seek jobs in the private sector. These initiatives are described in the following documents:

- Bahrain's Economic Vision 2030
- Kuwait's Vision Plan 2035
- Oman's Vision 2020
- Qatar's National Vision 2030
- The UAE's Vision 2021

Sources: Bahrain Economic Development Board (2008); Kingdom of Saudi Arabia (2016b); Kuwait General Secretariat of the Supreme Council for Planning, and Development (2010); Ministry of National Economy (1995); Qatar General Secretariat for Development Planning (2008); United Arab Emirates Cabinet (2010). .

Deployment of renewable energy can also have broader employment and labor market objectives, such as setting local content requirements to stimulate development of nascent industries. While targets and strategies on local content requirements have been implemented across GCC countries, examination of these developments is beyond the scope of this chapter.

The chapter is divided into five sections. The context for renewable energy across the GCC and its relationship to employment are outlined in the first section, followed by a brief overview of evidence on job creation in the sector. The third section identifies the opportunities and challenges related to GCC labor markets, while the subsequent section describes the policy mechanisms to address these labor needs. The last section offers some concluding thoughts.

Understanding the links between renewable energy and employment

It is important to stress at the outset that the employment situation of GCC economies was essentially shaped by the demands associated with rapid, oil based growth. Following the discovery of vast hydrocarbon resources, GCC countries built their industrial development strategies around low-cost, carbon-based energy. Although efforts towards diversification have been made by GCC countries in recent decades, many industries either remain linked directly to the oil and gas sector (e.g., petrochemicals) or continue to be sustained indirectly due to public spending derived by revenues from the sector.

Through oil and gas exports, and the competitive advantage low-cost domestic resources give other industries, these countries have been able to record rapid economic growth through notably the modernization of their economic infrastructure. In turn, the wealth generated has been redistributed through the provision of generous subsidies on utilities, especially electricity and water, free access to public services, and the promise of jobs in the public sector – hence greatly improving their citizens' living standards. In parallel, development led to a rapid increase in labor demand that could not be met by national workforces, which were either insufficient in size or lacking the necessary level of skills. It then became necessary to hire non-national (foreign) labor for both skilled and unskilled jobs in the private sector.

Over time, this strong economic growth, driven in part by the GCC economies' highly energy-intensive industrialization programs, led to a dramatic surge in energy consumption. At present, high shares of total final energy consumption (TFEC) are attributed to industry (50 per cent) and transport (32 per cent), with principal energy sources being natural gas (65 per cent) and oil (25 per cent) (IEA 2015). A steady rise in demand for electricity also contributes to high TFEC. Climate induced needs for year-round air conditioning and water desalination currently account for about 6 per cent of TFEC, with the share and absolute volume growing notably with population increase. On average across the GCC, electricity demand has steadily increased at an average annual rate of about 11 per cent over the last four decades, compared with just 3 per cent globally. Growth rates have been particularly high in Oman (19 per cent) and the UAE (16 per cent) (IEA 2015).

Overall demand for fossil fuels for power, industry, transportation and desalination is projected to continue rising rapidly across the GCC through to 2030 (IRENA 2016b). If left unchecked, such an increase in domestic consumption could reduce the volumes of oil and gas available for export, thereby reducing revenues and putting even more fiscal pressures on the government. This surging energy demand has led GCC governments to take action to temper growth. Efficiency measures and energy price reforms have been introduced as part of efforts to reduce consumption in the region, although the depth and breadth of reforms vary significantly across countries (Hvidt 2013; Côté and Wogan 2016; KSA 2016a, 2016b). Renewables based power generation is indeed seen as having potential to meet GCC members' commitments to sustainable development, while contributing to wider economic diversification. Historically, low-cost oil and gas have undermined the economic case for the uptake of alternative energy technologies. More recently, as the cost of manufacturing solar panels declines and GCC governments implement plans to increase energy tariffs, the emerging economic equation provides new opportunities for renewable energy.

The total share of renewables in the GCC energy mix will nonetheless remain small. Despite investments in renewables projects, the GCC region is projected to continue its high and ongoing reliance on fossil fuels until at least 2040 (OPEC 2016). At present, investment in renewable energy in Saudi Arabia represents less than 1 per cent of the total electricity produced. Future investments, which aim to bring capacity to 9.5 gigawatts (GW) by 2023, would represent about 4 per cent of production. According to estimates, the latest plan for renewable energy in Saudi Arabia would amount to savings of about 52,000 barrels of oil per day (bbl/d); considering production of around 10 million bbl/d, these savings remain small in terms of actual impact on exports (Blazquez et al. 2017).

Although the total share of renewables in the GCC energy mix will remain minor, these initiatives demonstrate a political and economic commitment to the transition towards low carbon energy systems. Going beyond the more obvious benefits of including renewables in the energy mix, i.e., reducing domestic oil and gas demand and meeting current and future climate change obligations, the next section explores the empirical evidence on the employment potential of renewable energy.

The empirical evidence on employment and renewable energy

Review of recent literature examining the relationship between renewable energy and employment paints a mixed picture in terms of the potential capacity for job creation. Whereas part of the literature makes the case that employment outcomes between renewables and job creation could be negative (Alvarez et al. 2009; Michaels and Murphy 2009; Morriss et al. 2009; Ragwitz et al. 2009; Hughes 2011; Furchtgott-Roth 2012; Böhringer et al. 2013; Cameron and Van der Zwaan 2015), numerous studies claim that, per unit of energy produced, renewable generation is more labor intensive than fossil fuel fired power plants – and thus the transition will create net new jobs.

One literature review carried out by the UK Energy Research Center (UKERC) cites sufficient evidence to support that, in general, investments in renewable energy are more job intensive than investments in coal or gas (Figure 10.4) (Blyth et al. 2014). The review covers 50 studies deemed to provide data in suitable detail to compare employment impacts of different types of electricity generation technology in different countries. Across all types of

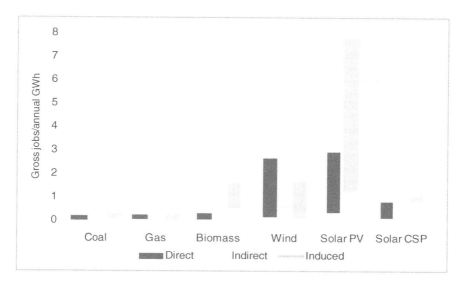

Figure 10.4 Range of estimates on gross jobs per annual GWh generated
Source: Blyth et al. 2014: 34.

employment gains – direct, indirect and induced[1] – the results presented below show labor intensity to be highest for renewable energy, particularly for solar photovoltaic (PV). In terms of direct jobs created, estimates for wind and solar PV are particularly significant, while concentrating solar power (CSP) appears to have a larger effect on indirect employment. Solar PV seems to have the greatest impact in terms of induced employment.

Figure 10.4 suggests that the positive effect in the case of renewable energy could be an order of magnitude of 0.65 jobs per gigawatt hour (/GWh). The average for fossil fuels from these figures is about 0.15 jobs/GWh, with coal being 0.15/GWh, gas 0.12/GWh and 0.18/GWh for carbon capture and storage (CCS). Assuming a production of 20,000 GWh/year over a 25-year period, the total gross job outcome in renewable energy would amount to about 325,000 jobs over the period — with most of the direct jobs created during the deployment and installation phases over the life of the project. This is a stark contrast to coal (75,000 jobs) and gas (60,000 jobs) over the same timeframe (Blyth et al. 2014).

Synthesizing data from 15 job studies covering renewable energy, energy efficiency, CCS and nuclear power, Wei et al. (2010) also find that all non-fossil fuel technologies (renewable energy, energy efficiency, low carbon technology) were shown to create more jobs per unit of energy than coal and natural gas in the United States. Kammen et al. (2004) review 13 independent reports and studies that analyze the economic and employment impacts of the clean energy industry in the United States and Europe. Across a broad range of scenarios, the key emerging result is that per unit of energy delivered, renewable energy generates more jobs than fossil fuel based energy. In terms of total employment outcomes, where gas and coal would create up to 86,400 jobs, renewable energy would generate about 188,000 jobs over a 25-year period.

Similar results have emerged from policy related institutions known to advocate green growth and renewable energy. In an assessment of the impact of renewable energies on employment, the German Ministry of the Environment, Nature Conservation, and Nuclear Safety (2006) concluded that investments in renewables in Germany resulted in a "clear and sustainable positive employment stimulus." Other studies also report positive effects of renewable energy on employment (UNEP 2008; OECD 2012; World Bank 2012). The International Renewable Energy Agency (IRENA) has also published comparable results, which are reviewed in more detail later in this section.

While most studies to date have focused on the United States, the United Kingdom and Germany, some evidence specific to GCC countries has emerged recently. Since 2012, IRENA has published several GCC focused reports examining the impact of renewable energy on employment. Using an employment factor approach (IRENA 2016a: 85–88), the Agency projects that investments in renewable energy in the GCC will create an average of 140,000 direct jobs per year, with a peak of 207,000 direct jobs in 2030 (Figure 10.5) (IRENA 2013: tables 1–3; 2016b: 14). Most of these jobs would be concentrated in the UAE (44 per cent), Saudi Arabia (39 per cent) and Qatar (12 per cent); the

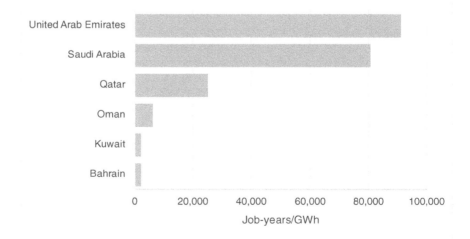

Figure 10.5 Projected direct jobs in renewable energy in GCC countries in 2030
Source: IRENA 2016b.

remaining 5 per cent would be distributed among the other GCC countries (Van der Zwaan et al. 2013).

Much as in the general literature, studies of the GCC region assume that solar PV (small and large) and CSP (utility scale) would be the leading technologies among renewables. In 2030, solar related technologies would create 177,000 direct jobs; together, the three subsectors would account for 86 per cent of renewable energy jobs in the region (Figure 10.6) (IRENA 2016b).

While the number of jobs created is important from the perspective of policymakers, it is equally imperative to identify the types of employment that will be created and the skills necessary to fill them. The dynamic dimensions of employment are therefore important to highlight. Indeed, time, transition and technology all play a role in the labor shift associated with the deployment of renewable energy.

Estimates of the renewable energy value chain provide a general idea of the distribution of occupations during different phases of a renewable energy project (IRENA 2017). Although IRENA uses a different measure of employment than applied above, the dimension of primary interest is the distribution of occupations, particularly during the different phases of the project. Technologies associated with solar PV typically involve jobs in the following areas: project planning and management; manufacture of technology and procurement; transport; installation and/or plant construction; operations and maintenance (O&M); and eventual plant decommissioning.

The time dimension of job creation in the renewables sector shows that employment outcomes can vary substantially across the different stages of a

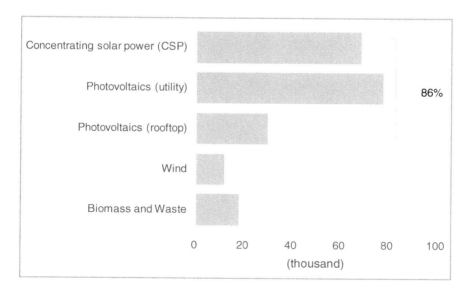

Figure 10.6 Breakdown of direct jobs in renewable energy in 2030, by technology
Source: IRENA 2016b.

project. Along the renewable energy value chain, most jobs will be linked to installations and equipment manufacturing. Analysis of the workforce requirement of a 50 MW solar PV plant project shows that three labor intensive phases generate 95 per cent of jobs, with operation and maintenance having the highest share (56 per cent), followed by manufacturing (22 per cent) and installation/grid connection (17 per cent) (IRENA 2017) (Figure 10.7).

Research also shows a concentration in certain occupations as well as a wide distribution in terms of skills (IRENA 2017). Analysis of workforce requirements during the various phases in the life of a solar PV project shows that diversity (Figure 10.8). For instance, during the planning phase, 39 per cent are occupations with expertise in the areas of finance, law, regulation, real estate and taxation while only 18 per cent are engineers and 4 per cent are environment experts. Although this is consistent with other findings that renewable energy also creates a number of indirect jobs, some of them referred to 'standard jobs' (Bezdek 2009), they still amount to a small proportion of the overall jobs during the life of the project.

Subsequent phases show a high distribution of jobs that would be considered low credentialed. This is particularly true during the deployment phases in manufacturing, with factory workers making up 62 per cent of the jobs, and installation, where 90 per cent are construction workers. Although the O&M phase still has a sizable proportion of construction workers (48 per cent), it also

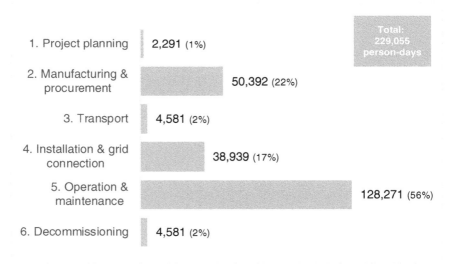

Figure 10.7 Workforce required at different stages of a wind power project (in person days)

Source: IRENA 2017.

Figure 10.8 Distribution of workforce requirements along a 50 MW solar PV value chain (percentage based on person days)

Source: IRENA 2017.

requires several more technical occupations in safety (19 per cent), engineering (15 per cent), operators (8 per cent) and technical personnel (8 per cent).

The distribution of jobs required is not static and may evolve with time. In the long run, research shows a clear trend towards fewer but more skilled employees. A detailed analysis of the electricity generation industry in the United States reports that the average number of employees per megawatt fell by about 50 per cent from 1990 to 2003, as a result of productive efficiency (Shanefelter 2008). Hughes (2011) also confirms an increase in annual productivity of 5.2 per cent in the sector, which led to a reduction in employment. In parallel, the content of many jobs can change as companies focus on being more productive and energy efficient. New occupations may also emerge, compounding labor shortages. Technology driven developments can have extensive effects on labor markets; over time, labor saving technologies may also play a role in reducing the demand for labor. This may help partly explain the large differences between the oil and gas sector and the renewable energy sector, since the former has benefited from decades of efficiency improvement.

Productivity warrants further consideration. Indeed, high labor intensity can contribute to increased labor productivity by raising overall employment and providing new job opportunities to previously unemployed or under-utilized workers (Pollin et al. 2009). Although, as will be elaborated later, GCC economies have much to gain in activating these groups into their labor markets, important limits are likely to emerge, some in low-skilled sectors.

Labor substitution is also an important factor to consider, as the labor adjustment which takes place across industrial sectors is usually slow and difficult. While some degree of labor market friction is always evident, in terms of search and matching, for general skilled jobs such as in administration, construction, or manufacturing, the adjustment cost remains larger for jobs that require sector specific knowledge and training (Cosar 2010; Dix-Carneiro 2010). In the case of the GCC countries, it is not clear substitution would amount to a significant challenge as the fossil fuel sector is expected to remain dominant in the medium term. It is thus more likely that the renewable energy sector would rely to a greater extent on newly trained workers rather than those switching from other energy related sectors.

While these studies identify the employment potential across various occupations, more comprehensive research is needed to examine more thoroughly the relationships among renewable energy, job creation and labor productivity. Further work is essential to estimate the size and composition of these various occupations across the renewables sector. In the case of the GCC, more accurate information is also needed, particularly regarding the identification of the number of higher value jobs that would appeal to nationals.

Turning now to the main questions of this chapter – i.e., whether a clean energy transition will create new jobs in the GCC and whether nationals within the GCC labor markets have the skills, capacity, and willingness to take advantage of these potential jobs – the following section highlights the structures of GCC labor markets and examines potential constraints from a supply-side perspective.

GCC labor markets: identifying the constraints

Labor markets in the GCC are unique for their very high rate of expatriates. From a 'lower' proportion of 56 per cent of the total population in Saudi Arabia, it reaches 83 per cent in Kuwait, and even 95 per cent in Qatar (Figure 10.9). In fact, nationals in these countries constitute a minority of the workforce, as many do not work at all, especially women and youths.

Additionally, employment rates for nationals are low, averaging around 50 per cent in the cases of Kuwait and Qatar and slipping further to below 40 per cent in Saudi Arabia and the UAE. By contrast, the rate for foreign workers is typically above 70 per cent (Figure 10.10). Data for Bahrain and Oman were not available at this level of disaggregation. This indicator provides valuable information on the level of utilization of the labor force.

Differences are also evident in the skill levels of nationals and foreign workers in the region (Figure 10.11). While data are lacking for some GCC countries, results for Kuwait, Saudi Arabia and Qatar provide some basis for comparison. Clearly, while nationals have the advantage in secondary education level skills, the proportion of non-nationals with primary education level skills is higher. The proportion of university level skills is mixed. The higher concentration of secondary level skills among nationals, as compared with foreign workers, should position them well for technical occupations requiring vocational training, which will be in high demand during further deployment of renewable energy technologies.

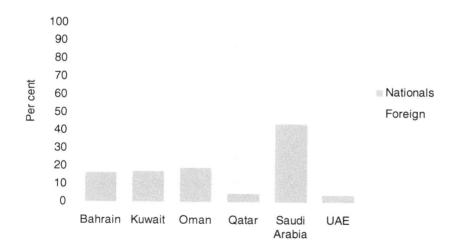

Figure 10.9 Labor force composition in GCC countries, 2016 (national statistical agencies)

Source: Labour Market Regulatory Authority, Bahrain (2014); Public Authority for Civil Information, Kuwait (2014); General Directorate of Civil Status, Oman (Mid-2014); Annual Bulletin of Labor Force Sample survey , Qatar (2016); General Authority for Statistics – Labor Force Survey, Saudi Arabia (2017 Q4, Table 32); Dubai Statistics Center – Labour Force Survey (2017).

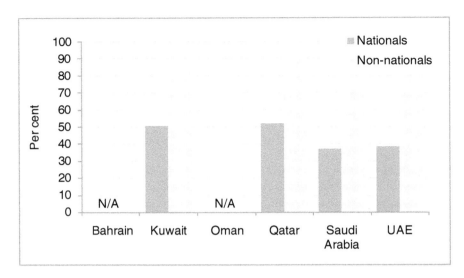

Figure 10.10 Employment rates of nationals and non-nationals in GCC countries, latest year or period available (national statistical agencies)

Source: Bahrain Central Informatics Organisation, Census (2010); Kuwait Public Authority for Civil Information (Dec. 2012); National Centre for Statistical Information, Statistical Yearbook (2013) (Data does not include nationals and non-nationals in the "Public administration and defense, compulsory social security"); Qatar Statistics Authority, Quarterly Labor Force Survey (Q4, 2013); General Authority for Statistics – Labor Force Survey, Saudi Arabia (2013); UAE National Bureau of Statistics, Labor Force Survey (2009).

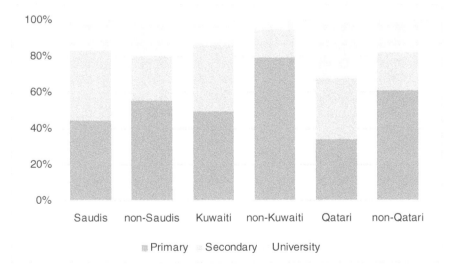

Figure 10.11 Working age population by level of education, selected GCC countries, latest year or period available (national statistical agencies)

Sources: Saudi Arabia General Authority for Statistics, 2014; Kuwait Public Authority for Civil Information, 2012; Qatar Statistics Authority, 2012).

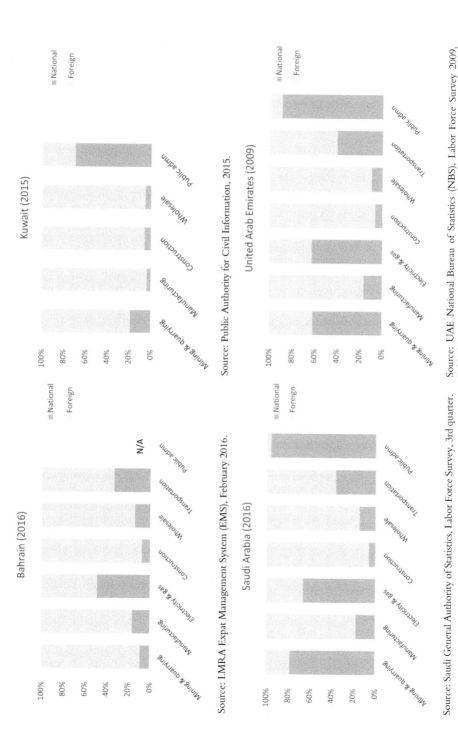

Kuwait (2015)

Source: Public Authority for Civil Information, 2015.

United Arab Emirates (2009)

Source: UAE National Bureau of Statistics (NBS), Labor Force Survey 2009, Table 21.

Bahrain (2016)

Source: LMRA Expat Management System (EMS), February 2016.

Saudi Arabia (2016)

Source: Saudi General Authority of Statistics, Labor Force Survey, 3rd quarter.

Figure 10.12 Distribution of employed population (15 years of age and over) by nationality group according to industry activity

A high degree of labor segregation between nationals and non-nationals is evident, with nationals highly concentrated in public administration. Indeed, the level of nationals within this sector reaches 90 per cent in Saudi Arabia and the UAE but is somewhat lower in Kuwait (70 per cent) (Figure 10.12). Electricity and gas, where the split is closer to 50 per cent, is perhaps the most balanced sector in terms of distribution between nationals and non-nationals, except for Kuwait, which relies entirely on non-nationals. These features are common in countries characterized by oil based rent distribution, which creates distortion resulting in an over-staffed public sector while stifling employment in the private sector (Eifert et al. 2003).

The vast majority of low-skilled and low-paying jobs – e.g., construction, manufacturing, and wholesale – in the private sector in GCC countries is filled by expatriates, reaching 85 per cent or more. The proportion of nationals in labor intensive sectors is correspondingly low. As discussed earlier, the concentration of secondary level skills among nationals could translate into an advantage in terms of expected labor productivity over lower skilled foreign workers in these sectors. The evidence, however, suggests otherwise. This has obvious implications for the employment of young nationals in the renewables sector, which relate to several market and behavioral failures, which will be discussed more thoroughly later.

These structural features of the GCC labor market are not expected to change quickly. This implies that, in construction and manufacturing – the two sectors in which most jobs in renewable energy would be created in the short term – the traditional practice of employing lower skilled foreign workers is likely to continue. The lower wages that can be paid to this group, along with the relative flexibility of labor contracts, remain attractive to employers.

The combination of high wage expectations of GCC nationals and easy access to low-cost foreign labor makes nationals less competitive in the private sector labor market. This is a tradeoff that employers have to consider when choosing which group of workers to hire. Policies to nationalize the labor force by favoring the employment of nationals, such as the Nitaqat program in Saudi Arabia, have had some degree of success. Due to costs and productivity considerations, however, employers in the GCC have historically shown some resistance to similar programs. Going forward, it is anticipated that progress will be more difficult to achieve in particular sectors.

Visualizing labor distribution in Saudi Arabia in another format delivers additional insights. In Figure 10.13, the magnitude of various sectors is indicated by the relative size of the bubbles, while shading indicates the concentration of Saudi nationals within each sector. A high concentration (dark bubbles) in sectors such as public administration and education can be partly explained by the fact that these sectors offer higher wages, better benefits and shorter working hours than are found in construction, manufacturing or wholesale, where concentration of Saudis is low (light colored bubbles). Social norms, for reasons explained later, are also likely to influence the labor market decisions of both national employers and employees. This confluence of factors and the corresponding labor market trends are unlikely to change in the short term, as these signals remain strong even among young workers.

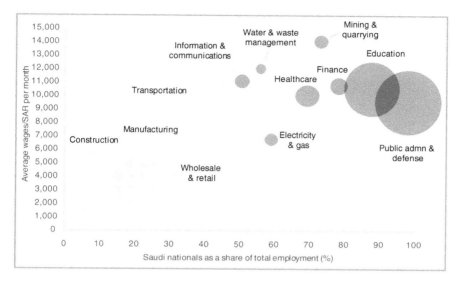

Figure 10.13 Labor distribution in Saudi Arabia, main sectoral industries, 2016
Source: Saudi General Authority for Statistics, Labor Force Survey, 3rd quarter.

GCC policies of rent distribution, which aim to provide public employment to local populations, have created some distortions in the labor market. The wide wage disparity between the public and private sectors leads to higher reservation wages for nationals. This situation creates a strong disincentive for nationals to seek private sector employment or become entrepreneurs in emerging sectors such as renewable energy.

Surveys show that over 60 per cent of GCC students still focus their job searches primarily on the public sector, which tends to offer attractive wages, good benefits, job security and relatively fewer working hours than the private sector. Queuing for public-sector jobs can then be seen as a rational strategy for young national job seekers. In Kuwait and Qatar, the proportion rises to over 70 per cent of students (E&Y 2015:24). As GCC nationals have traditionally shunned jobs outside in the public sector, exceptional efforts would have to be made to attract workers to sectors requiring technical and vocational training, which are among the requirements for many jobs in the renewables sector.

The preferences that drive national labor market searches carry more serious consequences. Over time, they have influenced human capital formation in the GCC region, resulting in a significant skills mismatch across the labor market: development of skills relevant to the public sector has been pursued at the expense of skills more aligned with the private sector.

As discussed earlier, many of the skill requirements for the renewables sector will be in science and engineering. However, the choice of fields of study among young people in the GCC (Figure 10.14) provides evidence that the

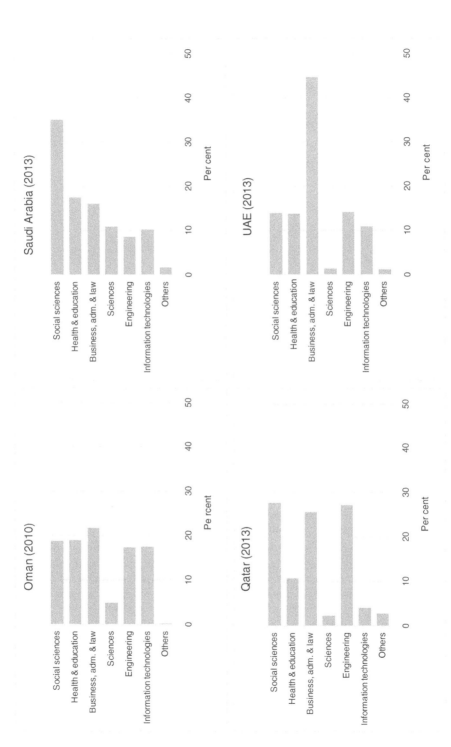

Figure 10.14 Distribution of university graduates across main fields of study

public sector has long been the main client of the education system. Social science, business, administration and law are the most popular fields of study in Saudi Arabia and the UAE, while enrollment in sciences and engineering is low. Oman and Qatar show a more balanced distribution.

Enrollment levels show that vocational and technical training remains largely neglected in the Gulf region. Bahrain appears to perform relatively well among GCC countries with a share of 16 per cent of its upper secondary education programs devoted to vocational training, against less than 5 per cent in other GCC countries. These estimates contrast sharply with levels of 46 per cent in China and 48 per cent in countries belonging to the Organisation for Economic Co-operation and Development (OECD) (Figure 10.15).

Faced with the potential demand for both skilled and unskilled workers in the renewables sector, the skill bias towards the public service and the lack of vocational training are problematic for the employment of GCC nationals in the emerging renewables sector. While university level qualifications will be necessary to fill positions in fields such as engineering, meteorology, project development and R&D, technical and vocational qualifications will be more relevant to jobs in system design and installation, as well as for indirect jobs in transport and administration.

While the opportunity for job creation in renewable energy appears important in the GCC, maximizing its potential will require appropriate policy development, particularly in terms of labor market structures and information,

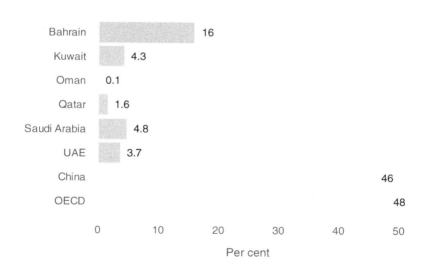

Figure 10.15 Share of vocational programs among upper secondary education programs, 2013

Source: OECD, World Indicators of Skills for Employment.

Note: data for Kuwait refer to 2012.

as well as skills development systems. The absence, or shortage, of a range of skilled workers could ultimately compromise the quality and performance of renewable energy systems, making it important to ensure the relevant range of professional, vocational, and technical training is available to nationals. Unless current job preferences can be altered among the local population, it seems likely that the bulk of jobs created in the short term, i.e., in the construction and manufacturing phase, would not require much training and are likely to continue to be occupied by low-skilled foreign workers.

Potential policy actions

To date, policy actions by governments to promote nationalization of GCC labor forces have been varied. They have included establishing quotas at the company and sector levels (Box 10.2) and restricted public sector hiring to nationals (Oman). In other case, they have provided for greater mobility of foreign workers among employers (Qatar, Saudi Arabia), have increased fees on foreign work visas (Bahrain, Oman, Saudi Arabia) or have imposed local content requirements (Oman, Saudi Arabia, the UAE). At the same time, another important objective has been to improve nationals' access to the private labor market – especially in new sectors being developed as part of efforts to diversify the economy away from oil. This would include renewable energy.

While many construction and manufacturing jobs arising from deployment of renewable energy will likely continue to be filled by low-skilled foreign workers, the sector is still expected to create some opportunities for nationals with appropriate professional, technical, and vocational training. To capture these opportunities and improve labor market outcomes for nationals, governments, in partnership with private stakeholders, may need to continue expanding efforts on complementary active labor market policies such as training programs and job search assistance targeting the skills required. The following briefly outlines measures that could help strengthen the incentives for, and abilities of, nationals to work in this emerging sector.

Addressing the problem of asymmetrical labor market information

Fewer than 30 per cent of GCC students claim to have sufficient information about the labor market in general. This is also true for job opportunities, qualification requirements, or application processes to enter the labor market (E&Y 2015). This asymmetrical labor market information, which arises mainly from the lack of access to and low interpretability of information, is known to lead to an inefficient allocation of jobs and workers in the labor market. Given the expectations of many nationals to work in the public service, it is important for governments and industry to send clear signals to potential workers about the demand for certain skills and potential opportunities in the renewables sector. In fact, as the renewable energy sector expands and creates more jobs, collecting relevant information on employment trends and requirements will be essential to inform labor market choices about this sector.

Educating young GCC nationals about employment opportunities in the renewable energy sector – which can include career choices – is crucial. As investment in human capital development implies an important time dimension, it is thus important to prepare and provide young people with relevant information about the workplace early on. This will help ensure alignment between education and training and the needs of employers in the sector. To encourage progress, governments and the private sector may need to continue working closely with schools, colleges and universities to ensure that potential job seekers have necessary information about the labor market and the career opportunities renewable energy might bring. This would imply further strategic investments in the education-to-employment ecosystem.

Dealing with sectoral and occupational biases

The clear preference of young nationals for jobs with certain characteristics creates additional challenges in the GCC context. In this case, measures to help reduce the distaste of GCC youth for certain types of private sector employment may be beneficial.

That GCC workers, including young people entering or planning to enter the workforce, have long had a strong bias for certain types of jobs in certain sectors is well documented. Their preference for public-sector employment in particular means much of the region's human capital investment has been directed toward specific fields of study and training. This situation has exacerbated the mismatch between the supply of skills and the demands of the labor market. In parallel, lower interest in medium skilled technical jobs has prevented nationals from taking employment opportunities even though their higher skill endowment ought to be a comparative advantage over low-skilled foreign workers.

Promoting certain jobs in the renewables sector as being socially acceptable to young GCC nationals may take time. It will, however, be necessary to continue enticing them towards jobs as skilled technicians in that sector. This promotional work could be complemented, under specific conditions, with incentives such as higher pay to help reduce the differentials with public employment. Such an approach may be challenging, however, as it would need to be done without imposing undue costs on businesses, which could erode competitiveness and potentially reduce economic growth. While promoting and subsidizing employment of nationals in the renewables sector could help reduce the distortion towards public-sector employment, it could also create a different kind of distortion in which nationals are preferred over more qualified foreign workers – perhaps resulting in a less economically efficient outcome.

Developing the workforce through education and training

Only 29 per cent of GCC employers currently feel that the education system in the Gulf region adequately prepares students with the right technical skills for the jobs available (E&Y 2015). Moreover, large numbers of nationals have little or no job skills, making them largely unemployable in any sector, including RE related jobs.

As diversification accelerates and GCC economies shift away from hydro-carbon industries, new and existing workers alike will need to develop new skills to succeed in the renewables sector. As businesses operating in the region consistently rank restrictive labor regulations and inadequately trained work-forces as their biggest barriers (World Economic Forum 2014), education, training, and retraining programs need to maintain their focus on reducing skill mismatches. It is therefore essential that stakeholders identify and communicate the specific needs of the renewable energy sector to job seekers.

Technical and vocational training programs still represent a relatively small proportion of secondary level education in the Gulf region. Further improv-ing the education and skill system is key to meeting the increasing needs for skilled workers in the renewable energy sector. While GCC governments have launched some programs to narrow the skill mismatches, more effort is needed. A case could also be made to integrate skills development for the renewable energy sector into the wider training and skills development policy. As it is important to build resiliency among workers to take advantage of wider opportunities, such approach would prevent the training system in the sector from becoming a separate form of skills development system isolated from the overall labor market.

Lack of adequate skills is a major barrier to renewables deployment in both industrialized and developing countries, including frequent shortages of engi-neers and technicians across all related technologies (ILO 2011). Yet demand is rising for workers with technical skills that can be applied in renewable energy and other sectors. This creates increased competition for such skills across the labor market which, in turn, could positively impact wages for these workers.

Although it can take time to realize returns on investments in human capi-tal, taking action to quickly expand technical and vocational training in the GCC could help address anticipated labor needs in the renewable energy sector in the immediate future. Expanding programs under the Saudi Technical and Vocational Training Corporation (TVTC), as well as the 'Duroob program' sponsored by the Saudi Ministry of Labor, could help narrow the skill gap. The Duroob program is a major initiative that specializes in addressing the needs of job seekers, most of whom fall into the youth age group.

Another positive step is that Saudi Arabia is in the early stages of expanding its vocational training system nearly fourfold in the next ten years through its Colleges of Excellence (COE) initiative, which offers quality vocational train-ing programs through public-private partnerships with top level global training providers in the Kingdom. With a focus on the employer's needs, the Colleges enable students to obtain world class qualifications. The Abu Dhabi Center for Technical and Vocational Education and Training, with its plans to open sev-eral centers, is another commendable attempt to address the challenge (Deloitte 2014). Faced with a similar shortage of sector relevant skills a few years ago, China took aggressive policy action to fill the gap (Box 10.2).

Box 10.2   China Wind Power Research and Training Project (CWPP)

With a strategy to rapidly increase wind-generated electrical power, the Chinese government recognized the need to improve the technical capacities of institutions involved in the expansion and upgrading of the national grid to accommodate this new source. In collaboration with industry, the government created intensive, tailor-made vocational training courses that would prepare workers to quickly be effective on the job.

The Suzhou Training Centre of CWPP is the only wind power O&M technician training institution of its kind in China. Estimating the number of technicians needed to grow from around 16,000 in 2009 to 86,000 in 2020, the Center provides fundamental training in wind power technology, and conveys highly sought-after understanding of specific methodologies and procedures needed for wind turbine testing and certification. Importantly, it also improves the trainees' practical skills through hands-on practice.

Source: China Wind Power Center

Optimizing public policy coordination

A comprehensive approach to policy, involving several stakeholders, would help to improve labor market information and to assess training needs associated with the renewable energy sector. For instance, with continued and further inputs from private actors, governments could better provide direction and coordination that would help drive vocational and technical training content toward the specific requirements of the industry.

By building on their experience in improving transparency about stimulation policies, ministries responsible for education and advanced training could further boost the participation of market actors in skill development activities. This, in turn, would allow private actors to make better investment decisions about growing businesses in the sector. This would also help GCC countries develop a workforce supply that more closely aligns with market demands. Collaboration across sectors could then help further promote a clear, consistent set of needs with the aim to support or create fast-track apprenticeships for participating students.

Conclusions

Evidence to date does suggest an overall positive potential for job creation as a result of the deployment of renewable energy – particularly solar. Yet the degree to which such a shift will influence employment effects in the GCC may be debated and warrants further assessment. Given the characteristics of GCC labor markets, a relevant issue for public policy is whether young nationals in these countries will be willing and able to take advantage of these job prospects.

This chapter has highlighted several constraints – including asymmetrical information and skill development as well as sectoral and occupational segregation – that might hamper the ability to realize these potential job opportunities through national workers. It also identifies some of the factors driving these changes in GCC countries and consequences that should be studied in more detail. The great majority of jobs in renewables will be in occupations such as laborers and installers. Historically, these have been unattractive to GCC nationals, which means employment opportunities for GCC nationals will be lower than if job creation is examined in the aggregate. Still, further deployment of renewable energy technologies will provide some valued added jobs that require more specific technical and vocational training. The estimated number of newly created jobs that could be, or are likely to be, filled by nationals is relevant for public authorities as it would directly impact, in terms of both quantity and quality, the training needs for national populations and the financial requirements to roll out such programs.

With demographic developments amplifying the pressure on GCC labor markets, an adequate policy response in these areas is vital. If no action is taken, the looming skills gap, reflecting the risk of skill shortages and/or deficiency in the quality of skills, in the renewable energy sector could slow the deployment and expansion of locally-developed technologies and related job creation. It could also represent a missed opportunity to train and employ a rising young population in this emerging sector.

Note

1 Direct employment refers to additional jobs created within the renewable energy sector (e.g., manufacturing or installation of solar panels). Indirect employment is measured as jobs created as other sectors expand their outputs to supply the renewable energy sector: e.g., providing raw materials (such as steel and other metals, basic electronic components, etc.). Induced employment refers to jobs created because of the increased household expenditure of direct and indirect employees. As a result, induced employment can include a wide range of non-industry jobs (e.g., teachers, retail jobs, postal workers) who benefit from the increased spending in the economy. See Wei et al. (2010) for more details about these distinctions.

References

Alvarez GC, Jara RM, Julián JRR et al. (2009) Study of the Effects on Employment of Public Aid to Renewable Energy Sources. *Procesos De Mercado* 7(1), Rey Juan Carlos University, Madrid. www.juandemariana.org/sites/default/files/investigacion/090327-employment-public-aid-renewable.pdf.

Bahrain Economic Development Board (2008) *From Regional Pioneer to Global Contender: The Bahrain Economic Vision 2030.* www.evisa.gov.bh/Vision2030English lowresolution.pdf.

Bezdek (2009) *Green Collar Jobs in the U.S., and Colorado: Economic Drivers for the 21st Century.* Prepared for the American Solar Energy Society (ASES), Boulder, CO.

Blazquez, J, Hunt LC, and Manzano B (2017) Oil Subsidies, and Renewable Energy in Saudi Arabia: A General Equilibrium Approach. *The Energy Journal* 38:1–17.

Blyth W, Gross R, Speirs J et al. (2014) *Low Carbon Jobs: The Evidence for Net Job Creation from Policy Support for Energy Efficiency, and Renewable Energy.* UK Energy Research Centre, London. www.ukerc.ac.uk/publications/low-carbon-jobs-the-evidence-for-net-job-creation-from-policy-support-for-energy-efficiency-and-renewable-energy.html.

Böhringer C, Keller A, and Van Der Werf E (2013) Are Green Hopes Too Rosy? Employment, and Welfare Impacts of Renewable Energy Promotion. *Energy Economics* 36:277–285.

Cameron L, and Van Der Zwaan B (2015) Employment Factors for Wind, and Solar Energy Technologies: A Literature Review. *Renewable and Sustainable Energy Reviews* 45:160–172.

China Wind Power Center (CWPC) www.cwpc.cn/cwpp/en/training/.

Cosar AK (2010) *Adjusting to Trade Liberalization: Reallocation, and Labor Market Policies.* University of Chicago, Booth School of Business, Chicago, IL. http://economics.yale.edu/sites/default/files/files/Workshops-Seminars/International-Trade/cosar-101103.pdf.

Côté S, and Wogan D (2016) *Opportunities, and Challenges in Reforming Energy Prices in GCC Countries.* KAPSARC discussion paper KS-1629-WB028A. KAPSARC, Riyadh. www.kapsarc.org/wp-content/uploads/2016/06/KS-1629-WB028A-Opportunities-and-Challenges-in-Reforming-Energy-Prices-in-GCC-Countries.pdf.

Deloitte (2014) School's Out, Now What? Meeting the Skills Challenge in A Middle East Point of View. *ME Point of View* issue 13. Spring 2014 issue. www2.deloitte.com/content/dam/Deloitte/xe/Documents/About-Deloitte/mepovdocuments/mepov13/dtme_mepov13_School%20is%20out.pdf.

Dix-Carneiro R (2010) *Trade Liberalization, and Labor Market Dynamics.* CEPS Working Paper 212, Princeton University, Department of Economics, Center for Economic Policy Studies, Princeton, NJ.

E&Y (Ernst & Young) (2015) *How Will the GCC Close the Skills Gap?* Available via Ernst & Young. www.ey.com/Publication/vwLUAssets/EY-gcc-education-report-how-will-the-gcc-close-the-skills-gap/$FILE/GCC%20Education%20report%20FINAL%20AU3093.pdf.

Eifert B, Gelb A, and Tallroth NB (2003) *Managing Oil Wealth. Finance and Development,* 40(1). www.imf.org/external/pubs/ft/fandd/2003/03/eife.htm, http://faculty.nps.edu/relooney/3040_c139.pdf.

Furchtgott-Roth D (2012) The Elusive, and Expensive Green Job. *Energy Economics* 34(Suppl. 1), S43–S52.

German Ministry of the Environment, Nature Conservation, and Nuclear Safety (2006) *Renewable Energy: Employment Effects.* Berlin, Germany, June.

Hughes G (2011) *The Myth of Green Jobs. The Global Warming Policy Foundation (GWPF) Report 2.* http://rpieu.org/Publications/2011/Gordon_Hughes_The_Myth_of_Green_Jobs_Sep2011.pdf.

Hvidt M (2013) *Economic Diversification in GCC Countries: Past Record, and Future Trends*. Research Paper Kuwait Programme on Development, Governance, and Globalisation in the Gulf States, vol 27. London School of Economics, and Political Science, London, pp 34–35. www.lse.ac.uk/middleEastCentre/kuwait/documents/Economic-diversification-in-the-GCC-countries.pdf.

IEA (International Energy Agency) (2015) *World Energy Statistics*. OECD/IEA, Paris.

International Labour Organisation (2011) *Skills for Green Jobs: A Global View*. Geneva: ILO.

IRENA (International Renewable Energy Agency) (2013) *Renewable Energy, and Jobs*. International Renewable Energy Agency, Abu Dhabi. www.irena.org/-/media/Files/IRENA/Agency/Publication/2013/rejobs.pdf.

IRENA (2016a) *Renewable Energy Benefits: Measuring the Economics*. International Renewable Energy Agency, Abu Dhabi. www.irena.org/DocumentDownloads/Publications/IRENA_Measuring-the-Economics_2016.pdf.

IRENA (2016b). *Renewable Energy Market Analysis: GCC Region*. International Renewable Energy Agency, Abu Dhabi. www.irena.org/DocumentDownloads/Publications/IRENA_Market_GCC_2016.pdf.

IRENA (2017) *Rethinking Energy 2017: Accelerating the Global Energy Transformation*. International Renewable Energy Agency, Abu Dhabi. www.irena.org/DocumentDownloads/Publications/IRENA_REthinking_Energy_2017.pdf.

Kammen DM, Kapadia K, and Fripp M (2004) *Putting Renewables to Work: How Many Jobs Can the Clean Energy Industry Generate?* Renewable, and Appropriate Energy Laboratory (RAEL) report, University of California, Berkeley, CA. http://community-wealth.org/sites/clone.community-wealth.org/files/downloads/paper-kammen-et-al.pdf.

Kingdom of Saudi Arabia (2016a) *National Transformation Program 2020*. Riyadh, KSA.

Kingdom of Saudi Arabia (2016b) *Vision 2030*. Riyadh, KSA. http://vision2030.gov.sa/en.

Kuwait General Secretariat of the Supreme Council for Planning, and Development (2010) *State Vision Kuwait 2035*. www.newkuwait.gov.kw/en/plan/.

McKinsey Global Institute (2015) *Saudi Arabia Beyond Oil: The Investment, and Productivity Transformation*.

Michaels R, and Murphy RP (2009) *Green Jobs: Fact or Fiction?* Institute for Energy Research, Houston, Texas. www.adapttech.it/old/files/document/1731GREEN_JOBS_FACT_.pdf.

Ministry of National Economy (1995) *Long-Term Development Strategy (1996–2020): The Vision for Oman's Economy – 2020*. Sultanate of Oman. www.scp.gov.om/PDF/NinthFiveYearPlan.docx.

Morriss AP, Bogart WT, Dorchak A et al. (2009) *Green Jobs Myths*. University of Illinois Law & Economics Research Paper No. LE09-001, and Case Western Reserve University Research Paper Series No. 09–15. University of Illinois, Case Western Reserve University, Champaign, IL.

OECD (2012) *The Jobs Potential of a Shift Towards a Low-Carbon Economy*. OECD, Paris.

OPEC (Organisation of the Petroleum Exporting Countries) (2016) *World Oil Outlook 2016*. October, OPEC, Vienna.

Pollin R, Heintz J, and Garrett-Peltier H (2009) *The Economic Benefits of Investing in Clean Energy: How the Economic Stimulus Program, and New Legislation can Boost U.S. Economic Growth, and Employment (June)*. Political Economy Research Institute, University of Massachusetts, Amherst, MA. www.peri.umass.edu/fileadmin/pdf/other_publication_types/green_economics/economic_benefits/economic_benefits.PDF.

Qatar General Secretariat for Development Planning (2008) *Qatar National Vision 2030*. Doha, Qatar. www.mdps.gov.qa/en/knowledge/HomePagePublications/QNV2030_English_v2.pdf.

Ragwitz M, Schade W, Breitschopf B et al. (2009). *The Impact of Renewable Energy Policy on Economic Growth, and Employment in the European Union*. European Commission, DG Energy, and Transport, Brussels. http://temis.documentation.developpement-durable.gouv.fr/docs/Temis/0064/Temis-0064479/17802.pdf.

Shanefelter JK (2008) *Restructuring, Ownership, and Efficiency: The Case of Labor in Electricity Generation*. Economic Analysis Group Discussion Paper EA 08–12. Department of Justice, Washington, DC. http://dx.doi.org/10.2139/ssrn.1313186.

United Arab Emirates Cabinet (2010) *UAE Vision 2021: United in Ambition, and Determination*. Abu Dhabi: Government of United Arab Emirates. https://www.vision2021.ae/en.

UNEP (United Nations Environment Programme) (2008) *Green Jobs: Towards Decent Work in a Sustainable Low Carbon World*. UNEP, Nairobi.

Van der Zwaan B, Cameron L, and Kober T (2013) Potential for Renewable Energy Jobs in the Middle East. *Energy Policy* 60:296–304.

Wei M, Patadia S, and Kammen DM (2010) Putting Renewables, and Energy Efficiency to Work: How Many Jobs can the Clean Energy Industry Generate in the US? *Energy Policy* 38(2):919–931.

World Bank (2012) *Inclusive Green Growth: The Pathway to Sustainable Development*. World Bank, Washington, DC. doi:10.1596/978-0-8213-9551-6.

World Bank (n.d.) World Development Indicators. *Accessed: 18 Jul* 2018. http://databank.worldbank.org/data/reports.aspx?source=world-development-indicators.

World Economic Forum (2014) *Rethinking Arab Employment: A Systemic Approach for Resource-Endowed Economies*.

11 Forging a more centralized GCC renewable energy policy

Omar Al-Ubaydli, Ghada Abdulla and Lama Yaseen

Abstract

Countries belonging to the Gulf Cooperation Council (GCC) have been planning to transform into knowledge economies for some time. Individually and collectively, however, they have faced difficulties in realizing their goals for several reasons, including a lack of expertise among citizens to support development of cutting-edge research and insufficient resources to compete with global leaders in research and development (R&D).

This chapter will explore how a more centralized GCC renewable energy policy can contribute to transforming the region into a knowledge economy, in part by addressing the shortcomings of previous efforts. In particular, GCC countries might opt to pool their resources to boost the effectiveness of their R&D, while also adopting technology nationalization policies to build the requisite homegrown talent as quickly as possible. The chapter will also explore how more centralized renewables policies can contribute to enhancing GCC economic integration.

Policy relevant insights

- In the absence of centralized policies and project coordination, the renewable energy sector in the GCC is operating below potential.
- Gains from greater centralization include minimization of research duplication and greater opportunity to exploit the economies of scale associated with joint efforts.
- Cooperation in renewable energy can serve as a pilot test for cooperation in other domains, ultimately contributing to GCC economic integration.
- Enhanced R&D on renewables can help GCC countries transition to knowledge-based economies.

Introduction

Renewable energy offers several advantages over traditional power sources, most notably lower environmental damage (Dincer 2000). Beyond this, energy security benefits stem from the diversification of energy sources (Valentine 2011), even in the case of energy-exporting countries, as energy sources vary in terms of susceptibility to threats such as natural disasters or terrorist attacks. Such advantages have motivated all six Gulf Cooperation Council (GCC) countries to invest significant resources in developing their own renewable energy projects, as they seek to shift away from dependence upon fossil fuels. In 2015, renewables investments in the GCC were around $900 million, with $400 million invested by the United Arab Emirates (UAE) in the Mohammed bin Rashid Al Maktoum (MBR) solar park and $400 million invested by Kuwait in the Shagaya Renewable Energy Park (IRENA 2016b). Similarly, in 2011, the UAE invested $800 million in the Shams 1 solar power project (IRENA 2016b).

A key challenge facing these projects is that the Gulf climate limits the effectiveness of many prevailing renewable energy technologies, creating a need for research and development (R&D) to adapt such technologies for GCC circumstances (Al Nasser 1995). For example, while many lay people, including GCC citizens, perceive the clear skies and blazing sun associated with the Gulf's arid climate as ideal for solar power generation, high temperatures (Skoplaki and Palyvos 2009) and dusty winds (Mani and Pillai 2010) seriously impair the efficiency of solar cells. Modifications to existing technologies will be necessary if solar energy is to constitute an economical alternative to fossil fuels (Al Nasser 1995).

While GCC countries have similar renewables goals and share similar challenges, a prevailing feature of current renewable energy efforts is that each country is operating unilaterally with, at best, minimal, and most frequently zero, collaboration or coordination with others. While decentralized competition among research units, whether or not they are separated by political boundaries, is generally a desirable trait (Hayek 1945), as it is conducive to higher research standards, it can also lead to wasteful replication of research (Bolton and Farrell 1990). Higher levels of centralization and coordination in research production can be especially useful due to the economies of scale it can bring to R&D (Henderson and Cockburn 1996). The benefits of cost-sharing R&D are most prominent when practitioners exhibit a homogenous skill set (Sakakibara 1997), which is likely to be the case in the nascent renewable energy efforts of the GCC countries.

This chapter argues that GCC countries might consider adopting a more centralized renewables policy to overcome three nominally independent problems that all six members currently face: insufficient R&D; poorly tailored renewable energy technologies; and partially malfunctioning economic integration.

Insufficient R&D, the first problem, relates to the GCC countries' desire to strengthen R&D output as part of a broader strategy to diversify their economies away from oil and toward knowledge economy activities. At present, GCC countries occupy low positions in global research output rankings, especially if analysis accounts for per capita income levels (McGlennon 2006). Ultimately, the economies of scale associated with centralized R&D efforts can also contribute to addressing the problem of undesirably low levels of research and innovation (R&I) (Fagerberg 1996).

Poorly tailored renewable energy technologies, the second problem, reflects the ineffectiveness of some existing renewable energy technologies in the Gulf climate, especially solar power. This presents a much more specific research challenge, which is likely best tackled by coordinating efforts to exploit economies of scale. The homogeneity of the climate across GCC countries means that required modifications are largely common and confirms the potential advantage of pooling research efforts.

Partially malfunctioning economic integration is the third problem hindering GCC countries' efforts to boost economic integration. While significant steps have been taken to integrate the six economies – including establishing a free trade area, a customs union, a single market and potential plans for a single currency – implementation difficulties have meant that the pace of actual integration has been slower than that of nominally legislated integration (Abdulghaffar et al. 2013). The slow pace can be attributed, at least in part, to the fact that the most important element of the GCC economy – energy exports – is almost completely decentralized. Increasing the degree of centralization in renewables research could be a first step towards a more centralized GCC energy sector and could therefore play a role in accelerating integration of the remaining elements of the economy.

This chapter is organized as follows: the next section examines these three challenges in greater detail. Subsequently, the chapter describes the GCC's renewables projects in their current, decentralized state. We then argue that a more centralized approach can yield significant returns in addressing all three problems identified, after which concluding statements are offered.

Background: three GCC challenges

Each of the three nominally unrelated challenges that GCC countries currently face warrants deeper examination. This section serves as a precursor to making the case that a more centralized renewables policy can potentially contribute to addressing all three.

Insufficient research and development

GCC states are among the countries with the highest gross domestic product (GDP) per capita in the world; however, they have not yet raised their R&D to be on a par with GDP (Figure 11.1). This is a missed opportunity, in light of

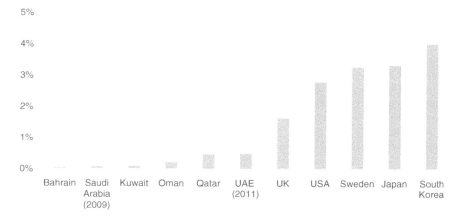

Figure 11.1 Gross domestic expenditure on R&D as a percentage of GDP, 2012
Source: UNESCO Institute for Statistics 2016a.

clear evidence that R&D delivers high private returns, which can be exceeded by social returns (Hall et al. 2009). R&D increases the productivity of the innovating firm, resulting not only in profit increases but also in cost reductions and spillover effects to other firms (Hall et al. 2009).

This underinvestment in R&D is reflected in the GCC countries' generally low rankings in numerous indicators relating to knowledge and innovation (Table 11.1). According to the World Economic Forum's 2015–2016 *Global Competitiveness Report*, among the 144 countries ranked for their quality of scientific research institutions, GCC countries ranked as follows: Qatar (14), the UAE (30), Saudi Arabia (49), Bahrain (87), Kuwait (96) and Oman (116) (WEF 2016). While Qatar and the UAE had substantially higher rankings, indicating superior performance, these can be attributed to the high number of foreign workers that dominate their labor forces (Baldwin-Edwards 2011), rather than to nationals. Anecdotally, local citizen contributions to R&D in these two countries are low – and potentially even lower than in the other GCC states.

A low number of researchers is further evidence of the GCC countries' modest dedication of resources to R&D (Figure 11.2). The four countries for which data are available have less than 600 researchers per million inhabitants, compared with over 4,000 in comparably rich countries such as the United Kingdom and the United States.

Data on scholarly scientific outputs paint a similar picture. The World Bank (2016) reports that in 2013 a total of 12,000 scientific and technical journal articles were published by GCC countries, with Saudi Arabia alone accounting for approximately two-thirds of this figure. In contrast, other countries such as Japan, Germany, the UK and India each published around 100,000 such articles in the same year, while the U.S. and China each published over 400,000.

Table 11.1 GCC country rankings, out of 144, for selected research indicators, 2015–2016 (WEF 2016)

Indicator	BAH	KUW	OMN	QAT	KSA	UAE
Capacity for innovation	70	101	119	12	57	28
Quality of scientific research institutions	87	96	116	14	49	30
Company spending on R&D	87	102	120	9	38	22
University-industry collaboration in R&D	90	107	69	8	38	22
Gov't procurement of advanced tech products	15	102	43	1	7	2
Availability of scientists and engineers	42	85	108	2	38	7
PCT* patents, applications/million pop	56	88	76	29	44	48
Secondary education enrollment	53	32	62	10	7	67
Tertiary education enrollment	73	80	82	103	44	99
Quality of the education system	26	88	106	2	47	12
Quality of math and science education	42	99	102	5	69	11

*Patent Cooperation Treaty (PCT)

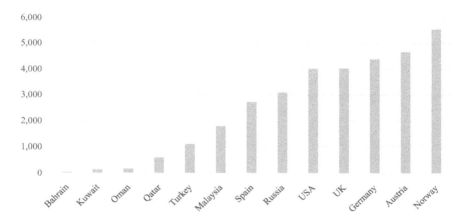

Figure 11.2 Researchers per million inhabitants, 2012
Source: UNESCO Institute for Statistics 2016b.

Patent applications are another alternative measure of research output. Data from the World Intellectual Property Organization (WIPO 2014) *WIPO Patent Report: Statistics on Worldwide Patent Activity* show that around 700 patent applications were received from the GCC in 2014. This can be compared with over 800,000 patent applications from China, around 290,000 from the U.S., and around 270,000 from Japan. In the case of both journal articles and patent applications, adjusting for population does not alter the fact that GCC countries rank low across these metrics.

The GCC countries are fully aware of their underperformance in the innovation domain and have made strengthening their R&D sectors a key goal in their economic visions. In fact, a common theme is the desire to transform into global leaders in innovation, as part of a transition from oil-based economies to knowledge-based ones.

In light of the relatively small size of GCC countries, any bid to make significant progress in knowledge production cannot be wide-ranging. Rather, these countries will have to focus on a relatively narrow range of technologies in which to advance. The next subsection discusses a domain where the returns to R&D are likely to be substantial.

Poorly tailored renewable energy technologies

Among the different sources of renewable energy, solar power has the best potential for GCC countries: long days and clear skies throughout the year give the region high solar radiation using two key measures. The average global horizontal irradiation (GHI) – which measures the total amount of shortwave radiation received by a surface parallel to the ground – is estimated at about 6 kilowatt hours per square meter (kWh/sq m) per day (Meltzer et al. 2014). GHI is the most important parameter used to estimate the average electricity yield from solar photovoltaic (PV) power systems. Direct normal irradiance (DNI), the most suitable measure of solar power for solar concentrating (CSP) technology, is around 4.5 kWh/sq m per day (Meltzer et al. 2014). By comparison, Germany, which is a leading country globally in solar energy deployment, has a GHI of around 3 kWh/sq m per day and a DNI of around 2.5 kWh/sq m per day (Solargis 2017). In terms of solar power potential, GCC countries are located in one of the most richly endowed regions in the world.

Considering this large solar power potential, investing in renewable energy technologies seems bound to be a logical step for GCC countries. However, the potential for profitability, and to secure large financial returns from such investment, depends not only on the solar radiance available but also on the efficiency of solar installations and other factors such as the ambient temperature, shading, local wind speed, glazing cover transmittance, plate absorbance, etc. As some of these factors are less favorable in the GCC region, existing technologies may need to be developed further to better suit the local climate.

Temperature, for instance, plays a key role in the solar PV conversion process; on average, PV cells typically convert 6 per cent to 20 per cent of the solar radiation received into electricity (Dubey et al. 2013). The rest of the solar radiation is converted into heat, resulting in an increase in the temperature of the panel. As the temperature increases, the efficiency of solar PV panels falls; every 1 Kelvin (K) increase in the temperature of a crystalline solar cell decreases its output power by 0.65 per cent (Radziemska 2003). In reality, the ideal environment for solar PV technologies is cold, sunny locations. Weather in GCC countries is hot most of the year, with summer noted for extreme temperatures that can exceed 50°C.

The climate in the GCC is also dusty (Touati et al. 2013), a condition that also has negative effects on the efficiency of solar cells and leads to increased maintenance costs. Dust accumulation, for example, has been found to reduce the performance of solar PV installations in Saudi Arabia by 32 per cent after just eight months (Salim et al. 1988). Similarly, in Kuwait, the accumulation of dust in just 38 days resulted in a 17 per cent to 65 per cent reduction in performance, depending on the tilt angles, ranging from 0° to 60° (Sayigh et al. 1985). The effect of dust on the capacity factor ratio – the ratio between actual energy output to maximum potential output over the same period of time – between a clean and a dust-covered panel is exponential, since dust attracts more dust (Kaldellis and Kapsali 2011).

Humidity, which is a factor in some areas of the GCC region, also affects solar panels in two ways. First, water vapor particles or water particles may refract, reflect, or diffract the sunlight, affecting the irradiance level received by panels and resulting in reduced efficiency (Mekhilef et al. 2012). Second, water droplets seeping into the solar cell enclosure cause degradation of the panel (Mekhilef et al. 2012). Research carried out in Oman found a significant negative relationship between humidity and solar PV efficiency for all three types of solar PV studied: polycrystalline, monocrystalline and amorphous silicon (Kazem et al. 2012). High humidity also leads to the formation of dew on solar cells, which increases the settlement of dust, thus creating a dual negative impact (Elminir et al. 2006).

A consequence of these environmental conditions in the GCC region is that frequent cleaning is required to maintain the high efficiency of solar cells. Considering the region's water scarcity, this is costly from financial and resource perspectives. It should be noted, however, that water consumption of solar technologies is less intense than for conventional oil and gas generation plants (Mielke et al. 2010).

Considering the mix of positive and negative climatic factors for solar generation, the opportunity for GCC countries may lie in designing innovative PV and CSP systems to better suit their climate or in modifying existing technologies. There is large potential, for example, to develop more efficient cleaning technologies. As other regions of the world have similar conditions, opportunity also exists to deploy new technologies beyond the GCC region.

Partially malfunctioning economic integration

A completely unrelated challenge facing GCC countries concerns their economic integration plan. Since its launch in 1981, the GCC has regarded economic integration as a key goal. Most likely, it drew inspiration from the path of the European Union (EU) toward greater cooperation, which started with a small free trade area for steel and, by the new millennium, had reached the highly advanced stage of a monetary union. In fact, many aspects of the GCC's institutional structure and operations seem to be overt or tacit efforts to copy the template provided by the European Union (Alasfoor 2007).

Economic integration confers a variety of benefits upon the integrating countries, most notably a larger opportunity to exploit economies of scale, and greater efficiency resulting from higher competition (Baldwin and Venables 1995). The prevailing exemplar for economic integration without full political integration, as reflected in improved levels of technical efficiency and better prices for consumers, is the European Single Market (Allen et al. 1998). But this approach also requires fiscal transfers to underperforming regions.

GCC economic integration started with a free trade area in 1982, before moving on to a customs union in 2003 and a single market in 2008; at present, there are potential plans to introduce a single currency (Rafiq 2011). Recent indicators of economic integration reflect a successful deepening of economic ties among the six countries; for example, intra-GCC trade has expanded from $8 billion in 1980 to $62 billion in 2010 – an average annual growth rate of 7 per cent (Basher 2015).

Despite the substantial progress achieved, however, significant room for improvement remains. In particular, a combination of bureaucratic delays and, on occasion, willful non-compliance show evidence that GCC governments have not always adhered to single market guidelines in the agreed upon manner (Abdulghaffar et al. 2013).

Of particular note is that representatives from the private sectors of the six member states have described a variety of barriers that continue to impede full functioning of the single market. Examples include fees imposed upon goods transported across GCC borders, restrictions on business activities that a GCC national can exercise in another GCC country, and job openings within the region that are clearly reserved for nationals of the host country (Abdulghaffar et al. 2013).

The perpetuation of such impediments represents a significant economic loss at the GCC level, counteracting precisely the reasons that GCC countries (and other blocs) pursue regional economic integration in the first place.

The GCC's current, decentralized approach to renewable energy

This chapter argues that a more centralized policy for renewable energy in the GCC could contribute to simultaneously tackling all three of the problems described above. Before exploring this argument in more detail, it is useful to examine current renewables policies being pursued by the six member states. The descriptions below are not intended to be exhaustive; rather, they provide a solid overview of the nature of the projects underway, which can be characterized as being completely decentralized.

Bahrain

Bahrain aims to achieve 5 per cent of its total electricity generation from renewable energy (Ferroukhi et al. 2016), as part of plans to boost the efficient use of power, a key component of the Bahrain National Vision 2030.

Among the initiatives is a project to deliver 5 megawatts (MW) of distributed PV solar systems using smart energy technology installations such as carports, solar trees, street light poles and ground mounts (Al Nasser et al. 2014). The project will be developed by The Bahrain Petroleum Company (BAPCO) in collaboration with Petra Solar, Caspain Energy Holdings and the National Oil and Gas Authority (NOGA).

The Askar Waste-to-Energy project, structured as a public-private partnership (PPP), is designed to treat 390,000 tons of water per year with an installed capacity of 25 MW connected to the grid. This planned initiative is currently on hold, but authorities are looking to revive it. The Municipalities and Urban Planning Affairs has already received nine bids (Sundar 2016).

Kuwait

According to its economic vision, Kuwait has set a target of using renewable energy to meet 15 per cent of its energy needs by 2030 (IRENA 2016b).

As part of implementing the vision, the Kuwait Institute for Scientific Research (KISR) is working with the Ministry of Electricity and Water (MEW) to develop the Shagaya Renewable Energy Park in western Kuwait, a 70 MW renewable project comprising 50 MW solar thermal, 10 MW wind and 10 MW solar PV (IRENA 2016a, 2016b).

The Partnership Technical Bureau has announced another planned project, an integrated solar combined cycle (ISCC) plant to be located in Al-Abdaliyah, with solar accounting for 60 MW of the total installed capacity of 280 MW. The project is being developed by the MEW, in partnership with Japan's Toyota Tsusho, and is expected to be commissioned by 2018 (Kuwait Partnerships Technical Bureau 2015).

Oman

Oman's Vision 2020 stipulates 10 per cent renewables contribution to energy needs (Sophia 2017). In 2013, Oman's GlassPoint Solar commissioned the first solar enhanced oil recovery (EOR) project in partnership with Petroleum Development Oman (PDO) in Amal. The project is a 7 MW solar plant that produces 11 tons per hour of high steam used to extract 33,000 barrels of oil (Meltzer et al. 2014). GlassPoint Solar also announced development of the second phase, which is a 1 gigawatt (GW) EOR project; measured by peak thermal capacity, it is considered the largest planned solar field in the world (Helman 2015).

Oman is also developing a 50 MW wind farm in Dhofar, through a joint agreement between Abu Dhabi's renewables company Masdar and the Rural Areas Electricity Company (RAECO). This will be the first large-scale wind farm in the GCC (Prabhu 2016).

Qatar

According to its National Vision 2030 (Qatar General Secretariat for Development Planning 2008), Qatar has targeted 20 per cent of its power generation from renewable energy. Additionally, Qatar's National Development Strategy 2011–2016 (Qatar General Secretariat for Development Planning 2011) highlighted the need for energy diversification and featured development plans for hosting the FIFA World Cup 2022. The policy paper also includes strategies for private sector participation in public projects. Qatar General Electricity and Water Corporation (KAHRAMAA) reported that it is planning to install 200 MW of renewable capacity by 2020 (Clover 2013). KAHRAMAA also announced its first solar station at Al-Duhail, which will add 10 MW to Qatar's 2020 goal (IRENA 2016b).

The Ministry of Municipality and Urban Planning has contracted Keppel Seghers Engineering to develop four waste transfer stations and one integrated Domestic Solid Waste Management Centre (DSWMC) located in Mesaieed, which will have a capacity of 40 MW.

Saudi Arabia

Saudi Arabia has set a target of 9.5 GW renewable energy installation by 2023 (Borgmann 2016). The recently published *Vision 2030* (Kingdom of Saudi Arabia 2016) outlines the country's aggressive approach to developing a renewables market. The upcoming launch of the King Salman Renewable Energy Initiative will apply strategies described in the paper as the government seeks to localize the renewables value chain within the economy through research and the development of necessary skillsets. The policy paper also speaks of encouraging PPPs and reviewing legal and regulatory frameworks to allow private sector participation through investment in renewable energy. The country is gradually transitioning toward a liberalized energy market.

Saudi Aramco's contribution to renewables targets so far consists of over 15 MW installed solar capacity, including the 10 MW solar car park commissioned in 2012 in Dhahran, which generates around 17.5 gigawatt hours (GWh) annually. In 2013, Aramco also launched Phase 1 of the solar project at the King Abdullah Petroleum Studies and Research Center (KAPSARC), with 3.5 MW of capacity commissioned; the second phase, commissioned in 2014, added another 1.8 MW.

Using Sun Power technology, the King Abdullah University of Science and Technology (KAUST) added a 2 MW rooftop solar PV project with annual electricity output of 3.3 GWh that supports campus facilities.

Saudi Arabia has a number of planned projects that could add up to 160 MW capacity of solar power in the near future, with major contributions from the Saudi Electric Company (SEC) and King Abdulaziz City for Science and Technology (KACST).

United Arab Emirates

The UAE also aims to decrease its reliance on oil by expanding strategies to adopt a sustainable range of energy sources. The Vision 2021 policy paper (UAE (United Arab Emirates) Government 2010) set an initial target of renewables generating 24 per cent of the total energy mix by 2021. As part of the UAE effort to fight global climate change through the COP21 Paris Agreement, the target was raised to 27 per cent (Abdul Kader 2016).

Shams 1, with an installed capacity of 100 MW of solar thermal, is one of the UAE's largest renewable energy projects to date. The project, located in Abu Dhabi, was commissioned in 2013, with Masdar owning 60 per cent while Spain's Abengoa Solar and Total each have 20 per cent (Masdar 2013).

The Dubai Electricity and Water Authority (DEWA; DEWA 2016) and First Solar completed the 13 MW Phase 1 of the Mohammed bin Rashid Al Maktoum (MBR) solar park in 2013. DEWA also managed to complete Phase 2, adding 200 MW which was commissioned in March 2017 (Graves 2017); Phase 3 is expected to add 800 MW by 2020. DEWA also announced Masdar as the selected bidder of Phase 3. Ultimately, the MBR solar park is expected to contribute 3 GW of installed solar capacity to help Dubai reach its 15 per cent renewables target by 2030.

Beyond leading the development of MBR Phase 3 for DEWA, Masdar developed a 10 MW solar PV plant at its own site. The project generates 17,500 megawatt hours (MWh) annually to power Masdar City. Masdar is also developing the planned 30 MW Wind Park in Sir Bani Yas Island in Abu Dhabi (Cronin 2014).

As noted earlier, while each GCC country is advancing renewable energy – with a strong emphasis on solar – there is very little cross-border activity and no evidence of any truly regional initiatives. A similar trend is seen in R&D activities. Several universities and institutions in the GCC are expanding research in renewable energy, and a number of specialized research institutions were established, such as MASDAR in the UAE and KAPSARC in Saudi Arabia. To date, the focus is local and cooperation among such institutions has been limited.

In summary, prevailing GCC renewables policy has three primary features. First, each country is devoting significant resources to expanding the role of renewable energy in domestic power generation. Second, these efforts reflect long-term strategies as spelled out in the GCC members' economic visions. Third, based on available documentation, very few joint renewables projects are under way in the GCC. In effect, each country is operating independently.

A more centralized GCC renewable energy policy

To advance to a more coordinated approach, it is helpful to explore key characteristics of a more centralized renewables policy.

Greater interaction is perhaps the most basic element of a more centralized renewables policy, starting with regular meetings during which those in charge of each GCC country's renewables policy would keep each other abreast of respective plans. This is already happening to some extent, in that the GCC Ministers of Energy and their undersecretaries have regular meetings to discuss matters of mutual interest. It is unclear, however, if the meeting agendas, which are likely to be dominated by oil matters, include explicit exchange of detailed plans regarding renewables projects.

One of the simplest benefits of such meetings would be to reduce the incidence of research duplication (Bolton and Farrell 1990). All six countries are likely working on developing the sorts of modifications needed to improve the efficiency of renewable energy technologies in the GCC, especially those relating to solar energy. While having multiple, competing teams working independently – as is the norm in science – has its virtues, it can also be wasteful, especially when it is something that can be predicted at the outset. Any decision to prefer competition over cooperation should be a deliberate one taken by GCC authorities, rather than the inadvertent consequence of lack of coordination in addressing common challenges.

Establishing centralized committees that propose joint projects would be the logical next step, with two primary reasons for explicit consideration of joint projects as against the existing, decentralized arrangement.

First, economies of scale (Stigler 1958). The mere act of pooling resources can lead to higher levels of productivity, often because large fixed costs can be defrayed over a wider base of operations. Economies of scale occur when two or more activities can share inputs with no or minimal additional costs. Experience in other regions confirms that this applies to R&D in renewable energy. For example, small research institutions with limited resources are often forced to restrict their researchers' access to a small number of academic journals, which constitutes a key constraint on input into the knowledge production process. If multiple small institutions cooperate under the umbrella of a larger organization, it may be possible to purchase overarching subscriptions to key journals at much lower costs than through individual subscriptions.

Similarly, research institutions can benefit significantly from cross-fertilization of ideas. *Ceteris paribus*, research programs located within larger institutions are significantly more productive than those within smaller institutions (Henderson and Cockburn 1996). This is especially important when considering that minimum efficient scale can act as a significant barrier to entry in markets (Schmalensee 1981). Given the immense costs associated with modern R&D, for example, it is unlikely that economies as small as Bahrain or Oman can summon the resources necessary to compete with the research output of scientists operating in the U.S. or China. International research collaboration is the sensible response and doing so within the GCC region makes the most sense in light of the legal, economic, cultural and linguistic ties that exist among the six members.

Economies of scale can also extend to procurement: GCC countries acting as a bloc when purchasing foreign renewable energy technologies are likely to obtain better prices. Moreover, if and when renewable energy R&D

undertaken in the GCC proves successful and can be exported to other arid climates – potentially providing a non-oil source of tradable exports (Cherif and Hasanov 2014), as developed in the German renewable energy sector (Blazejczak et al. 2014) – superior terms of trade can likely be secured if negotiations operate at the GCC level.

Second, joint projects can be the first step toward country level specialization, which could expand the renewables knowledge-production possibilities of GCC states (McKenzie 1955). Greater centralization may ultimately allow more strategic R&D in which countries leverage their comparative advantages, for example with Bahrain, an archipelago, focusing on wind technologies while Saudi Arabia, a largely terrestrial desert, dedicates resources to solar.

It should be noted that in private markets, if there are gains from centralizing and operating at a larger scale, firms are likely to organically deduce this – and to do so far more quickly than an overseeing civil servant. Due to the strength of the profit motive and the private returns associated with research, private sector actors tend to self-organize, without the need for government supervision (Kealey 1996). As renewables projects in the GCC are currently dominated by governments, government initiative is *de facto* required to exploit the efficiency opportunities offered by greater centralization.

In its weakest form, this class of centralization would see a committee established for cooperation and perhaps to make proposals to be considered and/ or adopted on an *ad hoc* basis, but keep resources decentralized. More evolved approaches would involve the central bodies controlling significant budgets, as well as having the executive power to provide legal and regulatory support, e.g., tax exemptions, subsidies and lifting visa restrictions.

The benefits associated with centralization can accrue to both basic and applied components of renewable energy research. In fact, basic research plays an important role in both laying a foundation for useful applied research, and for enabling researchers working in different institutions to benefit from each other's work (Cohen and Levinthal 1989).

Greater centralization of renewables policies can also help to embed renewable energy decisions into broader, more strategic government goals. Future plans for the GCC electricity grid, for example, should incorporate plans for renewable energy; in fact, this is already occurring to some extent (Farid and Muzhikyan 2013). More generally, all GCC energy planning should be done in conjunction with renewables plans, ideally with reference to a suite of centralized joint projects that are underway. The current GCC electricity grid serves as an excellent example of how greater cooperation and coordination among GCC governments has resulted in substantial economic gains. The process used to forge its relevant agreements could be considered as a template for other areas, including a more centralized renewable energy sector.

Several non-energy sectors also interact strategically with the renewable energy sector and would benefit from more centralized planning that enhances the overall performance by exploiting complementarities that exist at the regional level. For example, significant literature indicates the job-creating benefits of renewable energy (Lehr et al. 2012; Van der Zwaan et al. 2013). Realizing the full potential of these opportunities requires coordination among authorities overseeing renewable energy and those in charge of labor markets and the education sector.

An important qualifier in regard to centralization is the nature of funding. This chapter's recommendation that renewables policy be more centralized is restricted to publicly funded renewable energy, which essentially represents the entire GCC renewable energy sector. Historically and at present, private R&D is significantly more effective as a source of economically valuable innovations (Kealey 1996). In fact, publicly funded R&D is often wasteful, as its funders lack any strong commercial incentive; often, it tends to crowd out its more valuable sister, private R&D (Mamuneas and Nadiri 1996).

One of the virtues of private R&D is that the optimal level of intra-GCC cooperation and coordination will emerge organically, due to the presence of a profit motive (Romer 1994). Combined with the intensity of global competition, it may render proposals, such as the one made in this chapter, strictly academic. Yet it is critical that any efforts to encourage private R&D be based on creating a more commercially oriented research sector, such as via deregulation and a superior education system, rather than by providing government subsidies and artificial support. The latter approaches tend to undermine the effectiveness of the resultant private R&D (Kealey 1996). In the GCC case, it is clear that some publicly funded R&D will continue, in which case the primary argument holds for significantly higher levels of coordination and cooperation among the GCC governments, preferably under the umbrella of the GCC itself.

The remaining subsection spells out precisely how a centralized renewables policy can contribute to tackling the three problems described earlier in this chapter. This chapter makes the case that the renewable energy R&D productivity of GCC countries could be significantly enhanced by centralizing renewables policy, whether it simply limits duplication or actually involves exploiting the economies of scale that would result from pooling renewables budgets and decision-making. Even at these levels, such a policy could make a significant contribution to addressing R&D deficiencies currently exhibited by GCC countries.

The effect could be direct, reflecting a boost in RE's contribution to aggregate R&D. Or it could be indirect; for example, if a successful, more centralized renewables policy motivates the adoption of similar structures in other sectors, such as defense, manufacturing, or petrochemicals, since the same principles apply widely.

The benefits from higher levels of R&D in the renewable energy sector, and possibly beyond, would be amplified if GCC countries were to adopt the best practices associated with knowledge transfer. At present, the renewable energy sector is a microcosm of the GCC economy, in that it is dominated by foreigners, especially in areas where international-level scientific expertise is necessary. According to their economic visions for the future, GCC countries wish to see a greater role for local, national talent in all sectors, including technically advanced ones such as RE. This means that governments need to consider which policies facilitate the transfer of skills and knowledge possessed by these elite foreigners to their own workforces.

A large body of literature in business and economics examines the features of such policies (Dyer and Nobeoka 2000). Proven approaches include making knowledge-sharing tools more readily available (Brown and Duguid 1991), providing explicit rewards for knowledge sharing (Bartol and Srivastava 2002), and providing bonuses to teams based on the performance of the entire unit, where the unit comprises both foreigners and nationals (Dulebohn and Martocchio 1998).

Needless to say, by elevating the R&D productivity of the renewable energy sector, one would expect more rapid development of renewable energy technologies tailored to the specific, climate-related needs of the GCC renewable energy sector, including the previously mentioned inefficiencies associated with prevailing solar energy technologies.

In terms of the GCC countries' struggle to advance economic integration, a more centralized renewables policy can contribute in two ways. First, it can represent a step toward a centralized energy policy, which would include oil and gas, the most important and vibrant sector in the GCC economy. If and when GCC countries begin to coordinate decisions regarding key areas such as oil and gas, transportation and shipping, and electricity transmission and distribution, and also cooperate strategically in long-term investments, the level of economic integration will increase rapidly, as will trust in and between the central GCC institutions. Subsequently, member states will be more likely to adhere to integration directives issued by the GCC Supreme Council, which have been only partially implemented to date. While the prospect of such advanced levels of integration may seem dim at present, it is worth recalling just much the European Union achieved in the 30 years following World War II. The GCC countries have a much more favorable departure point.

Second, if a shared and more centralized renewable energy sector flourishes and creates significant jobs that match the aspirations of the citizens, as well as delivering important value to the sectors that consume energy, it will represent a significant form of economic integration, regardless of the inspiration drawn by other sectors that persist with decentralized (with respect to the GCC) strategic planning. This aspect will be boosted if the more centralized renewables policy also involves cooperation with labor market and education sector authorities.

Conclusions

This paper has two primary conclusions. First, renewables policy in the GCC is, at present, almost completely decentralized. Member states exhibit low levels of cooperation in their renewables projects, both at the planning and implementation stages. This is in stark contrast to the vision of collaboration and cooperation embodied in the GCC itself.

Second, forging a more centralized renewables policy can potentially yield substantial returns for the Gulf countries. In particular, it can contribute to tackling three unrelated challenges facing GCC countries: insufficient broad-based R&D and innovation; the need to modify prevailing renewable energy technologies to improve their operating efficiency in GCC climates; and the need to accelerate the pace of economic integration.

References

Abdulghaffar M, Al-Ubaydli O, and Mahmood O (2013) The malfunctioning of the Gulf Cooperation Council single market: features, causes and remedies. *Middle Eastern Finance and Economics* 19:54–67.

Abdul Kader B (2016) UAE raises clean energy target to 27% by 2021. *Gulf News* 23 Oct. Accessed Oct 2016. http://gulfnews.com/news/uae/environment/uae-raises-clean-energy-target-to-27-by-2021-1.1917569.

Alasfoor R (2007) *The Gulf Cooperation Council: Its Nature and Achievements.* Lund University, Lund, Sweden.

Allen C, Gasiorek M, and Smith A (1998) The competition effects of the Single Market in Europe. *Economic Policy* 13(27):440–486.

Al Nasser WE (1995) Renewable energy resources in the state of Bahrain. *Applied Energy* 50(1):23–30.

Al Nasser WE, Al Nasser NW, and Batarseh I (2014) Bahrain's BAPCO 5MWp PV grid-connected solar Project. *International Journal of Power and Renewable Energy Systems* 1:72–84.

Baldwin RE, and Venables AJ (1995) Regional economic integration. *Handbook of International Economics* 3:1597–1644.

Baldwin-Edwards M (2011) Labour immigration and labour markets in the GCC countries: National patterns and trends. Kuwait Programme on Development, Governance and Globalisation in the Gulf States 15. London School of Economics and Political Science, London.

Bartol KM, and Srivastava A (2002) Encouraging knowledge sharing: the role of organizational reward systems. *Journal of Leadership & Organizational Studies* 9(1):64–76.

Basher S (2015) Regional initiative in the Gulf Arab States: the search for a common currency. *International Journal of Islamic and Middle Eastern Finance and Management* 8(2):185–202.

Blazejczak J et al. (2014) Economic effects of renewable energy expansion: a model-based analysis for Germany. *Renewable and Sustainable Energy Reviews* 40:1070–1080.

Bolton P, and Farrell J (1990) Decentralization, duplication, and delay. *Journal of Political Economy* 98(4):803–826.

Borgmann M (2016) Potentially game-changing Saudi Arabian government restructuring bolsters 9.5 GW renewable energy target by 2023. *Apricum* 9 May. Accessed Sept 2016. www.apricum-group.com.

Brown JS, and Duguid P (1991) Organizational learning and communities-of-practice: toward a unified view of working, learning, and innovation. *Organization Science* 2(1):40–57.

Cherif R, and Hasanov F (2014) Soaring of the Gulf falcons: diversification in the GCC oil exporters in seven propositions. *IMF* working paper no. 14–177. International Monetary Fund, Washington, DC.

Clover I (2013) Qatar to install utility-scale reservoir rooftop solar panels. *PV-Magazine* 20 Nov. Accessed Sept 2016. www.pv-magazine.com.

Cohen WM, and Levinthal DA (1989) Innovation and learning: the two faces of R and D. *The Economic Journal* 99(397):569–596.

Cronin S (2014) UAE looks to tap vast potential of wind power. *The National: Business* 14 Jun. Accessed Oct 2016. www.thenational.ae/business.

DEWA (Dubai Electricity and Water Authority) (2016) DEWA announces selected bidder for 800 MW third phase of the Mohammed bin Rashid Al Maktoum solar park. DEWA 27 Jun. Accessed Oct 2016. www.dewa.gov.ae/en/about-dewa/news-and-media/press-and-news/latest-news/2016/06/dewa-announces-selected-bidder.

Dincer I (2000) Renewable energy and sustainable development: a crucial review. *Renewable and Sustainable Energy Reviews* 4(2):157–175

Dubey S, Narotam Sarvaiya J, and Seshadri B (2013) Temperature dependent photovoltaic (PV) efficiency and its effect on PV production in the world – a review. *Energy Procedia* 33:311–321.

Dulebohn JH, and Martocchio JJ (1998) Employee perceptions of the fairness of work group incentive pay plans. *Journal of Management* 24(4):469–488.

Dyer JH, and Nobeoka K (2000) Creating and managing a high-performance knowledge-sharing network: the Toyota case. *Strategic Management Journal* 21(3):345–367.

Elminir HK et al. (2006) Effect of dust on the transparent cover of solar collectors. *Energy Conversion and Management* 47(18):3192–3203.

Fagerberg J (1996) Competitiveness, scale and R&D. Norwegian Institute of International Affairs/Norsk utenrikspolitisk institutt (NUPI), Oslo.

Farid AM, and Muzhikyan A (2013) The need for holistic assessment methods for the future electricity grid. *GCC CIGRE Power* 2013:1–12.

Ferroukhi R, Khalid A, Hawila D, Nagpal D, El-Katiri L, Fthenakis V, Al-Fara A (2016) Renewable energy market analysis: the GCC region. IRENA, Abu Dhabi.

Graves, L (2017) Mohammed bin Rashid Al Maktoum solar park second phase now operational. *The National: Business*. Accessed May 2017. www.thenational.ae/business/energy.

Hall BH, Mairesse J, and Mohnen P (2009) Measuring the returns to R&D. No. w15622. National Bureau of Economic Research, Cambridge, MA.

Hayek FA (1945) The use of knowledge in society. *The American Economic Review* 35(4):519–530.

Helman C (2015) Ironic or economic? Oil giant to build world's largest solar project. *Forbes*. Retrieved 10 September 2016.

Henderson R, and Cockburn I (1996) Scale, scope, and spillovers: the determinants of research productivity in drug discovery. *Rand Journal of Economics* 1996:32–59.

IRENA (2016a) Renewable energy and jobs annual review 2016. IRENA, Abu Dhabi. www.irena.org/publications/2016/May/Renewable-Energy-and-Jobs--Annual-Review-2016. Accessed 1 Feb 2017.

IRENA (2016b) Renewable energy market analysis: the GCC region. IRENA, Abu Dhabi. Accessed 1 Mar 2017. www.irena.org/menu/index.aspx?mnu=Subcat&PriMenuID=36&CatID=141&SubcatID=691.

Kaldellis JK, and Kapsali M (2011) Simulating the dust effect on the energy performance of photovoltaic generators based on experimental measurements. *Energy* 36(8):5154–5161.

Kazem HA, et al. (2012) Effect of humidity on the PV performance in Oman. Accessed 18 Jul 2018. www.researchgate.net/publication/303516651.

Kealey T (1996) *The Economic Laws of Scientific Research*. Macmillan, London.

Kingdom of Saudi Arabia (2016) *Saudi Vision 2030*. Kingdom of Saudi Arabia, Riyadh.

Kuwait Partnerships Technical Bureau (2015) Al Abdaliyah Integrated Solar Combined Cycle (ISCC), Kuwait Partnerships Technical Bureau. Accessed 15 Sept 2016. www.ptb.gov.kw/en/Al-Abdaliyah-Integrated-Solar-Combined-Cycle-(ISCC).

Lehr U, Lutz C, and Edler D (2012) Green jobs? Economic impacts of renewable energy in Germany. *Energy Policy* 47:358–364.

Mamuneas TP, and Nadiri MI (1996) Public R&D policies and cost behavior of the US manufacturing industries. *Journal of Public Economics* 63(1):57–81.

Mani M, and Pillai R (2010) Impact of dust on solar photovoltaic (PV) performance: research status, challenges and recommendations. *Renewable and Sustainable Energy Reviews* 14(9):3124–3131.

Masdar (2013), Masdar launches Shams 1, the world's largest concentrated solar power plant in operation. Masdar, Abu Dhabi. Accessed 20 Sept 2016. www.masdar.ae/en/media/detail/masdar-launches-shams-1-the-worlds-largest-concentrated-solar-power-plant-i.

McGlennon D (2006) Building research capacity in the Gulf Cooperation Council countries: strategy, funding and engagement. Paper presented at the second international colloquium on research and higher education policy, UNESCO Headquarters, Paris, 29 Nov–1 Dec 2006.

McKenzie LW (1955) Specialization in production and the production possibility locus. *Review of Economic Studies* 23(1):56–64.

Mekhilef S, Saidur R, and Kamalisarvestani M (2012) Effect of dust, humidity and air velocity on efficiency of photovoltaic cells. *Renewable and Sustainable Energy Reviews* 16(5):2920–2925.

Meltzer J, Hultman NE, and Langley C (2014) Low-carbon energy transitions in Qatar and the Gulf Cooperation Council region. Brookings Papers on Economic Activity 7 Mar.

Mielke E, Diaz Anadon L, and Narayanamurti V (2010) Water consumption of energy resource extraction, processing, and conversion. *Belfer Center for Science and International Affairs Discussion Paper* 2010–15. President and Fellows of Harvard College, Cambridge, MA.

Prabhu C (2016) Masirah wind power project set to make headway in Oman. *Oman Observer* 13 Apr. http://2016.omanobserver.om/masirah-wind-power-project-set-to-make-headway/. Accessed 10 Sept 2016.

Qatar General Secretariat for Development Planning (2008) Qatar Vision 2030. Qatar General Secretariat For Development Planning, Doha. Accessed 1 Oct 2016. www.qdb.qa/English/Documents/QNV2030_English.pdf.

Qatar General Secretariat for Development Planning (2011) Qatar National Development Strategy 2011–2016. Qatar General Secretariat for Development Planning, Doha. Accessed 1 Oct 2016. www.mdps.gov.qa/en/knowledge/HomePagePublications/Qatar_NDS_reprint_complete_lowres_16May.pdf.

Radziemska E (2003) The effect of temperature on the power drop in crystalline silicon solar cells. *Renewable Energy* 28(1):1–12.

Rafiq MS (2011) The optimality of a Gulf currency union: commonalities and idiosyncrasies. *Economic Modelling* 28(1):728–740.

Romer PM (1994) The origins of endogenous growth. *Journal of Economic Perspectives* 8(1):3–22.

Sakakibara M (1997) Heterogeneity of firm capabilities and cooperative research and development: an empirical examination of motives. *Strategic Management Journal* 18(S1):143–164.

Salim AA, Huraib FS, and Eugenio NN (1988) PV power-study of system options and optimization. Paper presented at 8th EC photovoltaic solar conference, Florence, Italy, 9–13 May 1988.

Sayigh AAM, Al-Jandal S, and Ahmed H (1985) Dust effect on solar flat surfaces devices in Kuwait. In: Furlan G et al. (eds) *Proceedings of the international workshop on the physics of non-conventional energy sources and material science for energy*. Miramare-Trieste, Italy, 2–20 Sept 1985.

Schmalensee R (1981) Economies of scale and barriers to entry. *Journal of Political Economy* 89(6):1228–1238.

Skoplaki E, and Palyvos JA (2009) On the temperature dependence of photovoltaic module electrical performance: a review of efficiency/power correlations. *Solar Energy* 83(5):614–624.

Solargis (2017) Solar resource maps for Germany. Accessed 10 May 2017. http://solargis. com/products/maps-and-gis-data/free/download/germany.

Sophia M (2017) With an eye on energy savings, the Middle East is varying its power sources. *Forbes Middle East*. Accessed May 2017. www.forbesmiddleeast.com/en/with-an-eye-on-energy-savings-the-middle-east-is-varying-its-power-sources/.

Stigler GJ (1958) The economies of scale. *Journal of Law and Economics* 1(1):54.

Sundar S (2016) Bahrain halts $480 million waste management project-source. *Thomson Reuters Zawya* 3 Nov. Accessed Nov 2016. www.zawya.com/mena/en/story/Bahrain_halts_480_million_waste_management_project_source-ZAWYA20161103081201/.

Touati F et al. (2013) Effects of environmental and climatic conditions on PV efficiency in Qatar. Paper presented at International Conference on Renewable Energies and Power Quality (ICREPQ'13), Bilbao, Spain, 20–22 Mar 2013.

UAE (United Arab Emirates) Government (2010) *UAE Vision 2021*. UAE Government, Abu Dhabi.

UNESCO Institute for Statistics (2016a) Gross domestic expenditure on R&D. United Nations Statistics Division. Accessed 10 Aug 2016. http://data.un.org/Data. aspx?d=UNESCO&f=series%3aST_SCGERDGDP.

UNESCO Institute for Statistics (2016b) Researchers per million inhabitants in FTE. United Nations Statistics Division. Accessed 10 Aug 2016. http://data.un.org/Data. aspx?d=UNESCO&f=series%3aST_SCRMIFT.

Valentine SV (2011) Emerging symbiosis: renewable energy and energy security. *Renewable and Sustainable Energy Reviews* 15(9):4572–4578.

Van der Zwaan B, Cameron L, and Kober T (2013) Potential for renewable energy jobs in the Middle East. *Energy Policy* 60:296–304.

WEF (World Economic Forum) (2016) *The Global Competitiveness Report*. World Economic Forum, Geneva.

WIPO (World Intellectual Property Organization) (2014) WIPO Patent Report: Statistics on Worldwide Patent Activity. WIPO, Geneva.

World Bank (2016) Scientific and technical journal articles. World Bank. Accessed 10 Aug 2016. http://data.worldbank.org/indicator/IP.JRN.ARTC.SC/countries.

Index

Aarhus Convention (1998) 69
Abdul Latif Jameel 85
Abengoa Solar, S. A. 226
Abu Dhabi: electricity production 23;
     Energy Policy (2009) 66; GCC energy
     system 12, *13*; nuclear power 34; oil
     and gas production 27; PPP in water
     sector 88; reforms 94; renewable energy
     targets 2, 34; solar irradiance 29; water
     consumption 23; water prices 87; wind
     speeds 29–30
Abu Dhabi Center for Technical and
     Vocational Education and Training 210
Abu Dhabi Water and Electricity Authority
     (ADWEA) 88
access to electricity 154 *see also* electricity
     demand
ACWA Power 107, 157
AFEX 105
Agence Nationale pour la Maîtrise de l'Energie
     (Tunisia) 104
agriculture 23
air conditioning 193
airport privatizations 88
Al-Abdaliyah ISCC plant (Kuwait) 224
Al-Aflaj 50-MW solar PV plant (Saudi
     Arabia) 122
Algeria 131, 132, 135
Amal oilfield (Oman) 112, 224
analyzing risk environments 108
Arabian Company for Water and Power
     Development (ACWA) 85, 88
'Arab Spring' 128
Asia-Pacific region 134
Askar Waste-to-Energy project 224
asymmetrical labor market information 208–9
Atwa, Y. M. 172
auctions: accelerating renewables 161;
     MBR Solar Park 107, 124; processes

155–7; renewables support scheme
     criteria 128; tenders as 144–5

Bahrain: crude oil trade 27; Economic
     Vision 2030 192; energy price reforms
     129; energy-related activities 106; fuel
     mix 20, 21; fuel prices 49; funding gap
     92; GHG emissions 105, *106*; industrial
     fuel prices 31; installed renewables
     capacity 112; national plan for renewable
     energy (2017) 66; NDCs 114; oil and
     gas resources 26; power sector reforms
     35; privatization schemes *90*; renewable
     energy targets 2, 34; renewable projects
     223–4; RO and thermal desalination
     capacity 19; subsidy reforms 87; trade
     linkages and quantities *28*; vocational
     and technical training 207
Bahrain National Vision 2030 223–4
The Bahrain Petroleum Company
     (BAPCO) 224
Bahrain Sustainable Energy Unit 116
barriers to renewable investments 31,
     106–7, 130–4 *see also* fossil fuel subsidies
boom and bust cycles 14
buildings sector 158–9
bureaucratic barriers 132
business-as-usual (BAU) scenario 45, 50, 51

Canary Islands 171–2
capacity factor ratio 222
capacity targets 151
'cap and trade' *see* emission trading systems
     (ETS)
carbon dioxide (CO_2) emissions 17, 146,
     149–50, 169 *see also* greenhouse gas
     (GHG) emissions
carbon pricing 140, 146–7, 159–60, 161
     see also energy policies

carbon tax 173–4, 175–6, 181, 184
Caspain Energy Holdings 224
catalyzing private investments 103
centralization 216–31; committees 227;
    economic integration 230; funding 229;
    R&D 228; renewables policies 226–30;
    research production 217
China: ETS mechanisms 160, 162;
    medium-term plans 172; patient
    applications 220; vocational programs
    207; wind capacity 131
China Wind Power Research and Training
    Project (CWPP) 211
cities 66
citizen welfare 79
clean energy: health impacts 184;
    investments worldwide 101, *102*; job
    creation 153–4; reducing GHG 82;
    targets 154; transition 94, 153–4
climate: efficiency of solar cells 217, 221–2;
    energy intensities 105–6
climate change: energy policies 142–3;
    EU 2020 Energy Strategy 59, 70–2;
    mitigation 113–14, 141, 154, 160–1;
    policies 146–7; renewable energy
    mitigating 104 *see also* COP21 Paris
    Agreement (2015)
coal 196
coastal wind 29
cogeneration units 17–18, 80
collective working 59
combinatorial approaches 128–30, 136
combined cycle gas turbines (CCGTs)
    18, 171
community renewables projects 70
concentrating solar power (CSP): designing
    innovative systems 222; installed capacity
    28; job creation 197; measuring solar
    power 221; MENA countries
    121; Shams 1 project 94; thermal
    storage 51–3
construction jobs 208
consumers: costs of EVs 170; final cost to
    123–4; negative impacts of subsidies 145
    see also social contract
cooperation and coordination 62, 132
Cooperation Council of the Arab States
    of the Gulf *see* Gulf Cooperation
    Council (GCC)
COP21 Paris Agreement (2015) 1, 2,
    60, 113–14, 140, 146, 226 *see also*
    climate change; Nationally Determined
    Contributions (NDCs)
cornerstone instruments 109, 111

cost-competitiveness 143
cost of capital 134
coupled power and water production 19
    see also thermal cogeneration
Covenant of Mayors (EU) 66
credit ratings 107
credits (tax exemptions) 46
cross-border activities 226
cross-fertilization of ideas 227
crude oil *see* oil
currency and liquidity risks *133*, 134
customs unions 223

debt to GDP ratio 128
decarbonization 135
decentralized competition 217
decommissioning wind power projects
    198–9
demand management 66
'demographic dividend' 189
Denmark 131
deregulating fuel prices 50–4
de-risking low carbon investments 106–8
De-risking Renewable Energy Investment
    (DREI) methodology 100, *102*–5,
    108–13, 116
desalination *see* water desalination
descending bid (or clock) auction 156
developing countries 102, 107
Dhahran 225
Dhofar Power System 12
diesel 19–20; fuel consumption *21*; prices
    95 see also fossil fuels
direct carbon taxes 146, 159 *see also*
    carbon pricing
direct employment 189n1, 195, 196–7
direct financial incentives *109*, 110
direct normal irradiance (DNI) 221
discount rates 54
distribution of jobs 200, *203*
diversification 14, 79, 104, 148, 193, 210
Divisia index approaches 171
Dolphin pipeline 27, *28*
domestic consumption *see* households;
    residential consumption
drivers of energy demand growth 134
Dubai: fuel mix 20; GCC energy system
    12, *13*; net metering policy 158; oil and
    gas resources 27; reforms 94; renewable
    energy targets 2; solar water heating
    (SWH) 158–9; trade and industry
    model 95–6; utility scale solar PV
    development 157
Dubai Carbon Center 116

Dubai Electricity and Water Authority (DEWA) 20, 111, 157, 226
Dubai Green Fund 92
Dubai Supreme Council of Energy 82, 92
'Duroob program' (Saudi Ministry of Labor) 210
dust accumulation 222

Ease of Doing Business reports (World Bank) 92–3
economic and power system efficiency studies 171
economic development: MENA countries 134; oil and gas exports 14, 193; renewables deployment 60; transition to clean energy 153
economic efficiency 70–2
economic integration 218, 222–3, 230
economics of residential solar 47–9
economic top-down models 150–1
economic visions 229–30
economies of scale 227–8
education and training 205–7, 209–10
efficiency studies: energy distribution 172; oil/gas split 176; solar installations 217, 221–2
Electricity and Cogeneration Regulatory Authority (ECRA) 22–3, 36
electricity consumption *82*
electricity demand 3, 11, 23, 42 *see also* energy demand
electricity generation: Canary Islands 171–2; capacity by type *18*; and consumption 22–3; cost to Gulf governments 80; employees per megawatt 200; fuel mix 19–22, 121; geographic variations 12; low fuel prices 49–50; MENA countries 135; prices *95*; privatization 88; renewable energy 3, 60–1; 'replaced gas powered electricity' 174; state-owned operators 49; targets for renewable energy 151–2, 153; untenable use of oil and gas 81; using renewable energy 2; and water production 17–24
electricity loss 131
electricity subsidy reforms 54, 87
electricity supply industry: labor segregation 204; restructuring 135
electricity systems 12
electricity tariffs 16, 32, 46, 47
electric vehicles (EVs) 168, 169–70, 176
emissions of energy-intensive sectors 150, *151*

emission trading systems (ETS) 146–7, 159–60, 161–2
employment: foreign and national workers 201, *202*; job creation 197; occupational biases 209; productivity 200; and renewable energy 193–6
    see also education and training; job creation; labor markets
endogenous variables 174–17, 178
Energinet 131
energy and climate policy nexus 135, 142–8
energy consumption: climate induced 193; and economic growth 193; and energy intensities 105–6; final consumption (2004–2014) *82*; industrial sector 15–16; urbanization 15–16
energy demand 2, 12–16, 60, 80, 81, 104 *see also* electricity demand
energy distribution 172
energy efficiency 34, 59, 135
energy-intensive emissions 150, *151*
energy ministries 88, 132
energy policies: auctions 155–8; climate change 142–3; GHG emissions 143; net metering 158; solar thermal 158–9; three pillars 70–2 *see also* carbon pricing
energy pricing: barrier to coordination 30–2; government control 16; policies 147–8; product pricing *95*; reforms 43
energy production 17
energy security 70–2, 104, 217
energy subsidy reforms 148, 161
energy system 12
energy transformation 17–24
environmental factors *see* carbon dioxide (CO$_2$) emissions; climate; greenhouse gas (GHG) emissions
ethane 125
European Emissions Trading System 175–6
European Energy Research Alliance 66
European Industrial Initiatives 66
European Local Energy Assistance (ELENA) program 66
European Union (EU): climate and renewable energy policies 143; collective working 57, 58; demand management 66; Directive 2003/35/EC 69–70; economic integration 222; and GCC comparative analysis 4; legal and regulatory frameworks 64–6; literature review 63; main policy elements *71*; mandatory targets 64; policy transfer 62; Promotion of the Use of Biofuels

Directive (2003) 64; public participation
69–70; Renewable Electricity
Directive (2001) 64; renewable energy
deployment 62–72; renewable energy
production 58; renewables policies
timeline *65*; research, development,
and innovation 66–7; Strategic Energy
Technology Plan (2007) 67; two
thousand 2020 Energy Strategy 70;
voluntary measures 69
Eversheds 85
exchange rates 134
exogenous variables 176–7, 178
expatriates *see* foreign workers
export revenues 81 *see also* oil revenues
external financing 91

Fattouh, B. 128
favorable investment climates 105
Federal Electricity and Water Authority
(FEWA, UAE) 12, *13*, 20, 23
feed-in tariffs (FITs): and auctions 155–6;
bidding processes 109; payment rates
144–5; regulatory policy measures 67–9;
support schemes 46, 127–8
final cost to consumers 123–4
financial de-risking 109–10, 157 *see also*
auctions
financing offshore wind plants 107
financing renewable energy 4–5, 78
first price, sealed bid auctions 156
First Solar 158, 226
fiscal austerity 77–97; decline in oil
revenues 78, 80; disrupting role of
governments 79–80; MENA region
128; renewables strategy 80; water and
electricity pricing 87 *see also* oil revenues
fiscal incentives 144
foreign direct investment (FDI) 77, 78
foreign ownership 89–91
foreign workers 191, 193, 201–5
fossil fuels: continued reliance 194; demand
for 193; domestic consumption 134,
148, 193; dominating energy supply
61; electricity demand 42; fuel mix
for power and water 19–20; MENA
countries 134 *see also* diesel; oil and gas
fossil fuel subsidies 123–5, 136, 147–8 *see
also* barriers to renewable investments
fossil resource trade 27–8 *see also* transfer
of energy
Fotowatio Renewable Ventures B.V.
(FRV) 85
France 68

free trade areas 223
freshwater 23
fuel combustion emissions *149–50*
fuel consumption *21*
fuel displacement 180–1
fuel mix scenarios 181–2
fuel mix strategies 167–85; calculating
optimal mixes 172–83; constraints
177–8; cost-effectiveness 169; cost
savings 178; environmental factors
171; generating scenarios 177–8;
Malaysia 171; mathematical models
171; for power and water 19–22; power
generation 121; savings/returns 170;
studies 171–2
fuel prices 49, 54
fuel pricing policy scenarios 45
funding gaps 91–3
funding renewable energy 229

gas LCO&M 170, 177, 181
gasoline prices *95*
gasoline stations 170
'gas replaced' variables 173 *see also*
natural gas
general funds 147
Germany 128, 196, 221; Ministry of the
Environment, Nature Conservation, and
Nuclear Safety 196
GlassPoint Solar (Oman) 224
Global Competitiveness Report (WEF) 219
global horizontal irradiation (GHI) 221
'global sunbelt' 121
government budgets 129 *see also* fiscal
austerity; subsidies
government revenues 45 *see also* oil prices
government spending 85
gradual deregulation of fuel prices
scenario 50
green bonds 4, 92
greenhouse gas (GHG) emissions *17*,
60, 105–6, 146–7, 154 *see also* carbon
dioxide (CO_2) emissions
green spending 147
'Green sukuks' 92
grid connections 131–2
Gulf Cooperation Council (GCC) 1;
countries' goals 2–3; CSP potential 121;
economic reforms agenda *87*; energy
planning 228; energy system 12, *13*; and
EU practices 71; hub for low carbon
investments 113; Interconnector
23; regional and international
cooperation 62

health impacts of clean technology 184
heat recovery steam generators
 (HRSG) 18
heavy fuel oil (HFO) 19–20, *21*
Henry Hub spot prices 177
high gas prices/high gas subsidies
 scenario 183
high oil prices/high oil subsidies
 scenario 183
HOMER software 47
households 42, 44, 45–9, 47–9 *see also*
 residential consumption
Hughes, G. 200
human capital 209, 210
humidity 222
hybrid auctions 156
hybrid policies 145
hydrocarbon rich economies 126

IEA Price-Gap approach 174–5
immediate deregulation of fuel prices
 scenario 50–4
implicit fuel contracts scenario 50
incentives 123–30; combinatorial
 approaches 128–30; enabling markets
 125–6; subsidizing renewables 126–8
incentive schemes 46
independent power and water producers
 (IPWPS) 32, 34, 35
independent power producers (IPPs) 4, 88,
 89, 111, 123, 157
independent regulators 132
indigenizing labor forces 191
indirect employment 189n1, 195
induced employment 189n1, 195
industrial development strategies 126, 193
industrial energy consumption 15
industrial fuel prices 31–2
information gain 181–3
information gain ratio (IGR) 181, 182
innovation 66–7, 221
installed desalination capacity 18, *19*
installed electricity capacity 18, 122
installed renewables capacity 111
institutional barriers 132
institutional inertia 60, 85–6
insufficient R&D 217–21
insurance 134
integrated climate and energy policy tools
 140 *see also* carbon pricing
integrated GCC energy system 30
integrated solar combined cycle (ISCC)
 plants 224
integrating renewable energy 59

intended nationally determined
 contributions (INDCs) 113, 146, *154–5*
interest payments 91
inter-governmental cooperation 96
intermittent renewable capacity 44, 131
international cooperation 62
International Energy Agency (IEA) 101,
 174–5
International Finance Corporation (IFC) 88
International Institute for Sustainable
 Development (IISD) 147
International Monetary Fund (IMF) 148
International Renewable Energy Agency
 (IRENA): consultancy reports 63; job
 creation projections 82, 153–4, 196–8;
 REMap 2030 assessment 151
international research collaboration 227
 see also research and development (R&D)
investment credits 46
investment incentives *129*, 130
investment oriented approaches 127
investment risks 85–6, 108, *133*
investments in renewable energy 81–5,
 194, 196–7
Iran 129, 132, 135
Islamic bonds (*sukuks*) 4, 92
Islamic law 91–2

Japan 220
Jeddah 88
job creation: opportunity for 207–8;
 renewables industries 82; skills necessary
 197; time dimension 197–8; transition
 to clean energy 153 *see also* employment;
 labor markets
jobs: socially acceptable 209; studies 194–6
job searches 205
joint projects 228

Kammen, D. M. 195–6
KAPSARC Energy Model (KEM)
 49, 50, 52
Keppel Seghers Engineering 225
King Abdulaziz City for Science and
 Technology (KACST) 225
King Abdullah City for Atomic and
 Renewable Energy (KACARE)
 82, 85, 111
King Abdullah Petroleum Studies and
 Research Center (KAPSARC) 85, 225
King Abdullah University of Science and
 Technology (KAUST) 225
King Salman Renewable Energy
 Initiative 225

knowledge-sharing tools 230
Kuwait: electricity consumption 47; electricity tariffs 47; energy efficiency 34; energy-related activities 106; foreign investment 89; fuel mix 20, 21; fuel prices 49; GCC energy system 12, *13*; GHG emissions 105, *106*; industrial fuel prices 31; installed renewables capacity 112; ISCC plant 224; labor markets 201, 204, 205; liberalization 89; NDCs 114; oil and gas resources 26; population 14; power generation 148; PPP law 89; privatization schemes *90*; reform laws 135; reforms 35, 93–4, 129; renewable energy targets 2, 224; renewable projects 224; Shagaya Renewable Energy Park 112, 122, 217, 224; spending commitments 92–3; T&D losses 131; trade linkages and quantities *28*; Vision Plan 2035 192; water prices 87
Kuwait Authority for Public Partnerships 89
Kuwait Energy Center 116
Kuwait Institute for Scientific Research (KISR) 224

labor demand 193
labor distribution 204–5
labor forces: composition *201*; education and training 205–7, 209–10; policies 208–11; size *190*
labor intensive phases 198
labor market objectives 192
labor markets 188–212; constraints 201–8; friction 200; new occupations 200; objectives 192 *see also* employment; job creation
labor migration 14 *see also* foreign workers
labor nationalization initiatives 192
labor requirements: 50 MW solar PV value chain *199*; wind power project *198*
labor segregation 204
labor substitution 200
Lahn, G. 30
large-scale renewables projects 107
legal and regulatory frameworks: European Union (EU) 59, 64–6, *71*; GCC countries *71*; ownership structures 87–91
legal institutions 132
Leontief's input-output framework 171
levelized capital and the fixed operation and maintenance (LCO&M) costs 177, 182
levelized cost of electricity for renewables *130*

levelized cost of electricity (LCOE) 145; auction 107, 124; gas-fired power plants 177; renewables 129
liberalization: electricity markets 127, 136–7; energy prices 129; Kuwait 89; MENA countries 135; transition to a low carbon future 62
liquefied natural gas (LNG) 85, 149
Lisbon Strategy (EU) 66
load profiles 47
low carbon development 104, 106–7
low carbon investments 112–16
low-cost foreign labor 204, 208
low-cost oil and gas 194
low energy prices 79–80
low fuel prices 49–50
low gas prices and high oil prices scenario 183, 184
low hydrocarbon prices/low subsidies scenario 182–3
low oil prices 2, 108 *see also* fiscal austerity; oil revenues
low-skilled jobs 204, 208

Main Interconnected System 12
Malaysia 171
mandatory targets 59, 64, 72
manufacturing jobs *198–9*, 208
market distortions 124, 145 *see also* subsidies
Masdar 92, 107, 157, 224, 226
Masdar City (Abu Dhabi) 94
Matar, W. 28, 49
mathematical models 171
Mean-Variance Portfolio theory 171
Medina airport (Saudi Arabia) 88
methane 125
Mexico 147
Middle East and North Africa (MENA) 120–37; coordination by government bodies 132; economic and political characteristics 122–3; energy demand growth 134; energy intensive region 134; exchange rates 134; expansion of renewable energy 121–3; fiscal unsustainability 128; Grid connection 131; non-hydro renewables 122; pre-tax energy subsidies 148; renewable energy deployment 92; renewable energy targets *122*; renewable investment 121; resource rich countries 5, 121–3; revising energy policies 134–5; risks for renewables investors *133*; stakeholder confidence 135; subsidies 148

Middle East Solar Industry Association 85
Ministers of Energy 227
ministries of energy 86
moderate price increase and investment credits scenario 50
Mohammed bin Rashid Al Maktoum (MBR) Solar Park 92, 107, 111, 122, 157–8, 226
Moroccan Agency for Solar Energy (MASEN) 157
Morocco 156–7
motivations for renewable energy 44, 49, 150–5
multi-effect distillation (MED) 18
multistage flash (MSF) units 18
Muscat 12

national and subnational policy targets 151, *153*
national centers of excellence 115–16
Nationally Determined Contributions (NDCs) 11, 100, 101, 113–14, 146 *see also* COP21 Paris Agreement
National Oil and Gas Authority (NOGA) 224
national renewables targets 103
national workers 201–5
natural gas: employment outcomes 196; fuel consumption *21*; fuel mix for power and water 19–20; 'gas replaced' variables 173; price policy scenarios 51; prices *95*, 177, 180; production and exports *25*; Qatar 168; reserves 148–9; subsidies 181; trading 27 *see also* oil and gas
natural gas-fired electricity generation 85, 176, 177, 184
near-term energy policies 161
net metering 158
Nitaqat program (Saudi Arabia) 192, 204
non-associated gases 148–9
non-fossil fuel technologies 195–6
non-hydro renewables 122
nonlinear programming (NLP) 167, 168–9, 172
non-national labor 191, 193, 201–5
Noor 1 solar photovoltaic (PV) plant 122
nuclear power 34

occupational biases 209
offshore wind financing costs 107
oil: domestic consumption 148, 193; economic development 14; fuel consumption *21*; fuel mix for power and

water 19–20; production and exports *25*; replacing with solar PV 169–70; trade 27
oil and gas: boom period (2004–2013) 79; prices 177; Qatari subsidies *175*; resources 24–7; technological innovations 80; trading 27–8; vested interests 86 *see also* fossil fuels; natural gas
oil and gas exports 81, 82, 92, 193
oil-based economies 42
oil/gas split 176
oil prices: decline oil revenues 2, 128; exogenous variables 176–7; fiscal deficit 80; fuel mix strategies 170; government spending 85; 'new normal levels' 96; power sector 125; sensitivity analysis 179–80; utility function 178
'oil replaced' variables 173
oil reserves 24–7, 148
oil revenues 2, 78, 80, 81, 108, 128 *see also* fiscal austerity
oil subsidies 179–80
oil-to-electricity efficiency 176
oil versus gas prices sensitivity analysis 180–1
Oman: electricity production 23; Energy Ministry 88; energy price reforms 129; fuel mix 20, 21; funding gap 92; gas prices 49; gas supply 27; GCC energy system 12, *13*; GHG emissions 106; GHG reduction commitment 154; GlassPoint Solar 224; industrial fuel prices 32; IPP policy 112; natural gas uses 148; NDCs 114; oil and gas resources 26; power sector reforms 34–5; privatization schemes 88, *90*; quantifiable mitigation targets 114; renewable electricity generation 151; renewable energy targets 2; renewable projects 224; RO and thermal desalination capacity 19; trade linkages and quantities *28*; university graduates *206*; Vision 2020 192, 224; water consumption 24
onshore wind 29, 123
optimal generation portfolios 171
optimization models 182
Organisation for Economic Co-operation and Development (OECD): CO_2 emissions 171; liberalization 137; T&D losses 131; vocational and technical training 207
Ouarzazate Noor CSP project (Morocco) 157

parameter impact 179–83
Paris Agreement *see* COP21 Paris
  Agreement (2015)
Partnership Technical Bureau (Kuwait) 224
patient applications 220
pay-as-bid auctions 156
peak electricity demand 23 *see also*
  electricity demand
Pearson's correlation coefficient 177
The Peninsula (Qatar newspaper) 89
per capita electricity consumption 47
per capita income 189
Petra Systems, Inc. 224
Petroleum Development Oman
  (PDO) 224
policies 120–37; fuel price scenarios 50–3;
  labor forces 208–11; new frameworks
  5–6; optimizing coordination 211;
  regional approaches 141–2; and
  regulatory risks *133*, 134; separating
  energy carriers 134–5; supporting
  renewable energy 153; targets and
  reforms 33–6; working collectively 59
policy de-risking instruments 109
policy transfer 62
political risks *133*
Pollitt, M.G. 62
population 14, 23, 189, *190*
Poudineh, R. 136
power generation *see* electricity generation
power off-taker risks *133*, 134
power only thermal units 17–18
power purchasing agreements (PPAs): Abu
  Dhabi 36; auction prices 145, 156, 157;
  bidding processes 109; MBR Solar Park
  107; Oman 35; Saudi Arabia 110
power sector reforms 34–6
power systems 131–2
price determination and compensation
  schemes 144
'price-gap' approach 125
primary energy consumption *15*
private investment 103–4, 108, 123
private markets 228
private R&D 229
privatization 86, 87–91
procurement 227–8
production oriented approaches 127
productivity 200 *see also* employment
project planning *198–9*
Promotion of the Use of Biofuels Directive
  (EU 2003) 64
public bearing cost of transition 62
public criticism 93

public employment 205
public financing 144
publicly funded R&D 229
public participation and acceptance 59,
  69–70, *71*, 72
public-private partnerships (PPPs) 4,
  78; Abu Dhabi 88; Askar Waste-to-
  Energy project (Bahrain) 224; Kuwait
  89; models 87–8; national centers of
  excellence 115–16; renewable energy
  projects *90*, *91*; Saudi Arabia 89, 225
public-sector employment 205, 209
PV LCOE costs 170, 184 *see also*
  solar power
PwC 85

Qatar 167–85; carbon tax 175–6, 184;
  carbon tax savings 173–4; CO_2 emissions
  from oil and gas *176*; Domestic Solid
  Waste Management Centre (DSWMC)
  225; economic reforms 89; electricity
  and water tariffs 32; electricity
  consumption 47; electricity generation
  forecasts *169*; electricity production 23;
  endogenous variables 174–7; energy
  efficiency 34; energy-related activities
  106; exogenous variables 176–7; foreign
  ownership 89–91; fuel mix 21–2; fuel
  mix strategies 169; fuel prices 49;
  gas-fired power plants 176; gas
  production and exports 26–7, 168;
  GHG emissions 105, *106*; installed
  renewables capacity 112; labor markets
  201, 205; National Development
  Strategy (2011–2016) 225; National
  Vision 2030 192, 225; NDCs 114;
  oil and gas resources 26–7; oil and
  gas subsidies *175*; oil/gas split 176;
  policymaking 184–5; population 14;
  power sector reforms 35; privatizations
  89, *90*; renewable energy targets
  2, 6–7; renewable projects 225; solar
  energy adoption 168, 170–1; subsidies
  174–5; target for transport 151; trade
  linkages and quantities *28*; university
  graduates *206*; uses of natural gas 148;
  utility scale solar plants 185; waste
  transfer stations 225
Qatar Energy and Water Company
  (QEWC) 173
Qatar Fuel Company (Woqod) 173
Qatar General Electricity and Water
  Corporation (KAHRAMAA) 225
Qatari natural gas 94–5

reduced gas fired electricity generation 174
reform energy prices 125
reforms 86–94; electricity and water 33–6,
    87; energy prices 125, 129; funding gaps
    91–3; policy frameworks 93; power
    sector 34–6; privatization 87–91; public
    criticism 93; responses 93–4
Regional Center for Renewable Energy
    and Energy Efficiency (RCREEE) 63
regional cooperation 62
regional policy approaches 141–2
regulated price of energy 31
regulatory frameworks: European Union
    (EU) 64–6; partnerships and foreign
    investment 79
regulatory measures 59, 67–9,
    71, 72, *144*
REMap 2030 assessment (IRENA) 151
Renewable Electricity Directive (EU
    2001) 64
renewable energy: centralized policies
    226–30; and climate action 105–6;
    decentralized approaches 223–6; energy
    and climate policies 143–5; governance
    and policymaking 61; industry support
    nexus 93; integrating into conventional
    power systems 6; less expensive to
    produce 95; motivators 44, 45, 49,
    150–5; and non-energy sectors 228–9;
    plans and targets *152*; politically
    acceptable 85; resources 33–4; rising
    demand 81; stimulating 2, 3; support
    policies 127, 144, 153
renewable energy clusters 115
renewable energy deployment: drivers 60;
    European Union (EU) 62–4; and fossil
    fuels 146; and GCC countries
    140–2; policies 143–4, 155–60; skill
    shortages 210
renewable energy enhancement in power
    sector *124*
Renewable Energy Program Development
    Office (REPDO Saudi Arabia)) 115
renewable energy projects *83–4, 91*
renewable energy technologies 61–2, 82,
    123, 218
renewable resources 28–30
renewables based power generation 33, 194
renewable support mechanisms *127*
renewable water supply 23
rent distribution (rentier model) 79,
    125–6, 205
'replaced gas powered electricity'
    variable 174

research and development (R&D) 218–21;
    centralization 228; cost-sharing 217;
    country rankings *220*; decentralized
    competition 217; duplication 227;
    economies of scale 227–8; effectiveness
    of technologies 217; European Union
    (EU) 66–7, *71*, 72; GCC practices *71*;
    GDP per capita 218–19; insufficient
    217–21; policies to remove barriers
    59; private and public funding 229;
    procurement 227–8; productivity 230;
    regional cooperation 67, 72, 217, 226;
    underinvestment 219
research and innovation (R&I) 59,
    66, *71*, 72
researchers 219, *220*
residential consumption 15, 134, 148, 193
    see also households
residential electricity tariffs 44, 46
residential solar 46–9, 54
resource-rich MENA countries 121–3
results based financing (RBF) schemes 143
retail tariffs 124
revenue recycling 147
revenues *see* oil revenues
reverse osmosis (RO) 18–19
Rio Earth Summit (1992) 146
risk mitigation instruments 134
risks and uncertainties 133–4
Rural Areas Electricity Company
    (RAECO, Oman) 224
Rural Areas System (Oman) 12

al-Sabah, Sheikh Sabah al-Ahmed, Emir of
    Kuwait 94
Salalah 12
Saudi Arabia: centers of excellence 115–16;
    Colleges of Excellence (COE) 210;
    crude oil production 27; 'Duroob
    program' 210; economic reform
    agenda 88; electricity consumption 47;
    electricity generation 49–50; electricity
    production 22–3; energy efficiency
    34; energy pricing 16; energy-related
    activities 106; FITs and tradable green
    certificates 68–9; fuel mix 20, 22;
    funding new power plants 92; GCC
    energy system 12, *13*; GHG emissions
    105, *106*; gradual reform plan 129;
    industrial fuel prices 32; installed
    renewables capacity 111; institutional
    stakeholders 115; IPPs 89; job creation
    154; KACARE 82, 85, 111; KAPSARC
    85; labor distribution 204–5; labor

markets 201, 204; large-scale renewables projects 107, 122; Master Plan (2012) 66; NDCs 114; Nitaqat program 192, 204; nuclear power 34; oil and gas resources 27; population 14, 189; power and water desalination capacity 18; power sector oil prices 125; power sector reforms 35–6; PPPs and IPPs 89; privatization schemes *90*; reform laws 135; renewable energy investments 194; renewable energy targets 2, 34, 225; renewable projects 225; REPDO 115; residential solar 46–9; RO and thermal desalination capacity 19; scholarly scientific outputs 219; solar electricity generation 46–51; solar irradiance 29; tariff increases 93; trade linkages and quantities *28*; TVTC 210; university graduates *206*; uses of oil 148; utility scale solar 49–51; variable cogeneration plants 19; Vision 2030 89, 192, 225; vocational training system 210; water consumption 23–4; water distribution 88; wind speeds 29–30
Saudi Aramco 36, 88, 225
Saudi Company for Purchasing Power 36
Saudi Electric Company (SEC) 36, 115, 225
Saudi Energy Efficiency Center (SEEC) 115–16
Saudi Public Investment Fund 88
scientific research institutions 219
secondary level skills 204
second price, sealed bid auction 156
sectoral biases 209 *see also* employment
secure grid connections 131
sensitivity analysis 179–81
Shagaya Renewable Energy Park (Kuwait) 112, 122, 217, 224
shale oil 121
Shams 1 project (Abu Dhabi) 68, 94, 95, 111, 122, 226
Sharjah 12, *13*, 23
short-term liquidity 89
shortwave radiation 221
single-cycle gas turbines 18
single markets 223
Sir Bani Yas Island Wind Park (Abu Dhabi) 226
skilled workers 200, 207–8
social contract 79, 125
socially acceptable jobs 209
social spending programs 128
social welfare theory 125–6

solar car park 225
solar electricity generation: installed capacity 18; natural gas savings 169; political and economic sense 95; Saudi Arabia 46–51
solar enhanced oil recovery (EOR) 224
solar installations: efficiency 43, 217, 221–2; job creation 197; motivations for 43–6; payback period 54
solar irradiance 29, 221
solar photovoltaic (PV) cells: climate impairing efficiency 217; conversion process 221; electricity storage 44, 51–2; maintaining 221–2
solar power 28–9, 41–54; capacity targets 151; competitive pricing 126; costs 42–3, 85, 95, 123, 170, 183–4; fuel mix strategies 167–85; GCC solar deployment 42; GHI and electricity yield 221; intermittency 44; oil/gas split 176; Qatar 168; targets 42; viability 48
solar radiation 221
solar resources 1
solar thermal energy 151, 158–9
solar water heating (SWH) 158–9
stakeholder confidence 135
state capitalism 79
state-led growth 86
strategic price reform 46
'strategic triangle of energy policies' (Westphal) 70
strategic visions 2, 153, 160, 192
subsidies: barrier to renewable energy 151; cost-effectiveness of distributed renewables 158; defining 30, 125; energy pricing 147; market distortions 145; MBR Park bid for solar PV 157–8; measuring 125; Qatar 174–5; reforms and social order 80; social contract 124–5; supporting renewable energy 128
subsidy returns 173
sukuks (Islamic bonds) 4, 92
Sun Power technology 225
support policies 127, 144, 153
sustainability 70
Sustainable Development Goals (SDGs) 101
Suzhou Training Centre of CWPP 211
Sweden 147

Tamim bin Hamad al Thani, Sheikh, Amir of Qatar 89
targets: and defined policies and regulations 141; electricity generation from

renewables 151–2, 153; European Union (EU) 58–60, 64, 66; reforms of the power and water sectors 33–6; renewable energy *111*; requiring investments 96, 103
TAV Airports Holding Co 88
tax exemptions (credits) 46
Technical and Vocational Training Corporation (TVTC, Saudi) 210
technical skills 209–10
technical training 207, 210
technological bottom-up models 150–1
technological developments: labor markets 200; oil and gas extraction 80
technology risks *133*
temperature 221
thermal cogeneration 17–19
thermal power generation 17
thermal storage 52
thermal water only plants 19
three pillars of energy policies 70–2
Total 226
total final consumption (TFC) 175, 193
total primary energy supplies (TPES) 175
Toyota Tsusho Corporation 224
tradable green certificates 67–9
trade and industry economic model 95–6
trade linkages *28*
tradeoff curve *180*
training 209–10
transfer of energy 81 *see also* fossil resource trade
transition to low carbon development 1–2, 62, 106–8
transmission and distribution (T&D) losses 131
transport 15, 151, *198–9*
Tunisia 104–5
Tunisian Solar Plan (TSP) 104–5
21st Conference of the Parties (COP21) *see* COP21 Paris Agreement (2015)

UK Energy Research Center (UKERC) 194–5
unemployment 189–91
United Arab Emirates (UAE): Abu Dhabi reform law (1998) 135; auctions 124; case study 94–6; clean energy transition 94; cogeneration capacity 18; commitment to renewables 94; cross-border activities 226; electricity consumption 47; energy efficiency 34; energy-related activities 106; FEWA 12, *13*, 20, 23; fuel mix 20, 22; fuel prices 49; GCC energy system 12, *13*; GHG emissions 105, *106*; industrial fuel prices 32; installed renewables capacity 111; labor markets 204; liberalizing energy prices 129; MBR Solar Park 107; natural gas imports 94–5; NDCs 114; nuclear power 34; oil and gas resources 27; population 14; power sector reforms 36; privatization schemes *90*; renewable energy targets 2, 34; renewable projects 226; trade linkages and quantities *28*; university graduates *206*; use of natural gas 148; Vision 2021 192, 226
United Kingdom 68, 171, 196
United Nations Development Programme (UNDP) 100, 102, 116
United Nations Framework Convention on Climate Change (UNFCCC) 1, 113, 146
United Nations World Water Development Report 2016 23
United States (U.S.) 196; electricity industry employees 200; energy independence 80; job studies 195; natural gas power plants 176; patient applications 220; shale oil 121
university graduates *206*, 207
unskilled workers 207
urbanization 14–16, 23
utilities 44
utility function 173–4, 178 *see also* fuel mix strategy
utility scale adoption 46
utility scale deployment 43, 46
utility scale solar 44, 49–51

variable cogeneration plants 19
vehicle ownership 15
vision frameworks 2, 153, 160, 192
vocational training 207, 210
voluntary measures 59, 69, *71*, 72

wage expectations 204
wastewater 23
water desalination *24*, 80, 106, 193
water production: CO_2 emissions 17; and consumption 12, 23–4; demand 11; fuel mix 19–22; geographic variations 12; PPPs 88; reforms and targets 33–6; Saudi Arabia 88; state duty 79
water scarcity 23
water subsidy reforms 87
water tariffs 32

wealth redistribution 193 *see also* subsidies
welfare states 79
Westphal, K. 70
wholesale markets 135
wind power projects: Kuwait 224;
    offshore costs 107; onshore costs
    123; workforce requirements
    198–9
wind resources 1, 29–30, 131
WIPO Patent Report (WIPO 2014) 220

working age population *202 see also*
    labor forces
World Bank 107, 219; *Ease of Doing
    Business* reports 92–3
World Economic Forum (WEF) 219
World Energy Council 47
World Intellectual Property Organization
    (WIPO) 220

youth unemployment 191

For Product Safety Concerns and Information please contact our EU
representative GPSR@taylorandfrancis.com
Taylor & Francis Verlag GmbH, Kaufingerstraße 24, 80331 München, Germany